Imperial Cu[...]

IMPERIAL GLASS CORPORATION, BELL[...]

Elegant Glassware of the Depression Era

Depression Era

THIRTEENTH EDITION

IDENTIFICATION AND VALUE GUIDE

Cathy & Gene Florence

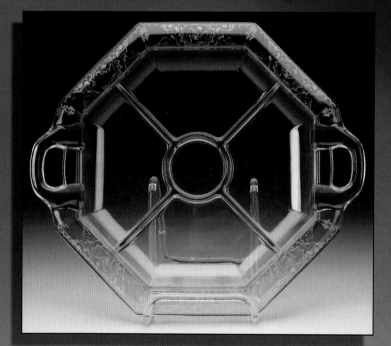

Cambridge,
Fostoria,
Heisey &
others

COLLECTOR BOOKS
A Division of Schroeder Publishing Co., Inc.

On the front cover: Lido cheese comport, $35.00. Jungle Assortment, 6", flat candy, $55.00. June #2496, 12" flared bowl, $200.00.

On the back cover: Ipswich, Heisey, candlestick center piece, $250.00. Bubble Girl, Heisey, five-part relish, pink, $110.00. Balda, sugar, amethyst, $35.00.

Cover design by Beth Summers
Book design by Heather Carvell
Cover photography by Charles R. Lynch

COLLECTOR BOOKS
P.O. Box 3009
Paducah, Kentucky 42002-3009

www.collectorbooks.com

Cathy & Gene Florence
P.O. Box 22186   P.O. Box 64
Lexington, KY 40522   Astutula, FL 34705

Copyright © 2009 Cathy & Gene Florence

The current values in this book should be used only as a guide. They are not intended to set prices, which vary from one section of the country to another. Auction prices as well as dealer prices vary greatly and are affected by condition as well as demand. Neither the authors nor the publisher assumes responsibility for any losses that might be incurred as a result of consulting this guide.

Searching for a Publisher?

We are always looking for people knowledgeable within their fields. If you feel that there is a real need for a book on your collectible subject and have a large comprehensive collection, contact Collector Books.

Proudly printed and bound in the
United States of America

CONTENTS

About the Authors

Gene M. Florence, Jr., a native Kentuckian, graduated from the University of Kentucky in 1967. He held a double major in mathematics and English that he immediately put to use in industry and subsequently, in teaching junior and senior high school.

A collector since childhood, Mr. Florence progressed from baseball cards, comic books, coins, and bottles to glassware. His buying and selling glassware "hobby" began to override his nine-year teaching career. In the summer of 1972, he wrote a book on Depression glassware that was well received by collectors in the field, persuading him to leave teaching in 1976 and pursue the antique glass business full time. This allowed time to travel to glass shows throughout the country, where he assiduously studied the prices of glass being sold... and of that remaining unsold.

Cathy Gaines Florence, a native of Owenton, Kentucky, graduated with honors and a coveted voice award from high school, attended Georgetown College where she obtained a French major and an English minor, and then married her high school sweetheart Gene Florence.

She taught for four years at the middle school level, and then worked part-time while raising two boys. In 1972, she typed her husband's first manuscript, written in "chicken scratch." The first three or four letters of each word would be legible and then it was up to her to guess what the last was. To their astonishment, the book sold well and a new career was born for her husband and their lives took different turns from the teaching careers they'd planned. In the mid-80s she authored a book on collecting quilts, harking back to skills taught her by her grandmothers; and she has since co-authored books on glass with husband Gene.

Books written by the Florences include the following titles: *Collector's Encyclopedia of Depression Glass, Stemware Identification, Pocket Guide to Depression Glass & More, Kitchen Glassware of the Depression Years, Collectible Glassware from the 40s, 50s, and 60s,* two volumes of *Glass Candlesticks of the Depression Era, Anchor Hocking's Fire-King & More,* four volumes of *Florences' Glassware Pattern Identification Guide, Florences' Big Book of Salt and Pepper Shakers, Florences' Glass Kitchen Shakers, 1930 – 1950s, Standard Baseball Card Price Guide,* two editions of *Collector's Encyclopedia of Akro Agate,* six editions of *Very Rare Glassware of the Depression Years,* and *Treasures of Very Rare Depression Glass, Hazel-Atlas Glass Identification and Value Guide* and *Florences' Ovenware from the 1920s to the Present.* They have also written five volumes of *Collector's Encyclopedia of Occupied Japan, Occupied Japan Collectibles,* and a book on Degenhart glassware for that museum.

Acknowledgments

From our first book in 1972, there have been a host of supportive people, many of whom went unrecognized. Some have contributed their glass, some, their time. Some traveled hundreds and even thousands of miles to bring valuable glass of theirs and their friends to photograph at the studio for your enjoyment. Some spent hours whipping out and recording prices, frequently late at night after exhausting show hours; others lent their talents and expertise in various contributing venues. Many readers sent lists of extra pieces from their collections that we had not yet recognized. These people have steadfastly remained friends and contributors even after grueling hours of packing, unpacking, arranging, sorting, and repacking glass. Please realize, as we do, that without these kind and extraordinary individuals, this book would not be the quality their encouragement and contributions made it.

An incomparable note of appreciation is owed Dick and Pat Spencer. It was Dick who first talked us into writing this book years ago by offering to provide glass (in particular Heisey, Fenton, Duncan, and Cambridge) and to help in pricing it. Twenty seven years later, we can honestly say that little did any of us know back then how much time and work that would entail! Today, our legend pictorials for Elegant glass take longer to do than writing and pricing the glass. We hope you will profit from everyone's long, mind-numbing days of numbering, researching, and labeling pieces herein. Readers have requested this exacting identification of photographed pieces over the years and the legends address that issue. The feedback to our doing this shows it has been very well received; but please know it has been quite an arduous task!

More generous people helping us with this particular book include John Knowles, Dan and Geri Tucker, Charles and Maxine Larson, and many readers from all over the U.S., Canada, and beyond who shared pictures and morsels of information about their collections and discoveries. Charles R. Lynch did most of the photography for this book. Thanks, also, to Heather Carvell of Collector Books for the layout you see herein. This time, this book has been a frustrating responsibility just trying to keep up with the price tweaking in the present-day rapidly descending market.

As it stands now, this is to be our last Elegant book. Our ages and growing list of health issues have factored into our decision to retire. Strangely, retirement does not seem to be such an unwelcoming word as it once was. (Of course, we still plan to be around buying and selling good glass when we find it, just not to the extent we did when we had 30 shows and 35,000 to 40,000 miles of driving each year.)

We had already been trying to slow down, but life seems to be telling us more insistently of late that it is time to pass this mantle to someone else. Cathy, who has always worked long hours beside me, has been stressed even harder this year by my health problems and subsequent surgeries. If we even knew the names of all the people who prayed for us both, we couldn't thank them enough! Now, we will try to take time to "smell the roses" without deadlines staring us in the face. Heartfelt thanks to all you readers whose responses to our books have literally made our writing careers possible. We thank you especially for your help and contributions. We are appreciative of each and every one and we hope our appreciation for this lovely older glass has helped enrich you as well!

Elegant glassware, as defined in this book, refers mostly to the hand worked, acid etched glassware that was sold by better department and jewelry stores during the Depression era through the 1960s. This separates it from the colored dime store and give-away glass that has become known as Depression glass. We have added an additional 16 pages to this book, all in photographs that we hope you will enjoy!

PRICING

All prices quoted are retail for mint condition glassware. This book is intended only as a guide to prices. There continue to be regional price disparities that cannot be adequately dealt with herein. We have always tried to report market prices as honestly as we could. Prices are extremely volatile in a changing market whether up or down, and, sadly, in today's economy, that trend is downward. We have stated in all our books that dealers will pay 30 to 60 percent less than the prices listed. However, today dealers tell us they have to quote 70 to 80 percent less than the prices listed in order to make even a meager profit. That tells us that our prices still need to be adjusted so that dealers will once again be able to afford to offer a fair price of what is listed. Thus, prices have again been readjusted so we believe a dealer can now offer a reasonable percentage of retail. However, with $4.00 gas on the horizon, food prices up, mortgage, credit card, and car payments, we feel only those dealers adjusting prices to the present market are likely to continue in business. You can find us on the internet at www.geneflorence.com. We readily acknowledge that we petition price information from persons acclaimed as authorities in certain areas of collecting to provide the latest, most accurate information. However, final decisions are always ours.

MEASUREMENTS AND TERMS

All measurements and terminology in this book are from factory catalogs and advertisements or actual measurements from the piece. It has been our experience that actual measurements vary slightly from those listed in most factory catalogs; so, do not get unduly concerned over slight variations. For example, Fostoria always seems to have measured plates to the nearest inch, but we have found that most Fostoria plates are never exact inches in measurement.

HOW TO USE THE PHOTO LEGENDS

To make this book easier to use and to provide more information, you will find photo legends with each pattern. Each piece is now identified either through the use of photo legends or through the use of numbers on shelf shots and individual shots. Each piece is numbered in the photo legends with corresponding numbers alongside the listings. Now you can tell exactly which piece is in the photo, and then refer to the listing to find size, color, price, and other information.

ACHILLES, ENGRAVING #698, CAMBRIDGE GLASS COMPANY, 1938 – EARLY 1950S

Color: crystal

We are continually surprised by the sheer number of readers who have thanked us for explaining the differences between Achilles and Adonis. These two engraved Cambridge patterns are similar, but they are often confused with each other. We were made aware of this a few years back when we purchased a dozen pieces of Adonis stemware in an antique shop and a Cambridge author strolled by, noticed them, and commented that we had quite a variety of stems; but he admitted that he needed a book to tell if they were Adonis or Achilles, as he always got them confused.

Achilles has a "shield" type design with a floral cut at its top. Think of "hill" within the name Achilles and the point of the shield as a "hill." That may help you identify Achilles.

Achilles is a wonderful design, but it remains difficult to find in quantity today. Apparently, more merchants were selling the heavily promoted, etched Rose Point, at the time, leaving less to be discovered today.

	Bonbon, 7½", 2-hdld., ftd. bowl, 3900/130	40.00			Plate, 13½", 2-hdld. cake, #3900/35	85.00
	Bowl, 12", 4-toed, flared, #3900/62	75.00			Plate, 14", rolled edge, #3900/166	75.00
	Candlestick, double, #399/72	50.00	5		Saucer, demi, #3400/69	20.00
	Candy box & cover, #3900/165	145.00			Stem, 1 oz., cordial, #3121	60.00
	Celery & relish, 8", 3-pt, #3900/125	65.00			Stem, 3½ oz., wine, #3121	50.00
	Celery & relish, 12", 3-pt, #3900/126	75.00			Stem, 3 oz., cocktail, #3121	25.00
	Celery & relish, 12", 5-pt, #3900/120	65.00			Stem, 4½ oz., claret, #3121	50.00
1	Cigarette holder, oval, #1066	85.00			Stem, 4½ oz., oyster cocktail, #3121	20.00
	Cocktail icer w/liner, #968	75.00			Stem, 5 oz., café parfait, #3121	40.00
	Comport, 5⅜", blown, #3121	65.00			Stem, 6 oz., high sherbet, #3121	15.00
	Comport, 5½", #3900/136	60.00			Stem, 6 oz., low sherbet, #3121	15.00
	Creamer, #3900/41	22.00			Stem, 10 oz., water goblet, #3121	38.00
5	Cup, demi, #3400/69	65.00			Sugar, #3900/41	22.00
	Mayonnaise, 2 part, #3900/11	35.00			Tumbler, 5 oz., ftd. juice, #3121	28.00
2	Mayonnaise liner, #3900/11	15.00			Tumbler, 10 oz., ftd. water, #3121	33.00
3	Mayonnaise, #3900/129	35.00			Tumbler, 12 oz., ftd. tea, #3121	40.00
	Mayonnaise liner, #3900/129	15.00			Vase, 11", ftd., #278	225.00
4	Pitcher, 80 oz., ball jug, #3400/38	265.00			Vase, 11", floral, ftd., #278	225.00
	Plate, 8", 2-hdld. ftd. bonbon, #3900/111	40.00	6		Vase, 18", floor vase, #1336	995.00
	Plate, 8½", luncheon, #3900/22	14.00				

ADONIS, ENGRAVING #740, CAMBRIDGE GLASS COMPANY, 1940S – EARLY 1950S

Color: crystal

Adonis, an engraved Cambridge pattern, appears to be easier to find than Achilles. You can identify Adonis by an oval in the design with a flower within that oval. Most tumblers and stems in Adonis are found on the #3500 line, pictured below. As with the majority of glassware patterns during this era, you will find stems in more copious amounts than any serving pieces. Stems were used with china settings. Fortunately, we have friends who collected both Adonis and Achilles; so, we were able to show you many examples of each pattern which you wouldn't have seen otherwise.

Cut patterns are usually acquired in sets or partial sets passed down within a family. Seldom do you find individual pieces for sale.

23

1   2   3   4   5   6   7   8

19	Bonbon, 7½", 2-hdld., ftd. bowl, 3900/130	40.00
18	Bowl, 9" ram's head, #3500/25	395.00
14	Bowl, 12", 4-toed, #3400/4	80.00
	Bowl, 12", 4-toed, flared, #3900/62	80.00
13	Candlestick, #627	35.00
	Candlestick, double, #399/72	65.00
12	Candlestick, double, ram's head, #657	85.00
	Candy box & cover, #3900/165	135.00
	Celery & relish, 8", 3-pt, #3900/125	60.00
	Celery & relish, 12", 3-pt, #3900/126	70.00
	Celery & relish, 12", 5-pt, #3900/120	75.00
	Cocktail icer w/liner, #968	75.00
	Comport, 5⅜", blown, #3500	65.00
	Comport, 5½", #3900/136	60.00
17	Comport, 8", 2-hdld., #3500	110.00
	Creamer, #3900/41	22.00
15	Cup, demi, #3400	75.00
9	Decanter, 28 oz., #1321	295.00
11	Ice pail, #1402/52	150.00
	Mayonnaise, 2 pt., #3900/11	35.00
	Mayonnaise liner, #3900/11	15.00
	Mayonnaise, #3900/129	35.00
	Mayonnaise liner, #3900/129	15.00
20	Plate, 6", bread, #3500	9.00
	Plate, 8", 2-hdld. ftd. bonbon, #3900/111	50.00

21	Plate, 8½", luncheon, #3500	14.00
10	Plate, 13", ftd., #3500/110	75.00
	Plate, 13½", 2-hdld. cake, #3900/35	85.00
	Plate, 14", rolled edge, #3900/166	75.00
23	Relish, 2-hdld., 2-pt.	75.00
15	Saucer, demi, #3400	15.00
22	Shaker, pr.	75.00
6	Stem, 1 oz., cordial, #3500	60.00
	Stem, 2 oz., sherry, #7966	50.00
4	Stem, 2½ oz., wine, #3500	50.00
5	Stem, 3 oz., cocktail, #3500	28.00
	Stem, 4½ oz., claret, #3500	50.00
	Stem, 4½ oz., oyster cocktail, #3500	20.00
	Stem, 5 oz., café parfait, #3500	40.00
7	Stem, 7 oz., high sherbet, #3500	15.00
8	Stem, 7 oz., low sherbet, #3500	15.00
1	Stem, 10 oz., water goblet, #3500	38.00
	Sugar, #3900/41	22.00
	Tumbler, 5 oz., ftd. juice, #3500	28.00
2	Tumbler, 10 oz., ftd. water, #3500	33.00
3	Tumbler, 13 oz., ftd. tea, #3500	40.00
16	Urn, 10" w/cover, #3500/41	395.00
	Vase, 10", ftd., bud, #274	85.00
	Vase, 11", ftd., #278	225.00
	Vase, 20", ftd.	1,095.00

ALEXIS, #1630, FOSTORIA GLASS COMPANY, 1909 – 1925

Color: crystal

Alexis is an earlier Fostoria design that was concluding its production about the time that most patterns in this book were being launched. Alexis has a timeless simplicity that sells well for us at shows across the country if we keep the price realistic. To our surprise, it has not become an exceptionally expensive pattern to amass. As usual, there are hard to find items that will be costly. Among these are pitchers, water bottles, and syrups or cruets, but various other items can be found without emptying your wallet. You will find many pressed and older glasswares gaining momentum in the collectibles market now that they are a century old. Production of Alexis began in 1909 and it was a long-lived pattern of a major company. Alexis serves as a link from the pattern glass era to that of Depression glass. Due to its age and design, wear and scratches are noticeable; so be cognizant of that.

You can find Alexis at most glass venues, antique malls, and antique shows as well as listed on internet auctions. Many times you will find it priced quite reasonably as it often goes unrecognized by sellers. Wines were bargain priced for $2.00 each in a furniture booth at a recent antique extravaganza we attended.

1	Bowl, 4½", high foot	15.00
9	Bowl, 4½", nappy	12.50
	Bowl, 5", nappy	15.00
	Bowl, 7", nappy	20.00
	Bowl, 8", nappy	20.00
10	Bowl, 8", nappy, shallow	20.00
12	Bowl, 9", nappy	25.00
	Bowl, crushed ice	25.00
	Bowl, finger (flat edge)	15.00
	Butter dish w/cover	75.00
	Catsup bottle	65.00
	Celery, tall	30.00
	Comport, 4½" high	22.50
4	Cream, short, hotel	20.00
	Cream, tall	20.00
11	Cup, hdld. custard	10.00
	Decanter w/stopper	110.00
17	Horseradish jar w/spoon	60.00
	Molasses can ewer, drip cut	65.00
	Mustard w/slotted cover	30.00
	Nut bowl	15.00
	Oil, 2 oz.	30.00
	Oil, 4 oz.	35.00
7	Oil, 6 oz.	45.00
	Oil, 9 oz.	55.00
	Pitcher, 16 oz.	45.00
	Pitcher, 32 oz.	75.00
	Pitcher, 64 oz., ice	85.00
	Pitcher, 64 oz., tall	100.00
14	Plate, crushed ice liner	10.00
	Salt shaker, pr. (2 styles)	33.00
8	Salt, individual, flat	20.00
	Salt, individual, ftd.	15.00

	Salt, table, flat	12.00
2	Spooner	25.00
	Stem, claret, 5 oz.	12.00
	Stem, cocktail, 3 oz.	10.00
	Stem, cordial, 1 oz.	12.00
	Stem, crème de menthe, 2½ oz.	12.00
13	Stem, egg cup	10.00
5	Stem, ice cream, high foot	12.00
	Stem, pousse café, ¾ oz.	14.00
	Stem, sherbet, high	10.00
	Stem, sherbet, low	8.00
	Stem, water, 10 oz.	12.00
6	Stem, wine, 2½ oz.	10.00
	Stem, wine, 3 oz.	10.00
	Sugar shaker	65.00
	Sugar, hdld., hotel	20.00
	Sugar, no handles w/lid	35.00
16	Sugar lid only	10.00
	Toothpick	30.00
	Tray, celery	25.00
	Tray, olive	20.00
	Tray, pickle	22.50
	Tumbler, ice tea	15.00
	Tumbler, ice tea, ftd., 10 oz.	18.00
15	Tumbler, water	12.00
	Tumbler, water, ftd., 8½ oz.	15.00
	Tumbler, whiskey	12.00
	Tumbler, wine	12.00
	Vase, 7", sweet pea, ftd.	50.00
3	Vase, 9", ftd.	60.00
	Vase, Nasturium (sic)	37.50
	Water bottle	85.00

17

AMERICAN, LINE #2056, FOSTORIA GLASS COMPANY, 1915 – 1986; 1987 – PRESENT

Colors: crystal; some amber, blue, green, yellow, pink tinting to purple in late 1920s; white, red in 1980s

American is Fostoria's most recognizable pattern, having been produced from 1915 until Fostoria's closing in 1986. After that, American was produced under the direction of the new owner, Lancaster Colony. Many items (particularly red colored) were subcontracted to Viking Glass Company (later Dalzell-Viking) and sold labeled Fostoria American by Lancaster Colony. The good news is that all Fostoria American forms of the pattern are no longer being made.

Don't be confused by the later designed Whitehall pattern that was produced by Indiana Glass Company and is similar to American. Whitehall's traits are inferior to that of American and shapes and sizes are dissimilar as well. Still, neophytes often fail to differentiate between the two patterns. A wealth of Whitehall is found in pink, avocado green, and several shades of blue. The glassware section of your local discount store was a good place to scrutinize colors and items being made. Whitehall's pink colored ware is frequently confused with Jeannette's Depression era Cube pattern judging by the numerous letters and e-mails we receive. There are no footed pitchers or tumblers in Jeannette's Cube, so any of those found are Whitehall. Look-alike American pieces are not marked in any way. American pieces that have been produced in recent years are indicated with an asterisk (*) in the price listing below. Most pieces found in green, pink, or blue are from Indiana's later manufactured ware.

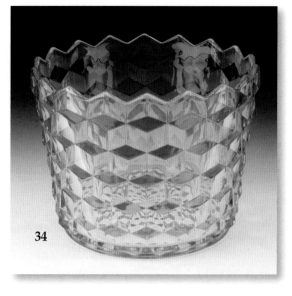

34

American, though appreciated by collectors, is beginning to be snubbed by some dealers because it is, currently, a sluggish seller due to its significant availability. Infrequently found items continue to sell well if priced within reason, but extravagantly priced items are wavering due, to a certain extent on the economy and collectors electing to do without those. In addition, the production of normally found pieces by Lancaster Colony kept supplementing an already bountiful supply.

Auction advertisements often announce Fostoria being sold when they mean the American pattern. That is generally recognized as Fostoria rather than the hundreds of other patterns that they made. These were the good "Sunday" dishes used by Mom or Grandma. When Fostoria was no longer available in the department or jewelry stores, the secondary market (glass shows, flea markets, local antique or thrift shops) became the means to replace missing or broken wares. The internet has added to the misadventures of finding true American, but the peril there is that many sellers are unprofessional or deceptive regarding glass condition (or identification). Recognize that most auctions on the internet that proclaim colored American are not Fostoria's American at all; however, having said that, an original flat, green pitcher and iced teas were recently offered and found new homes. Try to buy only from those who guarantee their merchandise. We have been told frequently that the shysters will not offer guarantees or returns.

Today, a bountiful supply of American pattern keeps a majority of the prices within reach of the typical collector. Harder to find pieces are almost out of the grasp of the ordinary collector. There are perceptible price corrections for American items being found in England. The internet has European antique dealers observing our glass collecting appetites. Those once hard-to-find English Fostoria American pieces are simpler to find here, since so many have been imported.

Reissued cookie jars continue to aggravate. A majority of the later issues have wavy lines in the pattern itself and bent or tilted knobs on the top. Old cookie jars do not. (A telling point that works more than half the time is to try to turn the lid around while it rests inside the cookie jar. The new lids seem to hang up and stop somewhere along the inside, making the whole cookie jar turn. The old jars will allow you to turn the lid completely around without catching on the sides.) However glass repairers have been known to eliminate that tell-tale problem for a fee.

If you get personal gratification from the splendor the American pattern exudes, then categorically buy it! Collecting what you like has always been primary! A little bliss in life should be courted whenever possible.

		*Crystal
	Appetizer, tray, 10½", w/6 inserts	240.00
	Appetizer, insert, 3¼"	25.00
	Ashtray, 2⅞", sq.	7.50
	Ashtray, 3⅞", oval	9.00
	Ashtray, 5", sq.	40.00
	Ashtray, 5½", oval	18.00
	Basket, w/reed handle, 7" x 9"	75.00
	Basket, 10", new in 1988 (glass handle)	40.00
	Bell	495.00
	Bottle, bitters, w/tube, 5¼", 4½ oz.	60.00
	Bottle, condiment/ketchup w/stopper	90.00
	Bottle, cologne, w/stopper, 6 oz., 5¾"	55.00
26	Bottle, cologne, w/stopper, 7¼", 8 oz.	60.00

		*Crystal
	Bottle, cordial, w/stopper, 7¼", 9 oz.	70.00
	Bottle, water, 44 oz., 9¼"	550.00
22	Bowl, banana split, 9" x 3½"	595.00
	Bowl, finger, 4½" diam., smooth edge	35.00
	Bowl, 3½", rose	15.00
	Bowl, 3¾", almond, oval	15.00
	Bowl, 4¼", jelly, 4¼" h.	12.00
	Bowl, 4½", 1 hdld.*	8.00
	Bowl, 4½", 1 hdld., sq.	8.00
	Bowl, 4½", jelly, w/cover, 6¾" h.	22.00
	Bowl, 4½", nappy*	10.00
	Bowl, 4½", oval	12.00
	Bowl, 4¾", fruit, flared	12.00

* See note in second paragraph above.

		*Crystal
	Bowl, 5", cream soup, 2 hdld.	40.00
	Bowl, 5", 1 hdld., tri-corner	10.00
	Bowl, 5", nappy*	8.00
	Bowl, 5", nappy, w/cover	22.00
	Bowl, 5", rose	25.00
	Bowl, 5½", lemon, w/cover	42.00
	Bowl, 5½", preserve, 2 hdld., w/cover	75.00
18	Bowl, 6", bonbon, 3 ftd.	12.00
	Bowl, 6", nappy*	12.00
	Bowl, 6", olive, oblong	10.00
	Bowl, 6½", wedding, w/cover, sq., ped. ft., 8" h.	90.00

		*Crystal
	Bowl, 6½", wedding, sq., ped. ft., 5¼" h.	60.00
	Bowl, 7", bonbon, 3 ftd.	11.00
	Bowl, 7", cupped, 4½" h.	48.00
	Bowl, 7", nappy*	22.00
	Bowl, 8", bonbon, 3 ftd.	15.00
	Bowl, 8", deep	55.00
	Bowl, 8", ftd.	75.00
	Bowl, 8", ftd., 2 hdld., "trophy" cup	90.00
15	Bowl, 8", nappy*	22.00
	Bowl, 8", pickle, oblong*	13.00
9	Bowl, 8½", 2 hdld.	40.00

		*Crystal
	Bowl, 8½", boat*	14.00
	Bowl, 9", boat, 2 pt.	11.00
	Bowl, 9", oval veg.*	28.00
	Bowl, 9½", centerpiece	40.00
	Bowl, 9½", 3 pt., 6" w.	30.00
16	Bowl, 10", celery, oblong	20.00
	Bowl, 10", deep*	35.00
	Bowl, 10", float	40.00
	Bowl, 10", oval, float	30.00
	Bowl, 10", oval, veg., 2 pt.	30.00
12	Bowl, 10½", fruit, 3 ftd.	35.00
	Bowl, 11", centerpiece	40.00
	Bowl, 11", centerpiece, tri-corner	40.00
	Bowl, 11", relish/celery, 3 pt.	28.00
	Bowl, 11½", float	60.00
	Bowl, 11½", fruit, rolled edge, 2¾" h.	40.00
13	Bowl, 11½", oval, float	40.00
	Bowl, 11½", rolled edge	45.00
	Bowl, 11¾", oval, deep	40.00
	Bowl, 12", boat	17.00
	Bowl, 12", fruit/sm. punch, ped. ft. (Tom & Jerry)*	185.00
	Bowl, 12", lily pond	50.00
	Bowl, 12", relish "boat," 2 pt.	20.00
	Bowl, 13", fruit, shallow	65.00
	Bowl, 14", punch, w/high ft. base (2 gal.)	300.00
	Bowl, 14", punch, w/low ft. base	275.00
	Bowl, 15", centerpiece, "hat" shape	175.00
	Bowl, 16", flat, fruit, ped. ft.	190.00
	Bowl, 18", punch, w/low ft. base (3¾ gal.)	395.00
	Box, pomade, 2" square	275.00
27	Box, w/cover, puff, 3⅛" x 2¾"	195.00
	Box, w/cover, 4½" x 4½"	195.00
25	Box, w/cover, handkerchief, 5⅝" x 4⅝"	250.00
	Box, w/cover, hairpin, 3½" x 1¾"	295.00
28	Box, w/cover, jewel, 5¼" x 2¼"	275.00
	Box, w/cover, jewel, 2 drawer, 4¼" x 3¼"	6,000.00
31	Box, w/cover, glove, 9½" x 3½"	275.00
	Butter, w/cover, rnd. plate, 7¼"*	80.00
19	Butter, w/cover, ¼ lb.*	16.00
	Cake stand (see salver)	
	Candelabrum, 6½", 2-lite, bell base w/bobeche & prisms	110.00
	Candle lamp, 8½", w/chimney, candle part, 3½"	135.00
	Candlestick, twin, 4⅛" h., 8½" spread	35.00
	Candlestick, 2", chamber with fingerhold	35.00
	Candlestick, 3", rnd. ft.**	12.00
	Candlestick, 4⅜", 2-lite, rnd. ft.	35.00
	Candlestick, 6", octagon ft.	20.00
2	Candlestick, 6½", 2-lite, bell base	65.00
	Candlestick, 6¼", round ft.	165.00
	Candlestick, 7", sq. column*	100.00
	Candlestick, 7¼", "Eiffel" tower	135.00
	Candy box, w/cover, 3 pt., triangular	70.00
	Candy, w/cover, ped. ft.	30.00

		*Crystal
	Cheese (5¾" compote) & cracker (11½" plate)	60.00
	Cigarette box, w/cover, 4¾"	30.00
	Coaster, 3¾"	6.00
	Comport, 4½", jelly	9.00
	Comport, 5", jelly, flared*	9.00
	Comport, 6¾", jelly, w/cover*	30.00
	Comport, 8½", 4" high	40.00
	Comport, 9½", 5¼" high	75.00
	Comport, w/cover, 5"	22.00
	Cookie jar, w/cover, 8⅞" h.**	225.00
	Creamer, tea, 3 oz., 2⅜" (#20561⁄2)	6.00
	Creamer, individual, 4¾ oz.	6.00
	Creamer, 9½ oz.	9.00
	Crushed fruit, w/cover & spoon, 10"	2,500.00
	Cup, flat	5.00
21	Cup, ftd., 7 oz.	5.00
	Cup, punch, flared rim	7.00
	Cup, punch, straight edge	7.00
	Decanter, w/stopper, 24 oz., 9¼" h.	70.00
	Dresser set: powder boxes w/covers & tray	475.00
1	Flower pot, w/perforated cover, 9½" diam., 5½" h.	1,750.00
5	Goblet, #2056, 2½ oz., wine, hex ft., 4½" h.	6.00
	Goblet, #2056, 4½ oz., oyster cocktail, 3½" h.	9.00
	Goblet, #2056, 4½ oz., sherbet, flared, 4⅜" h.	5.00
	Goblet, #2056, 4½ oz., fruit, hex ft., 4¾" h	5.00
	Goblet, #2056, 5 oz., low ft., sherbet, flared, 3¼" h	5.00
	Goblet, #2056, 6 oz., low ft., sundae, 3⅛" h.	5.00
	Goblet, #2056, 7 oz., claret, 4⅞" h.	40.00
	Goblet, #2056, 9 oz., low ft., 4⅜" h.*	7.00
	Goblet, #2056, 10 oz., hex ft., water, 6⅞" h.	7.00
	Goblet, #2056, 12 oz., low ft., tea, 5¾" h.	12.00
	Goblet, #2056½, 4½ oz., sherbet, 4½" h.	6.00
	Goblet, #2056½, 5 oz., low sherbet, 3½" h.	6.00
	Goblet, #5056, 1 oz., cordial, 3⅛", w/plain bowl	30.00
	Goblet, #5056, 3½ oz., claret, 4⅝", w/plain bowl	12.00
	Goblet, #5056, 3½ oz., cocktail, 4", w/plain bowl	8.00
	Goblet, #5056, 4 oz., oyster cocktail, 3½", w/plain bowl	8.00
	Goblet, #5056, 5½ oz., sherbet, 4⅛", w/plain bowl	6.00

1

AMERICAN

		*Crystal
	Goblet, #5056, 10 oz., water, 6⅛", w/plain bowl	10.00
	Hair receiver, 3" x 3"	395.00
	Hat, 2⅛" (sm. ashtray)	14.00
10	Hat, 3" tall	25.00
24	Hat, 4" tall	50.00
	Hat, western style	295.00
34	Hotel ice tub	3,500.00
	Hotel washbowl and pitcher	2,500.00
	Hurricane lamp, 12" complete w/chimney	150.00
	Hurricane lamp base	40.00
	Ice bucket, w/tongs	50.00
	Ice cream saucer (2 styles)	30.00
	Ice dish for 4 oz. crab or 5 oz. tomato liner	25.00
	Ice dish insert	6.00
	Ice tub, w/liner, 5⅝"	75.00
	Ice tub, w/liner, 6½"	75.00
	Jam pot, w/cover	50.00
	Jar, pickle, w/pointed cover, 6" h.	250.00
33	Liquor set in locking metal holder	250.00
	Marmalade, w/cover & chrome spoon	40.00
	Mayonnaise, div.*	14.00
	Mayonnaise, w/ladle, ped. ft.	50.00
	Mayonnaise, w/liner & ladle	30.00
	Molasses can, 11 oz., 6¾" h., 1 hdld.	450.00
	Mug, 5½ oz., Tom & Jerry, 3¼" h.*	30.00
	Mug, 12 oz., beer, 4½" h.*	50.00
	Mustard, w/cover	30.00
	Napkin ring	18.00
	Oil, 5 oz.	26.00
	Oil, 7 oz.	28.00
	Picture frame	12.00
	Pitcher, ½ gal. w/ice lip, 8¼", flat bottom	65.00
	Pitcher, ½ gal., w/o ice lip, 69 oz. (2056½)	225.00
8	Pitcher, ½ gal., 8", ftd.	60.00
	Pitcher, 1 pt., 5⅜", flat	25.00
	Pitcher, 2 pt., 7¼", ftd.	55.00
	Pitcher, 3 pt., 8", ftd.	60.00
	Pitcher, 3 pt., w/ice lip, 6½", ftd., "fat"	55.00
	Pitcher, 1 qt., flat*	28.00
	Plate, cream soup liner	7.00
	Plate, 6", bread & butter	7.00
	Plate, 7", salad	7.00
	Plate, 7½" x 4⅜", crescent salad	40.00
	Plate, 8", sauce liner, oval	15.00
	Plate, 8½", salad	8.00
	Plate, 9", sandwich (sm. center)	12.00
	Plate, 9½", dinner	16.00
	Plate, 10", cake, 2 hdld.	24.00
	Plate, 10½", sandwich (sm. center)	17.00
	Plate, 11½", sandwich (sm. center)	17.00
	Plate, 12", cake, 3 ftd.	25.00
	Plate, 13½", oval torte	45.00
	Plate, 14", torte	70.00
	Plate, 18", torte	125.00
	Plate, 20", torte	150.00

		*Crystal
	Plate 24", torte	195.00
	Platter, 10½", oval*	32.00
14	Platter, 12", oval	50.00
	Ring holder	200.00
	Salad set: 10" bowl, 14" torte, wood fork & spoon	125.00
	Salt, individual	8.00
23	Salver, 10", sq., ped. ft. (cake stand)	130.00
17	Salver, 10", rnd., ped. ft. (cake stand)	85.00
	Salver, 11", rnd., ped. ft. (cake stand)*	35.00
	Sauce boat & liner	40.00
21	Saucer	2.00
	Set: 2 jam pots w/tray	125.00
	Set: decanter, six 2 oz. whiskeys on 10½" tray	210.00
	Set: toddler, w/baby tumbler & bowl	90.00
	Set: youth, w/bowl, hdld. mug, 6" plate	100.00
	Set: condiment, 2 oils, 2 shakers, mustard w/ cover & spoon w/tray	300.00
	Shaker, 3", ea.	9.00
	Shaker, 3½", ea.*	6.00
	Shaker, 3¼", ea.	9.00
	Shakers w/tray, individual, 2"	17.00
	Sherbet, handled, 3½" high, 4½ oz.	75.00
	Shrimp bowl, 12¼"	295.00
29	Soap dish	995.00
	Spooner, 3¾"	35.00
	Strawholder, 10", w/cover**	250.00
	Sugar, tea, 2¼" (#2056½)	10.00
	Sugar, hdld., 3¼" h.	10.00
	Sugar shaker	55.00
	Sugar, w/o cover	8.00
	Sugar, w/cover, no hdl., 6¼" (cover fits strawholder)	55.00
	Sugar, w/cover, 2 hdld.	18.00
	Syrup, 6½ oz., #2056½, Sani-cut server	50.00
	Syrup, 6 oz., non pour screw top, 5¼" h.	225.00
11	Syrup, 10 oz., w/glass cover & 6" liner plate	150.00
	Syrup, w/drip proof top	30.00
	Toothpick	20.00
	Tray, cloverleaf for condiment set	135.00
	Tray, tidbit, w/question mark metal handle	30.00
	Tray, pin, oval, 5½" x 4½"	195.00
30	Tray, 5" x 2½", rect.	70.00
	Tray, 6" oval, hdld.	30.00
	Tray, 6½" x 9" relish, 4 part	40.00
	Tray, 9½", service, 2 hdld.	28.00
	Tray, 10", muffin (2 upturned sides)	30.00
	Tray, 10", square, 4 part	70.00
	Tray, 10½", cake, w/question mark metal hdl.	26.00
32	Tray, 10½" x 7½", rect.	60.00
	Tray, 10½" x 5", oval hdld.	40.00
	Tray, 10¾", square, 4 part	135.00
	Tray, 12", sand. w/ctr. handle	33.00
	Tray, 12", round	125.00
	Tray, 13½", oval, ice cream	150.00

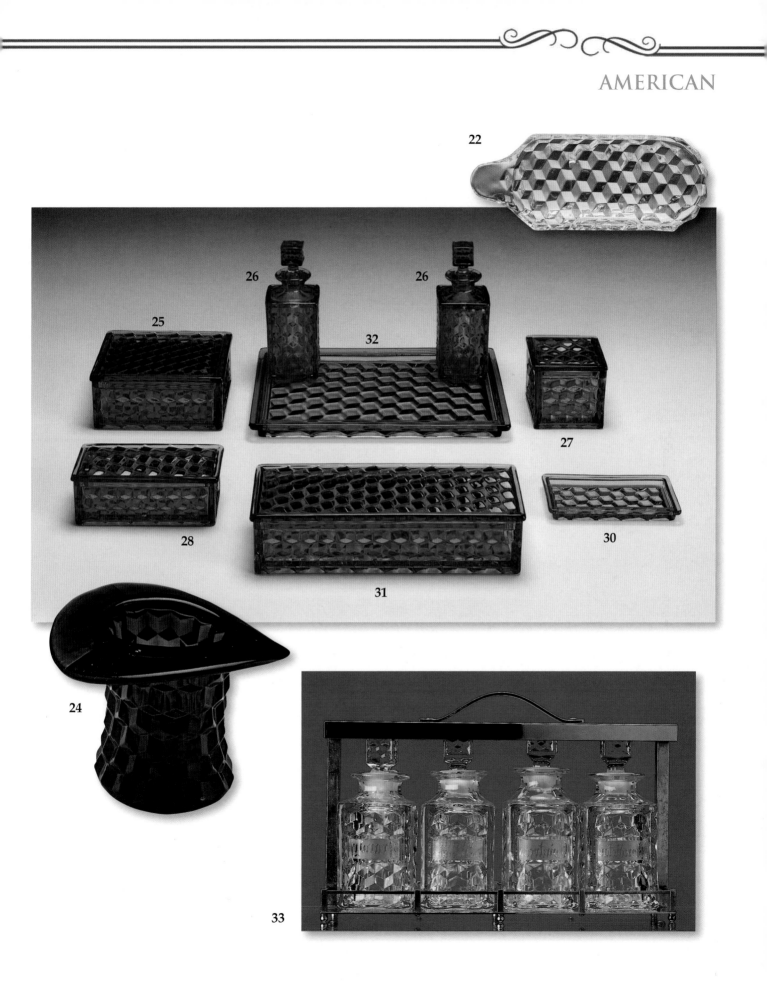

AMERICAN

29

29

		*Crystal
	Tray for sugar & creamer, tab. hdld., 6¾"	9.00
	Tumbler, hdld. iced tea	365.00
	Tumbler, #2056, 2 oz., whiskey, 2½" h.	8.00
	Tumbler, #2056, 3 oz., ftd. cone, cocktail, 2⅞" h.	9.00
	Tumbler, #2056, 5 oz., ftd., juice, 4¾"	9.00
6	Tumbler, #2056, 6 oz., flat, old-fashion, 3⅜" h.	12.00
	Tumbler, #2056, 8 oz. flat, water, flared, 4⅛" h.	12.00
7	Tumbler, #2056, 9 oz. ftd., water, 4⅞" h.*	9.00
	Tumbler, #2056, 12 oz., flat, tea, flared, 5¼" h.	12.00
	Tumbler, #2056½, 5 oz., straight side, juice	12.00
	Tumbler, #2056½, 8 oz., straight side, water, 3⅞" h.	10.00
	Tumbler, #2056½, 12 oz., straight side, tea, 5" h	15.00
	Tumbler, #5056, 5 oz., ftd., juice, 4⅛" w/plain bowl	5.00
	Tumbler, #5056, 12 oz., ftd., tea, 5½" w/plain bowl	6.00
	Urn, 6", sq., ped. ft	25.00
20	Urn, 7½", sq. ped. ft.	35.00
	Vase, 4½", sweet pea	65.00
4	Vase, 6", bud, ftd., cupped	15.00

		*Crystal
	Vase, 6", bud, flared*	15.00
	Vase, 6", straight side	30.00
	Vase, 6½", flared rim	14.00
	Vase, 7", flared	65.00
	Vase, 8", straight side*	35.00
	Vase, 8", flared*	75.00
	Vase, 8", porch, 5" diam.	495.00
	Vase, 8½", bud, flared	20.00
	Vase, 8½", bud, cupped	20.00
3	Vase, 9", w/sq. ped. ft.	40.00
	Vase, 9½", flared	135.00
	Vase, 10", cupped in top	295.00
	Vase, 10", porch, 8" diam.	795.00
	Vase, 10", straight side*	70.00
	Vase, 10", swung	195.00
	Vase, 10", flared	75.00
	Vase, 12", straight side	250.00
	Vase, 12", swung	250.00
	Vase, 14", swung	250.00
	Vase, 20", swung	395.00

AMERICAN BEAUTY, ETCHING #734, MORGANTOWN GLASS COMPANY

Colors: amber, blue, crystal, green, and pink

American Beauty evidently was widely dispersed in a quantity of stems and colors. Other items are rarely seen. The separate cordial pictured illustrates stem #7575 which has a rose vine climbing along the stem. Those stems are highly desired.

		*Crystal
	Candlestick, 3⅛", #7951 Stafford	100.00
	Compote, 5" w/8" diameter	40.00
	Compote, 6½" high, w/cover, #7941 Helena	195.00
	Custard liner, 5⅛"	15.00
	Custard, hdld. #8851	75.00
	Finger bowl liner	10.00
	Finger bowl, 4⅜", #2927	45.00
	Nappy, 6" diameter, w/cover, #7557 Savoy	155.00
	Nut, 4½" master w/cover, #7556	165.00
	Pitcher, 48 oz. 8"	210.00
	Pitcher, 54 oz. w/lid, #2 Arcadia	325.00
	Plate, 7¼"	10.00
5	Plate, 7½", #1511	10.00
	Stem, ¾ oz. cordial, #7565 Astrid	50.00
6	Stem, ¾ oz., 4⅜" cordial, #7575	75.00
	Stem, 1½ oz. port, #7565 Astrid	25.00
	Stem, 1 oz. pousse cafe, #7565 Astrid	40.00
	Stem, 2½ oz. sherry, #7565 Astrid	20.00
	Stem, 3 oz., 6" sherry, #7695 trumpet	40.00
3	Stem, 3 oz., 5" cocktail, Monroe cut stem	35.00
	Stem, 3 oz. wine, #7565 Astrid	20.00
	Stem, 3½ oz. cocktail, #7565 Astrid	12.00

		*Crystal
1	Stem, 3½ oz. cocktail, #7669 Grandure	16.00
	Stem, 4½ oz. parfait, #7565 Astrid	18.00
	Stem, 4½ oz., 5⅝", tall champagne, #7565 Astrid	18.00
	Stem, 4¼ oz. claret, #7565 Astrid	22.00
	Stem, 5 oz. deep champagne, #7565 Astrid	18.00
	Stem, 5 oz. hot whiskey, #7565 Astrid	14.00
	Stem, 5 oz. sherbet, #7565 Astrid	14.00
2	Stem, 5½ oz. saucer champagne, #7565 Astrid	18.00
	Stem, 6 oz., champagne	18.00
	Stem, 6½ oz., 4⅝" bowl champagne, #7565 Astrid	18.00
	Stem, 8½ oz., #7565 Astrid	26.00
4	Stem, 9 oz., 7" water	30.00
	Stem, 10 oz. water, #7565 Astrid	35.00
	Stem, 11 oz., 7½" water, #7695 trumpet	40.00
	Tumbler, 2¾ oz., 2¼" bar, #8107 Sherman	35.00
	Tumbler, 8 oz., 4⅛" water, #9001 Billings	30.00
	Tumbler, 9 oz, ftd. w/handle, #9069 Hopper	50.00
	Tumbler, 9 oz., 4⅝" water, #8701 Garrett	30.00
	Tumbler, 12 oz, 4⅞", #9715 Calhoun	30.00
	Tumbler, 12 oz, ftd. w/handle, #9069 Hopper	60.00
	Vase, 10", #25 Olympic	165.00
	Vase, 12" #25 Olympic	200.00

* Add 40% for colors.

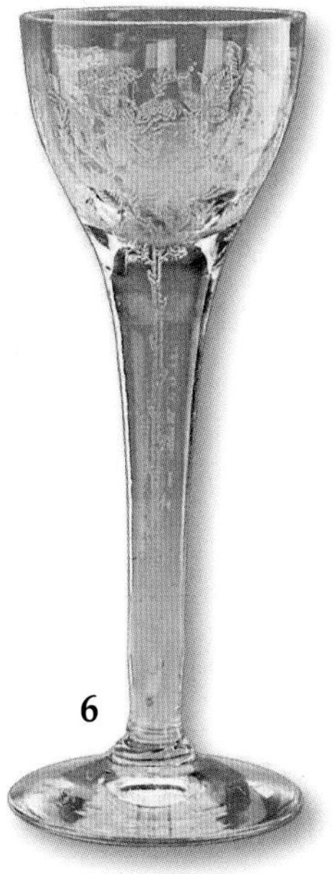

APPLE BLOSSOM, LINE #3400, CAMBRIDGE GLASS COMPANY, 1930S

Colors: amber, amethyst, crystal, crystal w/ebony stem, light and dark Emerald, Gold Krystol, Heatherbloom, Peach Blo, Royal blue, Willow blue

Apple Blossom's Gold Krystol (Cambridge's yellow) is the color most gathered by collectors. That color is found on a regular basis and is the most reasonably priced except for crystal. You can achieve a small set with luck; however, difficult to find items and serving pieces remain expensive. Notice the round casserole pictured. Luckily, we were able to obtain a photo, because it was broken in the shipment to us. Beverage items (tumblers and stems) can still be found in most colors. Buy every serving piece or dinner plate every time you have a chance.

Other colors can be found with patience (and funds); although, availability of pink, green, blue, and Heatherbloom is quite insufficient to those of yellow or crystal. Very little dark Emerald green, amethyst, or amber is uncovered. Pieces of blue produce a lot of excitement when displayed; but more often than not, the price makes viewers hesitate at buying those.

Apple Blossom was etched on several Cambridge stemware lines, but the #3130 line is predominantly found and collected. Some collectors presently mix stemware lines, but since bowl shapes differ, most still shy from that. One collector told us that she was collecting several yellow stem lines simultaneously because she loved Apple Blossom and bought everything she could find no matter what the stem line. That collecting mode may become more customary in the future, principally in Elegant patterns like this.

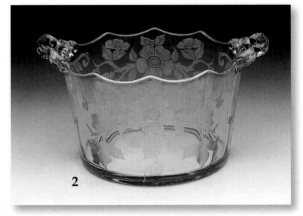

2

		Crystal	Yellow Amber	Pink *Green
14	Ashtray, 6", heavy	30.00	75.00	125.00
	Bowl, #3025, ftd., finger, w/plate	40.00	65.00	75.00
	Bowl, #3130, finger, w/plate	35.00	60.00	70.00
12	Bowl, 3", indiv. nut, 4 ftd., 3400/71	40.00	60.00	65.00
6	Bowl, 5¼", 2 hdld., bonbon, 3400/1180	22.00	40.00	45.00
3	Bowl, 5½", 2 hdld., bonbon, 3400/1179	22.00	40.00	40.00
	Bowl, 5½", fruit "saucer"	18.00	28.00	30.00
13	Bowl, 6", 2 hdld., "basket" (sides up), 3400/1182	30.00	48.00	50.00
	Bowl, 6", cereal	25.00	45.00	50.00
	Bowl, 9", pickle	30.00	55.00	60.00
	Bowl, 10", 2 hdld.	55.00	95.00	110.00
	Bowl, 10", baker	50.00	100.00	110.00
	Bowl, 10", oval baker	30.00	60.00	75.00
	Bowl, 11", fruit, tab hdld.	65.00	110.00	125.00
	Bowl, 11", low ftd.	60.00	100.00	120.00
9	Bowl, 12", relish, 5 pt., 3400/67	40.00	70.00	75.00
	Bowl, 12", 4 ftd.	60.00	100.00	125.00
	Bowl, 12", flat	55.00	90.00	95.00
38	Bowl, 12", oval, 4 ftd., 3400/1240	65.00	95.00	125.00
	Bowl, 12½", console	55.00	75.00	80.00
	Bowl, 13"	55.00	90.00	100.00
	Bowl, cream soup, w/liner plate	32.00	55.00	60.00
	Butter w/cover, 5½"	135.00	275.00	375.00
19	Cabinet flask, 12 oz., 3400/46	110.00	150.00	195.00
	Candelabrum, 3-lite, keyhole	35.00	45.00	70.00
43	Candlestick, 1-lite, keyhole, 3400/646	20.00	32.00	38.00
	Candlestick, 2-lite, keyhole	28.00	40.00	45.00
39	Candlestick, 4", #627	20.00	32.00	38.00
	Candy box w/cover, 4 ftd. "bowl"	85.00	145.00	195.00
1	Casserole, 10½", #912	195.00	400.00	
16	Cheese (compote) & cracker (11½" plate), 3400/6	40.00	75.00	95.00
	Comport, 4", fruit cocktail	16.00	25.00	28.00
	Comport, 7", tall	38.00	60.00	75.00

* Blue prices 25% to 30% more.

		Crystal	Yellow Amber	Pink *Green
4	Creamer, ftd., 3400/68	16.00	20.00	25.00
	Creamer, tall, ftd.	18.00	24.00	30.00
36	Cologne, 2 oz., 3400/97	60.00	90.00	120.00
17	Cup, 3400/75	12.00	22.00	30.00
24	Cup, A.D., 3400/83	40.00	60.00	75.00
	Ice bucket	65.00	100.00	150.00
2	Ice tub, #1147	60.00	95.00	135.00
	Fruit/oyster cocktail, #3025, 4½ oz.	18.00	22.00	28.00
	Mayonnaise, w/liner & ladle (4 ftd. bowl)	40.00	65.00	80.00
	Pitcher, 50 oz., ftd., flattened sides	195.00	295.00	395.00
	Pitcher, 64 oz., #3130	215.00	325.00	400.00
	Pitcher, 64 oz., #3025	215.00	325.00	400.00
	Pitcher, 67 oz., squeezed middle, loop hdld.	225.00	375.00	425.00
	Pitcher, 76 oz.	125.00	350.00	425.00
21	Pitcher, 80 oz., ball, 3400/38	175.00	350.00	495.00
	Pitcher w/cover, 76 oz., ftd., #3135	250.00	395.00	595.00
7	Plate, 6", bread/butter, 3400/60	6.00	8.00	10.00
	Plate, 6", sq., 2 hdld.	8.00	18.00	20.00
	Plate, 7½", tea	9.00	18.00	20.00
	Plate, 8½"	14.00	20.00	25.00
	Plate, 9½", dinner	40.00	65.00	80.00
	Plate, 10", grill, 3400/66, club luncheon	35.00	55.00	75.00

* Blue prices 25% to 30% more.

APPLE BLOSSOM

1

19

20

21

		Crystal	Yellow Amber	Pink *Green
	Plate, sandwich, 11½", tab hdld.	30.00	45.00	50.00
	Plate, sandwich, 12½", 2 hdld.	32.00	50.00	60.00
	Plate, sq., bread/butter	6.00	8.00	10.00
	Plate, sq., dinner	45.00	75.00	95.00
	Plate, sq., salad	10.00	20.00	22.00
	Plate, sq., servce	28.00	45.00	50.00
	Platter, 11½	50.00	85.00	105.00
	Platter, 13½" rect., w/tab handle	55.00	110.00	150.00
20	Puff Box, 3½", #3400/94	90.00	125.00	160.00
27	Relish, 8", 4-pt center handle, 3400/862	30.00	50.00	65.00
26	Salt & pepper, pr., 3400/77	40.00	95.00	125.00
18	Saucer, 3400/54 rnd.	3.00	5.00	6.00
25	Saucer, A.D., squared, 3400/83	16.00	25.00	30.00
	Stem, #1066, parfait	45.00	100.00	130.00
	Stem, #3025, 7 oz., low fancy ft., sherbet	14.00	22.00	25.00
	Stem, #3025, 7 oz., high sherbet	16.00	25.00	28.00
	Stem, #3025, 10 oz.	22.00	30.00	40.00
	Stem, #3130, 1 oz., cordial	40.00	75.00	120.00
11	Stem, #3130, 3 oz., cocktail	15.00	24.00	28.00
	Stem, #3130, 6 oz., low sherbet	11.00	18.00	20.00
22	Stem, #3130, 6 oz., tall sherbet	15.00	25.00	28.00
	Stem, #3130, 8 oz., water	20.00	25.00	38.00
29	Stem, #3135, 3 oz., cocktail	15.00	24.00	26.00
	Stem, #3135, 6 oz., low sherbet	11.00	18.00	20.00
	Stem, #3135, 6 oz., tall sherbet	15.00	25.00	28.00
	Stem, #3135, 8 oz., water	20.00	25.00	30.00
23	Stem, #3400, 6 oz., ftd., sherbet	12.00	16.00	20.00
10	Stem, #3400, 9 oz., water	16.00	28.00	40.00
37	Sugar, ftd., 3400/68	16.00	20.00	25.00
	Sugar, tall ftd.	16.00	24.00	30.00
	Tray, 7", hdld. relish	25.00	40.00	45.00
15	Tray, 11", ctr. hdld. sand., 3400/10	33.00	45.00	55.00
33	Tumbler, 9 oz., #321	25.00		
31	Tumbler, 10 oz., sham bottom	25.00	30.00	40.00
42	Tumbler, 2½ oz., #8161	15.00	30.00	40.00
	Tumbler, #3025, 4 oz.	15.00	24.00	28.00
	Tumbler, #3025, 10 oz.	20.00	30.00	35.00
	Tumbler, #3025, 12 oz.	25.00	40.00	45.00
8	Tumbler, #3130, 2½ oz.	14.00	25.00	45.00
34	Tumbler, #3130, 5 oz., ftd.	16.00	28.00	33.00
	Tumbler, #3130, 8 oz., ftd.	22.00	30.00	35.00
	Tumbler, #3130, 10 oz., ftd.	25.00	35.00	40.00
35	Tumbler, #3130, 12 oz., ftd.	30.00	40.00	50.00
	Tumbler, #3135, 5 oz., ftd.	16.00	30.00	35.00
	Tumbler, #3135, 8 oz., ftd.	22.00	35.00	40.00
40	Tumbler, #3135, 10 oz., ftd.	25.00	35.00	45.00
41	Tumbler, #3135, 12 oz., ftd.	30.00	40.00	50.00
	Tumbler, #3400, 2½ oz., flat	30.00	70.00	80.00
32	Tumbler, #3400, 12 oz., ftd.	22.00	30.00	35.00
	Tumbler, #3400, 14 oz., flat	30.00	40.00	50.00
30	Tumbler, 12 oz., flat, #9403 (2 styles) – 1 mid indent to match 67 oz. pitcher	25.00	50.00	60.00
	Tumbler, 6"	25.00	45.00	50.00
28	Vase, 5", #1309	65.00	110.00	145.00
	Vase, 6", rippled sides	95.00	145.00	195.00
	Vase, 8", 2 styles	100.00	175.00	225.00
	Vase, 12", keyhole base w/neck indent	125.00	195.00	265.00

"BALDA," ETCH #410, CENTRAL GLASS WORKS, 1920S – 1930S
Colors: Amber, Amethyst, black, blue, crystal, green, pink

"Balda" is a Central Glass Works pattern that was designed by Joseph Balda who was highly praised for his Heisey designs. Central Glass Works archives presented it as Etch #410; hence its designer's nomenclature thus far. As with other Elegant patterns, stems are the most frequently found items. Amazingly, Amethyst (lilac), as pictured here, is the often found color and consequently the most collected. Color and collectibility add to the higher price asked for amethyst. We created an "instant" collector in Michigan when a lady saw the Amethyst as the "loveliest pattern" she'd ever seen.

Internet auctions revealed "Balda" to masses of collectors. At first, there was a rash of activity with briskly escalating prices. Recently things have settled into more realistic realms and the collectors searching for "Balda" are able to shop for acceptable prices. There are almost certainly additional pieces and/or colors to those listed at this time. It is unlikely you will discover large groupings of "Balda," except for stemware or plates, but it does happen every so often.

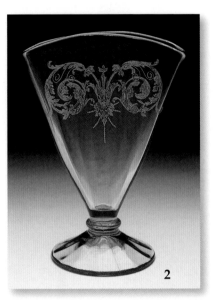

2

Morgan, another Central Glass pattern, is also found on the same #1428 stem and tumbler line pictured here in Amethyst. The Morgan pattern is etched on at least two additional stem lines (page 159), so "Balda" may also be found etched on other Central stemware lines. Let us know if you find additional pieces or other stemware lines etched with "Balda."

1

		Blue Amethyst	Pink Green Amber
	Bowl, 7" soup	55.00	45.00
	Candy and lid, cone shaped, 7⅝" tall	250.00	195.00
	Candlestick	65.00	45.00
	Creamer, ftd.	35.00	25.00
	Cup	25.00	20.00
	Decanter and stopper	450.00	325.00
6	Finger bowl	40.00	25.00
	Ice bucket	295.00	195.00
	Pitcher	795.00	595.00
	Plate, 6"	10.00	8.00
	Plate, lunch	15.00	12.00
4	Plate, dinner	65.00	45.00
	Platter	95.00	65.00
	Saucer	4.00	3.00
1	Server, center handled	75.00	55.00
	Shaker, pr		175.00
3	Stem, champagne/sherbet	20.00	15.00
	Stem, claret	70.00	35.00
	Stem, cordial	65.00	50.00
7	Stem, water	35.00	25.00
5	Stem, wine	35.00	25.00
	Suger, ftd.	35.00	25.00
	Tumbler, ftd. juice	22.00	18.00
	Tumbler, ftd. tea	30.00	28.00
	Tumbler, ftd. water	25.00	22.00
	Tumbler, ftd. whiskey	50.00	35.00
2	Vase, 7", fan	150.00	100.00
	Vase, 9"	195.00	135.00

BAROQUE, LINE #2496, FOSTORIA GLASS COMPANY, 1936 – 1966

Colors: crystal, Azure blue, Topaz yellow, amber, green, pink, red, cobalt blue, black amethyst

Baroque is mostly collected in Azure (blue) and Topaz (yellow), but there are a few seeking the more abundant crystal. Lancaster Colony produced a few pieces of Baroque in a color similar to Fostoria's Wisteria for Tiara. We have seen bowls and vases, but not the candle that was also made. Our old Tiara catalogs do not show the candle. These items do have a purple/pink tint; do not pay collectible prices for Baroque pieces in this color. Baroque was never made in the original Fostoria Wisteria, which, by the way, does change tints in natural or artificial light. However, this later made color does not.

Cream soups and individual shakers are hard to find in colors, and to some degree, crystal. These have always been expensive. The regular size shakers came with both metal and glass tops. Today, most collectors prefer glass lids, but they are found sporadically. Glass lids were easily broken by over tightening them. Fostoria switched to metal lids before Baroque production was discontinued. Replacement lids were always metal. Metal tops are typically found on the later crystal patterns of Navarre, Chintz, Lido, and Meadow Rose that were etched onto Baroque blanks.

28   29   28

Baroque pitchers and punch bowls are not abundant; but blue ones are, for all intents and purposes, impossible to find. Straight tumblers are more expensive and challenging to find than footed ones, but are preferred over cone-shaped, footed pieces although the flat ones are more expensive. Because the larger 9" sweetmeats are often misrepresented as the smaller covered 7½" jelly, we have pictured them above to show the size distinction.

Baroque has seven distinctive candlesticks, and candles are one item that buyers accumulate regardless of the pattern. There are many books out addressing this candlestick-collecting experience, two of which are ours (*Glass Candlesticks of the Depression Era, Volumes 1* and *2*).

You can find both 4" and 5½" single light candles and a 4½" double candle. The 6" three-light (triple) candlesticks are called candelabra when prisms are attached. Some collectors desire these elusive candelabra with original prism wires attached. However, collectors prefer newer wires and are exchanging them for the old, rusty ones. Once prisms are secured properly (try needle nose pliers or medical hemostats), they rarely come off, even if moved. New prisms and wires are obtainable at lamp and hardware stores.

Triple candlesticks without the prisms have been located in all the colors listed in the heading, but matching console bowls have never been seen in red, cobalt blue, or amethyst. Some pieces of Azure (blue) Baroque are found as a light green (bad batches of blue that were sold anyhow). This light green color is not as prized as Azure and even more difficult to find. Not all pieces occur in this hue.

		Crystal	Blue	Yellow
	Ashtray	10.00	20.00	15.00
19	Bowl, cream soup	30.00	75.00	60.00
	Bowl, ftd., punch, 1½ gal., 8¼" x 13¼"	395.00	995.00	
	Bowl, 3¾", rose	30.00	90.00	60.00
8, 12, 21	Bowl, 4", hdld. (4 styles: sq., rnd., tab hdld. mint, 4⅝" tricorn)	10.00	25.00	20.00
	Bowl, 5", fruit	12.00	33.00	25.00
	Bowl, 6", cereal	18.00	45.00	35.00
	Bowl, 6", sq., sweetmeat	12.00	25.00	22.00
22	Bowl, 6", 3-toe nut	12.00	28.00	18.00
11	Bowl, 6", 2-part relish, sq.	12.00	28.00	18.00
	Bowl, 6½", oblong sauce	14.00	28.00	18.00
	Bowl, 6½", 2 pt. mayonnaise, oval tab hdl.	15.00	30.00	20.00
	Bowl, 7", 3 ftd.	12.50	22.00	22.00
29	Bowl, 7½", jelly, w/cover	45.00	135.00	75.00
	Bowl, 8", pickle	15.00	30.00	25.00
	Bowl, 8½", hdld.	30.00	60.00	45.00
23	Bowl, 9½", veg., oval	40.00	80.00	60.00
	Bowl, 10", hdld.	35.00	90.00	65.00
24	Bowl, 10" x 7½", hdld.	30.00		
	Bowl, 10", relish, 3 pt.	22.00	40.00	30.00
	Bowl, 10½", hdld., 4 ftd.	35.00	75.00	60.00
	Bowl, 11", celery	28.00	40.00	33.00

		Crystal	Blue	Yellow
7	Bowl, 10½", salad	35.00	75.00	60.00
	Bowl, 11", rolled edge	30.00	80.00	55.00
	Bowl, 12", flared	30.00	45.00	35.00
	Candelabrum, 8¼", 2-lite, 16 lustre	90.00	175.00	135.00
	Candelabrum, 9½", 3-lite, 24 lustre	140.00	215.00	165.00
	Candle, 7¾", 8 lustre	45.00	80.00	70.00
	Candlestick, 4"	12.00	45.00	33.00
	Candlestick, 4½", 2-lite	20.00	50.00	40.00
	Candlestick, 5½"	30.00	55.00	40.00
13	Candlestick, 6", 3-lite*	30.00	75.00	55.00
3	Candy, 3 part w/cover	55.00	140.00	95.00
	Comport, 4¾"	16.00	40.00	30.00
	Comport, 6½"	20.00	50.00	35.00
	Creamer, 3¼", indiv.	8.00	18.00	16.00
2	Creamer, 3¾", ftd.	8.00	18.00	16.00
1	Cup	7.00	25.00	20.00
	Cup, 6 oz., punch	10.00	25.00	
	Ice bucket	50.00	120.00	75.00
9	Mayonnaise, 5½", w/liner	28.00	70.00	50.00
4	Mustard, w/cover	40.00	90.00	70.00
20	Oil, w/stopper, 5½"	60.00	295.00	140.00
	Pitcher, 6½"	75.00	695.00	395.00
	Pitcher, 7", ice lip	75.00	675.00	495.00
	Plate, 6"	4.00	10.00	8.00
	Plate, 7½"	7.00	14.00	9.00
	Plate, 8½"	8.00	18.00	15.00
	Plate, 9½"	17.00	55.00	40.00
18	Plate, 10", cake, hdld.	25.00	45.00	35.00
	Plate, 11", ctr. hdld., sandwich	28.00		
6	Plate, 14", torte	25.00	58.00	38.00
	Platter, 12", oval	33.00	75.00	50.00
16	Salt & pepper, 2¾", pr.	40.00	130.00	90.00
	Salt & pepper, indiv., 2", pr.	35.00	190.00	130.00
	Sauce dish	22.00	55.00	40.00
26	Sauce dish, divided	20.00	45.00	35.00
1	Saucer	2.00	6.00	5.00
	Sherbet, 3¾", 5 oz.	10.00	20.00	15.00
	Stem, 6¾", 9 oz., water	15.00	33.00	24.00
	Sugar, 3", indiv.	8.00	18.00	16.00
	Sugar, 3½", ftd.	8.00	18.00	16.00
28	Sweetmeat, covered, 9"	70.00	140.00	125.00
15	Tidbit, 3-toe flat	16.00	30.00	25.00
	Tray, 8" oblong, 7" w, tab hdl.	22.00	40.00	33.00
	Tray, 12½", oval	35.00	75.00	50.00
	Tray, 6¼" for indiv. cream/sugar	12.00	20.00	16.00
25	Tumbler, 3½", 6½ oz., old-fashion	20.00	75.00	55.00
14	Tumbler, 3", 3½ oz., ftd., cocktail	10.00	25.00	20.00
10	Tumbler, 6", 12 oz., ftd., tea	18.00	35.00	28.00
	Tumbler, 3¾", 5 oz., juice	12.00	40.00	30.00
5	Tumbler, 5½", 9 oz., ftd., water	10.00	28.00	22.00
27	Tumbler, 4¼", 9 oz., water	20.00	50.00	35.00
	Tumbler, 5¾", 14 oz., tea	30.00	85.00	55.00
	Vase, 6½"	40.00	100.00	90.00
17	Vase, 7"	50.00	135.00	95.00

* Red $150.00; Green $120.00; Black Amethyst $140.00; Cobalt Blue $140.00; Amber $75.00

BLACK FOREST, POSSIBLY PADEN CITY FOR VAN DEMAN & SON, LATE 1920S – EARLY 1930S

Colors: amber, black, ice blue, crystal, green, pink, red, cobalt

Black Forest items continue to attract appreciation in internet auctions, but prices have settled down and are reaching more reasonable levels than several years ago. Competition for pieces has subsided due to economic conditions as well as most collectors already owning all of the items being offered. Internet auction prices had blown the standard pricing of Black Forest out of the water. Internet activity also promoted sales of Deerwood, a pattern often offered incorrectly as Black Forest. The Black Forest etching consists of moose and trees, while Deerwood illustrates deer and trees.

We are frequently asked about the etched, heavy goblets pictured on page 27 that were made in the 1970s in amber, amberina, dark green, blue, crystal, and ruby by L. G. Wright. These are retailing in the $15.00 to $25.00 range with red and blue on the upper side of that price although you may see them priced for more by sellers who do not know their manufacturing history. These newer goblets have a heavy, prevalent "Daisy and Button" cubed stem and are not accepted as true Black Forest by most long-time collectors.

Notice the three styles of ice containers pictured on the bottom of page 27. That blue one sold to an avid ice bucket collector for a tidy sum — but it is the only one known! Sometimes collectors of particular items, such as ice buckets, are willing to pay more for items in a pattern than are collectors of said pattern.

8

		Amber	*Black	Crystal	Green	Pink	Red
	Batter jug			275.00			
	Bowl, 4½", finger				35.00		
	Bowl, 9¼", center hdld.				125.00	125.00	
4	Bowl, 11", console	75.00	135.00	55.00	110.00	110.00	
	Bowl, 11", fruit		135.00		110.00	110.00	
	Bowl, 13", console		150.00				
	Bowl, 3 ftd.			75.00			
11	Cake plate, 2" pedestal	75.00	135.00		110.00	110.00	
2	Candlestick, mushroom style, Line 210, 2⅜"		40.00	25.00	40.00	40.00	50.00
	Candlestick double			75.00			
3, 15	Candy dish, w/cover, several styles	125.00	225.00		200.00	200.00	
10	Creamer, 2 styles, Line 210 shown	40.00	60.00	25.00	50.00	50.00	
	Comport, 4", low ftd.				65.00	65.00	
12	Comport, 5½", high ftd.		110.00		90.00	90.00	
16	Cup and saucer, 3 styles		125.00		75.00	75.00	145.00
	Decanter, w/stopper, 8½", 28 oz., bulbous				395.00	395.00	395.00
	Decanter w/stopper, 8¾", 24 oz., straight				395.00	395.00	395.00
	Egg cup, Line 210				140.00		
6	Ice bucket		195.00		110.00	110.00	
1	Ice pail, 6", 3" high	125.00					
7	Ice tub, 3 styles (ice blue $1,000.00), Line 210	145.00	235.00		175.00	175.00	
	Mayonnaise, with liner		150.00		100.00	100.00	
	Night set: pitcher, 6½", 42 oz. & tumbler				650.00	650.00	
	Pitcher, 8", 40 oz. (cobalt $1,500.00)						
	Pitcher, 8", 62 oz., night set			295.00			
	Pitcher, 9", 80 oz.					450.00	
	Pitcher, 10½", 72 oz., T-neck, bulbous bottom				595.00	595.00	
	Plate, 6½", bread/butter		25.00		20.00	20.00	
	Plate, 8", luncheon		40.00		30.00	30.00	
8	Plate, 10", dinner		175.00				
14	Plate, 11", 2 hdld.		110.00		60.00	60.00	
	Plate, 13¾", 2 hdld., Line 210				95.00	95.00	
	Relish, 10½", 5 pt. covered				495.00	495.00	

*Add 20% for gold decorated.

		Amber	*Black	Crystal	Green	Pink	Red
	Salt and pepper, pr.			110.00		195.00	
5	Server, center hdld.	40.00	50.00	30.00	40.00	40.00	
	Shot glass, 2 oz., 2½"	35.00					
	Stem, 2 oz., wine, 4¼"			17.50	50.00		
	Stem, 6 oz., champagne, 4¾"			17.50		30.00	
	Stem, 9 oz., water, 6"			22.50			
9	Sugar, 2 styles, Line 210 shown	40.00	60.00	25.00	50.00	50.00	
13	Tumbler, 3 oz., juice, flat or footed, 3½"			40.00	75.00	75.00	
	Tumbler, 8 oz., old fashion, 3⅞"				95.00	95.00	
	Tumbler, 9 oz., ftd., 5½"	40.00					
	Tumbler, 12 oz., tea, 5½"				95.00	95.00	
17	Vase, 6½" (cobalt $300.00)		165.00	90.00	150.00	150.00	
	Vase, 8½", Line 210				150.00	150.00	
18, 19	Vase, 10", 2 styles in black, flat & bulbous base, Line 210		250.00		195.00	195.00	
	Whipped cream pail	95.00					

See page 26, second paragraph.

BO PEEP, DESIGN #854, MONONGAH, LATE 1920S
Colors: pink, amber, pink and green with crystal, green, all with Optic

In our previous book, we reported that we were contacted by a lady who said she had a set of green Tinkerbell which got us really excited. It turned out to be Bo Peep. That was fine since we can now show you several pieces of Bo Peep never pictured before. Notice the parfait, footed finger bowl, wine, and footed tea in green. Unfortunately, there were large amounts of damaged pieces in the set which were sold to a glass repairman. This set had been used by a relative as everyday ware and it showed. We had previously only viewed a large set of pink Bo Peep for sale in an antique mall. Prices for those pieces were more than we were willing to pay. Even today, we would have trouble selling the stemware for the prices being asked. We bought the vase and pitcher shown here. The pitcher lid is undecorated like Tiffin pitcher lids. Another collector was delighted we left that set since he negotiated a better price.

Monongah was forced out of business in the economic decline of the late 20s by the larger, more mechanized glass firms who were able to hang on after the Depression. It was taken over by Hocking Glass Company. For a long time, we thought Tiffin was the maker as all the shapes were typical of their moulds, but Bo Peep was made by Monongah, although the shapes are very similar to those we identify as Tiffin. Perhaps these moulds traveled.

		Pink Green
10	Finger bowl, ftd., #6102	65.00
7	Jug w/cover, #20	895.00
	Jug w/o cover, #20	795.00
3	Plate, 7½", salad	20.00
	Stem, cocktail, #6102	50.00
4	Stem, high sherbet, #6102	50.00
9	Stem, low sherbet, #6102	45.00
11	Stem, parfait, #6102	95.00
1	Stem, water, #6102	95.00
12	Stem, wine, #6102	75.00
8	Tumbler, 5 oz., ftd., juice/seltzer, #6102	65.00
5	Tumbler, 9 oz., ftd., water/table, #6102	55.00
6	Tumbler, 12 oz., ftd., iced tea, #6102	75.00
2	Vase, 9", ruffled edge, #0713	595.00

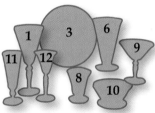

BROCADE, FOSTORIA GLASS COMPANY, 1927 – 1931

Colors: Azure blue, crystal, Ebony, green, Orchid, Rose

Pictured are a few of the more collected Fostoria Brocades. Designs are shown individually here and on the following pages. Hopefully, the sorting of small group shots will make recognition easier. You should know that Oak Leaf pattern with iridescence is correctly referred to as Oakwood and Paradise with iridescence is called Victoria, Decoration #71.

Grape

		Crystal	#290 Oakleaf Green/Rose	Ebony	#72 Oakwood Orchid/Azure	#289 Paradise Green/Orchid	#73 Palm Leaf Rose/Green	Blue	#287 Grape Green	Orchid
	Bonbon, #2375	30.00	45.00		50.00		50.00		40.00	
	Bowl, finger, #869	60.00	70.00		75.00					
	Bowl, 4½", mint, #2394	30.00	40.00							
	Bowl, 7½", "D," cupped rose, #2339							85.00	60.00	110.00
	Bowl, 10", scroll hdld, #2395	90.00	155.00	145.00			175.00			
	Bowl, 10", 2 hdld, #2375	80.00	125.00		175.00		165.00			
	Bowl, 10½", "A," 3 ftd., #2297					95.00		95.00	70.00	120.00
	Bowl, 10½", "C," sm roll rim, deep, #2297							95.00	70.00	120.00
	Bowl, 10½", "C," pedestal ftd., #2315					95.00				
	Bowl, 11", roll edge ctrpiece, #2329					100.00		155.00	135.00	175.00
	Bowl, 11", ctrpiece, #2375				195.00		155.00			
	Bowl, 11", cornucopia hdld, #2398	100.00	135.00							
8	Bowl, 12", 3 toe, flair rim, #2394	100.00	125.00		195.00		150.00			
	Bowl, 12", console, #2375	85.00	115.00							
2	Bowl, 12" low, "saturn rings," #2362					85.00		115.00	90.00	135.00
	Bowl, 12", hexagonal, 3 tab toe, #2342	110.00	135.00		210.00	100.00				
4	Bowl, 12", "A," 3 tab toe, #2297					115.00		125.00	110.00	135.00
	Bowl, 12½", "E," flat, shallow, #2297							125.00	100.00	135.00
	Bowl, 13", center piece rnd., #2329					140.00		225.00	195.00	235.00
	Bowl, center piece oval, #2375½		135.00		175.00		250.00			
	Bowl, 13", oval, roll edge w/ grid frog, #2371					175.00		225.00	185.00	250.00
	Bowl, #2415 comb, candle hdld.	120.00	175.00	185.00	295.00		250.00			
	Candlestick, 2", mushroom, #2372, pr						40.00	50.00	40.00	50.00
	Candlestick, 2", 3 toe, #2394, pr	40.00	55.00				70.00			
	Candlestick, 3", scroll, #2395, pr	50.00	70.00	95.00						
	Candlestick, 3", #2375, pr	45.00	60.00		65.00		75.00			
	Candlestick, 3", stack disc, #2362					50.00		40.00	40.00	40.00
1	Candlestick, 4", #2324, pr					40.00		40.00	40.00	40.00
	Candlestick, 5", 2395½, pr						135.00			
	Candlestick, hex mushroom, #2375½, pr	45.00	55.00		75.00					
	Candlestick, trindle, #2383 ea.						125.00			
9	Candy box, cov., 3 pt, #2331	100.00	150.00	200.00	250.00			185.00	145.00	200.00
	Candy, box, cone lid, #2380	100.00	145.00			115.00				
	Candy, cov., oval, #2395		135.00		200.00					
	Cheese & cracker, #2368	65.00	75.00							
	Cigarette & cov. (small), #2391	65.00	110.00	95.00	160.00					

		Crystal	#290 Oakleaf Green/Rose	Ebony	#72 Oakwood Orchid/Azure	#289 Paradise Green/Orchid	#73 Palm Leaf Rose/Green	Blue	#287 Grape Green	Orchid
	Cigarette & cov. (large), #2391	85.00	135.00	125.00	185.00					
	Comport, 6", #2400						125.00			
	Comport, 7" tall, twist stem, #2327					75.00		75.00	55.00	75.00
	Comport, 8", short, ftd., #2350					65.00				
	Comport, 8", pulled stem, #2400				115.00					
	Comport, 11", stack disc stem, ftd., #2362					100.00		125.00	100.00	120.00
10	Ice bucket, #2378	100.00	145.00		225.00		155.00	100.00	90.00	95.00
	Ice bucket, w/drainer, handle & tongs, #2378				150.00		140.00	125.00	130.00	
	Jug, #5000	395.00	595.00		995.00	695.00				
	Lemon, "bow" or open hdld, #2375	30.00	45.00		65.00	60.00	30.00		40.00	
	Mayonnaise, #2315	55.00	70.00		225.00					
	Plate, mayonnaise, #2332	20.00	30.00		35.00					
	Plate, 6", #2283	15.00	20.00							
	Plate, 7", #2283	20.00	25.00		35.00					
	Plate, 8", sq., #2419						30.00			
	Plate, 8", #2283	22.00	30.00		45.00					
12	Plate, 10", dinner, #2375	65.00	90.00		125.00		155.00			
	Plate, 12", salver, #2315	100.00	125.00		160.00					
	Plate, 13", lettuce, #2315	60.00	90.00		145.00					
	Stem, ¾ oz., cordial, #877	50.00			150.00					
	Stem, 2¾ oz., wine, #877	30.00			75.00					
	Stem, 3½ oz., cocktail, #877	20.00			55.00					
	Stem, 4 oz., claret, #877	30.00			75.00					
	Stem, 6 oz., high sherbet, #877	28.00			55.00					
	Stem, 6 oz., low sherbet, #877	20.00			50.00					
	Stem, 10 oz., water, #877	38.00			90.00					
	Sugar pail, #2378	105.00	150.00		225.00		250.00			
7	Sweetmeat, hex 2 hdld bowl, #2375	35.00	45.00		50.00		45.00		40.00	
	Tray, rnd, fleur de lis hdld., #2387							95.00	90.00	95.00
3	Tray, ctr, hdld., #2342, octagonal	65.00	95.00		150.00	75.00	100.00	95.00	90.00	95.00
	Tumbler, 2½ oz., ftd. whiskey, #877	30.00	75.00							
	Tumbler, 4½ oz., ftd. oyster cocktail	22.50								
	Tumbler, 5 oz., ftd. juice, #877	30.00								
	Tumbler, 5½ oz., parfait, #877	40.00	65.00							
	Tumbler, 9 oz., ftd., #877				90.00	60.00				
	Tumbler, 12 oz., ftd. tea, #877				120.00	65.00				

BROCADE

		#290 Oakleaf Green/Rose	Ebony	#72 Oakwood Orchid/Azure	#289 Paradise Green/Orchid	#73 Palm Leaf Rose/Green	Blue	#287 Grape Green	Orchid
		Crystal							
	Urn & cover, #2413		210.00		395.00		450.00			
	Vase, 3", 4", #4103, bulbous	50.00	60.00	75.00		70.00		85.00	70.00	80.00
	Vase, 5", 6", #4103, optic					75.00		105.00	90.00	100.00
	Vase, 6", #4100, flat straight side optic					85.00		105.00	90.00	100.00
	Vase, 6", #4105, scallop rim	65.00	85.00		140.00	85.00				
	Vase, 7", 9", ftd. urn, #2369	85.00	100.00		140.00	120.00	150.00			
14	Vase, 8", cupped melon, #2408						255.00			
	Vase, 8", #2292, ftd. flair flat, straight side	85.00	100.00	125.00						
	Vase, 8", #4100					95.00		125.00	115.00	135.00
	Vase, 8", #4105	70.00	95.00		265.00		250.00			
	Vase, 8", melon, #2387	90.00	115.00		210.00					
	Vase, 8½" fan, #2385	150.00	200.00		450.00		285.00			
	Vase, 10½" ftd., #2421						295.00			
	Vase, sm. or lg. window & cov., #2373	150.00	200.00	350.00	365.00		350.00			
	Whip cream, scallop 2 hdld. bowl, #2375	28.00	40.00		45.00		35.00			
	Whip cream pail, #2378	75.00	110.00		150.00				30.00	

BROCADE, MCKEE, 1930S

Colors: pink, green

McKee's Brocade only came in the one design unlike Fostoria's flock. We frequently hear it tendered by collectors as "Poinsettia" and on occasion "Palm Tree" though we have found no legitimate designation for either categorization. We have discovered a few more pieces and that no one seems to price Brocade moderately. Usually owners assume it to be rare or hard to get and price it accordingly!

		Pink/Green
	Bowl, 12", flared edge	40.00
	Bowl, center, hdld. nut	30.00
2	Bowl, 12", console, rolled edge	40.00
5	Candlestick, roll edge, octagonal	15.00
1	Candlestick, octagonal ft.	18.00
3	Candy box/cover	60.00
	Candy jar, ftd., w/cover	55.00
	Cheese and cracker	45.00
	Compote, 10", flared edge	40.00
	Compote, cone shape, octagonal	40.00
4	Mayonnaise, 3 pc., w/liner & spoon	40.00
	Salver, ftd. (cake stand)	40.00
	Server, center hdld.	30.00
	Vase, 11", bulbous	150.00

"BUBBLE GIRL" ETCHING (POSSIBLY LOTUS GLASS COMPANY) ON VARIOUS GLASS COMPANIES' BLANKS INCLUDING CAMBRIDGE, FRY, AND HEISEY

Colors: pink, crystal

"Bubble Girl" has been a mystifying pattern for glass dealers and collectors for almost 30 years. Our best supposition is that an etching company (most likely Lotus) utilized various mould blanks from Heisey, Cambridge, and Fry to market this pattern.

In the early 80s, several dealers at the Cambridge national show discussed this conundrum over dinner. Plates were being found marked Cambridge, but the stems all were Fry blanks which confused us terribly at that time. "Bubble Girl" was the name proposed (Opium Lady by one prankster) as the reclining woman looks to be blowing bubbles. We had jokes about Lawrence Welk and several other references to bubbles and champagne, but "Bubble Girl" seemed to win over "Champagne Lady." At that time, we were unaware of Heisey moulds also being used.

Subsequently, we purchased several different Fry stems for future photos. Later, still, we found a "Bubble Girl" Heisey candle and a friend found a Heisey Octagon bowl for us. It took some painstaking searching through dozens of boxes to exhume those previously found stems for photography, but during the intervening time we discovered footed water and tea tumblers, also of Fry origin.

A collector in Louisiana has since uncovered additional pieces on Cambridge moulds including cups and saucers. The newest discovery is a bonbon made by flattening the Heisey two-handled bowl making it 6½" long instead of 5⅜". Additionally, there has been a Cambridge mould platter uncovered. The internet has helped unearth pieces that may never have been discovered; so in that way, it has helped our business.

To summarize: stems and tumblers are Fry, with bowls and candles being Heisey. Most plates are unmarked, but others have Cambridge's triangle in a "C." All other pieces found are on Cambridge's mould shapes.

		Pink/Crystal
1	Bowl, 5⅜", 2-hdld., Heisey, Octagon, 1229 Jelly	45.00
3	Bowl, 11½", Octagon, 1229 Floral	55.00
	Bowl, 12", oval	100.00
4	Candlestick, 3½", Heisey, Pluto #114	33.00
	Cup	90.00
	Plate, 6¼", sherbet	10.00
	Plate, 6⅝", Octagon, 2-hdld.	35.00
2	Plate, 8½" luncheon	15.00
10	Relish, 5-part, Heisey, Octagon	110.00
	Saucer, 5¾"	15.00
	Shaker	150.00
	Stem, 3 oz., 4¾", wine	30.00
5	Stem, 3½ oz., 4⅜", cocktail	22.00
	Stem, 6 oz., 6¼", parfait	50.00
6	Stem, 7 oz., 5⅛", Fry stem, high sherbet	20.00
7	Stem, 9 oz., 7", Fry stem, water	32.00
8	Tumbler, 10 oz., 5⅛", Fry blank, ftd. water	22.00
9	Tumbler 15 oz., 6¼", Fry blank, ftd. ice tea	30.00

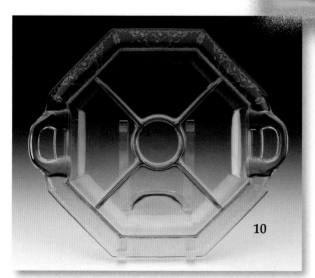

CADENA, TIFFIN GLASS COMPANY, EARLY 1930S

Colors: crystal, yellow; some pink

As with almost all Tiffin patterns of this era, Cadena stemware is a collectors' delight, but locating serving pieces is a chore. Even if you may be willing to pay the price for them, they appear infrequently. Notice the lack of those in our photo. We have spotted very few bowls in 29 years of searching; price was always prohibitive to have just for a photo. One bowl sat for years with a thumb-sized piece missing until the shop closed and our suspicious are that the owner may still have it. Even internet auctions have been a Cadena wasteland apart from the omnipresent stems.

A few pieces of pink have been surfacing, all stems. Tiffin pitchers were sold either with or without a lid. The top edge of pitchers without lids were often curved in or "cupped" so much that you cannot force a lid inside the lip. We found this out by buying a yellow lid separately for the pitcher shown. Remember that the Cadena pitcher cover will not have an etching.

We did purchase the rarely seen decanter pictured just for this book, but it sold the first time we displayed it. Never leave a rare piece if you come across it at a reasonable price. Someone desires it, even if you do not.

		Crystal	Pink Yellow
	Bowl, cream soup, #5831	20.00	40.00
	Bowl, finger, ftd., #041	20.00	40.00
	Bowl, grapefruit, ftd., #251	40.00	90.00
	Bowl, 6", hdld., #5831	16.00	26.00
	Bowl, 10", pickle, #5831	25.00	40.00
	Bowl, 12", console, ftd., #5831	33.00	58.00
	Candlestick, #5831	25.00	40.00
1	Creamer, #5831	18.00	25.00
	Cup, #5831	35.00	90.00
11	Decanter w/stopper	150.00	250.00
	Mayonnaise, ftd., w/liner, #5831	40.00	65.00
	Oyster cocktail, #065	15.00	26.00
3	Pitcher, ftd., #194	175.00	225.00
	Pitcher, ftd., w/cover, #194	225.00	350.00
	Plate, 6", #8814	6.00	12.00
	Plate, 7¾", #5831	8.00	16.00
	Plate, 9¼"	40.00	60.00
	Saucer, #5831	8.00	18.00
9	Stem, 4¾", sherbet/sundae	14.00	22.00
6	Stem, 5¼", cocktail	18.00	26.00
	Stem, 5¼", ¾ oz., cordial	55.00	95.00
	Stem, 6", wine	28.00	40.00
10	Stem, 6⁵⁄₁₆", 8 oz., parfait	30.00	50.00
5	Stem, 6½", champagne	18.00	24.00
4	Stem, 7½", water, #065	28.00	25.00
2	Sugar, #5831	18.00	25.00
12	Tumbler, 3¼", ftd., bar, #065	20.00	35.00
8	Tumbler, 4¼", ftd., juice, #065	20.00	25.00
7	Tumbler, 5¼", ftd., water, #065	22.00	28.00
	Vase, 9"	95.00	195.00

10

11   **12**

CANDLELIGHT, CAMBRIDGE GLASS COMPANY, 1940S – EARLY 1950S

Colors: crystal, crystal and Crown Tuscan with gold decoration

Pictured are the cover and a page from a 1951 Candlelight pamphlet of the style commonly offered to people who were registering a crystal pattern for bridal gift giving. We have copied one page to show you the #3776 stems typically found in Candlelight.

Through these brochure pages throughout the book and the legends for each item in our photographs, we hope we have solved those identification questions asked us over the years.

Candlelight appears on Cambridge stem line #3114, but it is not as prevalent as #3776. Candlelight is not as bountiful as other Cambridge patterns, so it may take some serious searching to accumulate a nice grouping. Candlelight was designed in two ways. The pattern was cut into some pieces, but was acid etched on others. The cut items are sparse; a wine and water goblet are pictured on page 36. There are fewer collectors for cut pieces due to their scarcity, but most Candlelight collectors like to own one piece to illustrate the difference. Etching was accomplished by covering the glass except where the design was desired and then dipping the glass into acid. Cutting was accomplished by a skilled hand on a wheel turning to form the design.

Dealers should note that, today, when people ask for wine goblets, you might need to find out if they want water goblets. Formerly, wine goblets held 2½ to 4 ounces; but now, many people think of wine goblets as holding 8 or 9 ounces. Thus, what they want for serving wine today is actually a water goblet.

Collectors hunting for this pattern should realize that there is a significant lack of shakers (both footed and flat), butter dishes, basic serving pieces, candlesticks, and even cups and saucers. Do not pass any of those items if you have a chance to buy them.

35

CANDLELIGHT

Cut Candlelight

1
16

		Crystal
	Bonbon, 7", ftd., 2 hdld., #3900/130	35.00
	Bowl, 10", 4 toed, flared, #3900/54	75.00
	Bowl, 11", 2 hdld., #3900/34	85.00
	Bowl, 11", 4 ftd., fancy edge, #3400/48	85.00
	Bowl, 11½", ftd., 2 hdld., #3900/28	75.00
	Bowl, 12", 4 ftd., flared, #3400/4	75.00
	Bowl, 12", 4 ftd., oblong, #3400/160	75.00
	Bowl, 12", 4 toed, flared, #3900/62	75.00
	Bowl, 12", 4 toed, oval, hdld., #3900/65	85.00
	Butter dish, 5", #3400/52	245.00
	Candle, 5", #3900/67	50.00
	Candle, 6", 2-lite, #3900/72	65.00
	Candle, 6", 3-lite, #3900/74	85.00
	Candlestick, 5", #646	55.00
	Candlestick, 6", 2-lite, #647	65.00
	Candlestick, 6", 3-lite, #1338	85.00
	Candy box and cover, 3-part, #3500/57	150.00
	Candy jar, 10", #3500/41	185.00
	Candy w/lid, rnd., div., #3900/165	85.00
	Cocktail shaker, 36 oz., #P101	195.00
17	Comport, 5", cheese, #3900/135	38.00
	Comport, 5⅜", blown, #3121	70.00
20	Comport, 5½", #3900/136	60.00
18	Creamer, #3900/41	22.00
	Creamer, indiv., #3900/40	22.00
	Cruet, 6 oz., w/stopper, #3900/100	135.00
19	Cup, #3900/17	28.00
	Decanter, 28 oz., ftd., #1321	250.00
6	Ice bucket, #3900/671	150.00
5	Icer, 2 pc., cocktail, #968	100.00
	Lamp, hurricane, #1617	195.00
	Lamp, hurricane, keyhole, w/bobeche, #1603	250.00
	Lamp, hurricane, w/bobeche, #1613	295.00
	Mayonnaise, 3 pc., #3900/129	65.00
	Mayonnaise, div., 4 pc., #3900/111	75.00
	Mayonnaise, ftd., 2 pc., #3900/19	65.00

		Crystal
	Nut cup, 3", 4 ftd., #3400/71	55.00
11	Pitcher, Doulton, #3400/141	395.00
	Plate, 6½", #3900/20	10.00
	Plate, 8", 2 hdld., #3900/131	25.00
	Plate, 8", salad, #3900/22	18.00
	Plate, 10½", dinner, #3900/24	65.00
	Plate, 12", 4 toed, #3900/26	65.00
	Plate, 13", torte, 4 toed, #3900/33	75.00
	Plate, 13½", cake, 2 hdld., #3900/35	75.00
	Plate, 13½", cracker, #3900/135	60.00
	Plate, 14", rolled edge, #3900/166	75.00
	Relish, 7", 2 hdld., #3900/123	35.00
	Relish, 7", div., 2 hdld., #3900/124	40.00
8	Relish, 8", 3 part, #3400/91	55.00
	Relish, 9", 3 pt., #3900/125	60.00
	Relish, 12", 3 pt., #3900/126	65.00
	Relish, 12", 5 pt., #3900/120	75.00
17	Salt & pepper, pr., #3900/1177	125.00
13	Salt & pepper, ftd., #3400/77	110.00
	Saucer, #3900/17	7.00
	Stem, 1 oz., cordial, #3776	75.00
1	Stem, 1 oz., cordial cut	150.00
	Stem, 2 oz., sherry, trumpet, #7966	75.00
2, 15	Stem, 2½ oz., wine, #3111 w/ball, 3114 w/rings	65.00
	Stem, 3 oz., cocktail, #3114	30.00
	Stem, 3 oz., cocktail, #3776	30.00
	Stem, 3½ oz., wine, #3776	50.00
	Stem, 4 oz., cocktail, #7801	28.00
	Stem, 4½ oz., claret, #3776	55.00
22	Stem, 4½ oz., oyster cocktail, #3114	28.00
23	Stem, 4½ oz., oyster cocktail, #3776	28.00
	Stem, 7 oz., low sherbet, #3114	16.00
	Stem, 7 oz., low sherbet, #3776	16.00
	Stem, 7 oz., tall sherbet, #3114	22.00
	Stem, 7 oz., tall sherbet, #3776	22.00
	Stem, 9 oz., water, #3776	40.00
16	Stem, 9 oz., water, cut	75.00
10	Stem, 10 oz., water, #3114	40.00
7	Sugar, #3900/41	22.00
	Sugar, indiv., #3900/40	22.00
4	Tumbler, 5 oz., ftd., juice, #3114	25.00
	Tumbler, 5 oz., juice, #3776	25.00
3	Tumbler, 10 oz., ftd., #3114	33.00
14	Tumbler, 12 oz., ftd., iced tea, #3114	40.00
24	Tumbler, 12 oz., iced tea, #3776	40.00
	Tumbler, 13 oz., #3900/115	45.00
	Vase, 5", ftd., bud, #6004	85.00
12	Vase, 5", globe, #1309	75.00
	Vase, 6", ftd., #6004	90.00
	Vase, 8", ftd., #6004	110.00
	Vase, 9", ftd., keyhole, #1237	125.00
	Vase, 10", bud, #274	95.00
	Vase, 11", ftd., pedestal, #1299	185.00
9	Vase, 11", ftd., #278	135.00
	Vase, 12", ftd., keyhole, #1238	175.00
	Vase, 13", ftd, #279	195.00

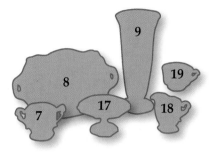

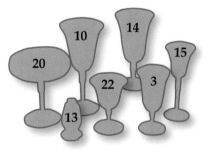

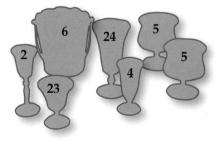

Colors: crystal, blue, pink, yellow, black, red, cobalt blue, green, caramel slag

We have dug through our archives to come up with as many new photos as possible for this book. Unfortunately, that means more hours of work for us writing the legends which identify each piece in the photographs. In all likelihood this will be our last Elegant book, so we wanted to leave with a book worthy of all those years of research and travel. New admirers should be aware that not all Candlewick has a ball in its stem. Note the Ritz blue oyster cocktail shown on page 40. We found a dozen of these gems at an antique show attended late where no one had recognized them. By viewing it, we are hoping you won't make that mistake.

Identification of tumbler and stemware styles is a concern of new collectors of Candlewick. Stemware line 400/190 comes with a hollow stem. Hollow stems should be easy to understand, and a couple are pictured on page 41. The tumblers designated 400/19 have flat bases with knobs around that base like the vases pictured on this page as opposed to 400/18 that have a domed foot. The 400/... was Imperial's factory designation for each piece. If you can find a copy of the first *Elegant Glassware of the Depression Era* book, there is a 15-page reprint of Imperial's Catalog B showing Candlewick listings as designated by the factory. Space does not permit the liberty of showing that catalog now.

The mid 30s Viennese Blue (light blue) Candlewick continues to sell well when priced appropriately; but higher priced red and black items have presently leveled or even dropped. One of the problems has been the many reproductions of Candlewick coming into the market. Candlewick was never made by Imperial in Jadite, but numerous Jadite pieces continue to plague the market from an Ohio glass company. Dalzell Viking made red and cobalt blue pieces (no stemware) before they went bankrupt a few years ago and many speculators rushed to their outlet store to buy these pieces including punch sets. Those items pictured on page 45 with the silver decorations were purchased at a discount store just a few years ago.

At present, there is not the demand for colored wares as in the past. Ruby and black fancy bowls used to sell in the ballpark of $250.00 with the Viennese blue pieces bringing 50% to 60% of that. Today, those prices are hoped for but seldom obtained. Ruby stems continue to be found in the 3400 and 3800 lines with most of these selling in the $45.00 to $100.00 range. However, cordials are selling in Ruby and Ritz blue (cobalt) from $100.00 to $150.00. Other Ritz blue stems are also fetching $100.00 to $150.00. All of these original colors of Candlewick were manufactured before 1943.

Collectors and non-collectors alike admire the 72-hole birthday cake plate. Imperial also made these cake plates in Cape Cod and Tradition. Candlewick ones are difficult to find without scratches or gouges from cake cuttings over the years (and the large plain center shows cuts easily). Be sure to notice the hanging lamp on page 39. Notice the matching cutting on the shades and the center piece. There is a gold chain which allows the electric wire to run down to the shade from the ceiling. It was spellbinding and heart stopping watching the photographers figure how to suspend it for a photo, although there were a few interesting expletives overheard while trying to do so. It was more unwieldy than it looked.

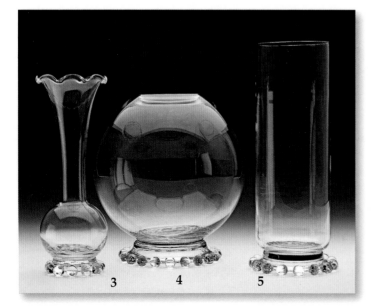

		Crystal
8	Ashtray, eagle, 6½", 1776/1	40.00
	Ashtray, heart, 4½", 400/172	7.00
	Ashtray, heart, 5½", 400/173	9.00
	Ashtray, heart, 6½", 400/174	11.00
	Ashtray, indiv., 400/64	6.00
	Ashtray, oblong, 4½", 400/134/1	4.00
56	Ashtray, round, 2¾", 400/19	6.00
57	Ashtray, round, 4", 400/33	8.00
	Ashtray, round, 5", 400/133	11.00
	Ashtray, square, 3¼", 400/651	22.00
	Ashtray, square, 4½", 400/652	22.00
	Ashtray, square, 5¾", 400/653	32.00
	Ashtray, 6", matchbook holder center, 400/60	140.00
	Ashtray set, 3 pc. rnd. nesting (crystal or colors), 400/550	28.00
	Ashtray set, 3 pc. sq. nesting, 400/650	80.00
	Ashtray set, 4 pc. bridge (cigarette holder at side), 400/118	40.00
	Basket, 5", beaded hdld., 400/273	165.00
72	Basket, 6½", hdld., 400/40/0	30.00
	Basket, 11", hdld., 400/73/0	225.00
	Bell, 4", 400/179	75.00
41	Bell, 5", 400/108	78.00
	Bottle, bitters, w/tube, 4 oz., 400/117	60.00
	Bottle, cologne, 4 bead, E408	60.00
	Bowl, bouillon, 2 hdld., 400/126	40.00
	Bowl, #3400, finger, ftd.	30.00
	Bowl, #3800, finger	30.00
	Bowl, 4½", nappy, 3 ftd., 400/206	60.00
	Bowl, 4¾", round, 2 hdld., 400/42B	10.00
74	Bowl, 5", cream soup, 400/50	35.00
	Bowl, 5", fruit, 400/1F	10.00
	Bowl, 5", heart w/handle, 400/49H	18.00
	Bowl, 5", square, 400/231	80.00
	Bowl, 5½", heart, 400/53H	18.00
	Bowl, 5½", jelly, w/cover, 400/59	65.00
	Bowl, 5½", sauce, deep, 400/243	35.00
	Bowl, 6", baked apple, rolled edge, 400/53X	30.00
	Bowl, 6", cottage cheese, 400/85	22.00
	Bowl, 6", fruit, 400/3F	10.00
	Bowl, 6", heart w/hand., 400/51H	28.00
	Bowl, 6", mint w/hand., 400/51F	20.00
20	Bowl, 6", round, div., 2 hdld., 400/52	18.00
	Bowl, 6", 2 hdld., 400/52B	12.00
	Bowl, 6", 3 ftd., 400/183	50.00
	Bowl, 6", sq., 400/232	100.00
	Bowl, 6½", relish, 2 pt., 400/84	20.00
	Bowl, 6½", 2 hdld., 400/181	22.00
	Bowl, 7", round, 400/5F	20.00
	Bowl, 7", round, 2 hdld., 400/62B	15.00
	Bowl, 7", relish, sq., div., 400/234	135.00
	Bowl, 7", ivy, high, bead ft., 400/188	285.00
	Bowl, 7", lily, 4 ft., 400/74J	70.00
	Bowl, 7", relish, 400/60	22.00
	Bowl, 7", sq., 400/233	135.00
	Bowl, 7¼", rose, ftd. w/crimp edge, 400/132C	595.00

		Crystal
	Bowl, 7½", pickle/celery, 400/57	25.00
	Bowl, 7½", lily, bead rim, ftd., 400/75N	395.00
	Bowl, 7½", belled (console base), 400/127B	60.00
	Bowl, 8", round, 400/7F	33.00
	Bowl, 8", relish, 2 pt., 400/268	18.00
	Bowl, 8", cov. veg., 400/65/1	325.00
	Bowl, 8½", rnd., 400/69B	30.00
	Bowl, 8½", nappy, 4 ftd., 400/74B	65.00
	Bowl, 8½", 3 ftd., 400/182	135.00
	Bowl, 8½", 2 hdld., 400/72B	20.00
	Bowl, 8½", pickle/celery, 400/58	20.00
	Bowl, 8½", relish, 4 pt., 400/55	22.00
60	Bowl, 9", fruit (like compote), 400/67B	65.00
	Bowl, 9", round, 400/10F	40.00
	Bowl, 9", crimp, ftd., 400/67C	175.00
59	Bowl, 9", sq., fancy crimp edge, 4 ft. 400/74SC	95.00
	Bowl, 9", heart, 400/49H	110.00
	Bowl, 9", heart w/hand., 400/73H	145.00
	Bowl, 10", 400/13F	40.00
	Bowl, 10", banana, 400/103E	1,500.00
	Bowl, 10", 3 toed, 400/205	160.00
	Bowl, 10", belled (punch base), 400/128B	75.00
	Bowl, 10", cupped edge, 400/75F	40.00
	Bowl, 10", deep, 2 hdld., 400/113A	150.00
	Bowl, 10", divided, deep, 2 hdld., 400/114A	150.00
	Bowl, 10", fruit, bead stem (like compote), 400/103F	210.00
	Bowl, 10", relish, oval, 2 hdld., 400/217	35.00
	Bowl, 10", relish, 3 pt., 3 ft., 400/208	100.00
	Bowl, 10", 3 pt., w/cover, 400/216	600.00
	Bowl, 10½", belled, 400/63B	50.00
	Bowl, 10½", butter/jam, 3 pt., 400/262	255.00
	Bowl, 10½", salad, 400/75B	35.00
21	Bowl, 10½", relish, 3 section, 400/256	28.00
	Bowl, 11", celery boat, oval, 400/46	50.00
58	Bowl, 11", centerpiece, flared, 400/13B	50.00
	Bowl, 11", float, inward rim, ftd., 400/75F	38.00
	Bowl, 11", oval, 400/124A	250.00
	Bowl, 11", oval w/partition, 400/125A	260.00
	Bowl, 12", round, 400/92B	40.00
	Bowl, 12", belled, 400/106B	85.00

73

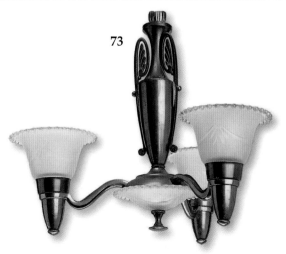

CANDLEWICK

30

		Crystal
51	Bowl, 12", cupped, float, console, rnd., 400/92F	38.00
	Bowl, 12", hdld., 400/113B	130.00
	Bowl, 12", shallow, 400/17F	40.00
	Bowl, 12", relish, oblong, 4 sect., 400/215	100.00
	Bowl, 13", centerpiece, mushroom, 400/92L	45.00
	Bowl, 13", float, 1½" deep, 400/101	50.00
	Bowl, 13½", relish, 5 pt., 400/209	70.00
	Bowl, 14", belled, 400/104B	75.00
	Bowl, 14", oval, flared, 400/131B	295.00
	Butter and jam set, 5 piece, 400/204	450.00
	Butter, w/cover, rnd., 5½", 400/144	30.00
36	Butter, w/cover, no beads, California, 400/276	120.00
31	Butter, w/bead top, ¼ lb., 400/161	28.00
	Cake stand, 10", low foot, 400/67D	50.00
	Cake stand, 11", high foot, 400/103D	60.00
	Calendar, 1947, desk	250.00
	Candleholder, 3 way, beaded base, 400/115	125.00
	Candleholder, 2-lite, 400/100	20.00
	Candleholder, flat, 3½", 400/280	35.00
	Candleholder, 3½", rolled edge, 400/79R	14.00
	Candleholder, 3½", w/fingerhold, 400/81	50.00
	Candleholder, flower, 4", 2 bead stem, 400/66F	55.00
75	Candleholder, urn, 4½", 400/129R	100.00
67	Candleholder, flower, 4½", 2 bead stem, 400/66C	55.00
	Candleholder, 4½", 3 toed, 400/207	95.00
	Candleholder, 3-lite on cir. bead. ctr., 400/147	40.00
	Candleholder, 5", hdld./bowled up base, 400/90	55.00
	Candleholder, 5", heart shape, 400/40HC	125.00
	Candleholder, 5½", 3 bead stems, 400/224	125.00
	Candleholder, flower, 5" (epergne inset), 400/40CV	195.00
	Candleholder, 5", flower, 400/40C	32.00
	Candleholder, 6½", tall, 3 bead stems, 400/175	150.00
	Candleholder, flower, 6", round, 400/40F	35.00
	Candleholder, urn, 6", holders on cir. ctr. bead, 400/129R	195.00
71	Candleholder, flower, 6½", square, 400/40S	75.00
	Candleholder, mushroom, 400/86	32.00
	Candleholder, flower, 9", centerpiece, 400/196FC	250.00
37	Candy box, round, 5½", 400/59	40.00
	Candy box, sq., 6½", rnd. lid, 400/245	395.00

		Crystal
	Candy box, w/cover, 7", 400/259	125.00
	Candy box, w/cover, 7" partitioned, 400/110	120.00
	Candy box, w/cover, round, 7", 3 sect., 400/158	200.00
	Candy box, w/cover, beaded, ft., 400/140	550.00
	Cigarette box w/cover, 400/134	30.00
66	Cigarette holder, Bicentennial	25.00
	Cigarette holder, 3", bead ft., 400/44	30.00
	Cigarette set: 6 pc. (cigarette box & 4 rect. ashtrays), 400/134/6	60.00
	Clock, 4", round	295.00
33	Coaster, 4", 400/78	6.00
	Coaster, w/spoon rest, 400/226	12.00
	Cocktail, seafood w/bead ft., 400/190	75.00
	Cocktail set: 2 pc., plate w/indent; cocktail, 400/97	35.00
	Compote, 4½", 400/63B	35.00
	Compote, 5", 3 bead stems, 400/220	80.00
	Compote, 5½", 4 bead stem, 400/45	25.00
55	Compote, 5½, low, plain stem, 400/66B	18.00
	Compote, 5½", 2 bead stem, 400/66B	20.00
	Compote, 8", bead stem, 400/48F	95.00
	Compote, 10", ftd. fruit, crimped, 40/103C	225.00
	Compote, ft. oval, 400/137	1,500.00
	Condiment set, 4 pc., 400/1769	70.00
	Creamer, domed foot, 400/18	90.00
	Creamer, 6 oz., bead handle, 400/30	7.00
52	Creamer, indiv. bridge, 400/122	8.00
45	Creamer, plain ft., 400/31	7.00
	Creamer, flat, bead handle, 400/126	30.00
	Cruet set, 3 pc., 400/2911	75.00
	Cruet w/stopper, 4 oz., 400/70	45.00
17	Cup, after dinner, 400/77	16.00
10	Cup, coffee, 400/37	5.00
	Cup, punch, 400/211	6.00
	Cup, tea, 400/35	5.00
	Decanter, w/stopper, 15 oz. cordial, 400/82/2	395.00
	Decanter, w/stopper, 18 oz., 400/18	295.00
	Decanter, w/stopper, 26 oz., 400/163	350.00
	Deviled egg server, 12", ctr. hdld., 400/154	90.00
	Eagle bookend, 777/3	350.00
	Egg cup, bead. ft., 400/19	50.00
	Fork & spoon, set, 400/75	28.00
	Hurricane lamp, 2 pc. candle base, 400/79	135.00
	Hurricane lamp, 2 pc., hdld. candle base, 400/76	210.00
	Hurricane lamp, 3 pc. flared & crimped edge globe, 400/152	225.00
	Ice tub, 5½" deep, 8" diam., 400/63	120.00
	Ice tub, 7", 2 hdld., 400/168	195.00
	Icer, 2 pc., seafood/fruit cocktail, 400/53/3	80.00
	Icer, 2 pc., seafood/fruit cocktail, #3800 line, one bead stem	65.00
	Jam set, 5 pc., oval tray w/2 marmalade jars w/ladles, 400/1589	135.00
	Jar tower, 3 sect., 400/655	495.00
	Knife, butter, 4000	400.00
	Ladle, marmalade, 3 bead stem, 400/130	10.00

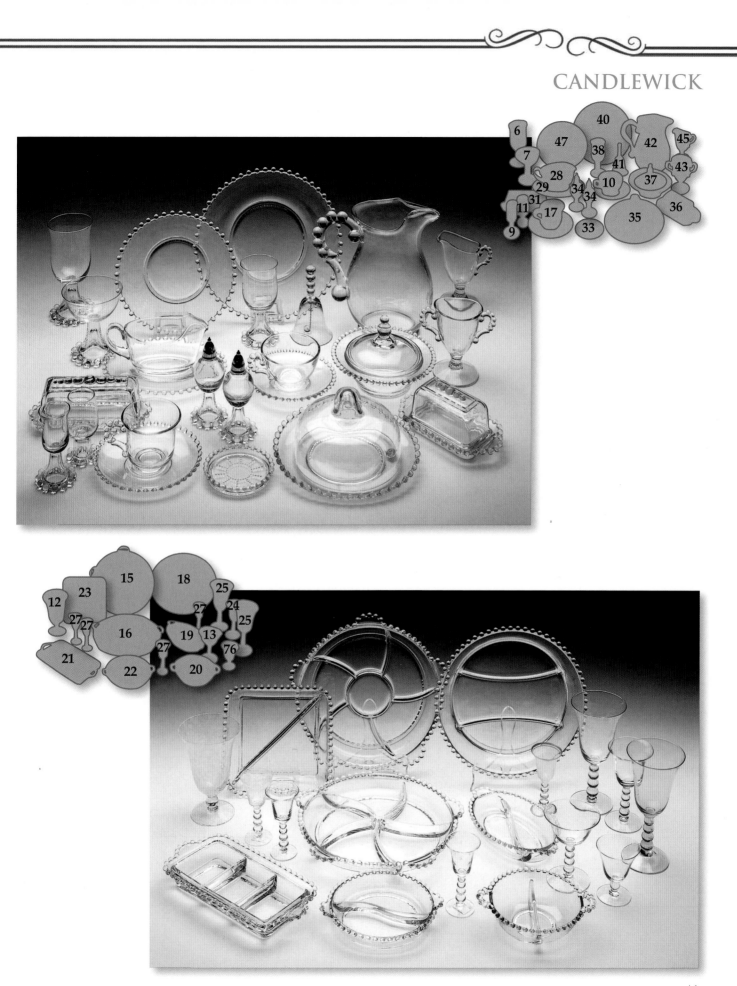

CANDLEWICK

		Crystal
	Ladle, mayonnaise, 3 knob, 400/165	10.00
	Ladle, mayonnaise, 6¼", 400/135	10.00
73	Lamp shade	85.00
	Marmalade set, 3 pc., beaded ft. w/cover & spoon, 400/1989	40.00
	Marmalade set, 3 pc. tall jar, domed bead ft., lid, spoon, 400/8918	90.00
69	Marmalade set, 3 pc. jar, lid, spoon, 400/289	48.00
	Mayonnaise set, 2 pc. scoop side bowl, spoon, 400/23	35.00
	Mayonnaise set, 3 pc. hdld. tray/hdld. bowl/ ladle, 400/52/3	48.00
	Mayonnaise set, 3 pc. plate, heart bowl, spoon, 400/49	35.00
	Mayonnaise set, 3 pc. scoop side bowl, spoon, tray, 400/496	130.00
49	Mayonnaise, 4 pc., plate, divided bowl, 2 ladles, rnd., 400/84	40.00
	Mirror, 4½", rnd., standing	165.00
	Muddler, 400/19	15.00
	Mustard jar, w/spoon, 400/156	35.00
	Oil, 4 oz., bead base, 400/164	45.00
	Oil, 6 oz., bead base, 400/166	65.00
	Oil, 4 oz., 400/177	45.00
26	Oil, 4 oz., bulbous bottom, 400/274	50.00
	Oil, 4 oz., hdld., bulbous bottom, 400/278	60.00
	Oil, 6 oz., hdld., bulbous bottom, 400/279	75.00
68	Oil, 6 oz., bulbous bottom, 400/275	55.00
	Oil, w/stopper, etched "Oil," 400/121	60.00
	Oil, w/stopper, etched "Vinegar," 400/121	60.00

		Crystal
	Party set, 2 pc., oval plate w/indent for cup, 400/98	25.00
	Pitcher, 14 oz., short rnd., 400/330	195.00
	Pitcher, 16 oz., low ft., Liliputian, 400/19	225.00
	Pitcher, 16 oz., no ft., 400/16	150.00
	Pitcher, 20 oz., plain, 400/416	40.00
	Pitcher, 40 oz., juice/cocktail, 400/19	195.00
	Pitcher, 40 oz., manhattan, 400/18	225.00
	Pitcher, 40 oz., plain, 400/419	50.00
	Pitcher, 64 oz., plain, 400/424	60.00
	Pitcher, 80 oz., plain, 400/424	70.00
42	Pitcher, 80 oz., 400/24	128.00
	Pitcher, 80 oz., beaded ft., 400/18	225.00
	Plate, 4½", 400/34	6.00
	Plate, 5½", 2 hdld., 400/42D	10.00
	Plate, 6", bread/butter, 400/1D	5.00
50	Plate, 6", canape w/off ctr. indent, 2 pc., 400/36	15.00
	Plate, 6¾", 2 hdld. crimped, 400/52C	25.00
47	Plate, 7", salad, 400/3D	6.00
	Plate, 7½", 2 hdld., 400/52D	10.00
	Plate, 7½", triangular, 400/266	95.00
	Plate, 8", oval, 400/169	20.00
	Plate, 8", salad, 400/5D	8.00
	Plate, 8", w/indent, 400/50	10.00
	Plate, 8¼", crescent salad, 400/120	55.00
	Plate, 8½", 2 hdld., crimped, 400/62C	25.00
	Plate, 8½", 2 hdld., 400/62D	11.00
	Plate, 8½", salad, 400/5D	9.00
	Plate, 8½", 2 hdld. (sides upturned), 400/62E	25.00
	Plate, 9", luncheon, 400/7D	12.00

		Crystal
	Plate, 9", oval, salad, 400/38	30.00
	Plate, 9", w/indent, oval, 400/98	20.00
	Plate, 10", 2 hdld., sides upturned, 400/72E	35.00
	Plate, 10", 2 hdld. crimped, 400/72C	35.00
	Plate, 10", 2 hdld., 400/72D	35.00
40	Plate, 10½", dinner, 400/10D	33.00
	Plate, 12", 2 hdld., 400/145D	40.00
	Plate, 12", 2 hdld. crimp., 400/145C	50.00
	Plate, 12", service, 400/13D	35.00
	Plate, 12½", cupped edge, torte, 400/75V	35.00
	Plate, 12½", oval, 400/124	78.00
	Plate, 13½", cracker, 400/145	40.00
	Plate, 13½", cupped edge, serving, 400/92V	47.00
	Plate, 14" birthday cake (holes for 72 candles), 400/160	495.00
	Plate, 14", 2 hdld., sides upturned, 400/113E	40.00
	Plate, 14", 2 hdld., torte, 400/113D	50.00
46	Plate, 14", service, 400/92D	50.00
	Plate, 14", torte, 400/17D	50.00
	Plate, 17", cupped edge, 400/20V	95.00
	Plate, 17", torte, 400/20D	95.00
	Platter, 13", 400/124D	95.00
	Platter, 16", 400/131D	195.00
	Puff box, E - 409	65.00
	Punch ladle, small 2 lip, 400/259	30.00
	Punch set, family, 8 demi cups, ladle, lid, 400/139/77	795.00
	Punch set, 15 pc. bowl on 18" plate, 12 cups, ladle, 400/20	225.00

		Crystal
	Relish & dressing set, 4 pc. (10½" 4 pt. relish w/marmalade), 400/1112	95.00
16	Relish, 10½", 5 pt., 5 hdld., 400/56	60.00
15	Relish, 10½", 6 pt., 5 hdld., 400/112	45.00
18	Relish, 13", 5 pt., 400/102	60.00
22	Relish, 6½", 2 pt., 400/54	18.00
23	Relish, 7" sq., div., 2 pt., 400/234	100.00
19	Relish, 10½", oval, 400/256	28.00
	Salad set, 4 pc. (buffet; lg. rnd. tray, div. bowl, 2 spoons), 400/17	125.00
	Salad set, 4 pc. (rnd. plate, flared bowl, fork, spoon), 400/75B	100.00
	Salt & pepper pr., bead ft., straight side, chrome top, 400/247	18.00
1	Salt & pepper pr., bead ft., bulbous, chrome top, 400/96	16.00
	Salt & pepper, 400/167	15.00
	Salt & pepper pr., bulbous w/bead stem, plastic top, 400/116	100.00
	Salt & pepper, pr., indiv., 400/109	14.00
34	Salt & pepper, pr., ftd. bead base, 400/190	50.00
	Salt dip, 2", 400/61	9.00
	Salt dip, 2¼", 400/19	8.00
	Salt "type" dip, 2¾", nut or sugar, 400/64	10.00
	Salt spoon, 3, 400/616	10.00
	Salt spoon, w/ribbed bowl, 4000	10.00
28	Sauce boat, 400/169	90.00
29	Sauce boat liner, 400/169	25.00

		Crystal				Crystal
17	Saucer, after dinner, 400/77AD	4.00		Tray, 10½", ctr. hdld. fruit, 400/68F		110.00
10	Saucer, tea or coffee, 400/35 or 400/37	2.00		Tray, 11½", ctr. hdld. party, 400/68D		55.00
	Set: 2 pc. hdld. cracker w/cheese compote, 400/88	60.00		Tray, 11½", 2 hdld., 400/145E		40.00
	Set: 2 pc. rnd. cracker plate w/indent; cheese compote, 400/145	60.00		Tray, 13½", 2 hdld., celery, oval, 400/105		30.00
				Tray, 13", relish, 5 sections, 400/102		55.00
	Snack jar w/cover, bead ft., 400/139/1	795.00		Tray, 14", hdld., 400/113E		75.00
9	Stem, 1 oz., cordial, 400/190	70.00		Tumbler, 3½ oz., cocktail, 400/18		40.00
11	Stem, 2 oz., 400/195	150.00		Tumbler, 3½ oz., juice, 400/112		12.00
	Stem, 4 oz., cocktail, 400/190	15.00		Tumbler, 5 oz., juice, 400/18		50.00
	Stem, 5 oz., tall sherbet, 400/190	12.00		Tumbler, 6 oz., sherbet, 400/18		50.00
38	Stem, 5 oz., wine, 400/190	18.00		Tumbler, 7 oz., old-fashion, 400/18		60.00
7	Stem, 6 oz., sherbet, 400/190	12.00		Tumbler, 7 oz., parfait, 400/18		65.00
6	Stem, 10 oz., water 400/190	18.00		Tumbler, 9 oz., water, 400/18		70.00
27	Stem, #3400, 1 oz., cordial	30.00		Tumbler, 12 oz., tea, 400/18		70.00
13	Stem, #3400, 4 oz., cocktail	12.00		Tumbler, 3 oz., ftd., cocktail, 400/19		14.00
30	Stem, #3400, 4 oz., oyster cocktail	10.00		Tumbler, 3 oz., ftd., wine, 400/19		18.00
14	Stem, #3400, 4 oz., wine	16.00		Tumbler, 5 oz., low sherbet, 400/19		11.00
24	Stem, #3400, 5 oz., claret	40.00		Tumbler, 5 oz., juice, 400/19		8.00
	Stem, #3400, 5 oz., low sherbet	7.00		Tumbler, 7 oz., old-fashion, 400/19		30.00
	Stem, #3400, 6 oz., parfait	48.00		Tumbler, 10 oz., 400/19		10.00
54	Stem, #3400, 6 oz., sherbet/saucer champagne	12.00		Tumbler, 12 oz., 400/19		18.00
25	Stem, #3400, 9 oz., goblet, water	15.00		Tumbler, 14 oz., 400/19, tea		18.00
	Stem, #3800, low sherbet	22.00		Tumbler, 12 oz., 400/195		42.00
	Stem, #3800, brandy	48.00		Tumbler, #3400, 5 oz., ft., juice		15.00
61	Stem, #3800, 1 oz., cordial	40.00		Tumbler, #3400, 6 oz., parfait		60.00
62	Stem, #3800, 4 oz., cocktail	20.00		Tumbler, #3400, 9 oz., ftd.		16.00
	Stem, #3800, 4 oz., wine	25.00		Tumbler, #3400, 10 oz., ftd.		16.00
	Stem, #3800, 6 oz., champagne/sherbet	24.00	12	Tumbler, #3400, 12 oz., ftd.		16.00
	Stem, #3800, 5 oz., claret	60.00	76	Tumbler, #3800, 5 oz., juice		24.00
64	Stem, #3800, 9 oz., water goblet	30.00	63	Tumbler, #3800, 9 oz.		24.00
	Stem, #4000, 1¼ oz., cordial	30.00		Tumbler, #3800, 12 oz.		30.00
	Stem, #4000, 4 oz., cocktail	18.00		Vase, 4", bead ft., sm. neck, ball, 400/25		55.00
	Stem, #4000, 5 oz., wine	22.00		Vase, 5¾", bead ft., bud, 400/107		55.00
	Stem, #4000, 6 oz., tall sherbet	18.00		Vase, 5¾", bead ft., mini bud, 400/107		55.00
	Stem, #4000, 11 oz., goblet	26.00		Vase, 6", flat, crimped edge, 400/287C		40.00
	Stem, #4000, 12 oz., tea	26.00		Vase, 6", ftd., flared rim, 400/138B		195.00
	Strawberry set, 2 pc. (7" plate/sugar dip bowl), 400/83	40.00		Vase, 6" diam., 400/198		350.00
				Vase, 6", fan, 400/287 F		35.00
	Sugar, domed foot, 400/18	90.00		Vase, 7", ftd., bud, 400/186		310.00
	Sugar, 6 oz., bead hdld., 400/30	6.00		Vase, 7", ftd., bud, 400/187		325.00
	Sugar, flat, bead handle, 400/126	28.00		Vase, 7", ivy bowl, 400/74J		165.00
32	Sugar, indiv. bridge, 400/122	7.00		Vase, 7", rolled rim w/bead hdld., 400/87 R		40.00
43	Sugar, plain ft., 400/31	6.00	2	Vase, 7", rose bowl, 400/142 K		300.00
	Tete-a-tete 3 pc. brandy, a.d. cup, 6½" oval tray, 400/111	110.00		Vase, 7¼", ftd., rose bowl, crimped top, 400/132C		525.00
			4	Vase, 7½", ftd., rose bowl, 400/132		495.00
	Tidbit server, 2 tier, cupped, 400/2701	50.00		Vase, 8", fan, w/bead hdld., 400/87F		30.00
	Tidbit set, 3 pc., 400/18TB	195.00		Vase, 8", flat, crimped edge, 400/143C		95.00
35	Toast, w/cover, set, 7¾", 400/123	295.00		Vase, 8", fluted rim w/bead hdlds., 400/87C		35.00
	Tray, 5½", hdld., upturned handles, 400/42E	20.00	3	Vase, 8½", bead ft., bud, 400/28C		110.00
	Tray, 5½", lemon, ctr. hdld., 400/221	28.00		Vase, 8½", bead ft., flared rim, 400/21		325.00
	Tray, 5¼" x 9¼", condiment, 400/148	40.00		Vase, 8½", bead ft., inward rim, 400/27		325.00
	Tray, 6½", 400/29	15.00		Vase, 8½", hdld. (pitcher shape), 400/227		595.00
	Tray, 6", wafer, handle bent to ctr. of dish, 400/51T	22.00	5	Vase, 10", bead ft., straight side, 400/22		295.00
	Tray, 9", oval, 400/159	35.00		Vase, 10", ftd., 400/193		295.00
70	Tray, 10", circular rings	50.00				

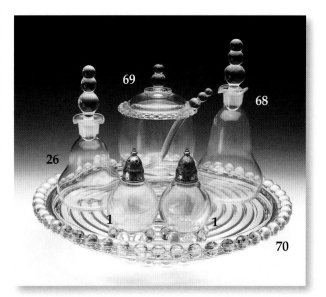

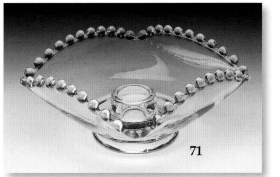

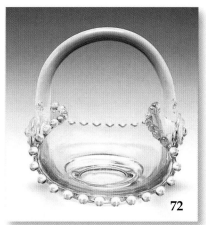

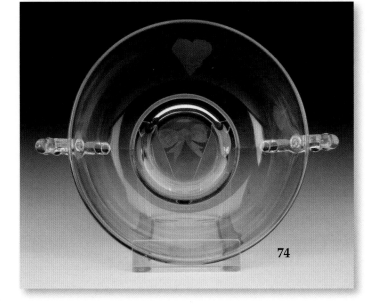

Reproductions made by Dalzell-Viking

26

69

68

1

1

70

67

71

72

74

75

CANTERBURY, NO. 115, DUNCAN & MILLER GLASS COMPANY, 1937 – 1950S

Colors: crystal, Sapphire blue, Cape Cod blue, Chartreuse, Ruby, Cranberry pink, Jasmine yellow

Canterbury, issued as Line No. 115, was the mould blank Duncan incorporated for some of their etched patterns; First Love is the most well-known. You can find First Love listed in our *Collectible Glassware of the 40s, 50s, and 60s* book. Duncan & Miller began Canterbury fabrication in 1937, but it had its primary manufacturing output through war years and early 1950s. Canterbury exemplifies that 50s love of fluid shapes. Later, moulds were transferred to Tiffin where most of the colored Canterbury was made. We see the yellow-green colored Canterbury (called Chartreuse) more than any other color in our travels. Maybe the few collectors of Chartreuse haven't found all those nooks and crannies where we shop. Those items being found in this color are Tiffin pieces manufactured from Duncan's moulds sometime after 1955. Often, you will find Tiffin labels still attached to these.

If you are a new collector and wish to see Canterbury catalog listings by Duncan, you will have to track down one of those earlier editions where we reproduced pages from old catalogs. You need to know that older editions have become collectible themselves and some sell at a premium price.

Duncan's light blue was called Sapphire and the opalescent blue was christened Cape Cod blue. The red was Ruby. You may find opalescent pieces of Canterbury in pink, called Cranberry, or yellow, called Jasmine. In Florida, crystal Canterbury pieces are habitually found cloudy or stained, which almost certainly indicates the hard water from wells here leaves residue that cannot be easily removed. There were several hard to find pieces at a flea market last week, but after the dew dried, the cloudiness showed quite clearly. Be aware of this problem especially when buying in the early morning dew by flashlight. If you know of additional pieces not listed or wish to share prices on colored wares, just drop us a postcard or email gflore@aol.com. The 64-ounce water pitcher and candlesticks have been the quick sell items for us when we have been able to find them.

We have mostly shown Canterbury crystal which is the most sought color. We have not seen enough Canterbury sold in colors to get a sense for those prices although 15% to 20% more than crystal seems to be normal except for Chartreuse and amber which sell in the range of crystal — or even less. We see Ruby pieces priced either very high or rather low. There does not seem to be any conformity. Time will determine whether Ruby is rare. Opalescent blue items seem to be priced three to four times those for crystal, but we have not found many customers buying or asking for them.

Canterbury is beginning to inch up in price with new collectors on the lookout for it since it is modestly priced when compared to patterns made by Cambridge, Heisey, or Fostoria. Pieces are heavier than most patterns, which bothers some, but which has also meant greater survival over the years. Another major concern is scratches from heavy use in the open plain areas. This pattern seems to have been bought for everyday use — and it is evident.

		Crystal
	Ashtray, 3"	5.00
	Ashtray, 3", club	7.00
	Ashtray, 4½", club	9.00
	Ashtray, 5"	12.00
	Ashtray, 5½", club	14.00
	Basket, 3" x 3" x 3¼", oval, hdld.	20.00
	Basket, 3" x 4", crimped, hdld.	30.00
	Basket, 3½", crimped, hdld.	35.00
	Basket, 3½", oval, hdld.	26.00
	Basket, 4½" x 4¾" x 4¾", oval, hdld.	42.00
	Basket, 4½" x 5" x 5", crimped, hdld.	48.00
	Basket, 9¼" x 10" x 7¼"	55.00
	Basket, 10" x 4¼" x 7", oval, hdld.	75.00
	Basket, 10" x 4½" x 8", oval, hdld.	78.00
	Basket, 11½", oval, hdld.	78.00
	Bowl, 4¼" x 2", finger	10.00
	Bowl, 5" x 3¼", 2 part, salad dressing	12.50
	Bowl, 5" x 3¼", salad dressing	12.50
	Bowl, 5½" x 1¾", one hdld., heart	9.00
	Bowl, 5½" x 1¾", one hdld., square	9.00
	Bowl, 5½" x 1¾", one hdld., star	10.00
	Bowl, 5½" x 1¾", one hdld., fruit	7.00
22	Bowl, 5½" x 1¾", one hdld., round	7.00
	Bowl, 5", fruit nappy	8.00
	Bowl, 6" x 2", 2 hdld., round	10.00
	Bowl, 6" x 2", 2 hdld., sweetmeat, star	15.00
	Bowl, 6" x 3¼", 2 part, salad dressing	14.00
	Bowl, 6" x 3¼", salad dressing	14.00

		Crystal
	Bowl, 6" x 5¼" x 2¼", oval olive	10.00
	Bowl, 7½" x 2¼", crimped	14.00
	Bowl, 7½" x 2¼", gardenia	17.50
6	Bowl, 8" x 2¾", crimped	20.00
	Bowl, 8" x 2½", flared	17.50
	Bowl, 8½" x 4"	22.00
	Bowl, 9" x 2", gardenia	27.50
12	Bowl, 9" x 4¼", crimped	27.50
	Bowl, 9" x 6" x 3", oval	30.00
	Bowl, 10" x 5", salad	30.00
	Bowl, 10" x 8½" x 5", oval	27.50
	Bowl, 10¾" x 4¾"	27.50
8	Bowl, 10½" x 5", crimped	30.00
7	Bowl, 11½" x 8¼", oval	32.50
	Bowl, 12" x 2¾", gardenia	30.00
	Bowl, 12" x 3½", flared	30.00
16	Bowl, 12" x 3¾", crimped	32.50
	Bowl, 13" x 8½" x 3¼", oval, flared	35.00
	Bowl, 13" x 10" x 5", crimped, oval	40.00
	Bowl, 15" x 2¾", shallow salad	42.00
20	Candle, 3", low	12.50
	Candle, 3½"	15.00
	Candlestick, 6", 3-lite	39.00
	Candlestick, 6"	25.00
	Candlestick, 7", w/U prisms	75.00
	Candy and cover, 8" x 3½", 3 hdld., 3 part	35.00
	Candy, 6½", w/5" lid	32.50
	Celery and relish, 10½" x 6¾" x 1¼", 2 hdld., 2 pt.	32.50

	Crystal		Crystal
Celery and relish, 10½" x 6¾" x 1¼", 2 hdld., 3 pt.	32.50	Cigarette jar w/cover, 4"	30.00
Celery, 9" x 4" x 1¼", 2 hdld.	22.50	Comport, high, 6" x 5½" high	20.00
Cheese stand, 5½" x 3½" high	15.00	Comport, low, 6" x 4½" high	18.00
Cigarette box w/cover, 3½" x 4½"	22.50	Creamer, 2¾", 3 oz., individual	6.00

CANTERBURY, NO. 115

		Crystal
5	Creamer, 3¾", 7 oz.	8.00
	Cup	8.00
	Decanter w/stopper, 12", 32 oz.	80.00
28	Ice bucket or vase, 6"	40.00
	Ice bucket or vase, 7"	45.00
	Lamp, hurricane, w/prisms, 15"	135.00
	Marmalade, 4½" x 2¾", crimped	20.00
	Mayonnaise, 5" x 3¼"	20.00
1	Mayonnaise, 5½" x 3¼", crimped	22.00
	Mayonnaise, 6" x 3¼"	24.00
	Pitcher, 16 oz., pint	55.00
	Pitcher, 9¼", 32 oz., hdld., martini	90.00
	Pitcher, 9¼", 32 oz., martini	80.00
	Pitcher, 64 oz.	250.00
	Plate, 6½", one hdld., fruit	6.00
15	Plate, 6", finger bowl liner	6.00
	Plate, 7½"	9.00
18	Plate, 7½", 2 hdld., mayonnaise	12.00
19	Plate, 8½"	12.00
	Plate, 11¼", dinner	25.00
	Plate, 11", 2 hdld. w/ring, cracker	20.00
17	Plate, 11", 2 hdld., sandwich	22.00
	Plate, 13½", cake, hdld.	40.00
	Plate, 14", cake	25.00
	Relish, 6" x 2", 2 hdld., 2 part, round	14.00
	Relish, 6" x 2", 2 hdld., 2 part, star	14.00
14	Relish, 7" x 5¼" x 2¼", 2 hdld., 2 part, oval	16.00
21	Relish, 8" x 1¾", 3 hdld., 3 part	17.50
23	Relish, 9" x 1½", 3 hdld., 3 part	22.00
	Relish, 11" x 2", 5 part	33.00
	Rose bowl, 5"	20.00
	Rose bowl, 6"	25.00
	Salt and pepper	22.50
	Sandwich tray, 12" x 5¼", center handle	50.00
	Saucer	3.00
	Sherbet, crimped, 4½", 2¾" high	10.00
	Sherbet, crimped, 5½", 2¾" high	11.00
25	Stem, 3¾", 6 oz., ice cream	5.00
	Stem, 4", 4½ oz., oyster cocktail	10.00
	Stem, 4¼", 1 oz., cordial, #5115	22.00
	Stem, 4¼", 3½ oz., cocktail	10.00
	Stem, 4½", 6 oz., saucer champagne	10.00
	Stem, 5", 4 oz., claret or wine	15.00
	Stem, 5¼", 3 oz., cocktail, #5115	12.00
	Stem, 5½", 5 oz., saucer champagne, #5115	10.00
	Stem, 6", 3½ oz., wine, #5115	22.00
24	Stem, 6", 9 oz., water	12.00
	Stem, 6¾", 5 oz., claret, #5115	20.00
	Stem, 7¼", 10 oz., water, #5115	16.00
	Sugar, 2½", 3 oz., individual	6.00
9	Sugar, 3", 7 oz.	8.00
	Top hat, 3"	20.00
26	Tray, 6", cream/sugar, shakers	15.00
13	Tray, 9", individual cream/sugar	9.00
	Tray, 9" x 4" x 1¼", 2 part, pickle and olive	17.50

		Crystal
3	Tumbler, 2½", 1½ oz., whiskey	11.00
	Tumbler, 2½", 5 oz., ftd., ice cream, #5115	8.00
27	Tumbler, 3¼", 4 oz., ftd., oyster cocktail, #5115	10.00
	Tumbler, 3¾", 5 oz., flat, juice	6.00
4	Tumbler, 4¼", 5 oz., ftd., juice	8.00
	Tumbler, 4¼", 5 oz., ftd., juice, #5115	10.00
10	Tumbler, 4½", 9 oz., flat, table, straight	10.00
	Tumbler, 4½", 10 oz., ftd., water, #5115	12.00
	Tumbler, 5½", 9 oz., ftd., luncheon goblet	12.00
	Tumbler, 5¾", 12 oz., ftd., ice tea, #5115	15.00
11	Tumbler, 6¼", 13 oz., flat, ice tea	15.00
	Tumbler, 6¼", 13 oz., ftd., ice tea	18.00
	Urn, 4½" x 4½"	15.00
	Vase, 3", crimped violet	15.00
	Vase, 3½", clover leaf	15.00
	Vase, 3½", crimped	15.00
	Vase, 3½", crimped violet	15.00
	Vase, 3½", oval	15.00
	Vase, 4", clover leaf	17.50
	Vase, 4", crimped	17.50
	Vase, 4", flared rim	17.50
	Vase, 4", oval	17.50
	Vase, 4½" x 4¾"	15.00
	Vase, 4½", clover leaf	20.00
2	Vase, 4½", crimped violet	17.50
	Vase, 4½", oval	17.50
	Vase, 5" x 5", crimped	17.50
	Vase, 5", clover leaf	25.00
	Vase, 5", crimped	17.50
	Vase, 5½", crimped	20.00
	Vase, 5½", flower arranger	27.50
	Vase, 6½", clover leaf	38.00
	Vase, 7", crimped	35.00
	Vase, 7", flower arranger	45.00
	Vase, 8½" x 6"	55.00
	Vase, 12", flared	80.00

CAPE COD, IMPERIAL GLASS COMPANY, 1932 – 1984

Colors: amber, Antique blue, Azalea, black, crystal, Evergreen, milk glass, Ritz blue, Ruby, Verde

As with Candlewick, we tried to clean out the closet of photos never used over the years. Crystal Cape Cod is most desired, since it can still be found while colored wares besides stems are difficult to gather. There are several hundred different pieces in crystal giving collectors a wide range of choices. As can be seen by our photos, stems and tumblers are what turn up regularly in color as well as crystal. The massive amount of crystal stems being unearthed is causing them to sell for lower prices than a few years ago. You can purchase many Cape Cod stems cheaper than newer glassware at your local department store. Rarely found items continue to soar in price, but those commonly seen have diminished in price due to lack of demand. You can buy most of the fundamental pieces of crystal Cape Cod inexpensively. How long that will hold true is a question. If you like it, buy it now.

Our picture illustrates the variety of colors found. In the top row is Ruby and crystal with red flashing as well as the pink that was called Azalea by Imperial. The trimmed pieces were made in the early 1940s and are difficult to find with that red flashing intact. Sellers, do not affix price stickers to the red flashing!

The second row shows pieces in Ebony, milk glass, Antique and Ritz blue, Emerald (dark), Verde (light) green, and amber in that order. Colored items were mostly made in the late 1960s and 1970s although Ruby and Ritz Blue first appeared in the 1930s.

Possibly, the color in which you could collect a small set would be Ruby, but it will not be inexpensive although there was enough made to find some. Most of the Ritz blue has disappeared into collections. If you like the Verde or Azalea, you could find enough stems to use.

		Crystal
	Ashtray, 4", 160/134/1	12.00
	Ashtray, 5½", 160/150	15.00
	Basket, 9", handled, crimped, 160/221/0	195.00
	Basket, 11" tall, handled, 160/40	175.00
48	Basket, 12", 160/73	150.00
	Bottle, bitters, 4 oz., 160/235	55.00
	Bottle, cologne, w/stopper, 1601	55.00
	Bottle, condiment, 6 oz., 160/224	60.00
	Bottle, cordial, 18 oz., 160/256	95.00
	Bottle, decanter, 26 oz., 160/244	115.00
	Bottle, ketchup, 14 oz., 160/237	175.00
	Bowl, 3", handled mint, 160/183	20.00
	Bowl, 3", jelly, 160/33	10.00
33	Bowl, 4½", finger, 1604½A	14.00
	Bowl, 4½", handled spider, 160/180	20.00
	Bowl, 4½", dessert, tab handled, 160/197	24.00
	Bowl, 5", dessert, heart shape, 160/49H	20.00
30	Bowl, 5", finger, 1602	15.00
	Bowl, 5", flower, 1605N	22.00
31	Bowl, 5½", fruit, 160/23B	8.00
	Bowl, 5½", handled spider, 160/181	22.00
40	Bowl, 5½", tab handled, soup, 160/198	20.00
	Bowl, 6", fruit, 160/3F	9.00
	Bowl, 6", baked apple, 160/53X	10.00
	Bowl, 6", handled, round mint, 160/51F	20.00
	Bowl, 6", handled heart, 160/40H	22.00
	Bowl, 6", handled mint, 160/51H	20.00
	Bowl, 6", handled tray, 160/51T	25.00

		Crystal
	Bowl, 6½", handled portioned spider, 160/187	25.00
	Bowl, 6½", handled spider, 160/182	28.00
	Bowl, 6½", tab handled, 160/199	28.00
	Bowl, 7", nappy, 160/5F	18.00
	Bowl, 7½", 160/7F	20.00
	Bowl, 7½", 2-handled, 160/62B	25.00
42	Bowl, 8½", portioned peanut butter or mint	15.00
	Bowl, 8¾", 160/10F	30.00
	Bowl, 9", footed fruit, 160/67F	65.00
	Bowl, 9½", 2 handled, 160/145B	40.00
	Bowl, 9½", crimped, 160/221C	100.00
	Bowl, 9½", float, 160/221F	65.00
	Bowl, 10", footed, 160/137B	75.00
	Bowl, 10", oval, 160/221	80.00
	Bowl, 11", flanged edge, 1608X	150.00
	Bowl, 11", oval, 160/124	70.00
	Bowl, 11", oval divided, 160/125	85.00
	Bowl, 11", round, 1608A	95.00
	Bowl, 11", salad, 1608D	60.00
	Bowl, 11¼", oval, 1602	80.00
	Bowl, 12", 160/75B	40.00
	Bowl, 12", oval, 160/131B	85.00
	Bowl, 12", oval crimped, 160/131C	175.00
	Bowl, 12", punch, 160/20B	65.00
	Bowl, 13", console, 160/75L	42.50
	Bowl, 15", console, 1601/0L	75.00
	Butter, 5", w/cover, handled, 160/144	28.00

MARTIN BRUEHL

		Crystal
	Butter, w/cover, ¼ lb., 160/161	45.00
	Cake plate, 10", 4 toed, 160/220	75.00
	Cake stand, 10½", footed, 160/67D	40.00
	Cake stand, 11", 160/103D	75.00
	Candleholder, twin, 160/100	85.00
	Candleholder, 3", single, 160/170	15.00
	Candleholder, 4", 160/81	25.00
	Candleholder, 4", Aladdin style, 160/90	125.00
	Candleholder, 4½", saucer, 160/175	25.00
	Candleholder, 5", 160/80	18.00
	Candleholder, 5", flower, 160/45B	50.00
	Candleholder, 5½", flower, 160/45N	100.00
	Candleholder, 6", centerpiece, 160/48BC	90.00
	Candy, w/cover, 160/110	75.00
	Carafe, wine, 26 oz., 160/185	235.00
	Celery, 8", 160/105	30.00
	Celery, 10½", 160/189	55.00
	Cigarette box, 4½", 160/134	40.00
	Cigarette holder, ftd., 1602	11.00
	Cigarette holder, Tom & Jerry mug, 160/200	25.00
	Cigarette lighter, 1602	30.00
	Coaster, w/spoon rest, 160/76	12.00
	Coaster, 3", square, 160/85	20.00
29	Coaster, 4", round, 160/78	15.00
	Coaster, 4½", flat, 160/1R	10.00
	Comport, 5¼", 160F	27.50
45	Comport, 5¾", 160X	30.00
	Comport, 6", 160/45	25.00
	Comport, 6", w/cover, ftd., 160/140	85.00
	Comport, 7", 160/48B	37.50
	Comport, 11¼", oval, 1602, 6½" tall	200.00
	Creamer, 160/190	25.00
36	Creamer, 160/30	6.00
	Creamer, ftd., 160/31	12.00
17	Cruet, w/stopper, 4 oz., 160/119	18.00
	Cruet, w/stopper, 5 oz., 160/70	30.00
49	Cruet, w/stopper, 6 oz., 160/241	40.00
	Cup, tea, 160/35	6.00
	Cup, coffee, 160/37	6.00
23	Cup, bouillon, 160/250	55.00
	Decanter, bourbon, 160/260	90.00
	Decanter, rye, 160/260	90.00
39	Decanter w/stopper, 30 oz., 160/163	60.00
	Decanter w/stopper, 24 oz., 160/212	65.00
43	Decanter, 26 oz., 160/244	90.00
	Egg cup, 160/225	22.00
	Epergne, 2 pc., plain center, 160/196	245.00
	Fork, 160/701	12.00
	Gravy bowl, 18 oz., 160/202	85.00
	Horseradish, 5 oz. jar, 160/226	75.00
	Ice bucket, 6½", 160/63	185.00
	Icer, 3 pc., bowl, 2 inserts, 160/53/3	55.00
	Jar, 12 oz., hdld. peanut w/lid, 160/210	65.00
	Jar, 10", "Pokal," 160/133	85.00
	Jar, 11", "Pokal," 160/128	90.00

		Crystal
	Jar, 15", "Pokal," 160/132	150.00
	Jar, candy w/lid, wicker hand., 5" h., 160/194	125.00
	Jar, cookie, w/lid, wicker hand., 6½" h., 160/195	150.00
	Jar, peanut butter w/lid, wicker hand., 4" h., 160/193	110.00
	Ladle, marmalade, 160/130	10.00
	Ladle, mayonnaise, 160/165	10.00
	Ladle, punch	25.00
	Lamp, hurricane, 2 pc., 5" base, 160/79	100.00
	Lamp, hurricane, 2 pc., bowl-like base, 1604	145.00
37	Marmalade, 3 pc. set, 160/89/3	32.50
	Marmalade, 4 pc. set, 160/89	40.00
	Mayonnaise, 3 pc. set, 160/52H	37.50
	Mayonnaise, 3 pc., 160/23	27.50
	Mayonnaise, 12 oz., hdld., spouted, 160/205	55.00
15	Mug, 12 oz., handled, 160/188	60.00
	Mustard, w/cover & spoon, 160/156	35.00
	Nut dish, 3", hdld., 160/183	30.00
	Nut dish, 4", hdld., 160/184	30.00
44	Pepper mill, 160/236	30.00
	Pitcher, milk, 1 pt., 160/240	55.00
	Pitcher, 36 oz., refrig. jug open lip, Tiars pro.	60.00
24	Pitcher, ice lipped, 40 oz., 160/19	85.00
	Pitcher, martini, blown, 40 oz., 160/178	200.00
	Pitcher, ice lipped, 2 qt., 160/239	85.00
	Pitcher, 2 qt., 160/24	85.00
	Pitcher, blown, 5 pt., 160/176	200.00
	Plate, 4½" butter, 160/34	6.00
	Plate, 6", cupped (liner for 160/208 salad dressing), 160/209	22.00
	Plate, 6½", bread & butter, 160/1D	6.00
	Plate, 7", 160/3D	7.00
	Plate, 7", cupped (liner for 160/205 mayo), 160/206	28.00

		Crystal
	Plate, 8", center handled tray, 160/149D	35.00
	Plate, 8", crescent salad, 160/12	70.00
	Plate, 8" cupped (liner for gravy), 160/203	28.00
	Plate, 8", salad, 160/5D	8.00
	Plate, 8½", 2 handled, 160/62D	25.00
	Plate, 9", 160/7D	18.00
	Plate, 9½", 2 hdld., 160/62D	35.00
	Plate, 10", dinner, 160/10D	30.00
	Plate, 11½", 2 handled, 160/145D	35.00
	Plate, 12½" bread, 160/222	60.00
	Plate, 13", birthday, 72 candle holes, 160/72	350.00
	Plate, 13", cupped torte, 1608V	35.00
	Plate, 13", torte, 1608F	40.00
	Plate, 14", cupped, 160/75V	50.00
	Plate, 14", flat, 160/75D	50.00
	Plate, 16", cupped, 160/20V	80.00
	Plate, 17", 2 styles, 160/10D or 20D	95.00
34	Platter, 13½", oval, 160/124D	80.00
	Puff box, w/cover, 1601	60.00
	Relish, 8", hdld., 2 part, 160/223	37.50
	Relish, 9½", 4 pt., 160/56	35.00
	Relish, 9½", oval, 3 part, 160/55	25.00
	Relish, 11", 5 part, 160/102	55.00
	Relish, 11¼", 3 part, oval, 1602	75.00
	Salad dressing, 6 oz., hdld., spouted, 160/208	65.00
	Salad set, 14" plate, 12" bowl, fork & spoon, 160/75	110.00
	Salt & pepper, individual, 160/251	18.00
10	Salt & pepper, pr., ftd., 160/117	18.00
	Salt & pepper, pr., ftd., stemmed, 160/243	40.00
	Salt & pepper, pr., 160/96	16.00
	Salt & pepper, pr. square, 160/109	25.00
44	Salt shaker, 160/237	15.00
	Salt dip, 160/61	20.00
	Salt spoon, 1600	8.00
	Saucer, tea, 160/35	2.00
	Saucer, coffee, 160/37	2.00
	Server, 12", ftd. or turned over, 160/93	75.00
	Spoon, 160/701	12.00
14	Stem, 1½ oz., cordial, 1602	5.00
21	Stem, 3 oz., wine, 1600	25.00
5	Stem, 3 oz., wine, 1602	4.00
18	Stem, 3½ oz., cocktail, 1602	3.00
28	Stem, 3½ oz., cocktail, 160B	3.00
7	Stem, 3½ oz., cocktail, 1600	3.00
12	Stem, 5 oz., claret, 1602	4.00
3	Stem, 6 oz., low sundae, 1602	2.00
	Stem, 6 oz., ftd., juice, 1602	3.00
20	Stem, 6 oz., parfait, 1602	6.00
	Stem, 6 oz., sherbet, 1600	10.00
25	Stem, 6 oz., sherbet, 3600	16.00
13	Stem, 6 oz., tall sherbet, 1602	3.00
	Stem, 8 oz., goblet, 160	5.00
4	Stem, 9 oz., water, 1602	4.00
	Stem, 10 oz., water, 1600	12.00

		Crystal
8	Stem, 11 oz., dinner goblet, 1602	5.00
27	Stem, 11 oz., goblet, 3600	16.00
26	Stem, 12 oz., tea, 3600	16.00
16	Stem, 14 oz., goblet, magnum, 160	30.00
42	Stem, oyster cocktail, 1602	5.00
	Sugar, 160/190	25.00
35	Sugar, 160/30	6.00
	Sugar, ftd., 160/31	12.00
	Toast, w/cover, 160/123	235.00
	Tom & Jerry footed punch bowl, 160/200	325.00
	Tray, sq. cov. sugar & creamer, 160/25/26	120.00
	Tray, 7", for creamer/sugar, 160/29	12.00
	Tray, 11", pastry, center hdld., 160/68D	50.00
	Tumbler, 2½ oz., whiskey, 160	8.00
11	Tumbler, 6 oz., ftd., juice, 1602	3.00
19	Tumbler, 6 oz., ftd., juice, 1600	15.00
2	Tumbler, 6 oz., juice, 160	3.00
1	Tumbler, 7 oz., old-fashion, 160	4.00
46	Tumbler, 9 oz., water, #1601	30.00
	Tumbler, 10 oz., ftd., water, 1602	4.00
41	Tumbler, 10 oz., water, 160	4.00
22	Tumbler, 12 oz., ftd., ice tea, 1600	5.00
9	Tumbler, 12 oz., ftd., tea, 160	9.00
6	Tumbler, 12 oz., ice tea, 160	9.00
32	Tumbler, 14 oz., double old-fashion, 160	22.00
38	Tumbler, 14 oz., 160	26.00
	Vase, 6¼", ftd., 160/22	35.00
	Vase, 6½", ftd., 160/110B	70.00
	Vase, 7½", ftd., 160/22	40.00
	Vase, 8", fan, 160/87F	215.00
	Vase, 8½", flip, 160/143	60.00
	Vase, 8½", ftd., 160/28	45.00
	Vase, 10", cylinder, 160/192	75.00
	Vase, 10½", hdld., urn, 160/186	200.00
47	Whimsey hat made from 10 oz. tumbler	65.00

QUICK MOTHER'S OATS

NET WEIGHT OF PRODUCT
3 LBS. 7 OZ.
(55 OUNCES)

CRYSTALWARE

42

Olde Thompson
PEPPER MILL
AND
SALT SHAKER

44

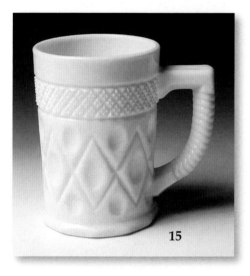

15

45

46

47

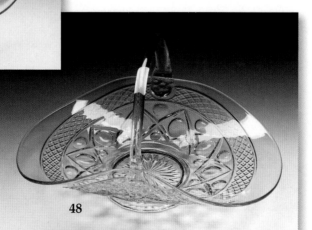

48

49

IMPERIAL
CAPE COD

160/73/0
11" Basket

160/186   10½"
2 Handled Urn Vase

160/79   2 pc.
Hurrican Lamp 9 inches Overall

160/24   60 oz.
Ice Lipped Pitcher

160/19   40 oz.
Ice Lipped Pitcher

160/196   2 pc. Epergne
Height-12 inches Overall

160/40   11"
Basket

160/63   6½"
Ice Bucket with Handle & Ice Tongs

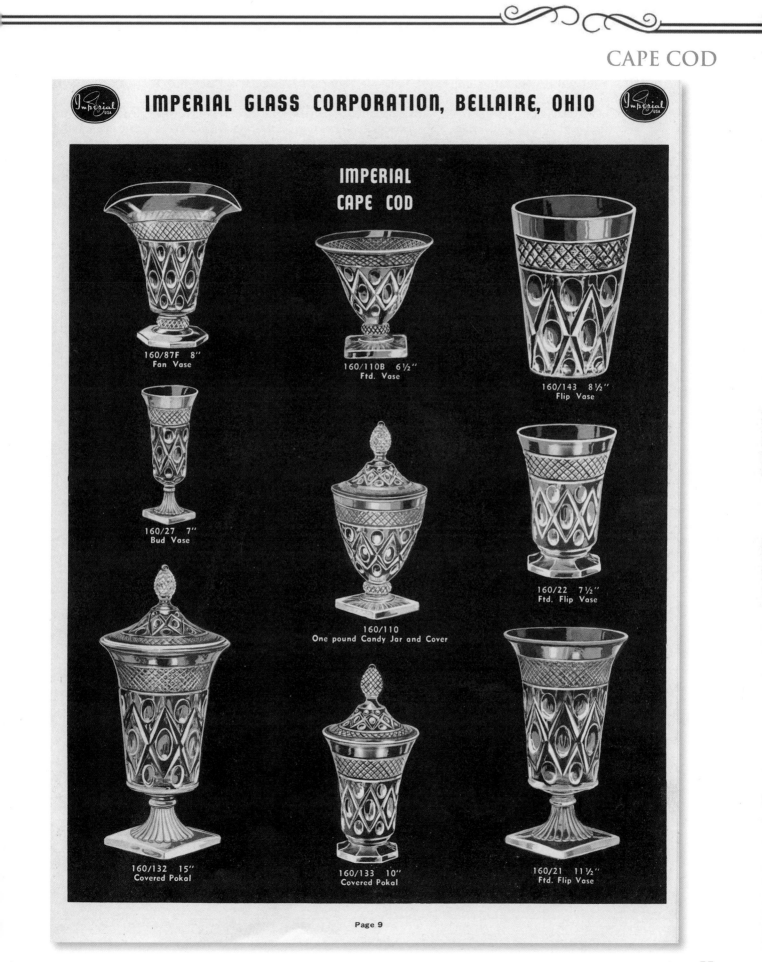

IMPERIAL GLASS CORPORATION, BELLAIRE, OHIO

IMPERIAL
CAPE COD

160/87F 8"
Fan Vase

160/110B 6½"
Ftd. Vase

160/143 8½"
Flip Vase

160/27 7"
Bud Vase

160/110
One pound Candy Jar and Cover

160/22 7½"
Ftd. Flip Vase

160/132 15"
Covered Pokal

160/133 10"
Covered Pokal

160/21 11½"
Ftd. Flip Vase

Page 9

CAPRICE, CAMBRIDGE GLASS COMPANY, 1940S – 1957

Colors: crystal, Moonlight Blue, amber, amethyst, La Rosa, Emerald green dark, Pistachio, Ritz blue, milk glass

Moonlight Blue and crystal Caprice are the colors routinely found and therefore, the most collected. Many items made in crystal and blue were never made in (La Rosa) pink, which limits collectors' options of collecting that color, although many do. Caprice can be found in a variety of colors listed above; only luncheon sets, a few stems, vases, bowls, and candles can be amassed in any color besides crystal, Moonlight Blue, and pink.

Pink is the color many new collectors first select, but most have given up the undertaking of putting a set together. Pink is as pricey as buying blue, but you will only discover a piece or two occasionally.

Prices for rarely seen colors of Caprice are similar to those of blue or pink. Collectors searching for amber or amethyst, should know those particular colors are priced closer to their crystal equivalent. Blue Caprice items have become hard to sell at prices they once fetched. Some items turned out to be more commonly found than previously thought which internet auctions have vividly pointed out.

Years ago, rare pieces were snatched up by the four or five determined collectors willing to pay whatever price was being asked. After those collectors satisfied their needs, prices adjusted — downward. Today, rarely found clarets, moulded, straight side, nine and twelve-ounce tumblers, footed whiskeys, and finger bowls are sitting in dealers' stock instead of being acquired for collections. That will likely change, but right now, we see collectors settling for not owning every piece in a pattern. Commonly found basic pieces are not selling well do to the lack of beginning collectors seeking them.

Blue bitters bottles and covered cracker jars have found new homes and most major collections now have a Doulton pitcher if the price met the buyer's expectations. The once overlooked Alpine Caprice items are being given a second look by beginners. Alpine pieces have satinized panels or bases and are found in both crystal and blue items. You should be aware that collector tastes change as more people come into our collecting fraternity. However, it is now possible to acquire this finish with chemicals from a craft shop. The satinized decoration on newly adorned pieces is pitted and rough and not as smooth a finish as it was originally, but the depressing circumstance is that it can now be done.

Crystal Caprice candle reflectors and punch bowls are seldom found; and there is serious money waiting for those who do find them. Should you desire, you could put a large set of crystal together for a reasonable price when compared to other patterns of this genre, if you avoid buying those rarely found items.

The non-designed centers on all flat pieces have a tendency to scratch with use or stacking. As long as you do not pay mint condition prices for items that are not mint, you will be fine.

		Crystal	Blue/Pink
45	Ashtray, 2¾", 3 ftd., shell, #213	4.00	6.00
3	Ashtray, 3", #214*	4.00	6.00
	Ashtray, 4", #215*	5.00	10.00
33	Ashtray, 4½", #210	9.00	15.00
	Ashtray, 5", #216*	6.00	15.00
	Bonbon, 6", oval, ftd., #155	20.00	40.00
	Bonbon, 6", sq., 2 hdld., #154	15.00	30.00
	Bonbon, 6", sq., ftd., #133	18.00	35.00
	Bottle, 7 oz., bitters, #186	195.00	695.00
	Bowl, 2", 4 ftd., almond, #95	15.00	35.00
	Bowl, 5", 2 hdld., jelly, #151*	12.00	25.00

		Crystal	Blue/Pink
	Bowl, 5", mayonnaise, #127	20.00	35.00
	Bowl, 5", fruit, #18	18.00	50.00
27	Bowl, 5", fruit, crimped, #19	22.00	55.00
	Bowl, 6", low ftd., compote, #130	20.00	40.00
	Bowl, 6", 2 hdld. bonbon	18.00	40.00
31	Bowl, 6¾", 2-part relish	14.00	25.00
32	Bowl, 7", low ftd. crimped jelly	18.00	40.00
	Bowl, 8", 4 ftd., #49	35.00	95.00
	Bowl, 8", sq., 4 ftd., #50	45.00	100.00
39	Bowl, 8", 3 pt., relish, #124*	18.00	38.00
	Bowl, 9½", crimped, 4 ftd., #52	40.00	85.00

		Crystal	Blue/Pink
	Bowl, 9", pickle, #102	22.00	40.00
	Bowl, 10", salad, 4 ftd., #57	40.00	90.00
	Bowl, 10", sq., 4 ftd., #58	40.00	90.00
13	Bowl, 10½", belled, 4 ftd., #54	38.00	75.00
	Bowl, 10½", crimped, 4 ftd., #53	38.00	90.00
	Bowl, 11", crimped, 4 ftd., #60	40.00	90.00
25	Bowl, 11", 2 hdld., oval, 4 ftd., #65*	40.00	90.00
10	Bowl, 11½", shallow, 4 ftd., #81	35.00	90.00
28	Bowl, 12", 4 pt. relish, oval, #126*	70.00	165.00
	Bowl, 12", relish, 3 pt., rect., #125*	40.00	110.00
	Bowl, 12½", belled, 4 ftd., #62	38.00	85.00
	Bowl, 12½", crimped, 4 ftd., #61	38.00	85.00
	Bowl, 13", cupped, salad, #80	65.00	140.00
	Bowl, 13", crimped, 4 ftd., #66	40.00	90.00
	Bowl, 13½", 4 ftd., shallow cupped, #82	42.00	90.00
	Bowl, 15", salad, shallow, #84	50.00	150.00
	Bridge set:		
	Cloverleaf, 6½", #173*	25.00	75.00
	Club, 6½", #170*	25.00	75.00
26	Diamond, 6½", #171	25.00	75.00
17	Heart, 6½", #169*	30.00	90.00
43	Spade, 6½", #172*	32.00	75.00
	Butter dish, ¼ lb., #52*	165.00	
	Cake plate, 13", ftd., #36	125.00	295.00
	Candle reflector, #73	295.00	
	Candlestick, 2½", ea., #67	12.00	18.00
	Candlestick, 2-lite, keyhole, 5", #647	15.00	45.00
29	Candlestick, 3-lite, #74	40.00	75.00
	Candlestick, 3-lite, keyhole, #638	20.00	50.00
50	Candlestick, 3-lite, #1338	35.00	60.00
30	Candlestick, 3-lite, #1357	45.00	110.00

		Crystal	Blue/Pink
	Candlestick, 5-lite, #1577	110.00	
	Candlestick, 5", ea., keyhole, #646	17.00	28.00
	Candlestick, 6", 2-lite, ea., arch, #72	30.00	75.00
	Candlestick, 7", ea., w/prism, #70	20.00	30.00
	Candlestick, 7½", dbl., ea., #69	150.00	500.00
	Candy, 6", 3 ftd., w/cover, #165	40.00	90.00
	Candy, 6", w/cover (divided), #168	75.00	135.00
	Celery & relish, 8½", 3 pt., #124	18.00	40.00
	Cheese stand comport, Alpine		200.00
22	Cigarette box, w/cover, 3½" x 2¼", #207	16.00	35.00
	Cigarette box, w/cover, 4½" x 3½", #208	20.00	45.00
	Cigarette holder, 2" x 2¼", triangular, #205	16.00	45.00
	Cigarette holder, 3" x 3", triangular, #204	20.00	40.00
16	Coaster, 3½", #13	14.00	25.00
	Comport, 6", low ftd., #130	20.00	40.00
	Comport, 7", low ftd., #130	30.00	60.00
	Comport, 7", tall, #136	33.00	85.00
14	Cracker jar & cover, #202	450.00	1,995.00
	Creamer, large, #41*	11.00	18.00
2	Creamer, medium, #38*	9.00	16.00
30	Creamer, ind., #40*	10.00	17.00
15	Cup, #17	10.00	22.00
	Decanter, w/stopper, 35 oz., #187	175.00	495.00
	Finger bowl & liner, #16	35.00	68.00
	Finger bowl and liner, blown, #300	38.00	68.00
5	Ice bucket, #201	60.00	135.00
52	Marmalade, w/cover, 6 oz., #89	60.00	175.00
	Mayonnaise, 6½", 3 pc. set, #129*	35.00	85.00
	Mayonnaise, 8", 3 pc. set, #106*	45.00	90.00
9	Mayonnaise, 8", 2-pt., 4 pc.	45.00	120.00
	Mustard, w/cover, 2 oz., #87	50.00	135.00

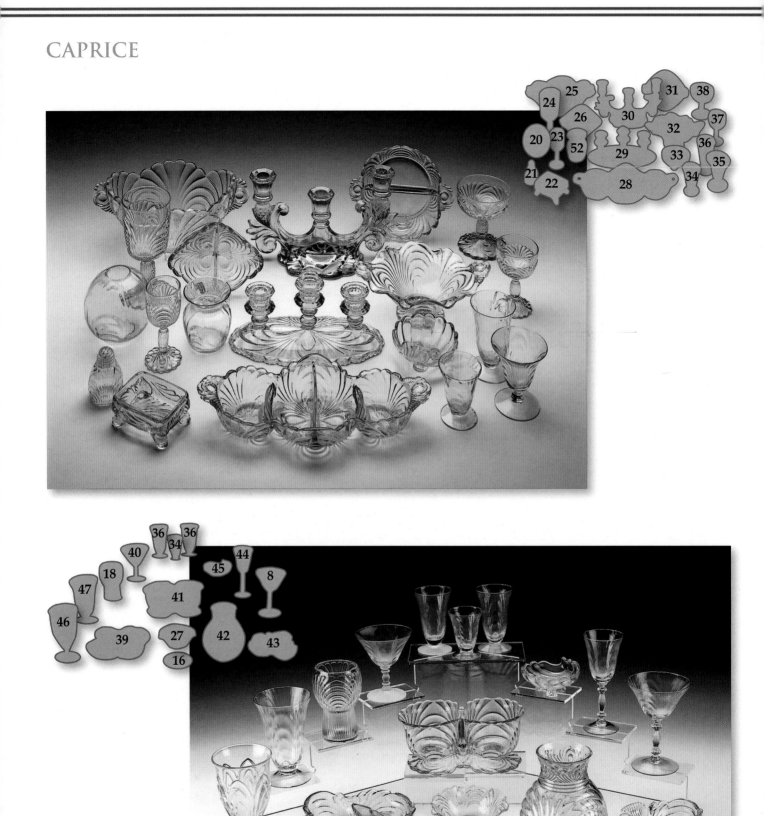

		Crystal	Blue/Pink
	Nut Dish, 2½", #93	18.00	35.00
	Nut dish, 2½", divided, #94	20.00	35.00
	Oil, 3 oz., w/stopper, #101*	30.00	60.00
	Oil, 3 oz., w/stopper, belled skirt, #117*	30.00	60.00
	Oil, 3 oz., w/stopper, #98*	30.00	60.00
	Oil, 5 oz., w/stopper, #100*	45.00	175.00
	Pitcher, 32 oz., ball shape, #179	90.00	235.00
	Pitcher, 80 oz., ball shape, #183	95.00	240.00
	Pitcher, 90 oz., tall Doulton style, #178	425.00	3,000.00
51	Plate, 5½", bread & butter, #20	7.00	12.00
	Plate, 6½", bread & butter, #21	7.00	12.00
	Plate, 6½", hdld., lemon, #152	8.00	18.00
	Plate, 7½", salad, #23	9.00	16.00
	Plate, 8½", luncheon, #22	9.00	18.00
	Plate, 9½", dinner, #24*	28.00	125.00
48	Plate, 11", cabaret, 4 ftd., #32	26.00	45.00
	Plate, 11½", cabaret, #26	26.00	45.00
11	Plate, 14", cabaret, 4 ftd., #33	34.00	50.00
	Plate, 14", 4 ftd., #28	30.00	55.00
	Plate, 16", #30	35.00	110.00
	Punch bowl, ftd., #498	2,750.00	
41	Salad dressing, 3 pc., ftd. & hdld., 2 spoons, #112*	175.00	335.00
	Salt & pepper, pr., ball, #91	35.00	90.00
21	Salt & pepper, pr., flat, #96*	28.00	60.00
	Salt & pepper, indiv., ball, pr., #90	40.00	90.00
	Salt & pepper, indiv., flat, pr., #92	35.00	90.00
	Salver, 13", 2 pc. (cake pedestal), #31	150.00	500.00
15	Saucer, #17	2.00	4.00
53	Stem, #300, blown, 1 oz., cordial	40.00	90.00
	Stem, #300, blown, 2½ oz., wine	20.00	45.00
	Stem, #300, blown, 3 oz., cocktail	18.00	30.00
44	Stem, #300, blown, 4½ oz., claret	60.00	115.00
	Stem, #300, blown, 4½ oz., low oyster cocktail	16.00	28.00
7	Stem, #300, blown, 5 oz., parfait	60.00	125.00
40	Stem, #300, blown, 6 oz., low sherbet	9.00	16.00
8	Stem, #300, blown, 6 oz., tall sherbet	9.00	20.00
6	Stem, #300, blown, 9 oz., water	14.00	30.00
	Stem, #301, blown, 1 oz., cordial	30.00	
	Stem, #301, blown, 2½ oz., wine	16.00	
	Stem, #301, blown, 3 oz., cocktail	16.00	
	Stem, #301, blown, 4½ oz., claret	30.00	
	Stem, #301, blown, 6 oz., sherbet	10.00	
	Stem, #301, blown, 9 oz., water	12.00	
23	Stem, 3 oz., wine, #6*	28.00	70.00
	Stem, 3½ oz., cocktail, #3*	16.00	40.00
	Stem, 4½ oz., claret, #5*	50.00	125.00
37	Stem, 4½ oz., fruit cocktail, #7	20.00	55.00
	Stem, 5 oz., low sherbet, #4	16.00	24.00
38	Stem, 7 oz., tall sherbet, #2*	14.00	26.00
24	Stem, 10 oz., water, #1	20.00	33.00
	Sugar, large, #41*	10.00	18.00

		Crystal	Blue/Pink
	Sugar, medium, #38*	9.00	16.00
1	Sugar, indiv., #40*	10.00	17.00
4	Tray, for sugar & creamer, #37*	12.00	24.00
	Tray, 9" oval, #42	16.00	35.00
	Tumbler, 2 oz., flat, #188*	18.00	70.00
	Tumbler, 3 oz., ftd., #12	24.00	75.00
	Tumbler, 5 oz., ftd., #11	15.00	55.00
	Tumbler, 5 oz., flat, #180	15.00	50.00
46	Tumbler, #200, iced tea	22.00	35.00
34	Tumbler, #300, 2½ oz., whiskey	35.00	160.00
36	Tumbler, #300, 5 oz., ftd., juice	15.00	35.00
47	Tumbler, #300, 10 oz., ftd. water	15.00	40.00
	Tumbler, #300, 12 oz., ftd. tea	15.00	40.00
35	Tumbler, #301, blown, 4½ oz., low oyster cocktail	14.00	
	Tumbler, #301, blown, 5 oz., juice	11.00	
19	Tumbler, #301, blown, 12 oz., tea	15.00	
	Tumbler, 9 oz., straight side, #14*	28.00	90.00
	Tumbler, 10 oz., ftd., #10*	15.00	28.00
18	Tumbler, 12 oz., flat., #184	35.00	40.00
	Tumbler, 12 oz., ftd., #9	18.00	35.00
	Tumbler, 12 oz., straight side, #15*	20.00	75.00
	Tumbler, #310, 5 oz., flat, juice	16.00	60.00
	Tumbler, #310, 7 oz., flat, old-fashion	25.00	90.00
	Tumbler, #310, 10 oz., flat, table	16.00	50.00
	Tumbler, #310, 11 oz., flat, tall, 4¹³⁄₁₆"	16.00	60.00
	Tumbler, #310, 12 oz., flat, tea	20.00	90.00
	Vase, 3½", #249	50.00	125.00
20	Vase, 4", blown, #251, blown	50.00	125.00
	Vase, 4¼", #241, ball	45.00	75.00
	Vase, 4½", #237, ball	55.00	150.00
	Vase, 4½", #252, blown	40.00	125.00
	Vase, 4½", #337, crimped top	40.00	100.00
	Vase, 4½", #344, crimped top	65.00	125.00
	Vase, 4½", #244	40.00	110.00
	Vase, 5", ivy bowl, #232	70.00	120.00
	Vase, 5½", #245	40.00	125.00
	Vase, 5½", #345, crimped top	65.00	170.00
	Vase, 6", #242, ftd.	60.00	150.00
	Vase, 6", blown, #254	150.00	335.00
	Vase, 6", #342, crimped top	75.00	150.00
	Vase, 6", #235, ftd., rose bowl	55.00	110.00
	Vase, 6½", #238, ball	40.00	125.00
	Vase, 6½", #338, crimped top	75.00	195.00
42	Vase, 7½", #246	50.00	150.00
	Vase, 7½", #346, crimped top	75.00	275.00
	Vase, 8", #236, ftd., rose bowl	75.00	195.00
	Vase, 8½", #243	85.00	170.00
	Vase, 8½", #239, ball	95.00	275.00
	Vase, 8½", #339, crimped top	95.00	250.00
	Vase, 8½", #343, crimped top	120.00	250.00
	Vase, 9¼" #240, ball	115.00	250.00
49	Vase, 9½" #340, crimped top	150.00	395.00

48

6   51   44   53

Viking cake salver

49

50

CARIBBEAN, LINE #112, DUNCAN MILLER GLASS COMPANY, 1936 – 1955

Colors: Amber, blue, cobalt blue, crystal, red

Caribbean crystal punch sets can be found with all crystal cups or with crystal cups with colored handles of red, cobalt blue, or amber. You can see one of these pictured here. With the colored handled punch cup and ladle, these sets sell for about $75.00 more than the plain crystal set priced below. Red and cobalt blue handled pieces appear to be more desirable than amber. Many collectors mix the colored punch cups so that they have four of each colored handle with their set as shown. In fact, we have seen so many with four of each cup that they may have been promoted like that in some areas.

We have seen a combination of blue and crystal Caribbean which made an alluring arrangement. Glass collectors commenced combining colors owing to a decorating inspiration initiated in women's magazines. Nowadays, combining glass colors has come about due to a lack of pieces available to acquire just one color. The practice is spawning some pleasingly innovative collections as we've witnessed in sent photos of artistic table arrangements.

Blue Caribbean dinner plates are challenging to find, but even more infuriating is finding them worn and defaced with mint condition prices on them. Collectors shopping for fundamental Caribbean dinnerware items (dinner plates, cups, and saucers) are finding few. When basic items are not found in quantity, new collectors tend to avoid the pattern. Prices for blue have remained fairly stable. So little is available for sale, there is no great rush of neophytes to purchase it. Neither do we see the crystal on the market that we once did. Of course, dealers have a tendency to avoid buying patterns that few collectors seek, creating a subsequent impediment for collecting crystal Caribbean. The blue punch bowl, pitchers, and some of the stemware, particularly cordials, will all cost you big monies, should you find them.

Amber Caribbean is rarely seen except for the cigarette jar and ashtrays pictured. Other amber pieces are uncommon; keep that in mind.

		Crystal	Blue
2	Ashtray, 6", 4 indent	15.00	30.00
	Bowl, 3¾" x 5", folded side, hdld.	15.00	30.00
	Bowl, 4½", finger	16.00	30.00
8	Bowl, 5", fruit nappy (takes liner), hdld.	12.50	25.00
7	Bowl, 5" x 7", folded side, hdld.	20.00	35.00
	Bowl, 6½", soup (takes liner)	16.00	40.00
17	Bowl, 7", hdld.	25.00	45.00
	Bowl, 7¼", ftd., hdld., grapefruit	20.00	45.00
	Bowl, 8½"	30.00	75.00
	Bowl, 9", salad	30.00	75.00
	Bowl, 9¼", veg., flared edge	32.50	75.00
13	Bowl, 9¼", veg., hdld.	40.00	90.00
	Bowl, 9½", epergne, flared edge	37.50	95.00
	Bowl, 10", 6¼ qt., punch	90.00	495.00
9	Bowl, 10", 6¼ qt., punch, flared top (catalog lists as salad)	90.00	400.00
	Bowl, 10¾", oval, flower, hdld.	40.00	95.00
	Bowl, 12", console, flared edge	50.00	110.00
	Candelabrum, 4¾", 2-lite	40.00	95.00
	Candlestick, 7¼", 1-lite, w/blue prisms	65.00	195.00
	Candy dish w/cover, 4" x 7"	50.00	120.00
	Cheese/cracker crumbs, 3½" h., plate 11", hdld.	50.00	100.00
4	Cigarette holder (stack ashtray top)	35.00	75.00
	Cocktail shaker, 9", 33 oz.	100.00	300.00
	Creamer	9.00	18.00
	Cruet	40.00	95.00
	Cup, tea	15.00	50.00
	Cup, punch	10.00	20.00
	Epergne, 4 pt., flower (12" bowl, 9½" bowl, 7¾" vase, 14" plate)	225.00	450.00
	Ice bucket, 6½", hdld.	65.00	195.00

		Crystal	Blue
	Ladle, punch	35.00	100.00
	Mayonnaise, w/liner, 5¾", 2 pt., 2 spoons, hdld.	40.00	90.00
3	Mayonnaise, w/liner, 5¾", hdld., 1 spoon	30.00	70.00
	Mustard, 4", w/slotted cover	35.00	55.00
	Pitcher, 4¾" 16 oz., milk	95.00	235.00
6	Pitcher, w/ice lip, 9", 72 oz., water	225.00	595.00
	Plate, 6", hdld., fruit nappy liner	4.00	9.00
	Plate 6¼", bread/butter	5.00	9.00
	Plate, 7¼", rolled edge, soup liner	5.00	10.00
	Plate, 7½", salad	8.00	16.00
	Plate, 8", hdld., mayonnaise liner	6.00	12.00
	Plate, 8½", luncheon	10.00	24.00
	Plate, 10½", dinner	40.00	110.00
15	Plate, 11", hdld., cheese/cracker liner	20.00	45.00
14	Plate, 12", salad liner, rolled edge	22.00	50.00
	Plate, 14"	25.00	80.00
	Plate, 16", torte	35.00	110.00
	Plate, 18", punch underliner	40.00	125.00
	Relish, 6", round, 2 pt.	12.00	25.00
	Relish, 9½", 4 pt., oblong	30.00	60.00
	Relish, 9½", oblong	25.00	60.00
	Relish, 12¾", 5 pt., rnd.	40.00	95.00
5	Relish, 12¾", 7 pt., rnd.	40.00	95.00
	Salt dip, 2½"	11.00	25.00
	Salt & pepper, 3", metal tops	32.00	95.00
	Salt & pepper, 5", metal tops	37.50	125.00
	Saucer	3.00	8.00
	Server, 5¾", ctr. hdld.	13.00	40.00
	Server, 6½", ctr. hdld.	22.00	50.00
	Stem, 3", 1 oz., cordial	40.00	150.00
	Stem, 3½", 3½ oz., ftd., ball stem, wine/cocktail	15.00	55.00
1	Stem, 3⅝", 2½ oz., wine (egg cup shape)	15.00	25.00
	Stem, 4", 6 oz., ftd., ball stem, champagne	10.00	25.00
	Stem, 4¼", ftd., sherbet	8.00	22.00
	Stem, 4¾", 3 oz., ftd., ball stem, wine	18.00	50.00
	Stem, 5¾", 8 oz., ftd., ball stem	18.00	40.00
	Sugar	9.00	18.00
	Syrup, metal cutoff top	110.00	250.00
	Tray, 6¼", hand., mint, div.	14.00	30.00
	Tray, 12¾", rnd.	25.00	50.00
	Tumbler, 2¼", 2 oz., shot glass	20.00	60.00
10	Tumbler, 3½", 5 oz., flat	20.00	55.00
	Tumbler, 5¼", 11½ oz., flat	20.00	55.00
	Tumbler, 5½", 8½ oz., ftd.	22.00	55.00
	Tumbler, 6½", 11 oz., ftd., ice tea	25.00	60.00
11	Vase, 5", hat shape	65.00	95.00
	Vase, 5¾", ftd., ruffled edge	22.00	55.00
	Vase, 7¼", ftd., flared edge, ball	27.50	75.00
	Vase, 7½", ftd., flared edge, bulbous	32.50	85.00
	Vase, 7¾", flared edge, epergne	40.00	125.00
12	Vase, 8", ftd., straight side	40.00	85.00
21	Vase, 9", 2 styles	50.00	225.00
16	Vase, 10", ftd.	55.00	195.00

21

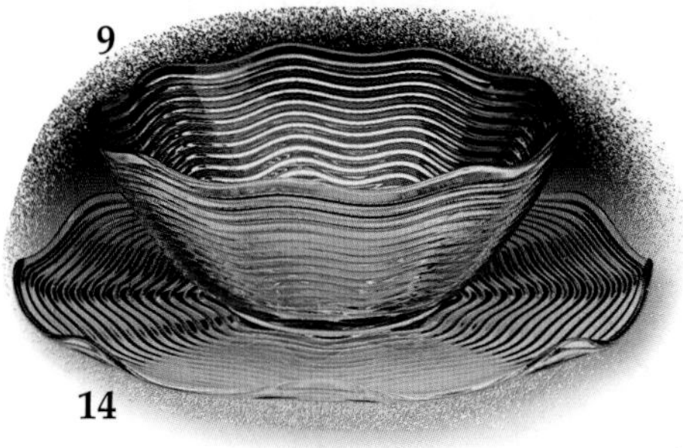

9

14

CATALONIAN (OLD SPANISH), CONSOLIDATED GLASS COMPANY, 1927 – 1940S

Brilliant Colors: Emerald Green, Spanish Rose, and Crystal (color of the glass itself)
Soft Colors: Honey, Amethyst, and Jade (ceramic wash over crystal)
Rare Colors: Ruby Stained (on crystal), Red (Ruby glass), Blue
(ceramic wash), and Rainbow (multiple color washed on crystal)

Catalonian was handmade glass pioneered in January 1927 and promoted as "a replica of seventeenth-century glass." Original labels found on several items read "Catalonian, A Reproduction of Old Spanish Glass."

Catalonian is characterized by bubbled and spiral ridges on the exterior surface of each piece. The gather of glass was sprinkled with raw "batch" and then dipped back into the molten glass. This caused the granules to bubble. As the glassmaker worked the glass, the bubbles would stretch and become larger.

13

All blown items always have a rough pontil mark on the base and in the case of Catalonian, the edges were generally not polished or shaped. The only exceptions to this are Ruby glass items, which commanded higher prices at the time of production and thus demanded extra attention. If you come across a piece of Catalonian other than Ruby with a ground edge, someone tried to repair a chip and didn't understand how it was made.

The Spanish Knobs line was based on the Catalonian appearance and glass formula. In addition to the bubbles, Spanish Knobs pieces have raised knobs molded into the glass. This line was sold along with Catalonian and original company ads combine the two in table settings. Today it's considered a part of the Catalonian line, not a separate pattern.

Usually, vases, candlesticks, and 8" plates are seen more often than other pieces. Other tableware is difficult to find, and cup and saucer sets, decanters, toilet bowls, covered cigarette boxes, and the whiskey set trays are rarely seen.

14

Crystal pieces were highlighted with one or more colors making a Rainbow color in the early 1940s. These colors were applied in bands, so that crystal became one of the colors in the "rainbow." Rare Rainbow items display three colors: blue, green, and red with no crystal band.

Pricing is similar for all the brilliant and soft colors (with crystal at least 50% less than the others). Spanish Rose (pink) is the hardest of the regular production colors to find. We typically discover green in our travels. Ruby Stained items are about 50% higher than listed prices. Blue ceramic, Rainbow colors, and Ruby glass are no less than 100% more. Rare colors are predominantly found on vases and occasional pieces such as console sets and pitchers.

Milk glass vases in Catalonian shapes were made in the 1950s, but are not accepted as Catalonian by collectors. Catalonian has been known to fetch higher prices in art glass markets than in Depression glass ones, but those markets are beginning to merge.

	Item	Price
	Ashtray, #1125	40.00
	Basket (made from fingerbowl), #1114	110.00
	Bottle, toilet water w/lid, #1175	125.00
	Bowl, bulb, #1178	65.00
10	Bowl, 4½", finger or mayo, #1114	45.00
11	Bowl, 9", straight-sided salad, #1115	125.00
	Bowl, 9½", flared salad, #1115B	125.00
	Bowl, 12", Lily, cupped, #1108	350.00
	Bowl, 12¾", flared, #1185	190.00
	Bowl, flower or low centerpiece, SK, #1130	375.00
	Candlestick, mushroom, SK, #1131, pr.	150.00
7	Candlestick, ftd., #1124, pr.	90.00
	Cigarette box and cover, #1107	165.00
	Comport, 6½", SK, #1145	85.00
	Creamer or mayonnaise boat, #1106	30.00
13	Creamer, 7 oz., triangular, #1103P	35.00
	Creamer, footed, SK, #1147	55.00

15

	Cup, #1179	75.00
	Goblet, parfait, low ftd., SK, #1141	75.00
1	Goblet, 10 oz., low ftd., #1120	40.00
	Goblet, 10 oz., low ftd., SK, #1142	65.00
2	Goblet, 12 oz., low ftd. iced tea, #1121	40.00
	Jug, 20 oz., 6", triangular, #1102P	150.00
	Jug, 72 oz., cylindrical, #1100P	225.00
	Jug, 72 oz., 10", triangular, #1101P	225.00
	Jug, 72 oz., squat triangular, #1109	225.00
	Jug, whiskey decanter & stopper, #1127	300.00
	Plate, 6", bread & butter, #1181	16.00
	Plate, 7", bread & butter, #1113	22.00
3	Plate, 8", salad, #1112	28.00
	Plate, 10", service, #1177	65.00
	Plate, 13", charger, #1111	110.00
	Plate, 16", #1194	150.00
	Relish tray, 3 part, #1191	350.00
	Relish tray, 6 part, #1192	450.00
	Saucer, #1180	50.00
15	Sugar, no handles, #1105B	30.00
	Sugar, two handles, #1105	35.00
	Sugar, footed, SK, #1146	55.00
12	Sundae (sherbet), 7 oz., ftd., #1123	40.00
	Sundae (sherbet), ftd. SK, #1140	65.00
	Tray, round whiskey set, #1128	300.00
9	Tumbler, 2 oz., whiskey, flat, #1119	40.00
	Tumbler, 2½ oz., whiskey, ftd., #1122	55.00
	Tumbler, 7 oz., flat, #1118	35.00
	Tumbler, 8 oz., flat, SK, #1138	60.00

6	Tumbler, 9 oz., flat, #1110	30.00
	Tumbler, 12. oz., tea, flat, #1117	40.00
5	Tumbler, 12. oz., hdld. tea, flat, #1117B	55.00
	Vase, 3 bulge rolled edge, #1182	200.00
	Vase, 3 bulge cupped edge, #1183	200.00
	Vase, 3 bulge flared edge, #1184	200.00
8	Vase, Nasturtium, 4 openings, bulbous, #1170	200.00
	Vase, 3¾", Violet, SK, #1171	90.00
	Vase, 4", fan, SK, #1174	90.00
	Vase, 4", flared (hat), SK, #1153	90.00
	Vase, 4", Sweet Pea SK, #1154	90.00
	Vase, 4", triangular, #1103	65.00
14	Vase, 6", flared (hat shape), #1116C	100.00
	Vase, 6", ftd., flared, SK, #1148	125.00
	Vase, 6", pillow (oblong), #1104	100.00
	Vase, 6", pinch bottle, triangular, SK, #1167	165.00
	Vase, 6", pinch bottle, 4-sided, SK, #1166	165.00
	Vase, 6", pinch bottle, 4 openings, SK, #1169	195.00
4	Vase, 6", triangular, #1102	90.00
	Vase, 6½", ftd. fan, #1172	90.00
	Vase, 7", fan, #1168	100.00
	Vase, 7", tumbler, #1116	100.00
	Vase, 8", fan, #1100B	125.00
	Vase, 8", flared (hat shape), #1100C	125.00
	Vase, 8", rose jar, #1109B	175.00
	Vase, 8", rose jar, SK, #1173	225.00
	Vase, 8", tumbler, #1100	125.00
	Vase, 10", triangular, #1101	165.00

CHANTILLY, CAMBRIDGE GLASS COMPANY, LATE 1930S – MID 1950S

Colors: crystal, Ebony (gold encrusted)

There is a more complete inventory for etched Cambridge items under Rose Point later in this book (pgs. 202 – 207). Numerous Chantilly pieces are not priced here, as our primary interest is to make you familiar with the pattern itself. If you are pricing unlisted Chantilly items by means of the Rose Point list, remember that Chantilly items are presently a minimum of 40% to 60% lower due to collector interest.

Although Chantilly was made and sold in conjunction with the well-liked Rose Point, it never captivated the number of patrons then or today as does the popular Rose Point. We have included a couple of fold out pages from a 1953 pamphlet showing the readily available #3625 Chantilly stems and an array of vases at the top of page 67. Hopefully, this will help anyone having difficulty distinguishing stemware or Cambridge line numbers.

		Crystal				Crystal
8	Bottle, French dressing, #1261	75.00		Plate, crescent, salad		95.00
	Bowl, 7", bonbon, 2 hdld., ftd.	20.00		Plate, 6½", bread/butter		6.00
	Bowl, 7", relish/pickle, 2 pt.	25.00		Plate, 8", salad		10.00
	Bowl, 7", relish/pickle	28.00		Plate, 8", tab hdld., ftd., bonbon		15.00
	Bowl, 9", celery/relish, 3 pt.	32.00		Plate, 10½", dinner		50.00
	Bowl, 10", 4 ftd., flared	40.00		Plate, 12", 4 ftd., service		40.00
	Bowl, 11", tab hdld.	40.00		Plate, 13", 4 ftd.		50.00
	Bowl, 11½", tab hdld. ftd.	45.00		Plate, 13½", tab hdld., cake		55.00
	Bowl, 12", celery/relish, 3 pt.	40.00		Plate, 14", torte		40.00
	Bowl, 12", 4 ftd., flared	45.00		Salad dressing bottle		135.00
	Bowl, 12", 4 ftd., oval	50.00		Salt & pepper, pr., flat		28.00
	Bowl, 12", celery/relish, 5 pt.	40.00		Salt & pepper, footed		30.00
	Butter, w/cover, round	150.00	21	Salt & pepper, handled		30.00
	Butter, ¼ lb.	245.00	20	Saucer, #3900/17		3.00
	Candlestick, 5"	22.00		Stem, #3080, 9 oz., water		30.00
	Candlestick, 6", 2-lite, "keyhole"	35.00		Stem, #3138, 6 oz., tall sherbet		14.00
	Candlestick, 6", 3-lite	40.00		Stem, #3600, 1 oz., cordial		38.00
	Candy box, w/cover, ftd.	65.00		Stem, #3600, 2½ oz., cocktail		16.00
29	Candy box, w/cover, rnd., 3900/165	85.00		Stem, #3600, 2½ oz., wine		26.00
	Cocktail icer, 2 pc.	50.00		Stem, #3600, 4½ oz., claret		30.00
9	Cocktail shaker, P 101, 32 oz.	75.00		Stem, #3600, 4½ oz., low oyster cocktail		12.00
	Comport, 5½"	30.00		Stem, #3600, 7 oz., tall sherbet		14.00
	Comport, 5⅜", blown	35.00		Stem, #3600, 7 oz., low sherbet		12.00
21	Creamer, 3900/41	14.00		Stem, #3600, 10 oz., water		22.00
	Creamer, indiv., #3900, scalloped edge	14.00	26	Stem, #3625, 1 oz., cordial		38.00
20	Cup, #3900/17	14.00		Stem, #3625, 3 oz., cocktail		18.00
	Decanter, ftd.	195.00		Stem, #3625, 4½ oz., claret		28.00
	Decanter, ball	225.00		Stem, #3625, 4½ oz., low oyster cocktail		12.00
	Hat, small	195.00	27	Stem, #3625, 7 oz., low sherbet		12.00
	Hat, large	295.00		Stem, #3625, 7 oz., tall sherbet		14.00
	Hurricane lamp, candlestick base	150.00	28	Stem, #3625, 10 oz., water		24.00
24	Hurricane lamp, keyhole base w/prisms, #1617	250.00		Stem, #3775, 1 oz., cordial		38.00
3	Ice bucket, w/chrome handle	95.00	19	Stem, #3775, 2½ oz., wine		22.00
	Marmalade & cover	50.00	16	Stem, #3775, 3 oz., cocktail		18.00
	Mayonnaise (sherbet type bowl w/ladle)	35.00		Stem, #3775, 4½ oz., claret		30.00
	Mayonnaise, div. w/liner & 2 ladles	55.00		Stem, #3775, 4½ oz., oyster cocktail		12.00
	Mayonnaise, w/liner & ladle	50.00	17	Stem, #3775, 6 oz., low sherbet		12.00
	Mustard & cover	75.00	18	Stem, #3775, 6 oz., tall sherbet		14.00
	Oil, 6 oz., hdld., w/stopper	95.00	6	Stem, #3779, 1 oz., cordial		45.00
23	Pickle tray, 9", 3400/59	30.00	4	Stem, #3779, 2½ oz., wine		22.00
	Pitcher, ball	150.00	5	Stem, #3779, 3 oz., cocktail		18.00
	Pitcher, Doulton	315.00		Stem, #3779, 4½ oz., claret		28.00
	Pitcher, upright	195.00		Stem, #3779, 4½ oz., low oyster cocktail		12.00
	Pitcher, 32 oz., martini jug, #3900/114	150.00	1	Stem, #3779, 6 oz., tall sherbet		14.00

		Crystal
	Stem, #3779, 6 oz., low sherbet	12.00
2	Stem, #3779, 9 oz., water	24.00
	Stem, #7801, 10 oz., goblet	24.00
12	Sugar, 3900/41	14.00
	Sugar, indiv., #3900, scalloped edge	14.00
14	Syrup, 1670, drip cut top	195.00
	Tumbler, #3600, 5 oz., ftd., juice	14.00
	Tumbler, #3600, 12 oz., ftd., tea	18.00
	Tumbler, #3625, 5 oz., ftd., juice	14.00
10	Tumbler, #3625, 10 oz., ftd., water	15.00
30	Tumbler, #3625, 12 oz., ftd., tea	20.00
	Tumbler, #3775, 5 oz., ftd., juice	14.00
25	Tumbler, #3775, 10 oz., ftd., water	15.00
	Tumbler, #3775, 12 oz., ftd., tea	18.00
11	Tumbler, #3779, 5 oz., ftd., juice	15.00
	Tumbler, #3779, 12 oz., ftd., tea	18.00
32	Tumbler, 13 oz., 3900/115	20.00
31	Tumbler, 14 oz., #498	30.00
	Vase, 5", globe	50.00
	Vase, 6", high ftd., flower	45.00
7	Vase, 8", high ftd., flower, 6004 with sterling base	60.00
	Vase, 9", keyhole base	60.00
	Vase, 10", bud	95.00
	Vase, 11", ftd., flower	95.00
	Vase, 11", ped. ftd., flower	115.00
	Vase, 12", keyhole base	95.00

		Crystal
	Vase, 13", ftd., flower	165.00
	Cordial, Sterling base	50.00
15	Wine, Farberware Trims	20.00
22	Sugar, Farberware Trims	20.00
13	Creamer, Farberware Trims	20.00

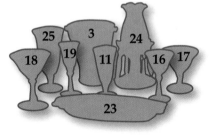

CHARTER OAK, #6632, A.H. HEISEY COMPANY, 1926 – 1935

Colors: Crystal, Flamingo, Moongleam, Hawthorne, Marigold

Flamingo (pink) Charter Oak pieces are found occasionally, but we seldom observe other colors. Pink stemware is often found in small groupings as opposed to a single piece. In the past, prices had remained steady for Charter Oak; but as with most patterns, there have been price decreases of late which often indicate more being found or fewer choosing to own it. Most pieces of Charter Oak are unmarked, and thus bargains can still be discovered. Acorns are characteristic of the pattern. Heisey Plantation with its pineapple stemware and Charter Oak with its acorns ought to be hard to miss.

Yeoman cups and saucers are regularly used with this set since there were no cups and saucers made. A Yeoman cup and saucer set is pictured below to show how well it matches this pattern.

You can see that clever "Acorn" #130, one-lite candleholder in our *Florences' Glassware Pattern Identification Guide, Volume 2.* The base is an oak leaf with stem curled up and an acorn for the candle cup. Honestly, this candle is not Charter Oak pattern, but most Charter Oak collectors try to obtain these to go with their sets. Heisey designed a number of candles to "blend" (their words) with numerous patterns. This candle was made during the same time as Charter Oak and mostly in the same colors.

		Crystal	Flamingo	Moongleam	Hawthorne	Marigold
	Bowl, 11", floral, #116 (oak leaf)	50.00	50.00	70.00	85.00	
4	Bowl, finger, #3362	10.00	17.50	20.00		
	Candleholder, 1-lite, #130, "Acorn"	150.00	400.00	500.00		
	Candlestick, 3", #116 (oak leaf)	25.00	35.00	45.00	100.00	
1	Candlestick, 5", 3-lite, #129, "Tricorn"	60.00	110.00	120.00	160.00	200.00+
11	Coaster, #10 (Oak Leaf)	10.00	20.00	25.00	45.00	
	Comport, 6", low ft., #3362	30.00	45.00	55.00	70.00	80.00
18	Comport, 7", ftd., #3362	35.00	55.00	70.00	100.00	150.00
7	Cup and saucer (#1184 Yeoman)	10.00	20.00	20.00	30.00	
	Lamp, #4262 (blown comport/water filled to magnify design & stabilize lamp)	1,000.00	1,500.00	1,500.00		
14	Pitcher, flat, #3362		140.00	160.00		
	Plate, 6", salad, #1246 (Acorn & Leaves)	5.00	10.00	12.50	20.00	
2	Plate, 7", luncheon/salad, #1246 (Acorn & Leaves)	8.00	12.00	17.50	22.50	
	Plate, 8", luncheon, #1246 (Acorn & Leaves)	10.00	15.00	20.00	25.00	
17	Plate, 10½", dinner, #1246 (Acorn & Leaves)	30.00	45.00	55.00	70.00	

CHARTER OAK

		Crystal	Flamingo	Moongleam	Hawthorne	Marigold
12	Stem, 3 oz., cocktail, #3362	10.00	20.00	25.00	40.00	40.00
10	Stem, 3½ oz., low ft., oyster cocktail, #3362	8.00	20.00	20.00	30.00	30.00
15	Stem, 4½ oz., parfait, #3362	15.00	20.00	30.00	50.00	40.00
6	Stem, 6 oz., saucer champagne, #3362	10.00	15.00	20.00	50.00	40.00
5	Stem, 6 oz., sherbet, low ft., #3362	7.00	10.00	18.00	40.00	30.00
16	Stem, 8 oz., goblet, high ft., #3362	10.00	20.00	20.00	80.00	40.00
3	Stem, 8 oz., luncheon goblet, low ft., #3362	10.00	30.00	35.00	75.00	40.00
13	Tumbler, 10 oz., flat, #3362	10.00	20.00	25.00	35.00	30.00
9	Tumbler, 12 oz., flat, #3362	12.50	20.00	25.00	40.00	35.00

CHEROKEE ROSE, TIFFIN GLASS COMPANY, 1940S – 1950S

Color: crystal

Cherokee Rose stemware line #17399 is the normally found teardrop style, alas not shown in our photo this time. Should you find a Cherokee Rose cup or saucer, please let us know. The #5902 line had scalloped and beaded edges on serving pieces. A few pieces are found with gold trim illustrated by the bell; and although the same etching, with gold trim, it was called Laurel by Tiffin.

2	Bell	65.00
	Bowl, 5", finger	25.00
	Bowl, 6", fruit or nut, #5902	25.00
	Bowl, 7", nappy, #5902	40.00
9	Bowl, 10", deep salad, cupped, #5902	60.00
6	Bowl, 10½", celery, rectangular, #5902	40.00
10	Bowl, 12", crimped, #5902	50.00
	Bowl, 12½", centerpiece, flared, #5902	50.00
	Bowl, 13", centerpiece, cone shape, #5902	55.00
	Cake plate, 12½", center hdld., #5902	45.00
	Candlesticks, pr., double branch, 7¼"	80.00
11	Comport, 6", #15082	45.00
4	Creamer, also bead hndl., #5902	16.00
1	Icer w/liner	100.00
5	Mayonnaise, liner and ladle, #5902	50.00
	Pitcher, sleek top dips to hndl., #5859	595.00
	Pitcher, 2 qt., straight top, ftd., #14194	400.00
	Plate, 6", sherbet	6.00
	Plate, 8", luncheon, plain or beaded rim, #5902	12.00
	Plate, 13½", turned-up edge, lily, #5902	40.00
	Plate, 14", sandwich, #5902	40.00
	Relish, 6½", 3 pt., #5902	32.00
	Relish, 12½", 3 pt., #5902	50.00
	Shaker, pr.	150.00
	Stem, 1 oz., cordial, #17399	30.00
	Stem, 2 oz., sherry, #17399	25.00
	Stem, 3½ oz., cocktail, #17399	14.00
7	Stem, 3½ oz., wine, #17399	24.00
	Stem, 4 oz., claret, #17399	30.00
	Stem, 4½ oz., parfait	35.00
	Stem, 5½ oz., sherbet/champagne, #17399	12.00
	Stem, 9 oz., water, #17399	22.00

3	Sugar, also w/beaded hndl., #5902	16.00
	Table bell, #9742 – lg.; #9743 – sm.	70.00
	Tumbler, 4½ oz., oyster cocktail, #14198	16.00
8	Tumbler, 5 oz., ftd., juice, #17399	16.00
	Tumbler, 8 oz., ftd., water, #17399	20.00
	Tumbler, 10½ oz., ftd., ice tea, #17399	30.00
	Vase, 6", bud, #14185	22.00
	Vase, 8", bud, #14185	30.00
	Vase, 8½", tear drop	75.00
	Vase, 9¼", tub, #17350, (1) ball stem, ftd.	95.00
	Vase, 10", bud, #14185	45.00
12	Vase, 11", bud, 6 beaded stem, flare rim	50.00
	Vase, 11", urn, #5943, (1) ball stem, ftd.	95.00
	Vase, 12", flared, #5855	135.00

1

2

CHINTZ, #1401 (EMPRESS BLANK) AND CHINTZ #3389 (DUQUESNE BLANK), A.H. HEISEY COMPANY, 1931 – 1938

Colors: crystal, Sahara yellow (Chintz only), Moongleam green, Flamingo pink, and Alexandrite orchid (all colors made in Formal Chintz)

Heisey's Chintz patterns are found as two different embellishments on Heisey mould blanks. Pieces pictured below are known as Chintz. Pieces with surrounding circles in the design are shown on page 73 and were labeled Formal Chintz. Both patterns are correspondingly priced. Formal Chintz tumblers and stemware were supposedly made on the #3390 Carcassone stem line, but we have never found any to picture. We find Chintz occasionally, but more often than not, it turns out to be stems.

Collectors have informed us that Chintz shakers have been found on #1401 Empress line, although we have not spotted them as yet. Items do occasionally slip through our listings until someone makes us aware so we can remedy omissions. We do thank our readers for that input.

Sahara is the color most preferred. A few collectors search for crystal. Alexandrite Formal Chintz is quite scarce and very striking when displayed in quantity. There is so little Alexandrite color that putting a set together would be a serious monetary drain.

Do not confuse this pattern with the Fostoria or Tiffin Chintz; and recognize that you must also *stipulate the company name when you request any pattern named Chintz.* It was a fashionable name and design used by various glass and pottery companies for their wares during that era.

		Crystal	Sahara
10	Bowl, cream soup	18.00	35.00
16	Bowl, finger, #4107	10.00	20.00
17	Bowl, nut, dolphin ftd., individual	40.00	60.00
	Bowl, 5½", ftd., preserve, hdld.	15.00	30.00
	Bowl, 6", ftd., mint	20.00	32.00
	Bowl, 6", ftd., 2 hdld., jelly	17.00	35.00
	Bowl, 7", triplex relish	20.00	40.00
	Bowl, 7½", Nasturtium	20.00	40.00
	Bowl, 8½", ftd., 2 hdld., floral	30.00	60.00

		Crystal	Sahara
15	Bowl, 10", oval, vegetable	20.00	35.00
	Bowl, 11", dolphin ft., floral	45.00	110.00
	Bowl, 13", 2 pt., pickle & olive	15.00	35.00
	Comport, 7", oval	45.00	85.00
7	Creamer, 3 dolphin ft.	20.00	50.00
	Creamer, individual	12.00	30.00
1	Cup	10.00	25.00
	Grapefruit, ftd., #3389, Duquesne	30.00	60.00
	Ice bucket, ftd.	75.00	155.00

		Crystal	Sahara
	Mayonnaise, 5½", dolphin ft.	35.00	65.00
	Oil, 4 oz.	60.00	135.00
	Pitcher, 3 pint, dolphin ft.	200.00	300.00
	Plate, 6", sq. or rnd., bread	6.00	15.00
	Plate, 7", sq. or rnd., salad	8.00	18.00
12	Plate, 8", sq. or rnd., luncheon	10.00	22.00
	Plate, 10½", sq. or rnd., dinner	40.00	85.00
	Plate, 12", two hdld.	25.00	47.50
14	Plate, 13", hors d' oeuvre, two hdld.	30.00	65.00
13	Platter, 14", oval	35.00	90.00
	Salt and pepper, pr.	40.00	95.00
2	Saucer	3.00	5.00
	Stem, #3389, Duquesne, 1 oz., cordial	50.00	100.00
6	Stem, #3389, 2½ oz., wine	18.00	40.00
	Stem, #3389, 3 oz., cocktail	12.00	30.00
	Stem, #3389, 4 oz., claret	18.00	40.00

		Crystal	Sahara
	Stem, #3389, 4 oz., oyster cocktail	10.00	22.00
5	Stem, #3389, 5 oz., parfait	12.00	20.00
	Stem, #3389, 5 oz., saucer champagne	10.00	15.00
4	Stem, #3389, 5 oz., sherbet	7.00	10.00
3	Stem, #3389, 9 oz., water	15.00	35.00
	Sugar, 3 dolphin ft.	20.00	50.00
8	Sugar, individual	12.00	30.00
	Tray, 10", celery	15.00	30.00
	Tray, 12", sq., ctr. hdld., sandwich	35.00	65.00
	Tray, 13", celery	18.00	45.00
	Tumbler, #3389, 5 oz., ftd., juice	10.00	20.00
	Tumbler, #3389, 8 oz., soda	11.00	22.00
11	Tumbler, #3389, 10 oz., ftd., water	12.00	22.00
9	Tumbler, #3389, 12 oz., iced tea	14.00	25.00
18	Tumbler, #3390, 2½ oz., bar	10.00	
	Vase, 9", dolphin ft.	140.00	200.00

CLASSIC, TIFFIN GLASS COMPANY, 1913 – 1930S

Colors: crystal, pink; crystal with Nile green trim

Classic is an older Tiffin pattern, but one where you never know what piece may still pop up. We have come upon an assortment of items in our travels. Dinner plates were a surprise find several years ago. A pink saucer to go with our cup has been elusive, but we did find a crystal one. Note the nicely bejeweled vase and cruet that recently found their way to the marketplace.

Pink Classic attracts admirers when displayed, but mostly stemmed beverage items are surfacing in that color. Some Tiffin pitchers (one pictured in pink) were sold with and without a lid. The one here has the top cupped inward so it will not take a lid. Remember that Tiffin pitcher lids have no pattern etched on them.

The crystal pitcher with lid at the bottom of page 75, is a different style from the pink, and holds approximately 60 ounces. Both pitcher styles are priced here as one listing. We have found few serving pieces in Classic other than a two-handled bowl, sandwich server, and a cheese and cracker.

Pink Classic stems are found on the same stem line (#17024) as those seen in Tiffin's Flanders pattern. Crystal stemmed items seem to surface on the #14185 line. There are size incongruities within these two stemware lines. We have measured both colors and documented them in our listings.

Other Classic items are found on the #15011 stem line which has a wafer beneath the flared rim bowl. On #15016, the bowl is cupped at the rim. With all these stems, you often come across the one you are not trying to locate.

32

		Crystal	Pink
21	Bowl, 9½" Nouvelle, #15361	90.00	
	Bowl, 2 hdld., 8" x 9¼"	125.00	
	Bowl, 11" centerpiece, #14185	100.00	
	Bowl, 13" centerpiece, rolled edge	110.00	
	Candy jar w/cover, ½ lb., ftd	135.00	

		Crystal	Pink
	Candle, 5", #9758	40.00	
28	Cheese & cracker set	100.00	
	Comport, 6" wide, 3¼" tall	65.00	
	Creamer, flat, #6	35.00	75.00
24	Creamer, ftd., #5931	30.00	
	Creamer, ftd., cone, #14185	30.00	
27	Cup, #8869	65.00	
	Finger bowl, ftd., #14185	20.00	40.00
29	Mayonnaise, or whipped cream w/ladle, ftd.		75.00

		Crystal	Pink
	Pitcher, ftd., hld., #194 (bulbous)	225.00	
4	Pitcher, 61 oz., (2 qt.) #114	250.00	595.00
25, 15	Pitcher, 61 oz., w/cover, #145 (subtract $50 w/out cover)	325.00	595.00
7	Plate, 6⅜", champagne liner, #23	8.00	
22	Plate, 7½", #8814	12.50	
	Plate, 8", #8833	15.00	25.00
23	Plate, 10", dinner, #8818	100.00	125.00
27	Saucer, #8869	10.00	
6	Sherbet, 3⅛", 6½ oz., short	14.00	*38.00
18	Stem, 3⅞", 1 oz., cordial	50.00	
19	Stem, 4¹⁵⁄₁₆", 3 oz., wine	25.00	*65.00
13	Stem, 4⅞", 3¾ oz., cocktail	25.00	
	Stem, 4⅞", 4 oz., cocktail	18.00	
14, 20	Stem, 6½", 5 oz., parfait	30.00	*75.00
	Stem, 6", 7½ oz., saucer champagne	18.00	*50.00
2	Stem, 7¼", 9 oz., water, 2 styles	28.00	*70.00
	Stem, 22 oz., grapefruit w/liner	65.00	

		Crystal	Pink
	Sugar, flat, #6	30.00	75.00
	Sugar, ftd.	30.00	
	Sugar, ftd., covered, #14185	35.00	
26	Tray, center handle	75.00	
5	Tumbler, 3½", 5 oz., ftd., juice	15.00	
8	Tumbler, 4½", 8½ oz., ftd., water	16.00	60.00
11	Tumbler, 4⅛", 10½ oz., flat, water	20.00	
	Tumbler, 5⁹⁄₁₆", 14 oz., ftd., tea	22.00	
	Tumbler, 6", 13 oz., ftd., iced tea		75.00
3	Tumbler, 6¹⁄₁₆", 14 oz., ftd., iced tea	25.00	
	Tumbler, 6¼", 6½ oz., ftd., Pilsner	30.00	
12	Tumbler, 10 oz., flat, table	25.00	
10	Tumbler, 12 oz., flat, tea	28.00	
	Tumbler, tea, hdld., #14185	33.00	
30	Vase, bud, 6½", #14185	33.00	
32	Vase, 8", wide optic	**160.00	
31	Vase, bud, 10½", #14185	35.00	

*Slight variation in size 40.00
**with decoration 350.00

CLEO, CAMBRIDGE GLASS COMPANY, INTRODUCED 1930

Colors: amber, Willow blue, crystal, Ebony, Emerald (light green), Gold Krystol (yellow), Peach Blo (pink)

Peach Blo (pink) and Emerald (light green) Cleo prices are slowly decreasing since supplies of those colors still appear in the market with fewer new collectors buying them. Regrettably, Emerald Cleo has almost been shunned by new collectors and is remaining in dealer inventories.

Cleo can be found in extensive sets of pink or green, but fewer pieces were made in the other colors. A few collections of Willow (blue) have surfaced in the market the last few years, and have been slowly assimilated into collections. A few years ago, those particular colored pieces would have sold quickly. Today's sellers are finding that collectors of blue Cleo are not as prevalent as they once were. Most blue is found on Cambridge's Decagon blank. Rarely found pieces of Cleo continue to reap serious prices — just not as speedily as in the past. There has always been a market for any rare or unusual glassware.

When we have spied rare pieces of Cleo in the past, they were generally amber rather than colors that charm collectors. Rare amber will sell — eventually! Cleo will doubtless continue to attract some collectors as long as the supply lasts. If this design appeals to you, you might consider choosing a combination of colors to collect which would make your search less arduous.

		Blue	Pink Green Yellow Amber
	Almond, 2½", individual	90.00	55.00
	Basket, 7", 2 hdld. (up-turned sides), Decagon	50.00	25.00
	Basket, 11", 2 hdld. (up-turned sides), Decagon	90.00	40.00
31	Bouillon cup, w/saucer, 2 hdld., Decagon	75.00	40.00
	Bowl, 2 pt., relish	40.00	20.00
	Bowl, 3½", cranberry	60.00	40.00
	Bowl, 5½", fruit	35.00	20.00
	Bowl, 5½" 2 hdld., bonbon, Decagon	50.00	20.00
	Bowl, 6", 4 ft., comport	55.00	30.00

		Blue	Pink Green Yellow Amber
32	Bowl, 6", cereal, Decagon	55.00	28.00
	Bowl, 6½", 2 hdld., bonbon, Decagon	35.00	18.00
	Bowl, 7½", tab hdld., soup	60.00	28.00
	Bowl, 8", miniature console		150.00
	Bowl, 8½"	75.00	33.00
	Bowl, 8½" 2 hdld., Decagon	90.00	40.00
24	Bowl, 9", covered vegetable, oval		325.00
	Bowl, 9½", oval veg., Decagon	120.00	65.00
8	Bowl, 9", pickle, Decagon, #1082	70.00	35.00

#		Blue	Pink Green Yellow Amber
28	Bowl, 10", 2 hdld., Decagon	110.00	60.00
3	Bowl, 11", oval, celery, #1083	110.00	60.00
	Bowl, 11½", oval	110.00	60.00
	Bowl, 12", console	115.00	60.00
7	Bowl, 12", #842	105.00	55.00
	Bowl, 15½", oval, Decagon		175.00
	Bowl, cream soup w/saucer, 2 hdld., Decagon	75.00	45.00
23	Bowl, finger w/liner, #3077	70.00	40.00
	Bowl, finger w/liner, #3115	70.00	40.00
21	Butter, #920		125.00
5	Candlestick, 1-lite, 2 styles, 4", #627	30.00	20.00
	Candlestick, 2-lite	100.00	50.00
	Candlestick, 3-lite	130.00	70.00
18	Candy box w/ 2 styles of lid	295.00	150.00
	Candy & cover, tall	325.00	175.00
	Comport, 7", tall, #3115	90.00	60.00
1	Comport, 12", #877	125.00	75.00
11	Creamer, Decagon/"Lightning"	28.00	16.00
	Creamer, ewer style, 6"	175.00	75.00
9	Creamer, ftd., #867	34.00	18.00
25	Cup, Decagon, #865	20.00	10.00
	Decanter, w/stopper		295.00
13	Gravy boat, w/liner plate, Decagon, #1091	500.00	250.00
	Gravy boat, 2 spout, #917		185.00
	Gravy boat liner, #167		70.00
16	Ice bowl, #844		130.00
17	Ice pail, #851	195.00	95.00
15	Ice tub, #394	185.00	95.00
20	Icer, w/liner, Decagon		60.00
	Mayonnaise, w/liner and ladle, Decagon, #983	125.00	65.00
	Mayonnaise, ftd.	60.00	35.00
	Oil, 6 oz., w/stopper, Decagon	595.00	175.00
	Pitcher, 3½ pt., #38		195.00
	Pitcher, w/cover, 22 oz.		240.00
	Pitcher, w/cover, 60 oz., #804		395.00
	Pitcher, w/cover, 62 oz., #955	595.00	350.00
	Pitcher, w/cover, 63 oz., #3077	895.00	395.00
	Pitcher, w/cover, 68 oz., #937		375.00
2	Plate, 6½", bread & butter, #809	9.00	6.00
	Plate, 7"	18.00	12.00
	Plate, 7", 2 hdld., Decagon	24.00	18.00
27	Plate, 8½", luncheon, Decagon	30.00	16.00
26	Plate, 9½", dinner, Decagon	110.00	55.00
	Plate, 9½", grill		75.00
	Plate, 11", 2 hdld., Decagon	90.00	45.00
	Platter, 12"	160.00	95.00
	Platter, 15", #1079	250.00	160.00
	Platter, w/cover, oval (toast)		395.00
	Platter, asparagus, indented, w/sauce & spoon		295.00
	Salt dip, 1½"	90.00	60.00
25	Saucer, Decagon, #865	6.00	4.00
	Server, 12", ctr. hand.	60.00	35.00
29	Stem, #3060, 9 oz., water		20.00

13

#		Blue	Pink Green Yellow Amber
	Stem, #3077, 1 oz., cordial	165.00	135.00
	Stem, #3077, 2½ oz., cocktail		22.00
	Stem, #3077, 3½ oz., wine	75.00	40.00
	Stem, #3077, 6 oz., low sherbet	30.00	15.00
	Stem, #3077, 6 oz., tall sherbet	38.00	18.00
	Stem, #3115, 9 oz.		22.00
	Stem, #3115, 3½ oz., cocktail		18.00
	Stem, #3115, 6 oz., fruit		12.00
	Stem, #3115, 6 oz., low sherbet		12.00
	Stem, #3115, 6 oz., tall sherbet		14.00
	Stem, #3115, 9 oz., water		20.00
	Sugar cube tray		150.00
4	Sugar, Decagon/"Lightning"	28.00	16.00
10	Sugar, ftd., #867	34.00	18.00
	Sugar sifter, ftd., 6¾"	750.00	275.00
	Syrup pitcher, drip cut		175.00
	Syrup pitcher, glass lid		225.00
	Toast & cover, round		400.00
	Tobacco humidor		450.00
	Tray, 12", handled serving		145.00
	Tray, 12", oval service, Decagon	195.00	110.00
	Tray, creamer & sugar, oval		30.00
12	Tray, hdld. for creamer/sugar	30.00	18.00
	Tumbler, #3077, 2½ oz., ftd.	90.00	40.00
6	Tumbler, #3077, 5 oz., ftd.	50.00	18.00
	Tumbler, #3077, 8 oz., ftd.	50.00	20.00
	Tumbler, #3077, 10 oz., ftd.	55.00	22.00
	Tumbler, #3022, 12 oz., ftd.	80.00	30.00
	Tumbler, #3115, 2½ oz., ftd.		40.00
	Tumbler, #3115, 5 oz., ftd.		18.00
	Tumbler, #3115, 8 oz., ftd.		18.00
	Tumbler, #3115, 10 oz., ftd.		30.00
	Tumbler, #3115, 12 oz., ftd.		28.00
30	Tumbler, #3400, 2½ oz., ftd.		25.00
	Tumbler, 12 oz., flat		48.00
	Vase, 5½"		90.00
	Vase, 9", ftd., #3450, Nautilis		225.00
19	Vase, 9½"		155.00
	Vase, 11"		195.00

CLEO

18

19

17

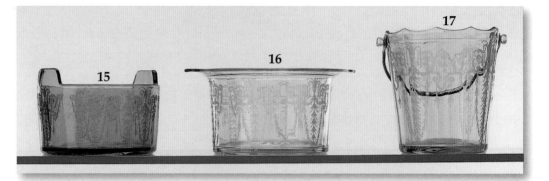

15

16

17

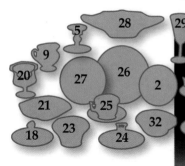

5
28
29
9
30
20
27
26
2
25
31
21
25
18
23
24
32

COLONY, LINE #2412, FOSTORIA GLASS COMPANY, 1930S – 1983

Colors: crystal; some yellow, opaque blue, green, white, amber, red in 1980s as Maypole

Fostoria's majestic Colony was developed and expanded from an earlier Fostoria pattern christened Queen Ann. A comport with an amber base is pictured here as an example of Queen Ann. A few Colony pieces were introduced as late as 1983. Fostoria listed colored pieces of Colony as Maypole in their 1980s catalogs. Red vases, candlesticks, and bowls now being found were produced by Viking for Fostoria in the early 1980s which we have shown in previous books.

Stems and tumblers with a thin, plain bowl and a Colony patterned foot (sold to go with this pattern) were christened Colonial Dame. You could find these stems with colored bowls of dark emerald green or amethyst. Unfortunately, only stems are found in these colors.

Colony experimental pieces such as opaque blue goblets turn up sporadically, but you could never accumulate many pieces in that color. Collectors often like to own an unusual colored item in their pattern. Colony prices have slowed dramatically indicating there is more than enough available for those wishing to own it. As with other Elegant patterns, stemware proliferates.

Some pieces you may have trouble turning up include finger bowls, cream soups, a punch bowl, an ice tub with flat rim, flat tumblers, and cigarette boxes. The supply of pitchers is adequate for now and we bought one for $9.00 in an antique mall. Obviously, that labeled "old twist pitcher" was not known to be Colony. All flat pieces with plain centers need to be scrutinized closely for scuffs, but that is always true for any pattern with clear centers. When stacking flat pieces, place a paper plate between each one to protect them for future generations.

Queen Anne Comport

		Crystal
1	Ashtray, 3", sq.	9.00
	Ashtray, 3", round, #2412½	12.00
28	Ashtray, 3½", sq.	14.00
	Ashtray, 4½", round, #2412½	18.00
	Ashtray, 6", round, #2412½	20.00
24	Bowl, 2¾" ftd., almond	12.00
10	Bowl, 4½", rnd.	8.00
	Bowl, 4¾", finger	35.00
27	Bowl, 4¾", hdld., whip cream	8.00
	Bowl, 5", bonbon, rolled edge	8.00
	Bowl, 5", cream soup	40.00
4	Bowl, 5", hdld., sweet meat	10.00
13	Bowl, 5½", sq.	16.00
	Bowl, 5⅝", 3 toe nut	16.00
	Bowl, 5¾", high ft.	12.00
6	Bowl, 5", rnd.	11.00
	Bowl, 6", rose	20.00
	Bowl, 7", 2 pt., relish, 2 hdld.	10.00
	Bowl, 7", bonbon, 3 ftd.	10.00
21	Bowl, 7", olive, oblong	10.00
	Bowl, 7¾", salad	18.00
	Bowl, 8", cupped	34.00
	Bowl, 8½", hdld.	30.00
	Bowl, 9", rolled console	30.00
17	Bowl, 9½", pickle	18.00
	Bowl, 9¾", salad	38.00
	Bowl, 8¾" x 9¾", w/rolled edge, muffin tray	24.00
	Bowl, 10", fruit	35.00
	Bowl, 10½", low ft.	55.00
	Bowl, 10½", high ft., #2412½, 6½" tall	90.00
	Bowl, 10½", oval	40.00
	Bowl, 10½", oval, 2 part	40.00

		Crystal
	Bowl, 11", oval, ftd.	55.00
	Bowl, 11", flared	33.00
	Bowl, 11½", celery	24.00
	Bowl, 13", console	35.00
	Bowl, 13¼", punch, ftd.	350.00
	Bowl, 14", fruit	55.00
3	Butter dish, ¼ lb.	30.00
	Candlestick, 3½"	11.00
	Candlestick, 6½", double	30.00
	Candlestick, 7"	30.00
	Candlestick, 7½", w/8 prisms	75.00
	Candlestick, 9"	33.00
	Candlestick, 9¾", w/prisms	100.00
	Candlestick, 14½", w/10 prisms	150.00
	Candy, w/cover, 6½"	38.00
	Candy, w/cover, ftd., ½ lb.	60.00
	Cheese & cracker	40.00
	Cigarette box	40.00
32	Comport, 4", low foot	12.00
	Comport, cover, 6½"	35.00
	Comport, 7"	45.00
	Comport, 7", w/plain top	75.00
29	Creamer, 3¼", indiv.	8.00
23	Creamer, 3¾"	6.00
18	Cup, 6 oz., ftd.	4.00
	Cup, punch	10.00
	Ice bucket	80.00
	Ice bucket, plain edge	195.00
	Lamp, electric	195.00
	Mayonnaise, 3 pc.	32.00
	Oil w/stopper, 4½ oz.	30.00
14	Pitcher, 16 oz., milk	48.00

		Crystal
	Pitcher, 48 oz., ice lip	125.00
	Pitcher, 2 qt., ice lip	75.00
	Plate, ctr. hdld., sandwich	26.00
	Plate, 6", bread & butter	4.00
	Plate, 6½", lemon, hdld.	8.00
22	Plate, 7", salad	6.00
	Plate, 8", luncheon	8.00
19	Plate, 9", dinner	18.00
	Plate, 10", hdld., cake	22.00
	Plate, 12", ftd., salver	65.00
	Plate, 13", torte	25.00
	Plate, 15", torte	48.00
	Plate, 18", torte	78.00
	Platter, 12"	42.00
2	Relish, 10", 3 part	18.00
	Salt, 2½" indiv., pr.	15.00
	Salt & pepper, pr., 3⅝"	20.00
18	Saucer	1.50
	Stem, 3½ oz., cocktail	7.00

		Crystal
5	Stem, 3⅜", 4 oz., oyster cocktail	7.00
	Stem, 3⅝", 5 oz., sherbet	5.00
	Stem, 4", 3½ oz., cocktail	7.00
7	Stem, 4¼", 3¼ oz., wine	12.00
8	Stem, 5¼", 9 oz., goblet	11.00
30	Sugar, 2¾", indiv.	8.00
20	Sugar, 3½"	6.00
31	Tray for indiv. sugar/cream, 6¾"	10.00
15	Tumbler, 3⅝", 5 oz., juice	18.00
12	Tumbler, 3⅞", 9 oz., water	16.00
16	Tumbler, 4⅞", 12 oz., tea	26.00
	Tumbler, 4½", 5 oz., ftd.	12.00
9	Tumbler, 5¾", 12 oz., ftd.	15.00
26	Vase, 6", bud, flared	12.00
25	Vase, 7", cupped, ftd.	38.00
	Vase, 7½", flared	50.00
	Vase, 9", cornucopia	75.00
	Vase, 12", straight	150.00

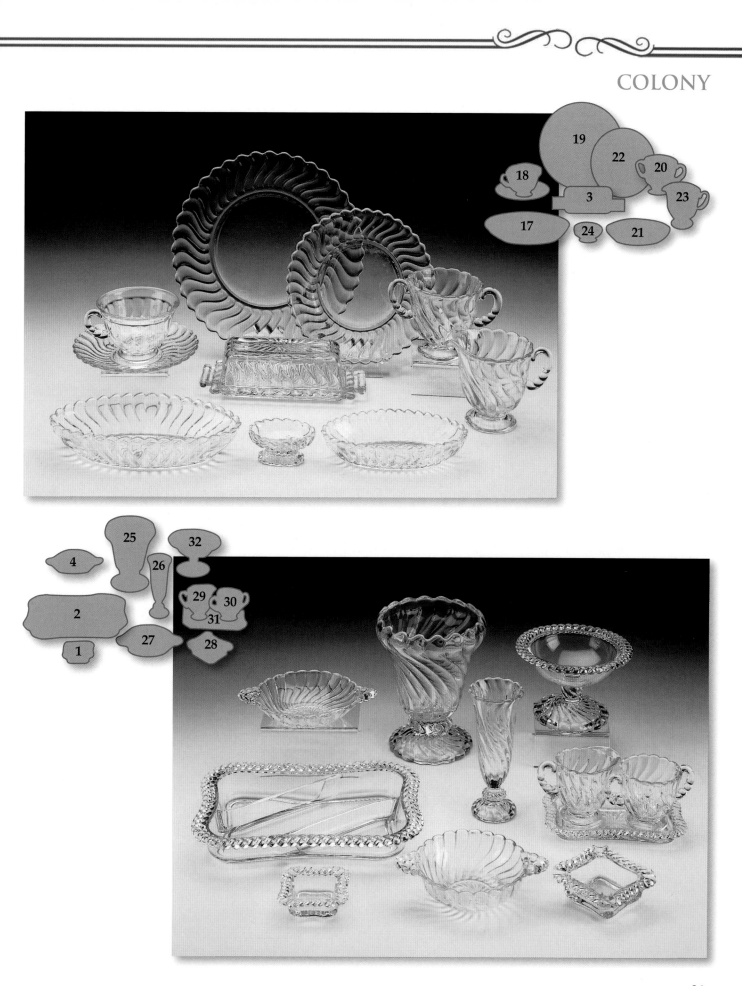

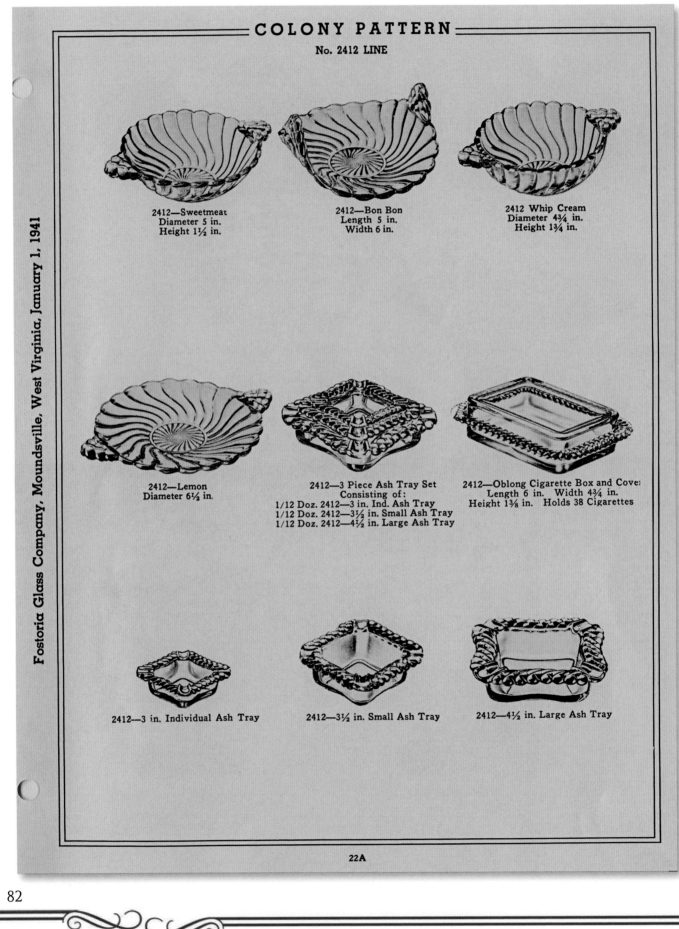

COLONY PATTERN
No. 2412 LINE

2412—Sweetmeat
Diameter 5 in.
Height 1½ in.

2412—Bon Bon
Length 5 in.
Width 6 in.

2412 Whip Cream
Diameter 4¾ in.
Height 1¾ in.

2412—Lemon
Diameter 6½ in.

2412—3 Piece Ash Tray Set
Consisting of:
1/12 Doz. 2412—3 in. Ind. Ash Tray
1/12 Doz. 2412—3½ in. Small Ash Tray
1/12 Doz. 2412—4½ in. Large Ash Tray

2412—Oblong Cigarette Box and Cover
Length 6 in.   Width 4¾ in.
Height 1⅜ in.   Holds 38 Cigarettes

2412—3 in. Individual Ash Tray

2412—3½ in. Small Ash Tray

2412—4½ in. Large Ash Tray

Fostoria Glass Company, Moundsville, West Virginia, January 1, 1941

22A

"COLUMBINE VARIANT," BLUEBELL, CUTTING ON TIFFIN AND FOSTORIA BLANKS, LATE 1920S

Colors: Fostoria Blue, Tiffin crystal with blue

"Columbine Variant" is a name we first used for this cutting, which is very close to Tiffin's Columbine and Double Columbine patterns. However, in researching, Cathy found the pattern called Bluebell in a 1928 Butler Brothers merchandising catalog and we should probably list it as such.

Bluebell cutting was created on both Fostoria and Tiffin mould blanks symptomatic of an independent cutting firm rather than production at either of these companies per se. This early color of Fostoria actually named Blue and the blue of Tiffin are virtually identical, so a variety of pieces could be used for this cutting. The name apparently came from the bluebell-like cutting or maybe from the color. Honestly, there does not seem to be much of this offered in the marketplace today, which lends credibility to its not being a major company's production.

The plate, candlestick, and comport are Fostoria mould blanks, but so far, all the other pieces we have found have been on Tiffin blanks. Additional pieces could be found, but our listing only includes those we could document. We could have purchased a creamer and sugar, priced as a pair, and the owner seemed to pretend that a customer would not notice the cracked handle on the sugar. Additional pieces have been observed, but they were priced in groups of six or eight with over half of them damaged. Pricing as group is a great idea for the seller, but not a buyer who does not want to pay mint prices for a group that is imperfect.

		Crystal
5	Candlestick, 4", #2324, Fostoria	22.00
4	Comport, 6¼" h x 7¼" w, #2327, Fostoria	60.00
	Creamer	30.00
2	Pitcher w/cover, 2 qt., #14194	250.00
3	Plate, 7⅛", #2350, Fostoria	11.00
	Stem, 3 oz., wine #50001	40.00
	Stem, 6 oz., low sherbet #50001	15.00
	Stem, 6 oz., high sherbet #50001	18.00
1	Stem, 9 oz., 7¼" water #50001	30.00
	Sugar	30.00

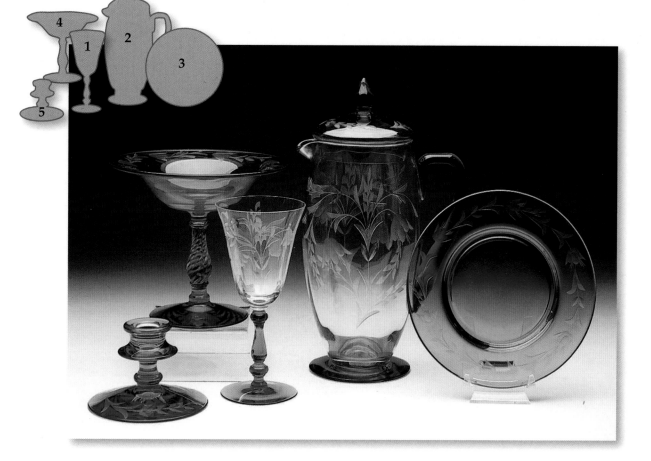

CRYSTOLITE, BLANK #1503, A.H. HEISEY COMPANY, LATE 1930S – 1957

Colors: crystal, Zircon/Limelight, Sahara, and rare in amber

Crystolite is one of the most identifiable Heisey patterns given that virtually all pieces are marked with the recognized **H** inside a diamond. That renowned mark signifies you will rarely find a good buy on a piece of Crystolite in today's market. Just because a piece of glass is Heisey does not mean it is rare or expensive as many sellers seem to assume. Over the years, we have encountered some ridiculous prices because of that Heisey mark. Many later patterns of Heisey were not marked and had paper labels that were removed with use. Those are the pieces where bargains can be acquired.

Pictured on page 85 is the swan handled Crystolite pitcher which brings big bucks, compared to the normal pitcher although those big bucks are not what they used to be. Crystolite is found only in crystal and should you spot colored pitchers, they are reproductions by Imperial from Heisey's moulds bought when Heisey closed its plant in 1957.

You can spot the harder to find items in the listing by their higher prices. Non-scratched dinner plates, 5" comport, 6" basket, rye bottle, cocktail shaker, and pressed tumblers have always been difficult to locate, but they are currently priced more moderately than in the past.

		Crystal				Crystal
	Ashtray, 3½", sq.	6.00	4	Candlestick, 2-lite, bobeche & 10 "D" prisms		65.00
	Ashtray, 4½", sq.	6.00		Candlestick and vase, 3-lite		45.00
	Ashtray, 4" x 6", oblong	50.00		Candlestick, w/#4233, 5", vase, 3-lite		55.00
	Ashtray, 5", w/book match holder	30.00		Candy, 5½", shell and cover		45.00
	Ashtray (coaster), 4", rnd.	8.00		Candy box, w/cover, 7", 3 part		60.00
	Basket, 6", hdld.	350.00	20	Candy box, w/cover, 7"		50.00
	Bonbon, 7", shell	20.00	14	Cheese, 5½", ftd.		20.00
	Bonbon, 7½", 2 hdld.	15.00		Cigarette box, w/cover, 4"		30.00
	Bottle, 1 qt., rye, #107 stopper	300.00		Cigarette box, w/cover, 4½"		35.00
	Bottle, 4 oz., bitters, w/short tube	140.00		Cigarette holder, ftd.		25.00
1	Bottle, 4 oz., cologne, w/#108 stopper	75.00		Cigarette holder, oval		20.00
	w/drip stop	140.00		Cigarette holder, rnd.		20.00
	Bottle, syrup, w/drip & cut top	135.00		Cigarette lighter		35.00
	Bowl, 7½ quart, punch	120.00		Coaster, 4"		10.00
	Bowl, 2", indiv. swan nut (or ashtray)	20.00		Cocktail shaker, 1 qt. w/#1 strainer, #86 stopper		350.00
	Bowl, 3", indiv. nut, hdld.	20.00		Comport, 5", ftd., deep, #5003, blown rare		300.00
	Bowl, 4½", dessert (or nappy)	20.00		Creamer, indiv.		20.00
	Bowl, 5", preserve	20.00		Creamer, reg.		25.00
	Bowl, 5", 1000 island dressing, ruffled top	30.00		Creamer, round		40.00
	Bowl, 5½", dessert	14.00		Cup		18.00
	Bowl, 6", oval jelly, 4 ft.	60.00		Cup, punch or custard		9.00
	Bowl, 6", preserve, 2 hdld.	20.00		Hurricane block, 1-lite, sq.		40.00
	Bowl, 7", shell praline	35.00		Hurricane block, w/#4061, 10" plain globe, 1-lite, sq.		120.00
	Bowl, 8", dessert (sauce)	30.00		Ice tub, w/silver plate handle		100.00
22	Bowl, 8", 2 pt. conserve, hdld.	55.00		Jar, covered cherry		85.00
	Bowl, 9", leaf pickle	30.00	18	Jam jar, w/cover		50.00
9	Bowl, gardenia, square 10"	95.00		Ladle, glass, punch		35.00
	Bowl, 10", salad, rnd.	50.00		Ladle, plastic		10.00
	Bowl, 11", w/attached mayonnaise (chip 'n dip)	140.00		Mayonnaise, 5½", shell, 3 ft.		35.00
	Bowl, 12", gardenia, shallow	65.00		Mayonnaise, 6", oval, hdld.		40.00
	Bowl, 13", oval floral, deep	50.00		Mayonnaise ladle		12.00
5	Candle block, 1-lite, melon	30.00	21	Mustard & cover		45.00
11	Candle block, 1-lite, rnd.	10.00		Nut, oval, footed		55.00
13	Candle block, 1-lite, sq.	20.00	23	Oil bottle, 3 oz.		45.00
12	Candle block, 1-lite, swirl	20.00		Oil bottle, w/stopper, 2 oz.		35.00
6	Candlestick, 1-lite, ftd.	25.00		Oval creamer, sugar, w/tray, set		70.00
10	Candlestick, 1-lite, w/#4233, 5", vase	35.00	17	Pitcher, ½ gallon, ice, blown		125.00
7	Candlestick, 2-lite	35.00				

		Crystal
24	Pitcher, 2 quart swan, ice lip	700.00
	Plate, 7", salad	15.00
	Plate, 7", shell	32.00
	Plate, 7", underliner for 1000 island dressing bowl	20.00
8	Plate, 7½", coupe	40.00
	Plate, 8", oval, mayonnaise liner	20.00
	Plate, 8½", salad	20.00
	Plate, 10½", dinner	100.00
	Plate, 11", ftd., cake salver	450.00
	Plate, 11", torte	40.00
	Plate, 12", sandwich	45.00
	Plate, 13", shell torte	100.00
	Plate, 14", sandwich	55.00
	Plate, 14", torte	50.00
	Plate, 20", buffet or punch liner	125.00
2	Puff box, w/cover, 4¾"	60.00
	Salad dressing set, 3 pc.	38.00
	Salt & pepper, pr.	40.00
	Saucer	4.00
	Stem, 1 oz., cordial, wide optic, blown, #5003	95.00
	Stem, 3½ oz., cocktail, w.o., blown, #5003	15.00
	Stem, 3½ oz., claret, w.o., blown, #5003	24.00
	Stem, 3½ oz., oyster cocktail, w.o. blown, #5003	15.00
	Stem, 6 oz., sherbet/saucer champagne, #5003	8.00
	Stem, 10 oz., water, #1503, pressed	500.00
16	Stem, 10 oz., w.o., blown, #5003	22.00
	Sugar, indiv.	20.00
	Sugar, reg.	25.00
	Sugar, round	40.00
	Syrup pitcher, drip cut	135.00
	Tray, 5½", oval, liner indiv. creamer/sugar set	40.00
	Tray, 9", 4 pt., leaf relish	40.00
	Tray, 10", 5 pt., rnd. relish	45.00

		Crystal
	Tray, 12", 3 pt., relish, oval	35.00
	Tray, 12", rect., celery	38.00
	Tray, 12", rect., celery/olive	35.00
3	Tray, 13", oval	50.00
	Tumbler, 5 oz., juice, blown	20.00
	Tumbler, 5 oz., ftd., juice, w.o., blown, #5003	38.00
	Tumbler, 8 oz., blown	25.00
	Tumbler, 8 oz., pressed, #5003	60.00
	Tumbler, 10 oz., pressed	70.00
	Tumbler, 10 oz., iced tea, w.o., blown, #5003	25.00
15	Tumbler, 12 oz., ftd., iced tea, w.o., blown, #5003	30.00
	Urn, 7", flower	75.00
	Vase, 3", short stem	45.00
19	Vase, 6", ftd.	40.00
	Vase, 12"	225.00
16	Vase, spittoon (whimsey)	400.00

24

DAFFODIL, CAMBRIDGE GLASS COMPANY, C. 1951

Colors: crystal, crystal w/gold encrusting

Daffodil is a 50s Cambridge pattern that attracts collectors with its depiction of those famous yellow spring flowers. When we sold glass in Cambridge, Ohio, last year, this was one of the patterns that completely sold out of our inventory. Don't pass by desirable items that someone will cherish.

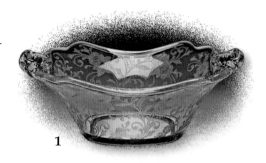

1

		Crystal
	Basket, 6", 2 hdld., low ft., #55	35.00
	Bonbon, #1181	28.00
1	Bonbon, 5¼", 2 hdld., #3400/1180	35.00
2	Bowl, 11" oval, tuck hdld., #384	60.00
	Bowl, 12", belled, #430	75.00
	Candle, 2 lite, arch, #3900/72	50.00
	Candlestick, 3½", #628	35.00
	Candy box & cover, cut hexagon knob, #306	135.00
11	Celery, 11", #248	50.00
	Comport, 5½", ftd., #533	40.00
	Comport, 6½", 2 hdld., low ftd., #54	50.00
3	Comport, 6" tall, pulled stem, #532	55.00
	Creamer, #254	20.00
9	Creamer, indiv., #253	25.00
	Cup, #11770	20.00
	Jug, #3400/140	275.00
	Jug, 76 oz., #3400/141	295.00
	Mayonnaise, 3 pc., ftd., w/ladle & liner plate, #533	70.00
7	Mayonnaise, ftd., w/ladle and plate	70.00
	Oil, 6 oz., #293	125.00
	Plate, #1174	25.00
	Plate, 6", 2 hdld., bonbon, #3400/1181	18.00
	Plate, 8½", salad	16.00
4	Plate, 8", sq., #1176	18.00
	Plate, 8", 2 hdld., low ft., #56	24.00
	Plate, 11½" cake, #1495	70.00
	Plate, 13½", cabaret, #166	90.00
12	Relish, 10", 3 pt., #214	55.00
6	Salad dressing set, twin, 4 pc. w/ladles & liner, #1491	95.00
	Salt & pepper, squat, pr., #360	50.00
	Saucer, #1170	4.00
	Stem, brandy, ¾ oz., #1937	60.00

		Crystal
	Stem, claret, 4½ oz., #3779	40.00
	Stem, claret, 4½ oz., #1937	40.00
	Stem, cocktail, 3½ oz., #1937	20.00
	Stem, cocktail, 3 oz., #3779	20.00
13	Stem, cordial, 1 oz., #3779	75.00
	Stem, cordial, 1 oz., #1937	75.00
	Stem, oyster cocktail, 5 oz., #1937	15.00
	Stem, oyster cocktail, 4½ oz., #3779	15.00
	Stem, sherbet, 6 oz., low, #1937	13.00
	Stem, sherbet, 6 oz., low, #3779	13.00
	Stem, sherbet, 6 oz., tall, #1937	16.00
	Stem, sherbet, 6 oz., tall, #3779	16.00
	Stem, sherry, 2 oz., #1937	50.00
	Stem, water, 9 oz., low, #3779	28.00
	Stem, water, 9 oz., tall, #3779	33.00
	Stem, water, 11 oz., #1937	40.00
	Stem, wine, 2½ oz., #3779	45.00
	Stem, wine, 3 oz., #1937	40.00
	Sugar, #254	20.00
8	Sugar, indiv., #253	25.00
	Tumbler, ftd., 5 oz., #1937	20.00
10	Tumbler, ftd., 5 oz., #3779	20.00
	Tumbler, ftd., 10 oz., #1937	22.00
5	Tumbler, ftd., 12 oz., iced tea, #3779	32.00
	Tumbler, ftd., 12 oz., #1937	32.00
	Vase, 8", ftd., #6004	115.00
	Vase, 11", ftd., #278	165.00

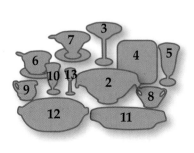

"DANCE OF THE NUDES," DANCING NYMPH, CONSOLIDATED LAMP AND GLASS COMPANY, 1928 – 1940S

Colors: crystal, French crystal, frosted crystal, green and frosted green, pink and frosted pink, Ruby flashed, white, and assorted ceramic colors

1

The "Dance of the Nudes" appellation has been used for as long as we have been researching glassware, although Dancing Nymph has emerged as the original Consolidated name. Traditional names are all but impossible to toss away in the collecting world, once they have been accepted, even after an original name has been uncovered. You will find both names used in the market.

When Consolidated's Deco-looking Ruba Rombic was first listed in this book 16 years ago, bargains in that pattern rapidly became few and far between. Dancing Nymph price hikes have not been quite so spectacular, since glassware portraying nude women has always been well-liked and pricey. People may not have known its proper name, but it caught their interest, and few assessed it strictly economically. Dancing Nymph prices are affordable when measured against other Consolidated patterns. Dancing Nymph is one of a few three-dimensional patterns that exist in this collecting field and was influenced by Lalique glassware and the graceful curves of the Art Nouveau period, trendy at that time. Today, prices have actually softened somewhat. However, you will still see some extraordinary prices on items sitting and not selling. When we decided to place our photography items of Dancing Nymph for sale, it only took two shows to deplete it. We know it will sell at a fair market price.

Dancing Nymph was introduced in 1926 and made until Consolidated closed in 1932. In 1936, the plant was restarted and a cupped saucer and sherbet plates were added to the line. These sherbet plates are like a shallow bowl and were often referred to as ice cream plates in other patterns of the period. The flatter version has no raised edge and is often used as sherbet liners. Salad plates usually came with basic sets, but sherbet plates were special order items, which makes them harder to find now. They should be priced more than the salad plates, and in this case, size does make a difference. Dancing Nymph candlesticks are rare.

The green color has an aqua cast to it as revealed in the photograph. French Crystal consists of clear nudes with satin background, exemplifying the Lalique influence. Other colors are self-explanatory except for the uncharacteristic ceramic colors which were achieved by covering the bottom of a crystal piece with color, wiping the nude designs clear, and firing the piece. The Honey (yellow) plate on page 88 and light green bowl pictured here are examples. Older glassware often involved several hand processes that would be prohibitive to perform today due to labor costs. Ceramic colors are highly desirable and costly. Other colors with this process are Sepia (brown), white, dark blue, light blue, pinkish lavender, and light green.

13

		Crystal	Frosted Crystal French Crystal	*Frosted Pink or Green	Ceramic Colors
5	Bowl, 4½", #3098	25.00	45.00	60.00	90.00
1	Bowl, 8", #3098½	55.00	90.00	150.00	210.00
	Bowl, 16", palace, #2795B	495.00	1,250.00		1,600.00
9	Candle, pr., #2840	300.00	450.00		750.00
6	Cup, #3099	25.00	35.00	60.00	90.00
10	Plate, 6", cupped, #3099½	12.00	18.00	26.00	40.00
4	Plate, 6", sherbet, flat, #3099½	16.00	30.00	45.00	90.00
8	Plate, 8", salad, #3096	25.00	45.00		110.00
7	Plate, 10", #3097	50.00	70.00	135.00	175.00
	Platter, 18", palace	495.00	900.00		1,100.00
6	Saucer, coupe	9.00		20.00	
3	Sherbet, #3094	26.00	50.00	70.00	
12	Tumbler, 3½", cocktail, #3094½	30.00	50.00		
2	Tumbler, 5½", goblet, #3080	40.00	55.00	110.00	165.00
13	Vase, 5½", crimped, #3080C	65.00	125.00		150.00
	Vase, 5½", fan, #3080F	65.00	125.00		150.00

*Subtract 10% to 15% for unfrosted.

DECAGON, CAMBRIDGE GLASS COMPANY, 1930S – 1940S

Colors: Amber, amethyst, crystal, Emerald (light green), Peach-Blo, Carmen, Royal blue, Willow blue, Ebony

Decagon is Cambridge's appellation for its 10-sided mould on which many of its etchings resided. The blank has added magnitude when etchings of Cleo, Rosalie, and Imperial Hunt Scene are featured. Collectors discern the pattern etching sooner than its Decagon blank. In spite of that, there are some passionate fans of this plain, geometric Decagon "pattern."

You will find that Peach-Blo (pink), Emerald (light green), and amber are more plentiful, but Willow (blue) remains the favored color, and therefore is more expensive to acquire. Pattern availability is only one influential factor in collecting. Color also plays an extremely important role, and blue colors repeatedly win collector interest. Amber Decagon has admirers, but not as many as Willow. Some Cleo collectors go for Decagon to augment their etched collections. Why splurge $500.00 for a blue gravy and liner when you can purchase a plain Decagon one for 25% of that — when you can find one!

Flat soups, cordials, and pitchers are not easily attained. Many collectors are on a mission for serving pieces not only for Decagon but the etched wares as well.

		Pastels	Blue
	Basket, 7", 2 hdld. (upturned sides), #760	12.00	30.00
	Bowl, bouillon, w/liner, #866	12.00	35.00
	Bowl, cream soup, w/liner, #1075	18.00	35.00
	Bowl, 2½", indiv., almond, #611	26.00	40.00
	Bowl, 3¾", flat rim, cranberry	16.00	30.00
	Bowl, 3½" belled, cranberry, #1102	16.00	30.00
	Bowl, 5½", 2 hdld., bonbon, #758	10.00	20.00
	Bowl, 5½", belled, fruit, #1098	8.00	20.00
	Bowl, 5¾", flat rim, fruit, #1099	8.00	20.00
	Bowl, 6", belled, cereal, #1011	16.00	30.00
	Bowl, 6", flat rim, cereal, #807	18.00	35.00
	Bowl, 6", ftd., almond, #612	26.00	40.00
3	Bowl, 6¼", 2 hdld., bonbon	10.00	20.00
20	Bowl, 8½", flat rim, soup, #808	22.00	40.00
	Bowl, 9", rnd., veg., #1085	30.00	50.00
	Bowl, 9", 2 pt., relish, #1067	28.00	33.00
	Bowl, 9½", oval, veg., #1087	35.00	45.00
	Bowl, 10", berry, #1087	35.00	45.00
	Bowl, 10½", oval, veg., #1088	35.00	45.00

		Pastels	Blue
	Bowl, 11", rnd. veg., #1086	35.00	45.00
	Bowl, 11", 2 pt., relish, #1068	35.00	35.00
	Comport, 5¾", #869	18.00	35.00
	Comport, 6½", low ft., #608	18.00	32.00
	Comport, 7", tall, #1090	22.00	45.00
	Comport, 9½", #877	35.00	60.00
	Comport, 11½", #877	45.00	70.00
5	Creamer, ftd., #979	9.00	18.00
	Creamer, bulbous, ftd., #867	8.00	16.00
15	Creamer, lightning bolt handles, #1096	9.00	15.00
	Creamer, tall, lg. ft., #814	9.00	24.00
11	Cup, #865	5.00	10.00
	Finger bowl	18.00	25.00
22	Gravy boat, w/2 hdld. liner (like spouted cream soup), #917/1167	90.00	135.00
	French dressing bottle, "Oil/Vinegar," #1263, ftd., #1261	75.00	135.00
10	Ice pail, #851	35.00	75.00
7	Ice tub	35.00	65.00

DECAGON

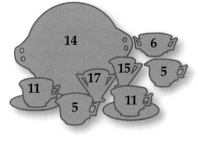

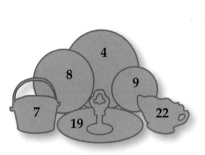

		Pastels	Blue
	Mayonnaise, 2 hdld., w/2 hdld. liner and ladle, #873	30.00	45.00
	Mayonnaise, w/liner & ladle, #983	30.00	58.00
	Oil, 6 oz., tall, w/hdld. & stopper, #197	50.00	160.00
9	Plate, 6¼", bread/butter	4.00	8.00
2	Plate, 7", 2 hdld.	8.00	12.00
	Plate, 7½"	7.00	16.00
8	Plate, 8½", salad, #597	10.00	18.00
12	Plate, 8½", snack w/ring		30.00
	Plate, 9½", dinner	35.00	50.00
	Plate, 10", grill, #1200	30.00	40.00
4	Plate, 10", service, #812	28.00	40.00
	Plate, 12½", service, #598	30.00	50.00
16	Relish, 6 inserts	100.00	120.00
	Salt dip, 1½", ftd., #613	22.00	38.00
	Salt & pepper, #396	30.00	75.00
	Sauce boat & plate, #1091	70.00	110.00
11	Saucer, #866	2.00	3.00
	Stem, 1 oz., cordial, #3077	30.00	50.00
	Stem, 3½ oz., cocktail, #3077	10.00	18.00
	Stem, 6 oz., low sherbet, #3077	6.00	14.00

		Pastels	Blue
18	Stem, 6 oz., high sherbet, #3077	10.00	18.00
1	Stem, 9 oz., water, #3077	14.00	25.00
17	Sugar, lightning bolt handles, #1096	9.00	12.00
6	Sugar, ftd., #979	8.00	16.00
	Sugar, bulbous, ftd., #867	8.00	20.00
	Sugar, tall, sifter, #813	35.00	50.00
	Tray, 8", 2 hdld., flat pickle, #1167	22.00	40.00
	Tray, 9", pickle, #1082	22.00	40.00
	Tray, 11", oval, service	28.00	45.00
	Tray, 11", celery, #1083	28.00	45.00
19	Tray, 12", center handled, #870	30.00	38.00
	Tray, 12", oval, service, #1078	25.00	40.00
14	Tray, 13", 2 hdld., service, #1084	32.00	48.00
	Tray, 15", oval, service, #1079	40.00	70.00
	Tumbler, 2½ oz., ftd., #3077	15.00	25.00
	Tumbler, 5 oz., ftd., #3077	10.00	20.00
	Tumbler, 8 oz., ftd., #3077	12.00	22.00
	Tumbler, 10 oz., ftd., #3077	14.00	25.00
13	Tumbler, 12 oz., ftd., #3077	15.00	30.00
21	Vanity set, 3 piece, #683	75.00	125.00

"DEERWOOD" OR "BIRCH TREE," U.S. GLASS COMPANY, LATE 1920S – EARLY 1930S

Colors: light amber, green, pink, black, crystal

Look on page 26 at the Black Forest pattern photo if you have a tendency to confuse these two patterns. *Deer* and trees are illustrated on "Deerwood"; *moose* and trees are presented on Black Forest. Some collectors have solved their confusion of the patterns by collecting both.

Know that some pieces similar to Deerwood (made at the Tiffin plant of U.S. Glass) have turned up on Paden City blanks as illustrated in the photograph of the pink candy on the left. We have cleaned out our photo file to give you more views of "Deerwood" this time.

Large sets can only be assembled in green and pink with patience. You will see amber and crystal only occasionally.

1

The black "Deerwood" pieces do not show the pattern very well unless gold decorated. Black "Deerwood" on Tiffin blanks is being acquired by admirers of that decorating genre who are not necessarily glass collectors per se, but who just admire this rich look. We recently sold a creamer and sugar to someone who had to be told what the pattern was named. She admired its look and bought it without batting an eye at the price. Incidentally, we have bought a creamer and sugar set in two of our last three trips to California. Evidently some store sold gold decorated "Deerwood" in the Los Angeles area.

Internet auctions have exposed "Deerwood" resulting in some price modifications. At first upward, but now reality has set in and prices are actually cheaper than before the internet auctions. "Deerwood" itself was not commonly found, but more pieces than dreamed of have surfaced in auctions. Since most collectors own many of the pieces being offered, prices are drifting downward with fewer bidders.

There is a little catalog documentation for "Deerwood," but not nearly enough. That is why unlisted pieces keep turning up after 40 years of serious collecting.

The conventional mayonnaise pictured in green was recorded by Tiffin as a whipped cream rather than a mayonnaise. Terminology within the old glass companies often deviated.

		*Black	Amber	Green	Pink
	Bowl, breakfast/cereal w/attched liner, #8133			50.00	50.00
	Bowl, 10", ftd.	165.00			
	Bowl, 10", straight edge, flat rim, salad, #8105			65.00	65.00
21	Bowl, 12", centerpiece, flat rim ftd.	85.00			
9	Bowl, 12", centerpiece, #8177, cupped	110.00		75.00	70.00
14	Cake plate, low pedestal, 10", #330, #8177			65.00	65.00
6	Candlestick, 2½"	60.00		35.00	
24	Candlestick, 5"				55.00
1	Candy dish, w/cover, 3 part, flat, #329, 6", 3 styles	195.00			125.00
23	Candy jar, w/cover, ftd. cone, #330			150.00	150.00
	Celery, 12", #151			70.00	
	Cheese and cracker, #330			90.00	90.00
3	Comport, 7", #8177	100.00			55.00
5	Comport, 9", low, ftd.	135.00			
20	Comport, 10", low, ftd., flared, #330	135.00			75.00
10	Creamer, 2 styles, #179	55.00		35.00	35.00
18	Cup, #9395				85.00
	Plate, 5½", #8836			12.00	12.00
22	Plate, 7½", salad, #8836				16.00
	Plate, 9½", dinner, #8859				90.00
	Plate, 10¼", 2 hdld., cake, #336	145.00			
18	Saucer, #9395				12.00
12	Server, center hdld., 10", #330			55.00	55.00
	Stem, 2 oz., cocktail, 4½", #2809				45.00
19	Stem, 3 oz., wine, 4¾", #2809			30.00	
11	Stem, 6 oz., saucer champagne, 5", #2809			30.00	
17	Stem, 9 oz., water, 7" or 8", #2809			50.00	50.00
8	Sugar, 2 styles, #179	55.00		35.00	35.00
	Tumbler, 9 oz., ftd., table, #2808			30.00	30.00
2	Tumbler, 12 oz., ftd., tea, 5½", #2808			50.00	

"DEERWOOD" OR "BIRCH TREE"

		*Black	Amber	Green	Pink
4	Tumbler, 12 oz., flat, tea		40.00	55.00	
15	Vase, 7", sweet pea, rolled edge, #151			195.00	195.00
	Vase, 10", ruffled top, #6471			195.00	195.00
7	Vase, 10", 2 handles, #15319	225.00			
13	Whipped cream pail, w/ladle			70.00	70.00

*Add 20% for gold decorated.

2

DIANE, ETCH 752, CAMBRIDGE GLASS COMPANY, 1934 – EARLY 1950S

Colors: crystal; some pink, yellow, blue, Heatherbloom, Emerald green, amber, Crown Tuscan with gold

Cambridge's Diane pattern can be found in all the colors listed; but only crystal can be gathered in a large set. You may be able to acquire a small luncheon set in color, but after that only an occasional bowl, candlestick, or tumbler will be seen. Notice the Willow Blue on page 95. This was part of a place setting for 24. It was originally ordered by two sisters who each received a 12 place setting. Since we couldn't find anyone willing to purchase our large expensive setting for eight, we have made a dozen or so collectors happy to own a few pieces of this rarely seen color. Seemingly, the price of making this colored, handmade glass contributed to its scarcity. At any rate, any colored Diane is in very short supply today.

On page 96 and 97 are samples of other colors found with Diane etchings. Hopefully these Diane listings and our legends will ease identification. As with other Cambridge patterns in this book, you will have to look at Rose Point listings for pricing any unlisted Diane items you come across. Diane will run 30% to 40% less than similar items listed in Rose Point. Remember that Rose Point is currently the highest priced etched crystal Cambridge pattern and other patterns sell for less.

The bitters bottle, cabinet flask, and pitchers are in demand. You have several alternatives for stemware in Diane; pick whichever you like. Each line enhances the set. In our travels, we see more #3122 stems than other stem lines; they might be easier to find. Be warned, once you settle on a stemware line you like, many times the stemware found will be another line. Of course, there is no rule stating you have to buy only one line.

21

		Crystal
29	Ashtray, 4"	10.00
	Basket, 6", 2 hdld., ftd.	26.00
19	Bottle, bitters	175.00
1	Bowl, #3106, finger, w/liner	40.00
	Bowl, #3122	22.00
10	Bowl, #3400, cream soup, w/liner	45.00
	Bowl, 3", indiv. nut, 4 ftd.	45.00
14	Bowl, 4½", finger, blown	25.00
	Bowl, 5", berry	25.00
	Bowl, 5¼", 2 hdld., bonbon	20.00
	Bowl, 6", 2 hdld., ftd., bonbon	20.00
	Bowl, 6", 2 pt., relish	20.00
	Bowl, 6", cereal	30.00
	Bowl, 6½", 3 pt., relish	32.00
	Bowl, 7", 2 hdld., ftd., bonbon	32.00
31	Bowl, 7", 2 pt., relish	30.00
	Bowl, 7", relish or pickle	32.00
	Bowl, 9", 3 pt., celery or relish	35.00
28	Bowl, 9½", oval	40.00
	Bowl, 9½", pickle (like corn)	28.00
	Bowl, 10", 4 ft., flared	55.00
	Bowl, 10", baker	50.00
7	Bowl, 10½", 3400/68	65.00
	Bowl, 11", 2 hdld., 2 pt. relish, #3400/89	50.00
	Bowl, 11", 4 ftd., fancy top, #3400/45	55.00
	Bowl, 11½", tab hdld., ftd.	55.00
15	Bowl, 11½", hdld., 3900/34	55.00
30	Bowl, 12", 3 pt., celery & relish	40.00
32	Bowl, 12", 4 ft., ruffled top	60.00
21	Bowl, 12", 4 ft., flared	70.00
	Bowl, 12", 4 ft., oval	60.00
	Bowl, 12", 4 ft., oval, w/"ears," hdld.	65.00
	Bowl, 12", 5 pt., celery & relish	55.00
	Bowl, 15", 3 pt. relish, #3500/112	65.00
11	Butter, rnd.	145.00
	Cabinet flask	295.00

		Crystal
	Candelabrum, 6", 2-lite, keyhole	40.00
	Candelabrum, 6", 3-lite, keyhole	50.00
8	Candlestick, 1-lite, keyhole	25.00
	Candlestick, 5"	25.00
34	Candy, 5½", blown, #3121/3	135.00
	Candy box, w/cover, rnd.	125.00
12	Candy Jar, 10", #3500/41	175.00
17	Candy Jar, 12", #3500/42	175.00
35	Cheese & cracker	55.00
18	Cigarette urn	50.00
	Cocktail shaker, glass top	235.00
	Cocktail shaker, metal top	135.00
3	Cocktail icer, 2 pc.	65.00
	Comport, 5½"	35.00
	Comport, 5⅜", blown	48.00
	Creamer, #3400	15.00
	Creamer, indiv., #3500 (pie crust edge)	15.00
	Creamer, indiv., #3900, scalloped edge	15.00
9	Creamer, scroll handle, #3400	18.00
2	Cup	14.00
	Decanter, ball, 16 oz., cordial, #3400/92	225.00
	Decanter, lg. ftd.	195.00
	Decanter, short ft., cordial	210.00
	Hurricane lamp, candlestick base	175.00
	Hurricane lamp, keyhole base w/prisms	235.00
	Ice bucket, w/chrome hand	90.00
	Mayonnaise, div., w/liner & ladles	55.00
	Mayonnaise (sherbet type w/ladle)	35.00
	Mayonnaise, w/liner, ladle	35.00
25	Oil, 2 oz., ball	40.00
13	Oil, 6 oz., w/stopper	110.00
16	Pitcher, ball	195.00
	Pitcher, Doulton	335.00
	Pitcher, martini	695.00
	Pitcher, upright	315.00
	Plate, 6", 2 hdld., plate.	12.00

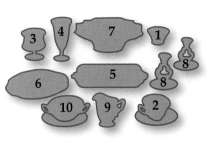

		Crystal
	Plate, 6", sq., bread/butter	6.00
	Plate, 6½", bread/butter	6.00
	Plate, 8", 2 hdld., ftd., bonbon	14.00
	Plate, 8", salad	10.00
27	Plate, 8½"	16.00
6	Plate, 10½", dinner, #3900/24	60.00
	Plate, 12", 4 ft., service	50.00
	Plate, 13", 4 ft., torte	50.00
	Plate, 13½", 2 hdld.	50.00
	Plate, 14", torte	58.00
5	Platter, 13½"	90.00
	Salt & pepper, ftd., w/glass tops, pr.	35.00
	Salt & pepper, pr., flat	35.00
26	Salt & pepper, pr., sterling base	40.00
2	Saucer	4.00
	Stem, #1066, 1 oz., cordial	45.00
	Stem, #1066, 3 oz., cocktail	18.00
	Stem, #1066, 3 oz., wine	24.00
	Stem, #1066, 3½ oz., tall cocktail	20.00
	Stem, #1066, 4½ oz., claret	33.00
	Stem, #1066, 5 oz., oyster/cocktail	16.00
	Stem, #1066, 7 oz., low sherbet	14.00
	Stem, #1066, 7 oz., tall sherbet	16.00
	Stem, #1066, 11 oz., water	24.00
36	Stem, #3122, 1 oz., cordial	45.00
	Stem, #3122, 2½ oz., wine	24.00
38	Stem, #3122, 3 oz., cocktail	16.00
	Stem, #3122, 4½ oz., claret	33.00
	Stem, #3122, 4½ oz., oyster/cocktail	16.00
	Stem, #3122, 7 oz., low sherbet	14.00
22	Stem, #3122, 7 oz., tall sherbet	16.00
23	Stem, #3122, 9 oz., water goblet	24.00
	Stem, #3575, tall sherbert/champagne	16.00
	Sugar, indiv., #3500 (pie crust edge)	16.00
	Sugar, indiv., #3900, scalloped edge	16.00
	Sugar, scroll handle, #3400	16.00
20	Sugar sifter	150.00

		Crystal
	Tumbler, 2½ oz., sham bottom	50.00
	Tumbler, 5 oz., ft., juice	30.00
	Tumbler, 5 oz., sham bottom	30.00
	Tumbler, 7 oz., old-fashion, w/sham bottom	45.00
	Tumbler, 8 oz., ft.	25.00
	Tumbler, 10 oz., sham bottom	30.00
	Tumbler, 12 oz., sham bottom	35.00
	Tumbler, 13 oz.	28.00
	Tumbler, 14 oz., sham bottom	36.00
	Tumbler, #1066, 3 oz.	23.00
	Tumbler, #1066, 5 oz., juice	20.00
	Tumbler, #1066, 9 oz., water	18.00
	Tumbler, #1066, 12 oz., tea	20.00
	Tumbler, #3106, 3 oz., ftd.	20.00
	Tumbler, #3106, 5 oz., ftd., juice	18.00
	Tumbler, #3106, 9 oz., ftd., water	18.00
	Tumbler, #3106, 12 oz., ftd., tea	20.00
	Tumbler, #3122, 2½ oz.	30.00
37	Tumbler, #3122, 5 oz., juice	16.00
	Tumbler, #3122, 9 oz., water	20.00
	Tumbler, #3122, 12 oz., tea	24.00
	Tumbler, #3135, 2½ oz., ftd., bar	36.00
	Tumbler, #3135, 10 oz., ftd., tumbler	18.00
4	Tumbler, #3135, 12 oz., ftd., tea	25.00
	Tumbler, #3575, 5 oz., ftd., juice	16.00
	Tumbler, #3575, 12 oz., ftd., tea	22.00
	Vase, 5", globe	50.00
	Vase, 6", high ft., flower	45.00
33	Vase, 8", high ft., flower	60.00
	Vase, 9", keyhole base	75.00
	Vase, 10", ftd., #1301	75.00
	Vase, 10", bud	60.00
	Vase, 11", flower	115.00
	Vase, 11", ped. ft., flower	110.00
	Vase, 12", keyhole base	115.00
	Vase, 13", flower	165.00

ELAINE, CAMBRIDGE GLASS COMPANY, 1934 – 1950S

Color: crystal

Elaine is frequently confused with Chantilly. The Elaine design has a thin, angled scroll like the top of the script capital letter "E." Compare the design shown at right with the one on the top of page 66. As with other patterns, we have emptied out the vault to show you as many photos as possible in this our last Elegant book before retirement.

Elaine is routinely found on Cambridge's #3500 Gadroon line that has the ornate "pie crust" edge. Several nationally known Cambridge dealers have found that description ("pie crust" edge) infuriating, but most customers distinguish it in that way. You may find some supplementary pieces unlisted here. Many pieces listed under Rose Point etch exist in Elaine. However, bear in mind that prices for Elaine will be 30% to 50% lower than those shown for Rose Point.

	Basket, 6", 2 hdld. (upturned sides)	28.00
	Bowl, #3104, finger, w/liner	40.00
	Bowl, 3", indiv. nut, 4 ftd.	45.00
	Bowl, 5¼", 2 hdld., bonbon	28.00
59	Bowl, 5½", 2 pt., relish, #3500/60	28.00
2	Bowl, 6", 1 hdld., 2 pt., relish, #3400/1093	28.00
	Bowl, 6", 2 hdld., ftd., bonbon	28.00
3	Bowl, 6", 2 pt., relish, "Gadroon"	26.00
51	Bowl, 6½", 3 pt., relish, #3400/91	28.00
	Bowl, 7", 2 pt., pickle or relish	30.00
	Bowl, 7", ftd., tab hdld., bonbon	32.00
	Bowl, 7", pickle or relish	28.00
24	Bowl, 8", 3 pt., relish, 2 hdld, #1402/91	40.00
58	Bowl, 9", 3 pt., celery & relish, #3500/164 "Gadroon"	40.00
	Bowl, 9½", pickle (like corn dish)	30.00
48	Bowl, 10", 4 ftd., flared, #3400/4	70.00
	Bowl, 11", tab hdld.	75.00
36	Bowl, 11", 3-pt relish, #3400/200	55.00
	Bowl, 11½", ftd., tab hdld.	70.00
	Bowl, 12", 3 pt., celery & relish	50.00
20	Bowl, 12", ftd., flared, #3500/17	65.00
	Bowl, 12", 4 ftd., oval, "ear" hdld.	70.00
7	Bowl, 12", 5 pt., celery & relish	45.00
44	Candlestick, 5", #3400/646, "Keyhole"	28.00
39	Candlestick, 6", 2-lite, #647	33.00
19	Candlestick, 6", 3-lite, #1338	40.00
6	Candlestick, 7", #3121	70.00
12	Candy box, w/cover, ftd., #3121/4	110.00
11	Candy box, 6", #306	95.00
54	Candy jar, 10", #3500/41	175.00
55	Candy jar, 12", #3500/42	235.00
25	Celery, 11", #3500	45.00
42	Cocktail icer, 2 pc., #3900/18	70.00
28	Comport, 4½", #1402	35.00
38	Comport, 5", 4-toed, #3400/74	40.00
1	Comport, 5½", #3600/136	30.00
	Comport, 5⅜", #3500 stem	35.00
	Comport, 5⅜", blown	45.00
23	Comport & cheese, #3400/7	35.00
33	Creamer (several styles)	18.00
41	Creamer, indiv., #3500/15	18.00
34	Cup, #3400/54	15.00
	Decanter, lg., ftd.	225.00
	Hat, 9"	395.00
	Hurricane lamp, candlestick base	175.00

	Hurricane lamp, keyhole ft., w/prisms	225.00
8	Ice bucket, w/chrome handle	80.00
43	Mayonnaise, #3900/128	40.00
	Mayonnaise (cupped sherbet w/ladle)	33.00
	Mayonnaise (div. bowl, liner, 2 ladles), #3900/111	48.00
	Mayonnaise, w/liner & ladle, #1532, "Pristine"	40.00
	Oil, 2 oz., handled w/stopper	40.00
	Oil, 6 oz., hdld., w/stopper	110.00
	Pitcher, ball, 80 oz.	195.00
	Pitcher, Doulton	325.00
52	Pitcher, 78 oz., #3400/100	195.00
50	Plate, mayo liner, #533	8.00
	Plate, 6", 2 hdld.	12.00
22	Plate, 6½", bread/butter, #3400/60	8.00
57, 30	Plate, 7½", dessert, #3500/4, #3400/176	10.00
49	Plate, 8", 2 hdld., ftd., bonbon, #3900/31	16.00
	Plate, 8", salad	15.00
	Plate, 8", tab hdld., bonbon	18.00
56	Plate, 8½", salad, #3500, "Gadroon"	15.00
	Plate, 10½", dinner	55.00
	Plate, 11½" 2 hdld., ringed "Tally Ho" sandwich	55.00
	Plate, 12", 4 ftd., service	50.00
	Plate, 13", 4 ftd., torte	50.00
9	Plate, 13", torte, #3500/38	75.00
	Plate, 13½", tab hdld., cake	55.00
46	Plate, 13½", cabaret plate, #1397	50.00
	Plate, 14", service, #3900/166, rolled edge	55.00
10	Salt & pepper, flat, pr.	33.00
5	Salt & pepper, ftd., pr	33.00
	Salt & pepper, hdld., pr	30.00
4	Salt & pepper, individual	18.00
34	Saucer, #3400/5447	3.00
47	Stem, #3035, 2½ oz. wine	30.00
16	Stem, #1402, 1 oz., cordial	75.00
	Stem, #1402, 3 oz., wine	35.00
	Stem, #1402, 3½ oz., cocktail	26.00
	Stem, #1402, 5 oz., claret	35.00
	Stem, #1402, low sherbet	14.00
	Stem, #1402, tall sherbet	16.00
	Stem, #1402, goblet	30.00
	Stem, #3035, cordial	45.00
	Stem, #3104 (very tall stems), ¾ oz., brandy	195.00
	Stem, #3104, 1 oz., cordial	195.00
	Stem, #3104, 1 oz., pousse-cafe	195.00
	Stem, #3104, 2 oz., sherry	195.00

	Stem, #3104, 2½ oz., creme de menthe	165.00
47	Stem, #3104, 3 oz., wine	165.00
	Stem, #3104, 3½ oz., cocktail	90.00
	Stem, #3104, 4½ oz., claret	165.00
	Stem, #3104, 5 oz., roemer	165.00
	Stem, #3104, 5 oz., tall hock	165.00
	Stem, #3104, 7 oz., tall sherbet	125.00
	Stem, #3104, 9 oz., goblet	195.00
	Stem, #3121, 1 oz., cordial	45.00
	Stem, #3121, 3 oz., cocktail	20.00
	Stem, #3121, 3½ oz., wine	26.00
	Stem, #3121, 4½ oz., claret	32.00
	Stem, #3121, 4½ oz., oyster cocktail	18.00
26	Stem, #3121, 5 oz., parfait, low stem	30.00
	Stem, #3121, 6 oz., low sherbet	16.00
	Stem, #3121, 6 oz., tall sherbet	18.00
	Stem, #3121, 10 oz., water	26.00
62	Stem, #3500, 1 oz., cordial	45.00
	Stem, #3500, 2½ oz., wine	28.00
	Stem, #3500, 3 oz., cocktail	22.00
61	Stem, #3500, 4½ oz., claret	33.00
	Stem, #3500, 4½ oz., oyster cocktail	18.00
	Stem, #3500, 5 oz., parfait, low stem	30.00
	Stem, #3500, 7 oz., low sherbet	14.00
	Stem, #3500, 7 oz., tall sherbet	16.00
60	Stem, #3500, 10 oz., water	28.00
14	Stem, #7801, champagne	110.00
17	Stem, #7966, 2 oz., sherry	60.00
	Sugar (several styles), #3500/14 (shown)	16.00
40	Sugar, indiv., #3500/15	16.00
29	Tray, #3500/67, 12"	70.00
18	Tumbler, 5 oz., ftd., juice	28.00
15	Tumbler, #498, 12 oz.	28.00
	Tumbler, #1402, 9 oz., ftd., water	18.00
	Tumbler, #1402, 12 oz., tea	30.00
	Tumbler, #1402, 12 oz., tall ftd., tea	30.00

32	Tumbler, #3000, 3 oz., ftd. cocktail	35.00
31	Tumbler, #3121, 5 oz., ftd., juice	22.00
	Tumbler, #3121, 10 oz., ftd., water	30.00
	Tumbler, #3121, 12 oz., ftd., tea	30.00
21	Tumbler, #3400/92, 2½ oz.	30.00
37	Tumbler, #3400/115, 13 oz.	35.00
	Tumbler, #3500, 5 oz., ftd., juice	22.00
27	Tumbler, #3500, 10 oz., ftd., water	24.00
	Tumbler, #3500, 12 oz., ftd., tea	30.00
	Vase, 6", ftd.	55.00
	Vase, 8", ftd.	85.00
	Vase, 9", keyhole, ftd.	110.00
45	Vase, 10", #1242	100.00
53	Vase, 10", cornucopia, #3900/575	195.00
13	Vase, 11", #278	110.00
	Vase, 12", #3400	175.00

ELIZABETH, ETCH #757, MORGANTOWN GLASS WORKS, EARLY 1930S

Colors: Crystal, and w/Ebony filament stem, Azure, Aquamarine and w/crystal stem, Spanish Red w/crystal stem

Elizabeth is another of Morgantown's smaller patterns which can be acquired on at least two different stem lines. An example of each is pictured. The twisted stem cocktail is from the #7664 Queen Anne line and the water goblet is #7630 Ballerina line commonly referred to as a "lady leg" stem. As with most Morgantown lines, stems can be uncovered but other than that, apparently only a salad plate and vases can be added to your search.

		Crystal
2	Plate, 7½", salad	15.00
	Stem, #7630, 1½ oz., cordial	75.00
	Stem, #7630, 2½ oz., wine	35.00
	Stem, #7630, 4 oz., cocktail	25.00
	Stem, #7639, 5 oz., parfait	35.00
	Stem, #7630, 6 oz., low sherbet	20.00
	Stem, #7630, 7 oz., 6¼" champagne	25.00
	Stem, #7630, 9 oz., 7¾", water goblet	38.00
	Stem, #7664, 1½ oz., cordial	75.00
	Stem, #7664, 2½ oz., wine	35.00
3	Stem, #7664, 4 oz., cocktail	25.00
	Stem, #7664, 6 oz., low sherbet	20.00
	Stem, #7664, 7 oz., 6¾" champagne	25.00
1	Stem, #7664, 10 oz., 8¼", water goblet	38.00
	Tumbler, #7664, 9 oz, 4¼", flair edge	30.00
	Vase, #7602, 6"	110.00
	Vase, #36 Uranus bud, 10"	85.00

* Add 50% for any color.

1   2   3

EMPIRE, TIFFIN GLASS CO., 1920S

Colors: Crystal, green, Rose

Empire is typically found in Rose (pink), even though it is cataloged as having been manufactured in green and crystal. We've heard this pattern presented as "one of those Tiffin bird patterns" several times. As we pursued this pattern, we only observed pink and not much of that. Jugs are listed as coming only with lid, so this may be one Tiffin pattern where jugs were only sold with a lid. You will generally find stems; but creamer, sugar, cup, and saucers are in diminutive supply. Although the #15018 stem line is pictured, you could find Empire etched on two other lines (#15024 and #15070).

		All Colors
	Bowl, finger, ftd.	40.00
	Comport, 7¼"	50.00
	Creamer	50.00
	Cup	55.00
	Jug w/cover	495.00
2	Plate, 8"	22.00
	Saucer	15.00
	Stem, #15018, 3 oz.., wine	60.00
	Stem, #15018, 4 oz., cocktail	40.00
1	Stem, #15018, 5 oz., café parfait	65.00
	Stem, #15018, 5 oz., claret	65.00
	Stem, #15018, 6 oz., champagne	45.00
	Stem, #15018, 6 oz., sherbet	35.00
3	Stem, #15018, 9 oz., goblet water	65.00
	Sugar	50.00
	Tumbler, water, ftd., 9 oz.	40.00

EMPRESS, BLANK #1401, A. H. HEISEY COMPANY, 1932 – 1934

Colors: Flamingo pink, Sahara yellow, Moongleam green, cobalt, and Alexandrite; some Tangerine

During the time colors were made, this Heisey pattern was listed as Empress; but later on, when crystal was produced, the pattern's name was changed to Queen Ann. Some Heisey people want to make great observational discrepancies in colored items and the crystal; they can do what they want as we are only listing Empress in color.

Be aware that Empress can be found on both round and square mould blanks as illustrated below. Many collectors have favored square plates.

Empress is shown below in Alexandrite which is Heisey's purple/pink color that changes colors depending upon the lighting source. Fostoria called their similar color Wisteria, Cambridge named theirs Heatherbloom, Tiffin's was Twilight, and Morgantown also used Alexandrite. Under natural light, this color appears pink; but, under florescent light, it appears blue. Our photographers and printers have always done an astonishing job in showing it accurately. That is not effortlessly accomplished. (Optimistically, that statement did not just jinx our photos.)

		Flamingo	Sahara	Moongleam	Cobalt	Alexandrite
12	Ashtray	100.00	100.00	150.00	200.00	200.00
	Bonbon, 6"	20.00	25.00	30.00		
	Bowl, cream soup	30.00	30.00	50.00		110.00
9, 10	Bowl, cream soup, with liner	40.00	40.00	55.00		175.00
	Bowl, frappe, w/center	45.00	60.00	75.00		
5	Bowl, nut, dolphin ftd., indiv.	30.00	32.00	45.00		150.00
	Bowl, 4½", nappy	40.00	40.00	60.00		
	Bowl, 5", preserve, 2 hdld.	20.00	25.00	30.00		
	Bowl, 6", ftd., jelly, 2 hdld.	20.00	25.00	30.00		
11	Bowl, 6", dolphin ftd., mint	35.00	40.00	45.00		275.00
15	Bowl, 6", grapefruit, ground bottom	12.50	20.00	25.00		
	Bowl, 6½", oval, lemon, w/cover	100.00	100.00	150.00		
	Bowl, 7", 3 pt., relish, triplex	40.00	45.00	50.00		175.00
21	Bowl, 7", 3 pt., relish, ctr. hand.	45.00	50.00	75.00		

		Flamingo	Sahara	Moongleam	Cobalt	Alexandrite
	Bowl, 7½", dolphin ftd., nappy	65.00	65.00	80.00	300.00	350.00
	Bowl, 7½", dolphin ftd., nasturtium	130.00	130.00	150.00	350.00	425.00
	Bowl, 8", nappy	35.00	37.00	45.00		
	Bowl, 8½", ftd., floral, 2 hdld	45.00	50.00	70.00		
	Bowl, 9", floral, rolled edge	40.00	42.00	50.00		
	Bowl, 9", floral, flared	70.00	75.00	90.00		
18	Bowl, 10", 2 hdld., oval dessert	50.00	60.00	70.00		
	Bowl, 10", lion head, floral	550.00	550.00	700.00		
	Bowl, 10", oval, veg.	50.00	55.00	75.00		
	Bowl, 10", square, salad, 2 hdld.	55.00	60.00	80.00		
	Bowl, 10", triplex, relish	50.00	55.00	65.00		
	Bowl, 11", dolphin ftd., floral	65.00	75.00	100.00	400.00	400.00
	Bowl, 13", pickle/olive, 2 pt.	35.00	45.00	50.00		
	Bowl, 15", dolphin ftd., punch	900.00	900.00	1,250.00		
	Candlestick, low, 4 ftd., w/2 hdld.	100.00	100.00	170.00		
20	Candlestick, 6", #135		50.00	190.00		275.00
17	Candlestick, 6", dolphin ftd.	170.00	125.00	155.00	260.00	400.00
	Candy, w/cover, 6", dolphin ftd.	150.00	150.00	350.00	600.00	
	Comport, 6", ftd.	110.00	70.00	100.00		
	Comport, 6", square	70.00	75.00	85.00		
	Comport, 7", oval	85.00	80.00	90.00		
	Compotier, 6", dolphin ftd.	260.00	225.00	275.00		
7	Creamer, dolphin ftd.	30.00	45.00	40.00		200.00
	Creamer, indiv.	45.00	45.00	50.00		210.00
	Cup	30.00	30.00	35.00		115.00

		Flamingo	Sahara	Moongleam	Cobalt	Alexandrite
	Cup, after dinner	60.00	60.00	70.00		
	Cup, bouillon, 2 hdld.	35.00	35.00	45.00		
	Cup, 4 oz., custard or punch	30.00	35.00	45.00		
	Cup, #1401½, has rim as demi-cup	28.00	32.00	40.00		
6	Grapefruit, w/square liner	30.00	30.00	35.00		
	Ice tub, w/metal handles, dolphin ftd.	100.00	150.00	350.00		3,000.00
	Hors d'oeuvre, 10", 7 compartments		75.00			
16	Jug, 3 pint, ftd.	200.00	210.00	250.00		
	Jug, flat			175.00		
	Marmalade, w/cover, dolphin ftd.	200.00	200.00	225.00		
14	Mayonnaise, 5½", ftd. with ladle	85.00	90.00	110.00		300.00
23	Mustard, w/cover and underplate	85.00	80.00	95.00		
	Oil bottle, 4 oz.	125.00	125.00	135.00		
	Plate, bouillon liner	12.00	15.00	17.50		25.00
	Plate, 4½"	10.00	15.00	20.00		
	Plate, 6"	11.00	14.00	16.00		40.00
4	Plate, 6", sq.	10.00	13.00	15.00		40.00
2	Plate, 7"	12.00	15.00	17.00		50.00
	Plate, 7", sq.	12.00	15.00	17.00	60.00	60.00
	Plate, 8", sq.	18.00	22.00	35.00	80.00	75.00
	Plate, 8"	16.00	20.00	24.00	70.00	75.00
	Plate, 9"	25.00	35.00	40.00		
	Plate, 10½"	100.00	100.00	140.00		335.00
3	Plate, 10½", sq.	100.00	100.00	140.00		335.00
	Plate, 12"	45.00	55.00	65.00		
	Plate, 12", muffin, sides upturned	55.00	80.00	90.00		
	Plate, 12", sandwich, 2 hdld.	35.00	45.00	60.00		180.00
	Plate, 13", hors d'oeuvre, 2 hdld.	50.00	60.00	70.00		
	Plate, 13", sq., 2 hdld.	40.00	45.00	55.00		
	Platter, 14"	40.00	45.00	80.00		
13	Salt & pepper, pr.	100.00	140.00	135.00		400.00
	Saucer, sq.	10.00	10.00	15.00		25.00
	Saucer, after dinner	10.00	10.00	15.00		
	Saucer, rnd.	10.00	10.00	15.00		25.00
	Stem, 2½ oz., oyster cocktail	20.00	25.00	30.00		
	Stem, 4 oz., saucer champagne	35.00	40.00	60.00		
	Stem, 4 oz., sherbet	22.00	28.00	25.00		
	Stem, 9 oz., Empress stemware, unusual	55.00	65.00	75.00		
	Sugar, indiv.	45.00	45.00	50.00		210.00
8	Sugar, dolphin ftd., 3 hdld.	30.00	45.00	40.00		200.00
	Tray, condiment & liner for indiv. sugar/creamer	75.00	75.00	85.00		
19	Tray, condiment & liner for cream & sugar	50.00	50.00	55.00		
	Tray, 10", 3 pt., relish	50.00	55.00	65.00		
	Tray, 10", 7 pt., hors d'oeuvre	160.00	150.00	200.00		
22	Tray, 10", celery	25.00	35.00	40.00		150.00
	Tray, 12", ctr. hdld., sandwich	48.00	57.00	65.00		325.00
	Tray, 12", sq. ctr. hdld., sandwich	52.00	60.00	67.50		
	Tray, 13", celery	30.00	40.00	45.00		100.00
	Tray, 16", 4 pt., buffet relish	75.00	75.00	86.00		160.00
	Tumbler, 8 oz., dolphin ftd., unusual	150.00	180.00	160.00		
	Tumbler, 8 oz., ground bottom	60.00	50.00	70.00		
	Tumbler, 12 oz., tea, ground bottom	60.00	50.00	75.00		
	Vase, 8", flared	140.00	150.00	190.00		
1	Vase, 9", dolphin ftd.	200.00	200.00	220.00		850.00

FAIRFAX NO. 2375, FOSTORIA GLASS COMPANY, 1927 – 1944

Colors: Blue, crystal, Azure blue, Orchid, amber, Rose, green, Topaz; some Ruby, Ebony, and Wisteria

Fairfax (the name of this Fostoria #2375 mould blank) was the mould shape used for most of Fostoria's well known etchings, including June, Versailles, and Trojan. Illustrated below is Azure (blue) and Orchid on page 108. Those are the colors most desired in Fairfax. Amber and Topaz (yellow) are readily available, but by and large have had fewer collectors seeking them which makes them less expensive to acquire. Some collectors of blue or pink June or Versailles are buying pieces of Fairfax to fill holes in their sets. Many Fairfax replacement pieces can be obtained for 25% – 40% of the cost of an etched piece. Thus, collectors prefer to have a non-etched piece than none at all, but in today's economic world many just do without owning every piece in the set.

Fortunately, Fairfax collectors have a choice of two stemware lines. The Fostoria stems and shapes shown on page 109 are the #5298 stem and tumbler line (even though the pieces shown are etched June, Trojan, and Versailles). More collectors embrace this line especially in pink and blue. The other stem line, #5299, is commonly found in Topaz with a Trojan etch and is shown at the bottom of page 109. Collectors dubbed this stem "waterfall." All Wisteria stems are found only on that #5299 line. Some collectors mix tumblers although they have a conspicuously different profile. The #5299 tumblers (oyster cocktail on page 109) are more flared at the top than the #5298 (all other tumblers on page 109).

We have shown an assortment of Fostoria's stemware on page 109 so that all shapes are profiled. The claret and high sherbets are major concerns. Each measures 6" high. The claret is shaped like the wine. We recently bought a set of blue June where the footed juices listed turned out to be parfaits. The parfait is taller than the juice, although shaped similarly; so check those measurements.

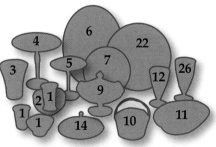

		Rose, Blue Orchid	Amber	Green Topaz
18	Ashtray, 2½"	12.00	5.00	9.00
	Ashtray, 4"	13.00	6.00	10.00
	Ashtray, 5½"	16.00	9.00	11.00
11	Baker, 9", oval	40.00	14.00	26.00
27	Baker, 10½", oval	45.00	16.00	26.00
	Bonbon	12.50	9.00	10.00
	Bottle, salad dressing	190.00	65.00	90.00
	Bouillon, ftd.	15.00	8.00	10.00
	Bowl, 9", lemon, 2 hdld.	20.00	10.00	13.00
	Bowl, sweetmeat	22.00	12.00	16.00
	Bowl, 5", fruit	16.00	8.00	10.00
15	Bowl, 6", cereal	24.00	10.00	12.00
	Bowl, 6⅞", 3 ftd.	25.00	15.00	20.00
	Bowl, 7", soup	40.00	20.00	30.00
	Bowl, 8", rnd., nappy	45.00	15.00	26.00
	Bowl, 8½", 2 pt., relish	30.00	15.00	20.00
	Bowl, lg., hdld., dessert	40.00	18.00	26.00

		Rose, Blue Orchid	Amber	Green Topaz
	Bowl, 12"	40.00	18.00	26.00
	Bowl, 12", ctrpiece, #2394	40.00	18.00	26.00
	Bowl, 13", oval, ctrpiece	40.00	18.00	26.00
	Bowl, 15", ctrpiece	45.00	20.00	28.00
14	Butter dish, w/ cover	130.00	50.00	75.00
24	Candlestick, 2"	15.00	9.00	12.00
17	Candlestick, 3"	18.00	9.00	12.00
	Candy w/cover, flat, 3 pt.	75.00	30.00	40.00
	Candy w/cover., ftd.	75.00	30.00	45.00
9	Candy jar, oval, #2395	65.00	45.00	55.00
	Celery, 11½"	28.00	12.00	15.00
	Cheese comport (2 styles), #2368	20.00	8.00	10.00
	Cheese & cracker set (2 styles)	40.00	18.00	20.00
	Cigarette box	30.00	14.00	20.00

FAIRFAX NO. 2375

		Rose, Blue Orchid	Amber	Green Topaz
5	Comport, 5"	30.00	12.00	18.00
	Comport, 6", #5299			22.00
4	Comport, 7", #2375	32.00	12.00	18.00
	Cream soup, ftd.	18.00	8.00	12.00
20	Creamer, flat		8.00	12.00
	Creamer, ftd.	12.00	6.00	8.00
	Creamer, tea	15.00	6.00	10.00
32	Cup, after dinner	15.00	6.00	10.00
16	Cup, flat		2.00	4.00
	Cup, ftd.	10.00	3.00	5.00
	Flower holder, oval, window box w/frog	125.00	60.00	75.00
	Grapefruit	30.00	15.00	20.00
	Grapefruit liner	25.00	9.00	15.00
	Ice bucket	65.00	30.00	40.00
2	Ice bowl, #2451	20.00	9.00	12.00
1	Ice bowl insert	15.00	5.00	*10.00
	Lemon dish, 6¾", 2 hndl.	22.00	12.00	18.00
21	Mayonnaise	22.00	10.00	12.00
	Mayonnaise ladle	23.00	12.00	16.00
23	Mayonnaise liner, 7"	8.00	3.00	4.00
	Nut cup, blown	20.00	9.00	11.00
	Oil, ftd.	150.00	60.00	75.00
	Pickle, 8½"	20.00	6.00	10.00
	Pitcher, #5000	195.00	65.00	100.00
	Plate, canape	20.00	9.00	10.00
	Plate, whipped cream	10.00	6.00	8.00
	Plate, 6", bread/butter	6.00	2.00	3.00
	Plate, 7½", salad	8.00	3.00	4.00
	Plate, 7½", cream soup or mayonnaise liner	8.00	3.00	4.00

		Rose, Blue Orchid	Amber	Green Topaz
7	Plate, 8¾", salad	12.00	5.00	6.00
	Plate, Mah Jongg (w/ sherbet), #2321	35.00	16.00	20.00
	Plate, 9½", luncheon	15.00	6.00	8.00
22	Plate, 10¼", dinner	33.00	10.00	20.00
	Plate, 10¼", grill	33.00	10.00	22.00
	Plate, 10", cake	22.00	10.00	14.00
	Plate, 12", bread, oval	40.00	16.00	20.00
	Plate, 13", chop	28.00	12.00	18.00
	Platter, 10½", oval	30.00	12.00	18.00
	Platter, 12", oval	35.00	14.00	20.00
6	Platter, 15", oval	75.00	25.00	40.00
	Relish, 3 part, 8½"	28.00	10.00	15.00
	Relish, 11½"	24.00	9.00	13.00
8	Sauce boat	35.00	15.00	20.00
	Sauce boat liner	15.00	5.00	10.00
32	Saucer, after dinner	4.00	1.00	2.00
19	Saucer	3.00	1.00	2.00
	Shaker, ftd., pr	50.00	25.00	30.00
	Shaker, indiv., ftd., pr.		15.00	20.00
	Stem, 4", ¾ oz., cordial, #5098	40.00	10.00	25.00
	Stem, 5½ oz., oyster cocktail	14.00	6.00	8.00
	Stem, 4¼", 6 oz., low sherbet	11.00	6.00	8.00
	Stem, 5¼", 3 oz., cocktail	14.00	8.00	10.00
	Stem, 5½", 3 oz., wine, #5098	20.00	12.00	14.00
	Stem, 6", 4 oz., claret	25.00	14.00	16.00
	Stem, 6", 6 oz., high sherbet, #5098	16.00	8.00	12.00
	Stem, 8¼", 10 oz., water	22.00	10.00	15.00

* topaz $10.00

		Rose, Blue Orchid	Amber	Green Topaz
13	Sugar, flat		8.00	12.00
	Sugar, ftd.	12.00	6.00	8.00
	Sugar cover	30.00	15.00	20.00

		Rose, Blue Orchid	Amber	Green Topaz
	Sugar pail	60.00	25.00	35.00
	Sugar, tea	15.00	6.00	10.00
25	Tray, 11", ctr. hdld.	30.00	15.00	20.00
	Tumbler, 2½ oz., ftd.	22.00	9.00	15.00
	Tumbler, 4½", 5½ oz., ftd., oyster cocktail, #5099	14.00	6.00	9.00
12	Tumbler, 5¼", 9 oz., ftd.	16.00	8.00	11.00
26	Tumbler, 6", 12 oz., ftd., #5098	22.00	9.00	15.00
3	Vase, 5", #4128	50.00	35.00	45.00
	Vase, 8" (2 styles)	85.00	30.00	40.00
10	Whipped cream pail	40.00	20.00	30.00

Cordial, 3⅞", #5099
"Waterfall" stemline

Fostoria Stems and Shapes

All are on #5098 "Petal" stems unless otherwise indicated.

Top Row: Left to Right
1. Water, 10 oz., 8¼", #5098
2. Claret, 4 oz., 6", #5098
3. Wine, 3 oz., 5½", #5098
4. Cordial, ¾ oz., 4", #5098
5. Sherbet, low, 6 oz., 4¼", #5098
6. Cocktail, 3 oz., 5¼", #5098
7. Sherbet, high, 6 oz., 6", #5098

Bottom Row: Left to Right
1. Grapefruit and liner, #877
2. Ice tea tumbler, 12 oz., 6", #5098
3. Water tumbler, 9 oz., 5¼", #5098
4. Parfait, 6 oz., 5¼", #5098
5. Juice tumbler, 5 oz., 4½", #5098
6. Oyster cocktail, 5½ oz., #5099 "Waterfall" stemline
7. Bar tumbler, 2½ oz., #5098

FIRST LOVE, DUNCAN & MILLER GLASS COMPANY, 1937

Color: crystal

First Love is almost certainly the most recognized Duncan & Miller etching. A variety of mould lines were incorporated into this bountiful design. Amongst those are #30 (Pall Mall), #111 (Terrace), #115 (Canterbury), #117 (Three Feathers), #126 (Venetian), and #5111½ (Terrace blown stemware). Canterbury shapes can be found on pages 46 to 48 and Terrace can be seen on pages 236 – 238.

Earlier editions of this book illustrated details of those other lines with catalog pages from Duncan. New patterns have been added which leaves little room for those pages now. We see most items of First Love on lines #111 or #115.

Roger Brothers First Love silver-plate was made to harmonize with this etching.

1

	Ashtray, 3½", sq., #111	12.00
	Ashtray, 3½" x 2½", #30	12.00
	Ashtray, 5" x 3", #12, club	20.00
	Ashtray, 5" x 3¼", #30	15.00
	Ashtray, 6½" x 4¼", #30	20.00
	Basket, 9¼" x 10" x 7¼", #115	150.00
2	Basket, 10" x 4¼" x 7", oval hdld., #115	155.00
	Bottle, oil w/stopper, 8", #5200	40.00
	Bowl, 3" x 5", rose, #115	30.00
	Bowl, 4" x 1½", finger, #30	26.00
	Bowl, 4¼", finger, #5111½	30.00
	Bowl, 6" x 2½", oval, olive, #115	20.00
	Bowl, 6¾" x 4¼", ftd., flared rim, #111	25.00
	Bowl, 7½" x 3", 3 pt., ftd., #117	30.00
	Bowl, 8" sq. x 2½", hdld., #111	50.00
	Bowl, 8½" x 4", #115	30.00
	Bowl, 9" x 4½", ftd., #111	33.00
	Bowl, 9½" x 2½", hdld., #111	35.00
	Bowl, 10" x 3¾", ftd., flared rim, #111	40.00
	Bowl, 10" x 4½", #115	40.00
	Bowl, 10½" x 5", crimped, #115	40.00
	Bowl, 10½" x 7" x 7", #126	50.00
	Bowl, 10¾" x 4¾", #115	40.00
	Bowl, 11" x 1¾", #30	45.00
	Bowl, 11" x 3¼", flared rim, #111	50.00
	Bowl, 11" x 5¼", flared rim, #6	55.00
	Bowl, 11½" x 8¼", oval, #115	40.00
	Bowl, 12" x 3½", #6	60.00
	Bowl, 12" x 3¼", flared, #115	50.00
	Bowl, 12" x 4" x 7½", oval, #117	52.00
	Bowl, 12½", flat, ftd., #126	60.00
	Bowl, 13" x 3¼" x 8¾", oval, flared, #115	48.00
	Bowl, 13" x 7" x 9¼", #126	55.00
	Bowl, 13" x 7", #117	55.00
	Bowl, 14" x 7½" x 6", oval, #126	55.00
	Box, candy w/lid, 4¾" x 6¼"	48.00
	Butter or cheese, 7" sq. x 1¼", #111	95.00
	Candelabra, 2-lite, #41	30.00
	Candelabrum, 6", 2-lite w/prisms, #30	50.00
8	Candle, 3", 1-lite, #111	22.00
	Candle, 3", low, #115	22.00
	Candle, 3½", #115	22.00
	Candle, 4", cornucopia, #117	22.00
	Candle, 4", low, #111	22.00

	Candle, 5¼", 2-lite, globe, #30	30.00
	Candle, 6", 2-lite, #30	30.00
	Candy box, 6" x 3½", 3 hdld., 3 pt., w/lid, #115	75.00
	Candy box, 6" x 3½", 3 pt., w/lid, crown finial, #106	75.00
	Candy jar, 5" x 7¼", w/lid, ftd., #25	75.00
	Candy, 6½", w/5" lid, #115	65.00
	Carafe, w/stopper, water, #5200	195.00
	Cheese stand, 3" x 5¼", #111	20.00
5	Cheese stand, 5¾" x 3½", #115	20.00
	Cigarette box w/lid, 4" x 4¼"	25.00
	Cigarette box w/lid, 4½" x 3½", #30	25.00
	Cigarette box w/lid, 4¾" x 3¾"	25.00
	Cocktail shaker, 14 oz., #5200	110.00
	Cocktail shaker, 16 oz., #5200	110.00
	Cocktail shaker, 32 oz., #5200	135.00
	Comport w/lid, 8¾" x 5½", #111	110.00
	Comport, 3½"x 4¾"w, #111	22.00
	Comport, 5" x 5½", flared rim, #115	24.00
	Comport, 5¼" x 6¾", flat top, #115	24.00
	Comport, 6" x 4¾", low, #115	30.00
	Creamer, 2½", individual, #115	15.00
	Creamer, 3", 10 oz., #111	15.00
11	Creamer, 3¾", 7 oz., #115	12.00
	Creamer, sugar w/butter pat lid, breakfast set, #28	75.00
	Cruet, #25	75.00
	Cruet, #30	75.00
	Cup, #115	10.00
	Decanter w/stopper, 16 oz., #5200	125.00
4	Decanter w/stopper, 32 oz., #30	150.00
	Decanter w/stopper, 32 oz., #5200	150.00
	Hat, 4½", #30	295.00
	Hat, 5½" x 8½" x 6¼", #30	250.00
	Honey dish, 5" x 3", #91	24.00
13	Ice bucket, 6", #30	90.00
	Lamp, hurricane, w/prisms, 15", #115	150.00
	Lamp shade only, #115	100.00
	Lid for candy urn, #111	35.00
	Mayonnaise, 4¾" x 4½", div. w/7½" underplate	30.00
	Mayonnaise, 5¼" x 3", div. w/6½" plate, #1153	30.00
	Mayonnaise, 5½" x 2½", ftd., hdld., #111	30.00
12	Mayonnaise, 5½" x 2¾", #115	30.00
	Mayonnaise, 5½" x 3½", crimped, #111	30.00
	Mayonnaise, 5¾" x 3", w/dish hdld. tray, #111	30.00

	Mayonnaise, w/7" tray hdld, #111	30.00
	Mustard w/lid & underplate	50.00
	Nappy, 5" x 1", w/bottom star, #25	16.00
	Nappy, 5" x 1¾", one hdld., #115	15.00
	Nappy, 5½" x 2", div., hdld., #111	15.00
	Nappy, 5½" x 2", one hdld., heart, #115	22.00
	Nappy, 6" x 1¾", hdld., #111	18.00
	Perfume tray, 8" x 5", #5200	22.00

	Perfume, 5", #5200	85.00
	Pitcher, #5200	150.00
15	Pitcher, 9", 80 oz., ice lip, #5202	175.00
	Plate, 6", #111	9.00
16	Plate, 6", #115, mayonnaise liner	9.00
	Plate, 6", hdld., lemon, #111	12.00
	Plate, 6", sq., #111	12.00
	Plate, 7", #111	14.00

	Item	Price
	Plate, 7½", #111	14.00
	Plate, 7½", #115	14.00
16	Plate, 7½", mayonnaise liner, hdld., #115	12.00
	Plate, 7½", sq., #111	15.00
	Plate, 7½", 2 hdld., #115	15.00
	Plate, 8½", #30	18.00
	Plate, 8½", #111	18.00
	Plate, 8½", #115	18.00
	Plate, 11", #111	36.00
	Plate, 11", 2 hdld., sandwich, #115	26.00
	Plate, 11", hdld., #111	33.00
6	Plate, 11", hdld., cracker w/ring, #115	33.00
	Plate, 11", hdld., cracker w/ring, #111	33.00
	Plate, 11", hdld., sandwich, #111	33.00
	Plate, 11¼", dinner, #115	45.00
3	Plate, 12", egg, #30	110.00
	Plate, 12", torte, rolled edge, #111	30.00
	Plate, 13", torte, flat edge, #111	40.00
	Plate, 13", torte, rolled edge, #111	45.00
	Plate, 13¼", torte, #111	48.00
	Plate, 13½", cake, hdld., #115	38.00
	Plate, 14", #115	38.00
	Plate, 14", cake, #115	38.00
	Plate, 14½", cake, lg. base, #30	38.00
	Plate, 14½", cake, sm. base, #30	42.00
	Relish, 6" x 1¾", hdld., 2 pt., #111	16.00
	Relish, 6" x 1¾", hdld., 2 pt., #115	16.00
	Relish, 8" x 4½", pickle, 2 pt., #115	22.00
	Relish, 8", 3 pt., hdld., #115	22.00
	Relish, 9" x 1½", 2 pt. pickle, #115	22.00
	Relish, 9" x 1½", 3 hdld., 3 pt., #115	28.00
	Relish, 9" x 1½", 3 hdld., flared, #115	28.00
	Relish, 10", 5 pt. tray, #30	50.00
	Relish, 10½" x 1½", hdld., 5 pt., #111	65.00
	Relish, 10½" x 1¼", 2 hdld, 3 pt., #115	55.00
	Relish, 10½" x 7", #115	30.00
	Relish, 11¾", tray, #115	38.00
	Relish, 12", 4 pt., hdld., #111	34.00
14	Relish, 12", 5 pt., hdld., #111	48.00
	Salt and pepper pr., #30	22.00
	Salt and pepper pr., #115	32.00
	Sandwich tray, 12" x 5¼", ctr. handle, #115	65.00
	Saucer, #115	3.00
	Stem, 3¾", 1 oz., cordial, #5111½	40.00
	Stem, 3¾", 4½ oz., oyster cocktail, #5111½	14.00
	Stem, 4", 5 oz., ice cream, #5111½	10.00
	Stem, 4¼", 3 oz., cocktail, #115	14.00
	Stem, 4½", 3½ oz., cocktail, #5111½	14.00
	Stem, 5", 5 oz., saucer champagne, #5111½	14.00
7	Stem, 5¼", 3 oz., wine, #5111½	20.00
	Stem, 5¼", 5 oz., ftd. juice, #5111½	16.00
	Stem, 5¾", 10 oz., low luncheon goblet, #5111½	14.00
	Stem, 6", 4½ oz., claret, #5111½	30.00
	Stem, 6½", 12 oz., ftd. ice tea, #5111½	22.00
	Stem, 6¾", 14 oz., ftd. ice tea, #5111½	22.00
	Stem, cordial, #111	16.00
	Sugar, 2½", individual, #115	12.00
10	Sugar, 3", 7 oz., #115	12.00
1	Sugar, 3", 10 oz., #111	12.00
	Tray, 8" x 2", hdld. celery, #111	14.00
	Tray, 8" x 4¾", individual sugar/cream, #115	14.00
	Tray, 8¾", celery, #91	26.00
	Tray, 11", celery, #91	33.00
	Tumbler, 2", 1½ oz., whiskey, #5200	40.00
	Tumbler, 2½" x 3⅜", sham, Teardrop, ftd.	38.00
	Tumbler, 3", sham #5200	26.00
	Tumbler, 4¾", 10 oz., sham, #5200	28.00
	Tumbler, 5½", 12 oz., sham, #5200	28.00
	Tumbler, 6", 14 oz., sham, #5200	28.00
	Tumbler, 8 oz., flat, #115	22.00
	Urn, 4½" x 4½", #111	22.00
	Urn, 4½" x 4½", #115	22.00
	Urn, 4¾", rnd ft.	22.00
	Urn, 5", #525	32.00
	Urn, 5½", ring hdld., sq. ft.	40.00
	Urn, 5½", sq. ft.	30.00
9	Urn, 7", sq. hdld., #545	55.00
	Urn, 7", #529	30.00
	Vase, 4", flared rim, #115	22.00
	Vase, 4½" x 4¾", #115	24.00
	Vase, 5" x 5", crimped, #115	32.00
	Vase, 6", green, #400	55.00
	Vase, 6", #507	48.00
	Vase, 8" x 4¾", cornucopia, #117	55.00
	Vase, 8", ftd., #506	80.00
	Vase, 8", ftd., #507	80.00
	Vase, 8½" x 2¾", #505	85.00
	Vase, 8½" x 6", #115	80.00
	Vase, 9" x 4½", #505	85.00
	Vase, 9", #509	80.00
	Vase, 9", bud, #506	70.00
	Vase, 9½" x 3½", #506	110.00
	Vase, 10" x 4¾", #5200	75.00
	Vase, 10", #507	80.00
	Vase, 10", ftd., #111	105.00
	Vase, 10", ftd., #505	105.00
	Vase, 10", ftd., #506	105.00
	Vase, 10½" x 12 x 9½", #126	145.00
	Vase, 10½", #126	165.00
	Vase, 11" x 5¼", #505	135.00
	Vase, 11½ x 4½", #506	130.00
	Vase, 12", flared #115	135.00
	Vase, 12", ftd., #506	135.00

FLANDERS, TIFFIN GLASS COMPANY, MID 1910S – MID 1930S

Colors: crystal, pink, yellow, and rare in green

We find that Tiffin's Flanders is often mistakenly displayed as Cambridge's Gloria and vice versa. Look at Gloria on pages 122 – 124 to see its curved stem floral design. In the past, we purchased a rare pink Gloria pitcher at a very reasonable price that was labeled Flanders.

Elegant patterns are being exposed world wide via the internet. This is affecting prices on previously scarce wares as well as illuminating some items we thought rare as being more abundant. More glassware has been assembled into collections through the internet than by any other means in the last few years. However, if you want any Elegant pattern, do not delay gathering it. We don't feel the unexpected internet supply is going to continue perpetually. An additional mode of collecting has been aided by internet buying. People are rarely trying to gather complete sets, but instead are purchasing only items they will immediately use instead of putting it in a cabinet to admire.

Flanders stemware is consistently found on Tiffin's #17024 blank. Usually these are found with a crystal foot and stem with tops of crystal, pink, or yellow. Color blending that is seen occasionally includes green foot with pink stems, and pink tumblers as well as pitchers with crystal handle and foot. A green Flanders vase was unearthed years ago and is pictured on the right. Round plates are Tiffin's line #8800 and each size plate has a different number. Scalloped plates are line #5831. We see more of the round plates than we do the scalloped ones with dinners rarely observed in either shape.

Crystal shakers are found once in a while, but seldom in pink. We have had reports of yellow, but have never seen one. Lamps are found only in crystal. That cylindrical shade is occasionally found over a candlestick and designated as a Chinese hurricane lamp. We have pictured one below.

		Crystal	Pink	Yellow
	Almond, ftd., nut, blown	25.00	50.00	40.00
	Ashtray, 2¼ x 3¾", w/cigarette rest	40.00		
	Bowl, 2 hdld., bouillon	40.00	120.00	75.00
2	Bowl, 2 hdld., cream soup	50.00		
4	Bowl, finger, ftd., 8 oz., #185	30.00	75.00	50.00
	Bowl, 2 hdld., bonbon	25.00	85.00	55.00
	Bowl, 8", ftd., blown	110.00	275.00	

		Crystal	Pink	Yellow
	Bowl, 11", ftd., console	65.00	135.00	75.00
	Bowl, 12", flanged rim, console	60.00	140.00	75.00
19	Candle, 2 styles, #5831 & #15360	35.00	65.00	40.00
	Candy box, w/cover, flat, #329	115.00	295.00	195.00
	Candy jar, w/cover, ftd.	90.00	210.00	175.00
	Celery, 11"	35.00	85.00	50.00

FLANDERS

		Crystal	Pink	Yellow
	Cheese & cracker	50.00	110.00	90.00
	Comport, 3½"	35.00	85.00	55.00
	Comport, 6"	55.00	155.00	85.00
	Creamer, flat	35.00	90.00	65.00
3	Creamer, ftd.	25.00	90.00	45.00
9	Cup, 2 styles, #8869 shown	40.00	90.00	55.00
	Decanter	145.00	295.00	195.00
	Electric lamp w/Chinese style shade	285.00		
22	Grapefruit, w/liner	60.00	155.00	100.00
15	Hurricane lamp, Chinese style	295.00		
	Mayonnaise, w/liner	45.00	110.00	70.00
	Oil bottle & stopper	95.00	250.00	165.00
20	Parfait, 5⅝", hdld.	55.00	135.00	90.00
	Pitcher & cover, 54 oz., #194	250.00	395.00	275.00
11	Plate, 6"	5.00	12.00	8.00
7	Plate, 8", #8833	8.00	16.00	11.00
16	Plate, 10¼", dinner, #8818	40.00	90.00	60.00
	Relish, 3 pt.	50.00	115.00	70.00
	Salt & pepper, pr., #2 (rare)	175.00	395.00	275.00
	Sandwich server, center hdld., octagon, #337		150.00	
9	Saucer, #8869 shown	5.00	10.00	7.00
	Stem, 4½", oyster cocktail	16.00	40.00	20.00
3	Stem, 4½", sherbet/sundae, 6 oz.	14.00	25.00	15.00
6	Stem, 4¾", cocktail, 3½ oz., #15024	17.00	35.00	25.00
	Stem, 5", cordial, 1½ oz., #15024	45.00	95.00	60.00

		Crystal	Pink	Yellow
14	Stem, 5⅝", parfait, cafe, 4½ oz., #15024	30.00	85.00	50.00
	Stem, 6⅛", wine, 3 oz.	25.00	65.00	35.00
	Stem, 6¼", saucer champagne, 6 oz.	14.00	32.00	20.00
	Stem, 7 oz., hdld., parfait		110.00	
18	Stem, claret, 5 oz., #15024	24.00	80.00	50.00
5	Stem, 8¼", water, 9 oz., #15024	24.00	45.00	30.00
	Stem, cordial, #15047	40.00	90.00	65.00
	Stem, sundae/sherbet, low ft., #15047	14.00	33.00	22.00
	Stem, sundae/sherbet, high ft., #15047	16.00	35.00	24.00
	Stem, 9 oz., water, #15047	28.00	45.00	30.00
	Sugar, flat, #6	35.00	90.00	65.00
12	Sugar, ftd., #185	25.00	90.00	45.00
21	Tumbler, 2¾", 2½ oz., ftd., whiskey, #020	28.00	65.00	35.00
8	Tumbler, 4¾", 9 oz., ftd., water	18.00	38.00	20.00
13	Tumbler, 4¾", 10 oz., ftd.	18.00	38.00	20.00
10	Tumbler, 5⅞", 12 oz., ftd., tea, #020	28.00	70.00	30.00
	Tumbler, 12 oz., tea, #14185	24.00	50.00	32.00
17	Tumbler, 12 oz., ftd., tea, #15071	26.00	60.00	32.00
	Vase, bud, 8" or 10", #14185	40.00	110.00	60.00
1	Vase, ftd., 8", #2	65.00	175.00	110.00
	Vase, 10½", Dahlia, cupped, ftd., #151	120.00	225.00	175.00
	Vase, fan, #15151	90.00	225.00	140.00

FONTAINE (FOUNTAIN), WIDE OPTIC, TIFFIN GLASS COMPANY, 1924 – 1931

Colors: crystal w/green, Twilight, Twilight w/crystal, pink, crystal w/amber

Fontaine is a Tiffin pattern that more collectors would love to find, but they rarely have that opportunity. The purple color shown below is Tiffin's earlier Wistaria color that does not change colors when placed under different light sources. Tiffin's later Twilight (1949 to 1980) does change from pink to purple depending upon fluorescent or natural light sources. We are having difficulty finding new Wistaria pieces to picture. We noticed some in a shop recently priced double and triple the normal selling prices and it was only labeled "pretty purple glass."

We have purchased other items including a covered pitcher with green accents. Although Tiffin sold pitchers with or without a lid, we have only seen three Fontaine pitchers in our travels and each has been complete with lids.

A fountain theme was popular and employed by several companies of this era (even on earlier carnival glass). As with other Tiffin etched patterns, cups and saucers are rarely spotted. We bought the set pictured about 20 years ago, before we had even considered this pattern a candidate for the book simply because we realized cups and saucers were hard to find in Tiffin patterns. Have you detected them in any other Fontaine colors?

Fontaine water goblets appear to be easier to find than other stemware. That is just as well, since, today, they are bought to use as wine goblets which more customers seem to want than water goblets.

		Amber Green Pink	Twilight
	Bowl, 8", deep, ftd., #14194	85.00	175.00
	Bowl, 13" ctrpc., #8153	75.00	175.00
	Candlestick, low, #9758	40.00	75.00
	Creamer, stem. ftd., #4	50.00	75.00
4	Cup, #8869	75.00	135.00
	Finger bowl, #022	45.00	85.00
	Grape fruit, #251 & footed liner, #881	65.00	195.00
8	Jug & cover, #194	495.00	1,095.00
	Plate, 6", #8814	10.00	12.00
	Plate, 8", #8833	15.00	24.00
	Plate, 10", #8818	75.00	125.00
	Plate, 10", cake w/ctr. hdld., oct., #345	65.00	150.00
4	Saucer, #8869	10.00	18.00
6	Stem, cafe parfait, #033	60.00	125.00
	Stem, claret, #033	55.00	95.00
	Stem, cocktail, #033	30.00	45.00
3	Stem, cordial, #033	110.00	210.00
9	Stem, saucer champagne, #033	25.00	45.00
2	Stem, sundae, #033	22.00	35.00
1	Stem, water, #033	65.00	90.00
	Stem, wine, 2½ oz., #033	60.00	90.00
	Sugar, ftd., #4	50.00	75.00
5	Tumbler, 9 oz. table, #032	35.00	60.00
7	Tumbler, 12 oz.	40.00	75.00
	Vase, 8" ftd., #2 (shown in Flanders)	95.00	250.00
	Vase, 9¼", bowed top, #7	125.00	250.00

FUCHSIA, ETCH #210, FOSTORIA GLASS COMPANY, C. 1931

Colors: crystal and crystal w/Wisteria base

Fostoria's Fuchsia was added to our book to help distinguish it from other Fuchsia patterns. Be sure to check out Tiffin's Fuchsia on the next page. Many companies made Fuchsia patterns. You need to be aware of this when shopping. Cambridge made Marjorie shown on 154 and 155 which is also a depiction of Fuchsia. Fostoria's Fuchsia pattern is mostly etched on Lafayette mould blank #2244, which can be seen on page 148. Stemware line #6044 was etched with Fuchsia. Notice that champagne with the Wisteria stem. Most of these are found with Lafayette Wisteria tableware that was non-etched. We have encountered more than one set of Lafayette that had Wisteria etched Fuchsia stems integrated with the plain Wisteria cups, saucers, plates, creamers, and sugars.

Over the years, we have met collectors who gather everything Fuchsia, including Fostoria's and Tiffin's as well as Cambridge's Marjorie. One has added a number of pottery designs highlighting Fuchsia as well.

The center surface areas of larger plates are commonly scratched from use. (Stacking due to the flat, ground bottoms can cause marks.) We have encountered dinner plates that were dull looking from all the marks. These will not sell for much in that condition, if at all. Many collectors do put a premium on mint condition and some will not buy any glassware that is not mint.

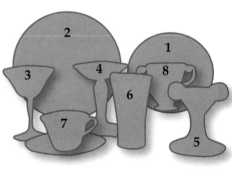

		Crystal	Wisteria
	Bonbon, #2470	30.00	
	Bowl, 10", #2395	75.00	
	Bowl, 10½", #2470½	70.00	
	Bowl 11½", "B," #2440	70.00	
	Bowl, 12" #2470	75.00	165.00
	Candlestick, 3", #2375	20.00	
5	Candlestick, 5", #2395½	25.00	
	Candlestick, 5½", #2470½	40.00	
4	Candlestick, 5½", #2470	40.00	175.00
	Comport, 6", low, #2470	30.00	100.00
	Comport, 6", tall, #2470	45.00	125.00
	Creamer, ftd., #2440	18.00	
7	Cup, #2440	15.00	
	Finger bowl, #869	25.00	
	Lemon dish, #2470	26.00	
	Oyster cocktail, 4½ oz., #6004	12.00	30.00
	Plate, 10", cake	50.00	
	Plate, 6", bread & butter, #2440	6.00	
	Plate, 7", salad, #2440	10.00	
1	Plate, 8", luncheon, #2440	15.00	

		Crystal	Wisteria
2	Plate, 9", dinner, #2440	40.00	
7	Saucer, #2440	4.00	
	Stem, ¾ oz., cordial, #6004	55.00	195.00
	Stem, 2½ oz., wine, #6004	25.00	40.00
	Stem, 3 oz., cocktail, #6004	18.00	40.00
	Stem, 4 oz., claret, #6004	33.00	50.00
	Stem, 5 oz., low sherbet, #6004	15.00	30.00
	Stem, 5½ oz., 6" parfait, #6004	24.00	65.00
3	Stem, 5½ oz., 5⅜", saucer champagne, #6004	18.00	40.00
	Stem, 9 oz., water, #6004	26.00	65.00
8	Sugar, ftd., #2440	18.00	
	Sweetmeat, #2470	24.00	
	Tumbler, 2 oz., #833	20.00	
	Tumbler, 2½ oz., ftd. whiskey, #6004	25.00	65.00
	Tumbler, 5 oz., #833	18.00	
	Tumbler, 5 oz., ftd. juice, #6004	16.00	45.00
	Tumbler, 8 oz., #833	18.00	
	Tumbler, 9 oz., ftd., #6004	14.00	50.00
6	Tumbler, 12 oz., #833	22.00	
	Tumbler, 12 oz., ftd., #6004	25.00	65.00

FUCHSIA, TIFFIN GLASS COMPANY, LATE 1937 – 1940

Colors: crystal; a few experimental Twilight pieces which were never marketed

Be sure to check out Fostoria's Fuchsia pattern listed on the previous page. The designs are similar, but the shapes differ. You need to be aware that pattern names were not exclusive to any particular company. Remember to state which company made the Fuchsia you collect when ordering or inquiring about collectible glassware.

Supplementary pieces of Fuchsia continue to be discovered. Cambridge's Rose Point pattern surfaces etched on almost every line that Cambridge made and Tiffin's Fuchsia seems to have followed this same path. Fuchsia has always attracted collectors; but, right now, price is a factor in slowing those actively pursuing it.

There are many rarely seen pieces in Fuchsia. These include the bitters bottle, icers with inserts, cocktail shaker, salt and pepper shakers, hurricane and electric lamps as well as the tall #17457 stems. The hurricane lamp consists of an etched shade over an etched candle as pictured. We sold the bitters bottle pictured to an avid collector on the West Coast a few years ago, but we were recently informed that it had a serious accident and no longer exists. It was the only one we have documented; so if you have one, it is extra rare now.

As with most Tiffin patterns, cups, saucers, and dinner plates are rarely encountered. There are footed as well as flat finger bowls; and there are three styles of double candlesticks. Today, collectors usually buy only one style candle and many ignore items such as finger bowls and buy only one or two different stems for their sets.

Serving bowls in Fuchsia abound unlike most other Tiffin patterns where serving items come at a premium. The large handled urn vase must have found favor with customers for years as we see that particular vase more than any other Tiffin vase made. We have also seen some amazingly high prices on it which we doubt is warranted. Our selling experience has been that they have a hard time attaining more than $75.00 on a good day.

	Ashtray, 2¼" x 3¾", w/cigarette rest	28.00		Bowl, 8⅜", 2 hdld., #5831	50.00
	Bell, 5", #15083	75.00		Bowl, 9¾", deep salad	60.00
18	Bitters bottle	495.00	20	Bowl, 10", salad, #5831	60.00
5	Bowl, 4", finger, ftd., #041	40.00		Bowl, 10½", console, fan shaped sides, #319	60.00
15	Bowl, 4½" finger, w/#8814 liner	55.00		Bowl, 11⅞", console, flared, #5902	65.00
	Bowl, 5³⁄₁₆", 2 hdld., #5831	25.00	27	Bowl, 12", flanged rim, ftd., console, #5831	55.00
	Bowl, 6¼", cream soup, ftd., #5831	45.00	31	Bowl, 12⅝", console, flared, #5902	65.00
	Bowl, 7¼", salad, #5902	32.00	25	Bowl, 13", crimped, #5902	70.00

FUCHSIA

9	Candlestick, 2-lite, w/pointed center, #5831	50.00
	Candlestick, 2-lite, tapered center, #15306	55.00
24	Candlestick, 5", 2-lite, ball center	55.00
23	Candlestick, 5⅝", 2-lite, w/fan center, #5902	55.00
	Candlestick, single, #348	24.00
	Celery, 10", oval, #5831	30.00
28	Celery, 10½", rectangular, #5902	35.00
	Cigarette box, w/lid, 4" x 2¾", #9305	110.00
	Cocktail shaker, 8", w/metal top	235.00
	Comport, 6¼", #5831	28.00
	Comport, 6½", w/beaded stem, #15082	32.00
	Creamer, 2⅞", individual, #5831	35.00
29	Creamer, 3⅜", flat w/beaded handle, #5902	16.00
26	Creamer, 4½", ftd., #5831	18.00
3	Creamer, pearl edge	26.00
22	Cup, #5831	85.00
	Electric lamp	350.00
11	Hurricane, 12", Chinese style	250.00
6	Icer, with insert	150.00
36	Mayonnaise, flat, w/6¼" liner, #5902 w/ladle	40.00
	Mayonnaise, ftd., w/ladle, #5831	40.00
	Nut dish, 6¼"	38.00
	Pickle, 7⅜", #5831	36.00
	Pitcher & cover, #194	395.00
14	Pitcher, flat	380.00
	Plate, 6¼", bread and butter, #5902	7.00
	Plate, 6¼", sherbet, #8814	8.00
	Plate, 6⅜", 2 hdld., #5831	9.00
8	Plate, 7", marmalade, 3-ftd., #310½	22.00
4	Plate, 7½", salad, #5831	12.00
	Plate, 7⅞", cream soup or mayo liner, #5831	9.00
	Plate, 7⅞", salad, #8814	10.00
	Plate, 8⅛", luncheon, #8833	16.00
	Plate, 8¼", luncheon, #5902	14.00
	Plate, 8⅜", bonbon, pearl edge	20.00
	Plate, 9½", dinner, #5902	60.00
	Plate, 10½", 2 hdld., cake, #5831	55.00
	Plate, 10½", muffin tray, pearl edge	40.00
	Plate, 13", lily rolled and crimped edge	50.00
32	Plate, 14", #5902	50.00
7	Plate, 14¼", sandwich, #8833	50.00
	Relish, 6⅜", 3 pt., #5902	26.00
	Relish, 9¼", sq., 3 pt.	40.00
	Relish, 10½" x 12½", hdld., 3 pt., #5902	40.00
	Relish, 10½" x 12½", hdld., 5 pt.	60.00
1	Salt and pepper, pr., #2	135.00
22	Saucer, #5831	8.00

	Stem, 4¹/₁₆", cordial, #15083	26.00
	Stem, 4⅜", sherbet, #15083	8.00
	Stem, 4¼", cocktail, #15083	10.00
	Stem, 4⅝", 3½ oz., cocktail, #17453	22.00
	Stem, 4⅞", saucer champagne, hollow stem	110.00
	Stem, 5¹/₁₆", wine, #15083	25.00
	Stem, 5¼", claret, #15083	28.00
	Stem, 5⅜", cocktail, "C" stem, #17457	45.00
	Stem, 5⅜", cordial, "C" stem, #17457	110.00
	Stem, 5⅜", 7 oz., saucer champagne, #17453	22.00
	Stem, 5⅜", saucer champagne, #15083	12.00
	Stem, 5⅜", saucer champagne, "C" stem, #17457	35.00
	Stem, 5⅝/₁₆", parfait, #15083	30.00
	Stem, 6¼", low water, #15083	20.00
12	Stem, 7⅜", 9 oz., water, #17453, cupped bowl	30.00
	Stem, 7½", water, high, #15083	22.00
	Stem, 7⅝", water, "C" stem, #17457	65.00
	Sugar, 2⅞", individual, #5831	30.00
30	Sugar, 3⅜", flat, w/beaded handle, #5902	16.00
	Sugar, 4½", ftd., #5831	18.00
2	Sugar, pearl edge	26.00
21	Tray, sugar/creamer, ind.	40.00
	Tray, 9½", 2 hdld. for cream/sugar	30.00
17	Tumbler, 2⁷/₁₆", 2 oz., bar, flat, #506	50.00
19	Tumbler, 3⁵/₁₆", oyster cocktail, #14196	10.00
	Tumbler, 3⅜", old-fashioned, flat, #580	40.00
	Tumbler, 4³/₁₆" flat, juice	30.00
34	Tumbler, 4⁵/₁₆", 5 oz., ftd., juice, #15083	20.00
	Tumbler, 5⅛", water, flat, #517	25.00
35	Tumbler, 5⁵/₁₆", 9 oz., ftd., water, #15083	20.00
33	Tumbler, 6⁵/₁₆", 12 oz., ftd., tea, #15083	26.00
13	Vase, 6½", bud, #14185	26.00
	Vase, 8¹³/₁₆", flared, crimped	110.00
	Vase, 8¼", bud, #14185	32.00
	Vase, 10½", bud, #14185	40.00
	Vase, 10¾", bulbous bottom, #5872	195.00
	Vase, 10⅞", beaded stem, #15082	65.00
10	Vase, 11¾", urn, 2 hdld., trophy.	90.00
16	Whipped cream, 3-ftd., #310	22.00

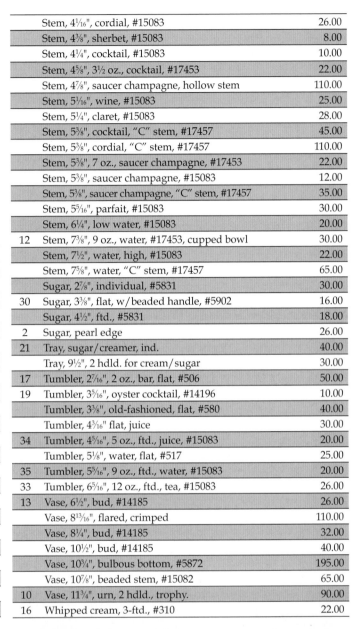

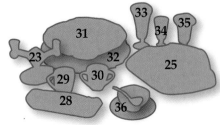

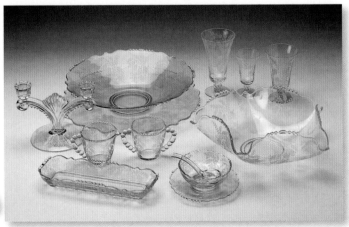

GAZEBO, PADEN CITY GLASS COMPANY, 1930S

Colors: black, blue, crystal, green, red, and yellow

1   1

Gazebo and another Paden City pattern, Utopia, are two like designs, which we are combining for the time being. In the pattern shot of heart candy tops at right, Utopia is on the left and Gazebo on the right. The etchings on Utopia are larger and more detailed than those of Gazebo. Utopia may have been altered from Gazebo for use on larger items or Gazebo scaled back from Utopia. Theory today is just that, as no one knows why the glass companies did most of the things they did. In the panhandle of Florida, we recently encountered a crystal, rolled edge console bowl in Gazebo for $45.00. The coat of dust on it indicated it had been sitting there for quite a while.

The inadequate quantities of Paden City's patterns generate major concerns for collectors today. There is scarcely enough existing to stimulate your enthusiasm. Fortunately, there seems to be an ample supply of crystal Gazebo for the present. Before we added Gazebo to our book, you could find most pieces priced around $45.00, evidently due to size. Most people selling Gazebo had no idea what they had. It was old, elegant, and infrequently priced inexpensively.

Colored Gazebo items are highly desired but rarely found. The blue cheese dish and yellow vases found new homes as soon as they were offered for sale.

Several different Paden City mould lines were used for this etching. All measurements in our listing are taken from actual pieces. We have yet to find a punch bowl to go with our punch cups, although they do exist in crystal.

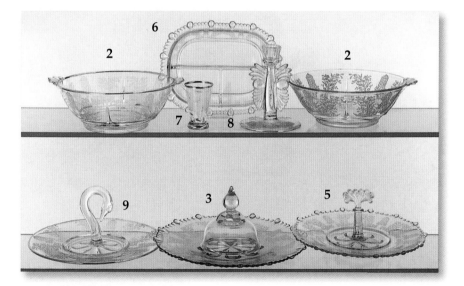

		Crystal	Blue
2	Bowl, 9", fan handles	30.00	
	Bowl, 9", bead handles	30.00	65.00
	Bowl, 13", flat edge	40.00	
	Bowl, 14", low flat	38.00	
	Cake stand	40.00	
8	Candlestick, 5¼"	25.00	
12	Candlestick, double, 2 styles, #555	28.00	48.00
15	Candy dish, flat, clover	65.00	
14	Candy dish, flat, square	65.00	
1	Candy dish w/lid, "heart"	68.00	195.00
4	Candy w/lid, 10¼", small, ftd., #444	55.00	100.00
13	Candy w/lid, 11", large, ftd.	65.00	
3	Cheese dish and cover, #555	75.00	250.00
17	Cocktail shaker, w/glass rooster stopper	110.00	
	Creamer	12.00	

		Crystal	Blue
	Mayonnaise liner	7.00	
	Mayonnaise, bead handles	18.00	
	Plate, 10¾"	28.00	
	Plate, 12½", bead handles	32.00	70.00
	Plate, 13", fan handles	38.00	
	Plate, 16", beaded edge, #555		75.00
6	Relish, 9¾", three part, #555	22.00	50.00
16	Relish, 12", 3-pt., rectangular	60.00	
9	Server, 10", swan handle	35.00	
5	Server, 11", center handle, #555	28.00	60.00
	Sugar	12.00	
7	Tumbler, ftd. juice	12.00	
11	Vase, 10¼"	60.00	395.00*
10	Vase, 12"	65.00	450.00

*Black or yellow

10 11

12

13 4

1

14 15

16

11 17

1

GLACIER, #2510, FOSTORIA GLASS COMPANY, 1935 – 1943

Color: crystal Sunray with Silver Mist ribbing (See page 226 – 227)

	Item	Price		Item	Price
	Ashtray, individual	15.00		Plate, 9½"	20.00
	Ashtray, square	12.00		Plate 11", torte	30.00
	Bowl, 5" fruit	12.00		Plate 12", sandwich	30.00
9	Bowl, 5", hdld., round or square	15.00		Plate, 15", torte	40.00
	Bowl, 5", hdld., triangular	14.00		Plate, 16"	40.00
	Bowl, 10", hdld.	35.00		Relish, 6½", 3-part	27.50
	Bowl, 12", salad	40.00		Relish, 8", 4-part	35.00
	Bowl, 13", rolled edge	40.00		Relish, 10", 2-part	25.00
	Bowl, custard or frozen dessert	12.00		Salt dip	15.00
	Butter w/lid, ¼ lb.	40.00		Saucer	3.00
	Candelabra. 2-lite w/prisms	95.00		Shaker, pr.	35.00
4	Candlestick, 3"	18.00		Stem, 3½", 5½ oz., sherbet	10.00
	Candlestick, 5½"	30.00		Stem, 3¼", 3½", fruit cocktail	11.00
	Candlestick, duo	45.00		Stem, 4⅞", 4½ oz., claret	14.00
	Candy w/lid	65.00		Stem, 5¾", 9 oz., water	15.00
5	Celery, 10", hdld.	30.00		Sugar, ftd.	15.00
	Cigarette & cover	50.00		Sugar, ind., ftd.	15.00
	Comport, 5" w. x 4" h.	30.00		Sweetmeat, 6", divided	22.00
1	Cream soup	20.00		Tray, 6½" for cream/sugar	20.00
	Creamer, ftd.	15.00		Tray, 7", oval hdld.	22.00
	Creamer, ind., ftd.	15.00		Tray, 8½", condiment	50.00
	Cup	10.00		Tray, 10", square	50.00
	Decanter, rectangular	90.00		Tray, 10½", oblong	45.00
2	Ice bucket	60.00		Tumbler, 2¼", 2 oz., whiskey	10.00
	Jelly w/cover, 7¼"	50.00		Tumbler, 3½", 5 oz., juice	12.00
	Mayonnaise, 3-pc. set	42.00		Tumbler, 3½", 6 oz., old-fashion	12.00
	Mustard w/cover and ladle	38.00		Tumbler, 3", 4 oz., ftd. cocktail	12.50
	Oil bottle w/stopper, 3 oz.	45.00		Tumbler, 4⅛", 9 oz., water	10.00
	Onion soup w/cover	50.00	6	Tumbler, 4¾", 9 oz., ftd. water	12.50
8	Pickle, 6"	18.00		Tumbler, 4⅝", 5 oz., ftd. juice	15.00
	Pitcher, 2-quart	75.00		Tumbler, 5¼", 13 oz., ftd. ice tea	15.00
	Plate, 6"	6.00		Tumbler, 5⅛", 13 oz., ice tea	15.00
7	Plate, 6½", hdld.	8.00		Vase, 3½, rose bowl	33.00
	Plate, 7½"	9.00		Vase, 5½, rose bowl	40.00
	Plate, 8½"	10.00	3	Vase, 9", sq. ftd.	50.00

GLORIA, ETCHING 1746, CAMBRIDGE GLASS 3400 LINE DINNERWARE, INTRODUCED 1930

Colors: crystal, Topaz (yellow), Peach-Blo (pink), green, Emerald green (light and dark), amber, blue, Heatherbloom, Ebony with white gold

Cambridge's Gloria pattern is time and again confused with Tiffin's Flanders. Look closely at our photos and notice that the flower on Gloria bends the stem. Both are interpretations of poppies, a flower suggestive of WWI and European poppy fields.

We have tried to illustrate a diversity of colors in our photos here. If you wish to own a set you will have to stick to Topaz (yellow) or crystal as a great variety of pieces were manufactured in those colors. Our experiences have shown yellow Gloria is more available than is crystal; so if you like that color, buy it now when you can. A luncheon set in blue or Peach-Blo (pink) may turn up sporadically, but larger sets appear impossible to pull together. The dark Emerald green really shows off the etched design better than other hues, but it is rarely found.

6

6

Gold encrusted items bring 20% to 25% more than those without gold. However, pieces with worn gold are not easy to sell at present. Gloria might make an ideal candidate for merging colors, since there are so many from which to choose. As with other Cambridge patterns in this book, not all Gloria pieces are listed. A more complete listing of Cambridge etched pieces is found under Rose Point. Prices for crystal Gloria will run 30% to 40% less than the prices listed for Rose Point.

		Crystal	Green Pink Yellow
	Basket, 6", 2 hdld. (sides up)	28.00	45.00
	Bowl, 3", indiv. nut, 4 ftd.	45.00	65.00
	Bowl, 3½", cranberry	30.00	50.00
	Bowl, 5", ftd., crimped edge, bonbon	26.00	40.00
	Bowl, 5", sq., fruit, "saucer"	18.00	30.00
	Bowl, 5½", bonbon, 2 hdld.	22.00	35.00
	Bowl, 5½", bonbon, ftd.	23.00	33.00
	Bowl, 5½", flattened, ftd., bonbon	22.00	33.00
	Bowl, 5½", fruit, "saucer"	18.00	30.00
	Bowl, 6", rnd., cereal	30.00	45.00
	Bowl, 6", sq., cereal	30.00	45.00
	Bowl, 8", 2 pt., 2 hdld., relish	30.00	42.00
	Bowl, 8", 3 pt., 3 hdld., relish	35.00	45.00
	Bowl, 8¾", 2 hdld., figure "8" pickle	28.00	40.00
	Bowl, 8¾", 2 pt., 2 hdld., figure "8" relish	28.00	40.00
	Bowl, 9", salad, tab hdld.	45.00	80.00
	Bowl, 9½", 2 hdld., veg.	60.00	90.00
	Bowl, 10", oblong, tab hdld., "baker"	55.00	90.00
	Bowl, 10", 2 hdld.	45.00	75.00
	Bowl, 11", 2 hdld., fruit	55.00	90.00
12	Bowl, 11", ped. ft., #3400/3	60.00	100.00
	Bowl, 12", 4 ftd., console	55.00	90.00
	Bowl, 12", 4 ftd., flared rim	55.00	90.00
	Bowl, 12", 4 ftd., oval	65.00	120.00
	Bowl, 12", 5 pt., celery & relish	45.00	75.00
	Bowl, 13", flared rim	55.00	95.00
	Bowl, cream soup, w/rnd. liner	38.00	65.00
	Bowl, cream soup, w/sq. liner	38.00	65.00
	Bowl, finger, flared edge, w/rnd. plate	30.00	55.00
	Bowl, finger, ftd.	25.00	45.00
6	Bowl, finger, w/rnd. plate	33.00	55.00

		Crystal	Green Pink Yellow
8	Butter, w/cover, 2 hdld.	160.00	325.00
	Candlestick, 6", ea., keyhole	28.00	48.00
20	Candlelabra, 3 lite, keyhole, #638	30.00	50.00
	Candy box, w/cover, 4 ftd., w/tab hdld.	100.00	175.00
18	Cheese compote w/11½" cracker plate, tab hdld.	50.00	75.00
	Cocktail shaker, ground stopper, spout (like pitcher)	110.00	195.00
	Comport, 4", fruit cocktail	15.00	28.00
	Comport, 5", 4 ftd.	22.00	60.00
	Comport, 6", 4 ftd.	26.00	65.00
	Comport, 7", low	30.00	75.00
	Comport, 7", tall	33.00	100.00
	Comport, 9½", tall, 2 hdld., ftd. bowl	65.00	145.00
9	Creamer, 6 oz., ftd., #3400/16	17.00	25.00
	Creamer, tall, ftd.	18.00	30.00
11	Cup, rnd. or sq.	15.00	25.00
	Cup, 4 ftd., sq.	30.00	60.00
	Cup, after dinner (demitasse), rnd. or sq.	50.00	80.00
	Fruit cocktail, 6 oz., ftd. (3 styles), #3135 shown	12.00	20.00
	Ice pail, metal handle w/tongs, #3400/851	60.00	125.00
	Icer, w/insert	45.00	78.00
	Mayonnaise, w/liner & ladle (4 ftd. bowl)	35.00	75.00
	Oil, w/stopper, 6 oz., tall, ftd., hdld.	85.00	195.00
	Oyster cocktail, #3035, 4½ oz.	15.00	23.00
	Oyster cocktail, 4½ oz., low stem	15.00	23.00
	Pitcher, 64 oz., #935	195.00	295.00
	Pitcher, 67 oz., middle indent	195.00	335.00
16	Pitcher, 80 oz., ball	225.00	395.00
	Pitcher, w/cover, 64 oz.	275.00	595.00
	Plate, 6", 2 hdld.	9.00	15.00

		Crystal	Green Pink Yellow
	Plate, 6", bread/butter	6.00	12.00
19	Plate, 7½", tea, #3400/60	6.00	12.00
	Plate, 8½", salad, #3400/62	12.00	18.00
28	Plate, 9½", dinner	50.00	75.00
	Plate, 10", tab hdld., salad	38.00	55.00
	Plate, 11", 2 hdld.	45.00	65.00
	Plate, 11", sq., ftd. cake	80.00	195.00
25	Plate, 11½", tab hdld., sandwich	55.00	75.00
	Plate, 14", chop or salad	55.00	80.00
	Plate, sq., bread/butter	9.00	13.00

	Crystal	Green Pink Yellow
Plate, sq., dinner	45.00	15.00
Plate, sq., salad	12.00	18.00
Plate, sq., service	35.00	65.00
Platter, 11½"	65.00	140.00
Salt & pepper, pr., short	38.00	75.00
Salt & pepper, pr., w/glass top, tall	60.00	100.00
Salt & pepper, ftd., metal tops	40.00	100.00
Saucer, rnd.	3.00	5.00
Saucer, rnd. after dinner	8.00	15.00
Saucer, sq., after dinner (demitasse)	10.00	18.00
Saucer, sq.	3.00	5.00
Stem, #3035, 2½ oz., wine	23.00	45.00

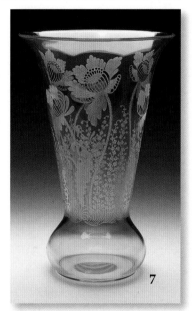

		Crystal	Green Pink Yellow
	Stem, #3035, 3 oz., cocktail	15.00	25.00
	Stem, #3035, 3½ oz., cocktail	15.00	25.00
	Stem, #3035, 4½ oz., claret	30.00	48.00
	Stem, #3035, 6 oz., low sherbet	13.00	18.00
	Stem, #3035, 6 oz., tall sherbet	15.00	22.00
	Stem, #3035, 9 oz., water	23.00	40.00
	Stem, #3035, 3½ oz., cocktail	15.00	25.00
	Stem, #3115, 9 oz., goblet	23.00	40.00
4	Stem, #3120, 1 oz., cordial	45.00	150.00
2	Stem, #3120, 3 oz., cocktail	15.00	25.00
1	Stem, #3120, 4½ oz., claret	30.00	48.00
	Stem, #3120, 6 oz., low sherbet	14.00	18.00
5	Stem, #3120, 6 oz., tall sherbet	15.00	22.00
3	Stem, #3120, 9 oz., water	23.00	40.00
	Stem, #3130, 1 oz., cordial	45.00	150.00
	Stem, #3130, 2½ oz., wine	23.00	40.00
	Stem, #3130, 6 oz., low sherbet	14.00	20.00
21	Stem, #3130, 6 oz., tall sherbet	15.00	22.00
22	Stem, #3130, 8 oz., water	23.00	40.00
	Stem, #3135, 6 oz., low sherbet	14.00	18.00
	Stem, #3135, 6 oz., tall sherbet	15.00	20.00
	Stem, #3135, 8 oz., water	23.00	40.00
10	Sugar, ftd., #3400/16	17.00	25.00
	Sugar, tall, ftd.	18.00	30.00
	Sugar shaker, w/glass top	185.00	295.00
	Syrup, tall, ftd.	75.00	160.00
	Tray, 11", ctr. hdld., sandwich	32.00	50.00
	Tray, 2 pt., ctr. hdld., relish	25.00	40.00
	Tray, 4 pt., ctr. hdld., relish	30.00	50.00
	Tray, 9", pickle, tab hdld.	30.00	60.00
	Tumbler, #3035, 5 oz., high ftd.	15.00	25.00

		Crystal	Green Pink Yellow
	Tumbler, #3035, 10 oz., high ftd.	18.00	33.00
15	Tumbler, #3035, 12 oz., high ftd.	23.00	40.00
	Tumbler, #3115, 5 oz., ftd., juice	18.00	30.00
	Tumbler, #3115, 8 oz., ftd.	18.00	30.00
	Tumbler, #3115, 10 oz., ftd.	20.00	32.00
	Tumbler, #3115, 12 oz., ftd.	24.00	35.00
23	Tumbler, #3120, 2½ oz., ftd. (used w/ cocktail shaker), flat, #1070	25.00	50.00
	Tumbler, #3120, 5 oz., ftd.	18.00	28.00
	Tumbler, #3120, 10 oz., ftd.	20.00	32.00
17	Tumbler, #3120, 12 oz., ftd.	23.00	38.00
26	Tumbler, #3130, 5 oz., ftd.	18.00	30.00
14	Tumbler, #3130, 10 oz., ftd.	22.00	38.00
27	Tumbler, #3130, 12 oz., ftd.	24.00	38.00
	Tumbler, #3135, 5 oz., juice	18.00	30.00
	Tumbler, #3135, 10 oz., water	20.00	32.00
	Tumbler, #3135, 12 oz., tea	24.00	40.00
	Tumbler, 12 oz., flat (2 styles), one indent side to match 67 oz. pitcher	25.00	45.00
13	Tumbler, #3120, 2 oz., whiskey, #3400/92	26.00	50.00
24	Vase, 6", #1308	50.00	75.00
	Vase, 9", oval, 4 indent	115.00	195.00
	Vase, 10", keyhole base	85.00	150.00
	Vase, 10", squarish top	140.00	295.00
	Vase, 11"	110.00	195.00
	Vase, 11", neck indent	135.00	210.00
7	Vase, 12", #407	150.00	250.00
	Vase, 12", keyhole base, flared rim	150.00	250.00
	Vase, 12", squarish top	195.00	325.00
	Vase, 14", keyhole base, flared rim	165.00	240.00

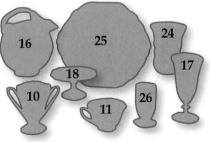

GOLF BALL, #7643, MORGANTOWN GLASS WORKS, LATE 1920S – EARLY 1930S

Colors: crystal, Spanish Red, Ritz Blue, Stiegel Green, 14K Topaz, Anna Rose, Old Amethyst, India Black, Venetian (shamrock) Green, Azure blue, Aquamarine, Peach, Caramel, Meadow Green, Copen Blue, Smoke, light Amethyst, Mission Gold, Milk

Morgantown's Golf Ball pattern is the most recognized and collected design of this company. It is often confused with Cambridge's line #1066, which is similar to Golf Ball at first glance; Cambridge's #1066 has cut indentations at intervals around the ball portion of the stem. Morgantown's Golf Ball has symmetrical bumps spread over the surface of the ball of the stem. Candles in #1066 are not nearly as pricey as those of Golf Ball.

As a general rule, pieces of Golf Ball are hard to find except for stems and most vases. Prices for stems have drifted from earlier levels due both to quantities found and proliferation of stems in collections. The Dupont (inverted two tiers) candle is not easily found. You should note the Irish coffee (second from right in Ritz blue row on page 126). This item became a creamer when a spout was added. The sugar is handleless.

The Harlequin pastel colors, often marketed in sets of eight, are Amethyst, Copen Blue, Gloria Blue, Peach, Smoke, Topaz Mist, Shamrock Green, and Iridized Yellow. Some are illustrated in the row above the Ritz blue on page 126. Some Harlequin sets included Coral and Pink Champagne colors.

Note the three Spanish red stems in the middle of the next page. The cocktail is first, followed by the champagne; the third item is a rarely seen grapefruit. We have only been able to find two collectors who own grapefruits. One has eight and the other only had one.

To be consistent in terminology for collectors, our listings have used name designations found in Gallagher's *Handbook of Old Morgantown Glass* that unfortunately is no longer in print.

		Spanish Red *Ritz Blue	Other Colors
	Amherst water lamp, super rare	1,000.00+	
	Bell	100.00	50.00
	Candle, pr., 4⅝", Dupont (inverted 2 tier)	175.00	90.00
	Candle, 6" torch	135.00	75.00
3	Candlestick, 4" Jacobi (top flat rim)	100.00	60.00
	Candy, flat w/golf ball knob cover, 6"x 5½" (Alexandra)	1,000.00	750.00
	Creamer	150.00	
	Compote, 10" diam., 7½" high, w/14 crimp rim (Truman)	395.00	295.00
	Compote w/cover, 6" diam. (Celeste)	750.00	550.00
2	Compote, 6" diam. (Celeste)	395.00	250.00
16	Irish coffee, 5¼", 6 oz.	150.00	100.00
	Pilsner, 9⅛", 11 oz.	130.00	80.00
	Schooner, 8½", 32 oz.	295.00	195.00

		Spanish Red *Ritz Blue	Other Colors
	Stem, brandy snifter, 6½", 21 oz.	125.00	100.00
13	Stem, cafe parfait, 6¼", 4 oz.	75.00	45.00
11	Stem, champagne, 5", 5½ oz.	15.00	10.00
10	Stem, champagne, "Old English"	20.00	14.00
	Stem, claret, 5¼", 4½ oz.	35.00	20.00
8	Stem, cocktail, 4⅛"	12.00	10.00
6	Stem, cordial, 3½", 1½ oz.	30.00	20.00
17	Stem, grapefruit, 4¼", 9 oz.	85.00	
	Stem, oyster cocktail, 4⅜", 4½ oz.	30.00	18.00
	Stem, oyster cocktail, 4¼", 4 oz., flared	26.00	16.00
	Stem, sherbet/sundae, 4⅛", 3½ oz.	12.00	9.00
	Stem, sherry, 4⅝", 2½ oz.	30.00	20.00
9	Stem, water, 6¾", 9 oz.	25.00	15.00
7	Stem, water, 10 oz., "Old English"	24.00	14.00
14	Stem, wine, 4¾", 3 oz.	22.00	15.00
	Sugar, no handles, cone	150.00	
20	Tumbler, 4⅜", ftd., wine	20.00	12.00
15	Tumbler, 5", 5 oz., ftd., juice	20.00	12.00
4	Tumbler, 6⅛", 9 oz., ftd., water	25.00	14.00
5	Tumbler, 6¾", 12 oz., ftd., tea	30.00	20.00
19	Urn, 6½" high	75.00	50.00
	Vase, 4", Ivy ball, ruffled top	300.00	150.00
12	Vase, 4", Ivy ball w/rim (Kimball)	48.00	32.00
18	Vase, 4", Ivy ball, no rim (Kennon)	45.00	30.00
	Vase, 8" high, Charlotte w/crimped rim	225.00	145.00
1	Vase, 8" high, flair rim flute (Charlotte)	175.00	125.00
	Vase, 10½", #78 Lancaster (cupped w/tiny stand up rim)	425.00	250.00
	Vase, 11", #79 Montague (flair rim)	450.00	300.00

*Add 10% for Ritz Blue.

GREEK KEY, PATTERN #433, A. H. HEISEY & CO., 1912 – 1930S

Colors: crystal; Flamingo pink punch bowl and cups only

Greek Key is an older Heisey pattern that is loved and easily recognized as most pieces are marked with that familiar diamond within an H. Other companies made similar patterns, but Heisey's is the celebrity in the collecting field. Stemware in all sizes is taxing to find and the prices signify that.

1

	Bowl, finger	40.00
	Bowl, jelly, w/cover, 2 hdld., ftd.	145.00
26	Bowl, indiv., ftd., almond	22.00
10	Bowl, 4", nappy	25.00
	Bowl, 4", shallow, low ft., jelly	40.00
	Bowl, 4½", nappy	25.00
	Bowl, 4½", scalloped, nappy	25.00
	Bowl, 4½", shallow, low ft., jelly	40.00
	Bowl, 5", ftd., almond	40.00
	Bowl, 5", ftd., almond, w/cover	110.00
7	Bowl, 5", hdld., jelly	65.00
	Bowl, 5", low ft., jelly, w/cover	75.00
	Bowl, 5", nappy	30.00
	Bowl, 5½", nappy	40.00
	Bowl, 5½", shallow nappy, ftd.	65.00
	Bowl, 6", nappy	30.00
	Bowl, 6", shallow nappy	30.00
	Bowl, 6½", nappy	35.00
	Bowl, 7", low ft., straight side	90.00
	Bowl, 7", nappy	80.00
	Bowl, 8", low ft., straight side	70.00
	Bowl, 8", nappy	70.00
	Bowl, 8", scalloped nappy	65.00
	Bowl, 8", shallow, low ft.	75.00
	Bowl, 8½", shallow nappy	75.00
	Bowl, 9", flat, banana split	45.00
11	Bowl, 9", ftd., banana split	40.00
	Bowl, 9", low ft., straight side	65.00
9	Bowl, 9", nappy	70.00
	Bowl, 9", shallow, low ft.	70.00
	Bowl, 9½", shallow nappy	70.00
	Bowl, 10", shallow, low ft.	85.00
	Bowl, 11", shallow nappy	70.00
	Bowl, 12", orange bowl	500.00
	Bowl, 12", punch, ftd., Flamingo	750.00
	Bowl, 12", orange, flared rim	450.00
	Bowl, 14½", orange, flared rim	500.00
	Bowl, 15", punch, ftd.	400.00
	Bowl, 18", punch, shallow	400.00
	Butter, individual (plate)	35.00
	Butter/jelly, 2 hdld., w/cover	200.00
6	Candy, w/cover, ½ lb.	140.00
	Candy, w/cover, 1 lb.	170.00
	Candy, w/cover, 2 lb.	210.00
16	Cheese & cracker set, 10"	175.00
	Compote, 5"	75.00
	Compote, 5", w/cover	130.00
	Creamer	50.00
	Creamer, oval, hotel	45.00
	Creamer, rnd., hotel	40.00

12	Cup, 4½" oz., punch	18.00
	Cup, punch, Flamingo	40.00
	Coaster	20.00
	Egg cup, 5 oz.	80.00
	Hair receiver	170.00
	Ice tub, lg., tab hdld.	150.00
15	Ice tub, sm., tab hdld.	130.00
	Ice tub, w/cover, hotel	225.00
13	Ice tub, w/cover, 5", individual, w/5" plate	200.00
	Jar, 1 qt., crushed fruit, w/cover	400.00
3	Jar, 2 qt., crushed fruit, w/cover	450.00
	Jar, cherry + cover	125.00
	Jar, lg. cover, horseradish	140.00
4	Jar, sm. cover, horseradish	130.00
	Jar, w/knob cover, pickle	160.00
	Oil bottle, 2 oz., squat, w/#8 stopper	90.00
	Oil bottle, 2 oz., w/#6 stopper	100.00
24	Oil bottle, 4 oz., squat, w/#8 stopper	90.00
20	Oil bottle, 4 oz., w/#6 stopper	80.00
21	Oil bottle, 6 oz., w/#6 stopper	80.00
	Oil bottle, 6 oz., squat, w/#8 stopper	80.00
	Pitcher, 1 pint (jug)	130.00
	Pitcher, 1 quart (jug)	180.00
	Pitcher, 3 pint (jug)	200.00
	Pitcher, ½ gal. (tankard)	240.00
	Plate, 4½"	15.00
	Plate, 5"	18.00
	Plate, 5½"	20.00
	Plate, 6"	30.00
	Plate, 6½"	30.00
	Plate, 7"	45.00
	Plate, 8"	60.00
	Plate, 9"	90.00
	Plate, 10"	110.00
	Plate, 16", orange bowl liner	180.00
	Puff box, #1, w/cover	175.00
	Puff box, #3, w/cover	175.00
	Salt & pepper, pr.	135.00
2	Sherbet, 4½ oz., ftd., straight rim	20.00
8	Sherbet, 4½ oz., ftd., flared rim	20.00
	Sherbet, 4½ oz., high ft., shallow	20.00
	Sherbet, 4½ oz., ftd., shallow	20.00
	Sherbet, 4½ oz., ftd., cupped rim	20.00
	Sherbet, 6 oz., low ft.	20.00
	Spooner, lg.	110.00

	Spooner, 4½" (or straw jar)	110.00
	Stem, ¾ oz., cordial	225.00
	Stem, 2 oz., wine	100.00
	Stem, 2 oz., sherry	200.00
	Stem, 3 oz., cocktail	35.00
	Stem, 3½ oz., burgundy	125.00
	Stem, 4½ oz., saucer champagne	40.00
	Stem, 4½ oz., claret	140.00
	Stem, 7 oz., goblet	95.00
	Stem, 9 oz., goblet	160.00
	Stem, 9 oz., low ft., goblet	145.00
5	Straw jar, w/cover	425.00
	Sugar	50.00
	Sugar, oval, hotel	45.00
14	Sugar, rnd., hotel, and cover	40.00
	Sugar & creamer, oval, individual	90.00
25	Tray, 9", oval celery	50.00
23	Tray, 12", oval celery	60.00

22	Tray, 12½", French roll	150.00
	Tray, 13", oblong	260.00
	Tray, 15", oblong	300.00
	Tumbler, 2½ oz. (or toothpick)	900.00
	Tumbler, 5 oz., flared rim	50.00
	Tumbler, 5 oz., straight side	50.00
	Tumbler, 5½ oz., water	50.00
	Tumbler, 7 oz., flared rim	60.00
	Tumbler, 7 oz., straight side	60.00
	Tumbler, 8 oz., w/straight, flared, cupped, shallow	60.00
	Tumbler, 10 oz., flared rim	90.00
	Tumbler, 10 oz., straight wide	90.00
	Tumbler, 12 oz., flared rim	100.00
	Tumbler, 12 oz., straight side	100.00
	Tumbler, 13 oz., straight side	100.00
	Tumbler, 13 oz., flared rim	100.00
	Water bottle	220.00
1	Whimsey (vase)	165.00

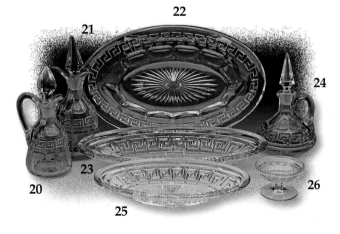

"HARDING," NO. 401 DEEP PLATE ETCH OPTIC, CENTRAL GLASS WORKS, PAT. JUNE 1, 1920

Colors: amber, amethyst, green, pink, crystal, crystal with black, gold, and green trim

Central's No. 401 etch was given the name "Harding" when President and Mrs. Harding chose this exclusive "Dragon" design set for use at the White House. That set of over 300 pieces was etched with gold, and we assume it was gold on crystal. We have never seen Harding decorated in gold. Afterward, Central advertised it as glass "for America's first families."

Few pieces are being advertised or displayed at present. It has taken us nine years to accumulate the pieces of "Harding" pictured here. We did see a few other pieces, but the price being asked became a hindrance to owning them. In any case, these few pieces should give you a clue of scarcity. You must remember, though, we are discussing nearly 90 year old glassware which nobody dreamed would have intrinsic value all these years later. It was used, broken, given or thrown away, and replaced by something more up-to-the-minute. It had to be easy on the pocket at that time. The traditional viewpoint was that china had value, but glass dishes were disposable.

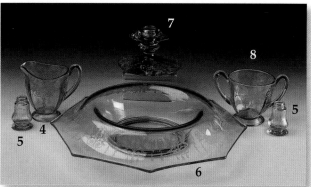

		*All Colors
6	Bowl, 12", console, octagon	60.00
	Bowl, finger, #800	25.00
	Bowl, soup, flat	40.00
	Bowl, soup, 2 hdld. cream	30.00
7	Candlestick, octagon collar	30.00
11	Candlestick, rnd. collar	28.00
	Candy, ftd. cone w/etched lid	100.00
	Cheese & cracker	35.00
2	Comport, 4½", short stem	35.00
	Comport, 6", short stem	35.00
	Comport, 6", 10 oz., tall stem	45.00
4	Creamer, ftd.	22.00
	Cup, handled custard	15.00
	Decanter, qt., w/cut stop	250.00
	Ice tub, 2 hdld.	350.00
1	Jug, tall, flat bottom	300.00
	Oil & vinegar bottle	145.00
	Plate, 5" sherbet	6.00
	Plate, 6" finger bowl liner	8.00
3	Plate, dinner	50.00

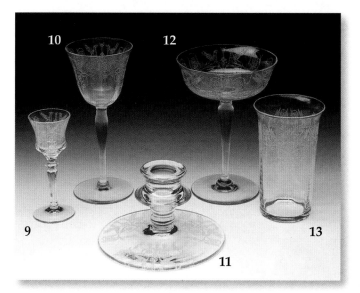

		*All Colors
	Plate, lunch	18.00
	Server, center handle	35.00
5	Shaker, ftd. individual	85.00
	Stem style, individual, almond	22.00
	Stem, 5½ oz. sherbet	12.00
12	Stem, 6 oz., saucer champagne, #780	15.00
	Stem, 9 oz., water, #780	20.00
9	Stem, cordial	50.00
	Stem, oyster cocktail	12.00
10	Stem, wine	18.00
8	Sugar, ftd.	22.00
	Tumbler, 5 oz	16.00
	Tumbler, 8 oz.	18.00
	Tumbler, 10 oz., #530	22.00
13	Tumbler, 12 oz.	24.00
	Tumbler, ftd., hdld., tea	30.00
	Vase, 8"	150.00
	Vase, 10", ruffled top	195.00

* 25% less for crystal

HERMITAGE, #2449, FOSTORIA GLASS COMPANY, 1932 – 1945

Colors: Amber, Azure (blue), crystal, Ebony, green, Topaz, Wisteria

Hermitage presently is admired by a small number of collectors; however, a few of those are beginning to set their sights on Wisteria. Other Fostoria patterns in Wisteria are being priced somewhat lavishly. Hermitage prices are reasonably priced at the moment, so if you like the Wisteria color now is the time to start while it can be found.

Our listings are derived from a Fostoria catalog that had January 1, 1933, entered on the front page in pencil. Be sure to note the stacking ashtrays in holder on page 131. Fostoria took advantage of the colors being made for that set.

		Crystal	Amber, Green Topaz	Azure	Wisteria
23	Ashtray holder, #2449	4.00	6.00	10.00	
24	Ashtray, #2449*	3.00	5.00	8.00	
5	Bottle, 3 oz., oil, #2449	15.00	32.00		
	Bottle, 27 oz., bar w/stopper, #2449	35.00			
16	Bowl, 4½", finger, #2449½	3.00	6.00	10.00	15.00
	Bowl, 5", fruit, #2449½	4.00	7.00	12.00	
	Bowl, 6", cereal, #2449½	5.00	8.00	15.00	
	Bowl, 6½", salad, #2449½	5.00	8.00	15.00	
15	Bowl, 7", soup, #2449½	6.00	10.00	20.00	32.00
	Bowl, 7½", salad, #2449½	6.00	12.00	24.00	
	Bowl, 8", deep, pedestal, ft., #2449	15.00	30.00	50.00	
1	Bowl, 10", ftd., #2449	18.00	30.00		75.00
	Bowl, grapefruit, w/crystal liner, #2449	18.00	28.00		
	Candle, 6", #2449	11.00	16.00	28.00	
	Coaster, 5⅝", #2449	4.00	6.00	9.00	
6	Comport, 6", #2449	10.00	15.00	22.00	30.00
	Creamer, ftd., #2449	3.00	5.00	10.00	20.00
	Cup, ftd., #2449	5.00	8.00	12.00	15.00
19	Decanter, 28 oz., w/stopper, #2449	35.00	60.00	110.00	
7	Fruit cocktail, 2⅜", 5 oz., ftd., #2449	4.00	6.00	10.00	
3	Ice tub, 6", #2449	15.00	40.00	65.00	150.00
10	Icer, w/insert, #2449	15.00	30.00	45.00	15.00
	Mayonnaise, 5⅝" w/7" plate, #2449	18.00	30.00		
18	Mug, 9 oz., ftd., #2449	12.00			
	Mug, 12 oz., ftd., #2449	15.00			
	Mustard w/cover & spoon, #2449	15.00	30.00		
	Pitcher, pint, #2449	20.00	32.00	50.00	
2	Pitcher, 3 pint, #2449	45.00	70.00	110.00	300.00
	Plate, 6", #2449½	2.00	4.00	6.00	
	Plate, 7", ice dish liner	2.00	4.00	6.00	12.00
	Plate, 7", #2449½	4.00	6.00	10.00	
	Plate, 7⅜", crescent salad, #2449	8.00	14.00	25.00	50.00
21	Plate, 8", #2449½	5.00	8.00	12.00	15.00
	Plate, 9", #2449½	10.00	16.00	24.00	
	Plate, 12", sandwich, #2449		12.50	20.00	
	Relish, 6", 2 pt., #2449	5.00	10.00	14.00	18.00
14	Relish, 7¼", 3 pt., #2449	7.00	11.00	16.00	35.00
	Relish, 8", pickle, #2449	7.00	11.00	16.00	
11	Relish, 11", celery, #2449	9.00	14.00	22.00	36.00

* Ebony – $15.00

		Crystal	Amber, Green Topaz	Azure	Wisteria
8	Salt & pepper, 3⅜", #2449	15.00	30.00	50.00	70.00
	Salt, individual, #2449	3.00	5.00	9.00	
	Saucer, #2449	1.00	2.50	4.00	4.00
23	Sherbet, 3", 7 oz., low, ftd., #2449	4.00	6.00	10.00	12.00
	Stem, 3¼", 5½ oz., high sherbet, #2449	6.00	9.00	15.00	15.00
	Stem, 4⅝", 4 oz., claret, #2449	8.00	14.00		
22	Stem, 5¼", 9 oz., water goblet, #2449	8.00	14.00	18.00	20.00
4	Sugar, ftd., #2449	3.00	5.00	10.00	20.00
	Tray, 6½", condiment, #2449	6.00	10.00	18.00	20.00
12	Tumbler, 2½", 2 oz., #2449½	6.00	9.00	18.00	28.00
	Tumbler, 2½", 2 oz., ftd., #2449	5.00	9.00		
9	Tumbler, 3", 4 oz., cocktail, ftd., #2449	4.00	7.00	11.00	15.00
13	Tumbler, 3¼", 6 oz. old-fashion, #2449½	5.00	8.00	12.00	20.00
	Tumbler, 3⅞", 5 oz., #2449½	4.00	7.00	11.00	18.00
	Tumbler, 4", 5 oz., ftd., #2449	4.00	7.00	11.00	18.00
20	Tumbler, 4⅛", 9 oz., ftd., #2449	5.00	9.00	12.00	20.00
17	Tumbler, 4¾", 9 oz., #2449½	5.00	9.00	12.00	22.00
	Tumbler, 5¼", 12 oz., ftd., iced tea, #2449	8.00	14.00	20.00	
	Tumbler, 5⅞", 13 oz., #2449½	8.00	14.00	20.00	30.00
	Vase, 6", ftd.	18.00	30.00		

IMPERIAL HUNT SCENE, #718, CAMBRIDGE GLASS COMPANY, LATE 1920S – 1930S

Colors: amber, black, crystal, Emerald green, Peach Blo, Willow blue

Internet auctions have influenced prices on Imperial Hunt Scene. A few years ago a piece would fetch a tidy sum due to several bidders wanting it, and now the same item will receive few bids since those collectors wanting to own every piece do or have decided to be more frugal in today's market. That makes for interesting buying and selling as well as our pricing for this book.

In selling Cambridge the last two years, we noticed gold encrusted Imperial Hunt Scene sold first and well. Other pieces did sell, except crystal that we still own.

Collectors have a tendency to stalk glassware that portrays animals, in particular horses. On Imperial Hunt Scene, you get the bonus benefit of a fox. Cups, saucers, sugars, and shakers have always been scarce. Today, owning those does not seem to be as much a detriment as in the past. Most collectors are not trying to own everything made for a set.

Has anyone found a pink creamer to match the sugar and lid we have pictured previously? None of the Cambridge catalogs we own illustrate either a sugar or creamer with this etching, but we'd be highly shocked if they made a sugar without a creamer.

Stems are abundant in most sizes with the exception of cordials and clarets. There are cordial collectors to diminish that small supply, but demand for clarets is way down in all patterns. Stemware is plentiful contrasted to serving pieces rather than plentiful in comparison to other patterns. We did not allege economically priced! You may find bi-colored Hunt Scene stemware. A pink bowl with a green stem or foot is the typical form — as illustrated by the jug below.

Ebony and Emerald green (light or dark) with gold encrustations retail 25% to 50% higher than prices listed should you come across those.

		Crystal	Colors
	Bowl, 6", cereal	18.00	35.00
	Bowl, 8"	35.00	75.00
	Bowl, 8½", 3 pt.	40.00	80.00
	Candlestick, 2-lite, keyhole	28.00	50.00
	Candle 3-lite, keyhole, #638	33.00	70.00
	Comport, 5½", #3085		50.00
	Creamer, flat	15.00	50.00
	Creamer, ftd.	20.00	60.00
16	Cup, #933/481	25.00	50.00
5	Decanter		250.00
6	Finger bowl, w/plate, #3085		60.00
	Humidor, tobacco		495.00
15	Ice bucket, #851 scallop edge	85.00	150.00
	Ice bucket, #2978 plain edge	80.00	150.00
	Ice tub	50.00	125.00
	Mayonnaise, w/liner	35.00	75.00
11	Pitcher, w/cover, 63 oz., #3085		395.00
	Pitcher, w/cover, 76 oz., #711	175.00	350.00

		Crystal	Colors
	Plate, 6", #668	8.00	12.00
	Plate, 7", #554	10.00	15.00
	Plate, 8", #556	12.00	16.00
19	Plate, 8½", #559	14.00	20.00
	Plate, 9½", #810	22.00	45.00
	Plate, 10½", #244	25.00	40.00
	Salt & pepper, pr., #396	100.00	250.00
16	Saucer, #1481	6.00	10.00
	Stem, 1 oz., cordial, #1402	50.00	
	Stem, 2½ oz., wine, #1402	40.00	
	Stem, 3 oz., cocktail, #1402	30.00	
13	Stem, 6 oz., tomato, #1402	25.00	
	Stem, 6½ oz., sherbet, #1402	22.00	
	Stem, 7½ oz., sherbet, #1402	25.00	
14	Stem, 10 oz., water, #1402	30.00	
	Stem, 14 oz., #1402	35.00	
	Stem, 18 oz., #1402	45.00	
	Stem, 1 oz., cordial, #3075		125.00
7	Stem, 2½ oz., cocktail, #3075		35.00
21	Stem, 2½ oz., wine, #3085*		40.00
20	Stem, 4½ oz., claret, #3075		45.00
	Stem, 5½ oz., parfait, #3085		60.00
10	Stem, 6 oz., low sherbet, #3085		20.00
18	Stem, 6 oz., high sherbet, #3075		28.00
2	Stem, 9 oz., water, #3085		48.00
	Sugar, flat w/lid, #842	40.00	125.00
	Sugar, ftd.	18.00	60.00
	Tumbler, 2½ oz., 2⅞", flat, #1402	18.00	
3	Tumbler, 5 oz., flat, #3085	16.00	
	Tumbler, 7 oz., flat, #1402	16.00	
4	Tumbler, 10 oz., flat, #3075, cupped rim	18.00	
1	Tumbler, 10 oz., flat, tall, #1402	20.00	
12	Tumbler, 15 oz., flat, #1402	25.00	
	Tumbler, 2½ oz., ftd., #3085		45.00
17	Tumbler, 5 oz., 3⅞", ftd., #3085 (cone w/flare rim)		35.00
8	Tumbler, 8 oz., ftd., #3085		35.00
	Tumbler, 10 oz., ftd., #3075 (cone w/cupped rim)		40.00
9	Tumbler, 12 oz., 5⅜", ftd., #3075		40.00

* with bicolor add 50%

IPSWICH, BLANK #1405, A. H. HEISEY & CO., 1931 – LATE 1940S

Colors: crystal, Flamingo pink, Sahara yellow, Moongleam green, cobalt, and Alexandrite

We cannot stress enough that if you see any colored piece of Ipswich, other than colors listed above, it was produced at the Imperial factory and not Heisey. It may even be marked Heisey, but it was created at Imperial from purchased Heisey moulds after Heisey closed and is ignored at this point by serious Heisey collectors. Mostly, we get letters on Alexandrite candy jars that are actually Imperial's Heather (purple) color. Imperial is now out of business; their wares are collectible; but, so far, not the Heisey patterns Imperial made in other colors. That, of course, could change.

Moongleam (green) is preferred by collectors of Ipswich. Note the lack of a vase atop the cobalt candlestick at right. That is harder to find today than the candles.

		Crystal	Flamingo	Sahara	Moongleam	Cobalt	Alexandrite
	Bowl, finger, w/underplate	40.00	80.00	70.00	100.00		
2	Bowl, 11", ftd., floral	70.00		200.00	600.00	350.00	
	Candlestick, 6", 1-lite	150.00	275.00	200.00	300.00	400.00	
1	Candlestick centerpiece, ftd., vase, "A" prisms, complete w/inserts	160.00	300.00	350.00	450.00	550.00	
	Candy jar, ¼ lb., w/cover	175.00			450.00		
	Candy jar, ½ lb., w/cover	175.00	325.00	400.00	500.00		
	Cocktail shaker, 1 quart, strainer, #86 stopper	225.00	600.00	700.00	800.00		
4	Creamer	35.00	70.00	90.00	100.00		
	Oil bottle, 2 oz., ftd., #86 stopper	125.00	285.00	275.00	300.00		
	Pitcher, ½ gal.	350.00	600.00	550.00	950.00		
	Plate, 7", sq.	30.00	60.00	50.00	70.00		
	Plate, 8", sq.	35.00	65.00	55.00	75.00		
	Sherbet, 4 oz., ftd. (knob in stem)	5.00	35.00	30.00	65.00		
	Stem, 4 oz., oyster cocktail, ftd.	25.00	60.00	30.00	70.00		
	Stem, 5 oz., saucer champagne (knob in stem)	25.00	60.00	50.00	70.00		
	Stem, 10 oz., goblet (knob in stem)	35.00	70.00	60.00	150.00		750.00
	Stem, 12 oz., schoppen, flat bottom	100.00					
3	Sugar	35.00	70.00	90.00	100.00		
	Tumbler, 5 oz., ftd. (soda)	30.00	45.00	40.00	85.00		
5	Tumbler, 8 oz.	45.00	95.00	95.00	175.00		
	Tumbler, 8 oz., ftd. (soda)	30.00	40.00	40.00	100.00		
	Tumbler, 10 oz., cupped rim, flat bottom	70.00	110.00	100.00	140.00		
	Tumbler, 10 oz., straight rim, flat bottom	70.00	110.00	100.00	140.00		
2	Tumbler, 12 oz., ftd. (soda)	40.00	80.00	70.00	95.00		

JANICE, LINE 4500, NEW MARTINSVILLE GLASS CO., 1926 – 1944; VIKING GLASS CO., 1944 – 1970; DALZELL VIKING GLASS CO., 1996

Colors: crystal, Cobalt, Ruby, light Blue, Emerald, Amethyst

Janice once had a crowd of collectors seeking blue or Ruby; but recently that has thinned somewhat. Although a few pieces were made in cobalt, it is the light blue that can be gathered as a set. Few seek crystal and those who do are deterred when a desired piece is uncovered with an etching rather than without one.

We informed you that Dalzell Viking had remade both single candlesticks pictured in blue. These were redone in crystal, cobalt blue, and red. As much as we can verify, the light blue was not redone; but be circumspect of paying high prices for other colors. They were using original New Martinsville moulds so the only significant difference is that the newer ones are slightly heavier and not as fire polished as the old. The reissued ones have a greasy, oily feel, as does most recently made glass. If price stickers are sliding off or stuck on with tape, be extra suspicious as to age.

Ice buckets are rare in Janice, but you couldn't prove it from our photo. The glass handled one that looks like a basket rather than a bucket is exceptional. That the glass handle is still attached all these years later is a wonder.

A separate line of swan handled items with the Janice pattern are not listed as many do not consider them a part of the set. They are usually gathered by collectors of glass animals; but they can add some fun to sets of Janice.

		Crystal	Blue, Red				Crystal	Blue, Red
	Basket, 6½", 8" high	55.00	135.00	27	Creamer, tall, #4549		15.00	45.00
	Basket, 6½", 9" high, 4 toe	65.00	155.00	11	Cup, #4580		8.00	23.00
25	Basket, 11", #4552	65.00	225.00		Guest set: bottle w/tumbler		85.00	
	Basket, 12", oval, 10" high	75.00	265.00	36	Ice pail, 10", hdld., #4589		250.00	595.00
	Bonbon, 5½", 2 hdld., 4½" high	16.00	30.00	17	Ice tub, 6", ftd., #4584		100.00	275.00
35	Bonbon, 6", 2 hdld., 4" high	18.00	33.00		Jam jar w/cover, 6", #4577		20.00	55.00
	Bonbon, 7", 2 hdld., 4¾" high	22.00	40.00		Mayonnaise liner, 7", 2 hdld.		9.00	14.00
	Bowl, 5", sterling base	24.00			Mayonnaise plate, 6"		6.00	12.50
19	Bowl, 5½", flower, w/eight crimps	20.00	40.00		Mayonnaise, 6", 2 hdld.		15.00	30.00
	Bowl, 6", 2 hdld., crimped	18.00	33.00		Mayonnaise, round, #4522		15.00	27.50
	Bowl, 6½", shallow, swan hdl.	45.00		10	Oil, 5 oz., w/stopper, #4583		35.00	100.00
	Bowl, 9½", cupped	30.00	65.00	8	Pitcher, 15 oz., berry cream, #4576		45.00	165.00
	Bowl, 9½", flared	30.00	65.00	14	Plate, 7", 2 hdld., #4520		7.00	14.00
	Bowl, 9", 2 hdld., #4591	32.00	75.00	3	Plate, 8½", salad, #4579		9.00	17.50
	Bowl, 10"	32.00	75.00	34	Plate, 11", cheese, swan hdld., #4528-25J		22.50	40.00
	Bowl, 10½", cupped, 3 toed, #4512	40.00	75.00		Plate, 11", ftd., rolled edge		25.00	50.00
	Bowl, 10½", flared, 3 toed, #4511	40.00	85.00		Plate, 12", 2 hdld.		25.00	55.00
	Bowl, 11", oval	35.00	95.00	2	Plate, 13"		25.00	60.00
	Bowl, 11", cupped, ftd.	40.00	85.00	26	Plate, 13", 2 hdld., #4529		28.00	65.00
	Bowl, 11", flared	35.00	65.00		Plate, 14", ftd., rolled edge		35.00	85.00
	Bowl, 11", floral, swan hdl.	65.00	125.00		Plate, 15"			40.00
18	Bowl, 12", flared, #4513	38.00	90.00		Plate, 15", rolled edge torte			50.00
	Bowl, 12", fruit, ruffled top	45.00	110.00	20	Platter, 13", oval, #4588		30.00	90.00
	Bowl, 12", oval, #4551	40.00	70.00	13	Relish, 6", 2 part, 2 hdld.		12.00	37.50
	Bowl, 12", salad, scalloped top	45.00	85.00		Salt and pepper, pr.		35.00	85.00
	Bowl, 12", six crimps, 3½"t, #4515	48.00	125.00	12	Saucer, #4580		2.00	4.50
	Bowl, 13", flared	45.00	100.00	9	Sherbet, #4582, low ft.		10.00	26.00
	Canape set: tray w/ftd. juice	25.00			Stem, cordial		100.00	
16	Candelbra, 5", 2-lite, 5" wide, #4536	35.00			Sugar, 4-footed		20.00	
15	Candlestick, 5½", 1-lite, 5" wide, #4554	30.00	50.00	30	Sugar, 6 oz.		10.00	20.00
	Candlestick, 6", 1-lite, 4½" wide, "flame"	35.00	60.00		Sugar, individual, flat, #4532		10.00	22.00
	Candy box w/cover, 5½"	60.00	155.00	7	Sugar, individual, ftd., #4586		11.00	25.00
	Celery, 11", oblong, #4521	15.00	45.00	28	Sugar, tall, #4549		15.00	45.00
	Comport, cracker for cheese plate	12.00	25.00		Syrup, w/dripcut top		75.00	
1	Condiment set: tray and 2 cov. jars	47.00	125.00	5	Tray, oval, 2 hdld., ind. sugar/cream		10.00	20.00
	Creamer, 4-footed	20.00		29	Tray, oval, 2 hdld., cream/sugar		12.00	25.00
31	Creamer, 6 oz.	10.00	20.00	4	Tumbler, #4551/23 luncheon		14.00	30.00
	Creamer, individual, flat, 6 oz., #4532	10.00	22.00		Vase, 4", ivy, 3½" high, #4575		20.00	50.00
6	Creamer, individual, ftd.	11.00	25.00		Vase, 4", ivy, 4½" high, w/base peg, #4575		23.00	60.00

JANICE

	Crystal	Blue, Red
Vase, 7", ftd.	32.00	75.00
Vase, 8", ball, 7½" high, #4565	42.00	115.00
Vase, 8", cupped, 3 toed	45.00	135.00

	Crystal	Blue, Red
Vase, 8", flared, 3 toed, #4527	45.00	135.00
Vase, 9", ball	50.00	135.00

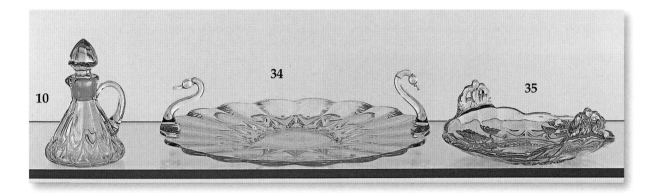

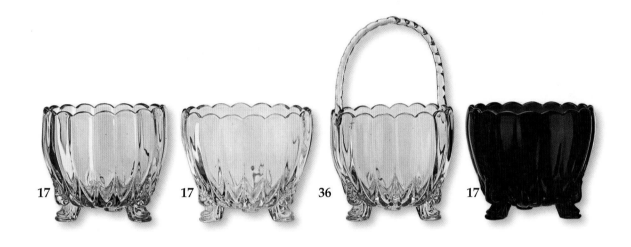

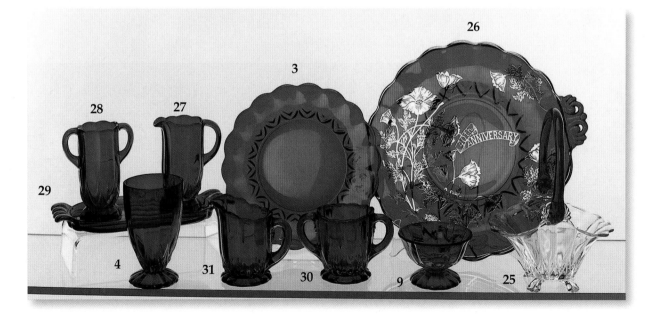

JULIA, TIFFIN GLASS COMPANY, C. 1930

Color: crystal w/amber trim, wide optic

Julia is a Tiffin pattern that is attractive to collectors. Unfortunately, it is only found in amber or with amber trim which limits its appeal. In writing since 1972, we have been told that amber is the next *big* color to collect, but we are still awaiting that trend. It obviously was charming in the 30s and Julia is one of the era's better examples.

A Tiffin expert told us that Julia was only manufactured for about five years. Observe that the plates are totally amber while stems and other pieces are crystal with amber stems, feet, or handles. Unfortunately, the pattern does not show well on those amber flat pieces. When sitting flat, the design basically disappears. However, it really stands out against the crystal.

It was the fad in the late 20s and early 30s to make bi-colored glass. There are collectors whose entire focus is bi-colored glass. Few Tiffin patterns can be found in amber; so, if you like this Tiffin color and design, this would be a pattern to seek.

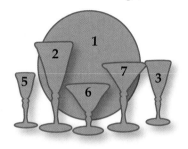

	Bowl, finger		20.00	5	Stem, cordial, #15011	50.00
	Candy jar and cover, ftd., #9557		110.00	7	Stem, saucer champagne, #15011	16.00
9	Creamer, #6		30.00	6	Stem, sundae, #15011	12.00
	Jug and cover, ftd., #194		295.00	2	Stem, water, #15011	24.00
1	Plate, 8", luncheon, #8833		15.00	3	Stem, wine, #15011	30.00
12	Plate, dessert, #8814		10.00		Sugar, #6	30.00
13	Plate, dinner, #8818		25.00	10	Tumbler, ftd., seltzer, #14185	18.00
4	Stem, cafe parfait, #15011		25.00	8	Tumbler, ftd., table, #14185	20.00
	Stem, claret, #15011		30.00	11	Tumbler, ftd., tea, #14185	25.00
	Stem, cocktail, #15011		16.00			

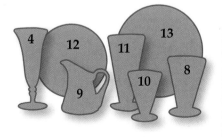

JUNE, ETCH #279, FOSTORIA GLASS COMPANY, 1928 – 1944

Colors: crystal, Azure blue, Topaz yellow, Rose pink

June is Fostoria's etched Depression era pattern collected by more people than any other. It is gathered in all four colors which were widely distributed. Azure and Rose have more admirers but supplies used to be insufficient to satisfy everyone. In view of the fact that collectors are adjusting their traditions from acquiring everything in a set to setting goals of smaller proportions, price changes have occurred in the last few years. Some rarer items have actually decreased in price. Prices for crystal and Topaz have also fallen some, but a steady supply of those are more available. Be sure to examine the Baroque mould blank bowl pictured right which is the only one of those we have ever documented in June.

An ongoing dilemma for dealers in Elegant glass involves stemware. The wines and clarets of this era held three to four ounces and were not made in quantities of other stems; so prices have traditionally been high. However, today's buyers want larger wine goblets; so they buy waters and not wines or clarets. That is causing the price of water goblets to escalate while prices for true clarets and wines are dropping due to a lack of buyers.

Shakers are found with both glass and metal tops. Collectors prefer the glass ones first used. In later years, only metal tops were made and all replacement tops were metal. If you will refer to Versailles (page 253), we have listed all the Fostoria line numbers for each piece. Since these are fundamentally the same listings as June, you can use the ware number listings from Versailles should you want them. See the stemware illustrations on page 109. You would not want to pay for a 6" claret and receive a 6" high sherbet simply because you didn't realize they were shaped differently.

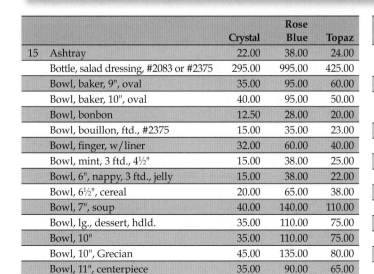

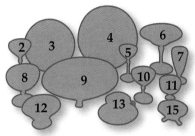

		Crystal	Rose Blue	Topaz
15	Ashtray	22.00	38.00	24.00
	Bottle, salad dressing, #2083 or #2375	295.00	995.00	425.00
	Bowl, baker, 9", oval	35.00	95.00	60.00
	Bowl, baker, 10", oval	40.00	95.00	50.00
	Bowl, bonbon	12.50	28.00	20.00
	Bowl, bouillon, ftd., #2375	15.00	35.00	23.00
	Bowl, finger, w/liner	32.00	60.00	40.00
	Bowl, mint, 3 ftd., 4½"	15.00	38.00	25.00
	Bowl, 6", nappy, 3 ftd., jelly	15.00	38.00	22.00
	Bowl, 6½", cereal	20.00	65.00	38.00
	Bowl, 7", soup	40.00	140.00	110.00
	Bowl, lg., dessert, hdld.	35.00	110.00	75.00
	Bowl, 10"	35.00	110.00	75.00
	Bowl, 10", Grecian	45.00	135.00	80.00
	Bowl, 11", centerpiece	35.00	90.00	65.00

		Crystal	Rose Blue	Topaz
9	Bowl, 12", centerpiece, three types, #2394 shown	50.00	110.00	65.00
25	Bowl, 12", #2396 (Baroque)		200.00	
	Bowl, 13", oval centerpiece, w/flower frog	80.00	210.00	130.00
15	Candlestick, 2", #2394	12.00	20.00	15.00
	Candlestick, 3", #2394	16.00	28.00	18.00
	Candlestick, 3", Grecian "Scroll"	18.00	35.00	25.00
	Candlestick, 5", Grecian "Scroll"	22.00	40.00	28.00
	Candy, w/cover, 3 pt.		350.00	
	Candy, w/cover, ½ lb., ¼ lb.			175.00
	Celery, 11½"	25.00	75.00	50.00
19	Cheese & cracker set, #2368 or #2375	45.00	100.00	65.00
6	Comport, 5", #2400	25.00	50.00	40.00

		Crystal	Rose Blue	Topaz
	Comport, 6", #5298 or #5299	28.00	60.00	45.00
	Comport, 7", #2375	32.00	90.00	60.00
	Comport, 8", #2400	40.00	120.00	65.00
	Cream soup, ftd.	20.00	40.00	28.00
14	Creamer, ftd., #2375½	12.00	22.00	16.00
	Creamer, tea	18.00	50.00	30.00
	Cup, after dinner	18.00	60.00	38.00
13	Cup, ftd., #2375½	10.00	22.00	18.00
	Decanter	395.00	2,000.00	595.00
	Goblet, claret, 6", 4 oz.	28.00	75.00	60.00
5	Goblet, cocktail, 5¼", 3 oz.	15.00	28.00	22.00
	Goblet, cordial, 4", ¾ oz.	40.00	90.00	50.00
	Goblet, water, 8¼", 10 oz., #5298	20.00	60.00	38.00
	Goblet, wine, 5½", 3 oz.	18.00	65.00	33.00
8	Grapefruit	25.00	90.00	50.00
11	Grapefruit liner	20.00	60.00	30.00
1	Ice bucket	55.00	110.00	65.00
	Ice dish	15.00	50.00	30.00
	Ice dish liner (tomato, crab, fruit)	5.00	15.00	5.00
12	Mayonnaise, w/liner	30.00	65.00	48.00
	Oil, ftd.	150.00	595.00	250.00
	Oyster cocktail, 5½ oz.	12.00	28.00	20.00
	Parfait, 5¼"	25.00	60.00	50.00
	Pitcher, ftd., #5000	195.00	595.00	350.00
	Plate, canape	15.00	40.00	25.00
	Plate, lemon	14.00	25.00	20.00
16	Plate, 6", bread/butter	5.00	12.00	8.00
	Plate, 6", finger bowl liner	4.00	12.00	8.00
	Plate, 7½", salad	7.00	14.00	11.00
	Plate, 7½, cream soup	6.00	14.00	11.00
3	Plate, 8¾", luncheon, #2375	6.00	22.00	17.00
4	Plate, 9½", sm. dinner	12.00	35.00	25.00
	Plate, 10", cake, hdld. (no indent)	30.00	55.00	40.00
	Plate, 10", cheese with indent, hdld.	30.00	55.00	40.00
	Plate, 10¼", dinner, service	30.00	80.00	65.00

		Crystal	Rose Blue	Topaz
	Plate, 10¼", grill	30.00	100.00	75.00
	Plate, 13", chop	25.00	75.00	60.00
	Plate, 14", torte		110.00	65.00
	Platter, 12", #2375	30.00	90.00	65.00
	Platter, 15"	60.00	195.00	95.00
20	Relish, 8½", 2 part	28.00		50.00
	Sauce boat	28.00	250.00	90.00
	Sauce boat liner	12.00	50.00	35.00
	Saucer, after dinner	5.00	15.00	9.00
13	Saucer, #2375	3.00	5.00	4.00
	Shaker, ftd., pr., #2375	50.00	150.00	110.00
2	Sherbet, high, 6", 6 oz., #5298	15.00	25.00	18.00
10	Sherbet, low, 4¼", 6 oz., #5298	14.00	22.00	16.00
24	Sugar, ftd., straight or scalloped top	12.00	22.00	18.00
	Sugar cover	50.00	200.00	100.00
	Sugar pail	50.00	195.00	125.00
	Sugar, tea	18.00	50.00	30.00
	Sweetmeat	20.00	30.00	20.00
	Tray, service and lemon		325.00	250.00
	Tray, 11", ctr. hdld.	25.00	40.00	35.00
	Tumbler, 2½ oz., ftd.	15.00	60.00	40.00
	Tumbler, 5 oz., 4½", ftd.	12.00	33.00	20.00
7	Tumbler, 6 oz., 5¼", ftd., #5098	12.00	35.00	20.00
	Tumbler, 9 oz., 5¼", water	13.00	30.00	20.00
	Tumbler, 12 oz., 6", ftd., tea	18.00	50.00	35.00
	Vase, 8", 2 styles	75.00	295.00	195.00
	Vase, 8½", fan, ftd.	80.00	250.00	150.00
	Whipped cream bowl	10.00	24.00	18.00
	Whipped cream pail	75.00	195.00	140.00

Note: See stemware identification on page 109.

JUNE NIGHT, TIFFIN GLASS COMPANY, 1940S – 1950S

Color: crystal

June Night stemware is easy to get and reasonably priced. We seldom see serving pieces, however. June Night was etched on several stemware lines, but the one most often displayed is Tiffin's #17392 that we picture below. You may find stem line #17378 (prism stem with pearl edge top), #17441 (quadrangle flowing to hexagonal cut), and #17471. That last line has a bow tie stem, but we never catch a glimpse of June Night on it. Even though listed in Tiffin catalogs, no one has been able to find one for us to photograph.

More June Night is being exhibited at shows, but again mostly stems. As far as we know, Tiffin advertised this competitor of Cambridge's Rose Point for consumers to use with their china. We've noticed that comparable pieces in Cherokee Rose pattern have caused some confusion with novices and part-time dealers. Although similar in shapes, there is a flower encircled on June Night but an urn on Cherokee Rose. Shapes are significant, but it is the etched design that makes the pattern. Since both of these patterns are on the same Tiffin mould blank, pay attention to which one it is! Just a few months ago at a flea market, we observed a dealer bargaining on a price for several June Night items, which she had labeled Rose Point. Not only is June Night confused with Cherokee Rose, but apparently, even Cambridge's Rose Point.

Pitchers and shakers are problematic to acquire. The pitcher has the encircled flower below the ice lip (design shown at right). The side of the pitcher does not have this etch which may cause you to pass it by should you not know that.

Tiffin dubbed gold-trimmed June Night stemware Cherry Laurel. Name variation within same patterns was another glass company gimmick. Any apparent process done to a pattern induced a separate name, often completely different from the original. In the case of gold trim, frequently they would just add "golden" to the pattern name. Remember that gold trim does not hold up well with frequent use. Never put gold-trimmed items in the dishwasher especially if you use any soap with lemon in it. Lemon will remove gold trim extremely well — if you so wish.

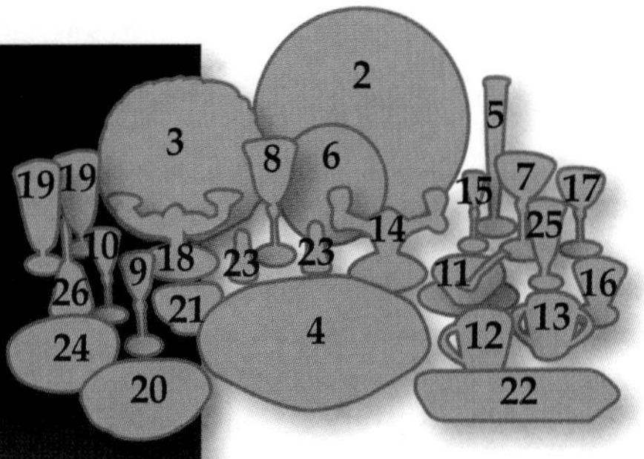

1

21	Bowl, 5", finger.	20.00
	Bowl, 6", fruit or nut	25.00
20	Bowl, 7", salad	35.00
	Bowl, 10", deep salad	60.00
	Bowl, 12", crimped	60.00
	Bowl, 12½" centerpiece, flared	60.00
4	Bowl, 13", centerpiece, #5902, cone	60.00
14	Candlestick, double branch, #5902	32.00
18	Candlestick, 9", 2-lite	35.00
22	Celery, 10½", oblong	32.00
12	Creamer	16.00
11	Mayonnaise, liner and ladle	35.00
1	Pitcher, #5859	595.00
6	Plate, 6", sherbet	6.00
	Plate, 8", luncheon	10.00
2	Plate, 13½", turned-up edge, lily, #5902	35.00
	Plate, 14", sandwich	35.00
24	Relish, 6½", 3 pt.	28.00
3	Relish, 12½", 3 pt., #5902	55.00

23	Shaker, pr., #2	195.00
15	Stem, 1 oz., cordial	30.00
9, 10	Stem, 2 oz., sherry, 10 is Cherry Laurel	25.00
17	Stem, 3½ oz., cocktail	12.00
	Stem, 3½ oz., wine	16.00
	Stem, 4 oz., claret	22.00
	Stem, 4½ oz., parfait	28.00
7	Stem, 5½ oz., sherbet/champagne, #17441	12.00
8	Stem, 9 oz., water, #17441	18.00
13	Sugar	16.00
26	Table bell, #9742	75.00
16	Tumbler, 4½ oz., oyster cocktail	15.00
25	Tumbler, 5 oz., ftd., juice	12.00
	Tumbler, 8 oz., ftd., water	14.00
19	Tumbler, 10½ oz., ftd., ice tea	16.00
	Vase, 6", bud	22.00
5	Vase, 8", bud, #14185	28.00
	Vase, 10", bud	38.00

JUNGLE ASSORTMENT, SATIN DECORATED #14 PARROT, TIFFIN GLASS COMPANY, ET. AL., C. 1922 – 1934

Colors: green, pink, and crystal satin; various flashed colors

Jungle Assortment is a pattern that has fascinated collectors. There is a likelihood that the flashed items are Lancaster wares.

Below is an assortment of poses which are named for what the bird's holding. The bottom of page 143 shows "Bird on a Bar," the top of page 144 is "Bird on a Branch," and the bottom of page 144 illustrates "Bird on a Perch."

It would appear flashed colors did not hold the hand-painted patterns any better than Tiffin's satinized versions. This is one pattern where you might like to pick up some gently used pieces until mint condition ones appear. You will find that many of the birds have all but flown the decorations at this stage.

The cologne bottle, cigarette set, night set, basket, lamp, and vase in metal holder appear to be difficult to find. Notice the 1928 Sears catalog ad for the night set calling it a "Bed Room Water Bottle and Tumbler." They also called the bird a cockatoo.

We have found three styles of candleholders. Additional items may be seen, so keep looking!

		All Colors
1	Basket, 6", #151	100.00
	Bonbon & cover, 5½" high ftd., #330	50.00
	Bonbon and cover, 5", low ftd., #330	50.00
	Bowl, centerpiece, #320	40.00
12	Candle, hdld., #330	28.00
22	Candle, hdld. tall, octagonal base	40.00
16	Candle, low, #10	25.00
5	Candy and cover, ftd., #15179	65.00
9	Candy box & cover, flat, 5½"	50.00
7	Candy box & cover, flat, 6", #329	55.00
15	Candy jar and cover, ftd., cone, #330	60.00
20	Candy jar and cover, ftd., #179	55.00
27	Candy jar and cover, ftd.	55.00
10	Cologne bottle, #5722	90.00
19	Decanter & stopper	110.00
26	Jug and cover, 2 quart, #127	195.00
24	Lamp	125.00

		All Colors
	Marmalade & cover, #330	40.00
2	Night cap set, #6712	125.00
29	Perfume	100.00
14	Puff box and cover, hexagonal, #6772	75.00
21	Puff box	38.00
8	Shaker, ftd., #6205	40.00
	Smoking set, 3 pc., #188	40.00
25	Tumbler, 12 oz., #444	25.00
3	Vase, 5½", ftd., rose bowl	65.00
6	Vase, 6", 2 hdld., #151	40.00
17	Vase, 6⅜", flat	40.00
13	Vase, 7" ftd., flair from base, #330	55.00
11	Vase, 7" ftd., flair rim, #151	55.00
4	Vase, 7" sweet pea, #151	65.00
18	Vase, 8", flat	55.00
	Vase, wall, #320	110.00
23	Vase in metal stand	50.00

JUNGLE ASSORTMENT

9

KALONYAL, #1776, A.H. HEISEY COMPANY, 1905 – 1907

Color: crystal

Kalonyal was created in crystal; however, some pieces with ruby stain have emerged which was an old procedure used to get "color" on the glass. Most early Heisey patterns, and this is quite early, are marked with the Heisey insignia, consisting of an H enclosed in a diamond. Because of its pattern number (1776), it became extremely popular with collectors during the bicentennial in 1976, and it has remained in style since that time.

	Bottle, hdld., molasses, 13 oz.	250.00
	Bottle, hdld., oil, 2 oz.	150.00
	Bottle, hdld., oil, 4 oz.	100.00
	Bottle, hdld., oil, 6 oz.	100.00
	Bottle, water	350.00
	Bowl, 4½", deep	30.00
	Bowl, 5", deep	35.00
8	Bowl, 5", flared	35.00
	Bowl, 5", hdld.	38.00
	Bowl, 5", crimped	35.00
	Bowl, 6", shallow	35.00
	Bowl, 7", deep, straight sided	45.00
	Bowl, 7", deep, flared	45.00
	Bowl, 8", flared	65.00
	Bowl, 9", shallow	65.00
9	Bowl, 10", shallow	70.00
	Bowl, 11", shallow	70.00
	Bowl, 12", punch and stand	250.00
	Butter and cover, domed	150.00
1	Cake stand, 9", ftd.	275.00
2	Celery, tall	100.00
	Celery tray, 12"	55.00
	Comport, deep ftd. jelly, 5"	110.00
	Comport, shallow ftd. jelly, 5½"	110.00
	Comport, deep or shallow, 8", ftd.	225.00
	Comport, deep or shallow, 9", ftd.	225.00
3	Comport, deep or shallow, 10", ftd.	300.00
	Creamer, tall	90.00
	Creamer, hotel	70.00

	Cup, punch, 3 oz.	30.00
	Cup, punch, 3½ oz.	30.00
	Mug, hdld., 8 oz.	175.00
	Mustard and cover	235.00
	Pickle jar and cover	195.00
	Pickle tray	65.00
5	Pitcher, ½ gallon	350.00
	Plate, 5½"	30.00
	Plate, 6"	35.00
	Plate, 8", fruit	55.00
	Shaker, salt & pepper, 3 styles, pr.	225.00
	Shaker, sugar	145.00
	Spoon tray	60.00
	Spooner, tall	95.00
	Stem, egg cup, 9½ oz.	45.00
6	Stem, goblet, 9 oz.	150.00
	Stem, champagne, 6½ oz.	65.00
	Stem, sherbet, 6 oz.	40.00
	Stem, sherbet, 5½ oz., straight sided or scalloped	40.00
	Stem, claret, 5 oz.	85.00
	Stem, sherbet, 4½ oz., scalloped	40.00
	Stem, sherbet, 3½ oz., scalloped	40.00
4	Stem, burgundy, 3 oz.	50.00
11	Stem, wine, 2 oz.	110.00
10	Stem, cordial, 1¼ oz.	375.00
	Sugar and cover, tall	95.00
	Sugar, hotel (no cover)	70.00
7	Toothpick	375.00
	Tumbler, 8 oz.	95.00

KASHMIR, ETCH #283, FOSTORIA GLASS COMPANY, 1930 – 1933

Colors: Topaz yellow, Azure blue, some green

Kashmir was not as extensively dispersed as were many Fostoria patterns; therefore finding it will probably take longer than other patterns. Blue Kashmir would be a Fostoria pattern to own if you like that color. Other Azure Fostoria etched patterns have many collectors hunting them; but a lack of attention is given to Kashmir. Of course, finding Azure Kashmir is the problem. We displayed our accumulation after photographing it, and the blue sold but not as well as we thought it would. The yellow had to be discounted heavily to make a few happy collectors visiting our booth. You could gather yellow Kashmir more economically than any other etched, yellow Fostoria pattern could you find it.

We found our Kashmir in the Midwest; you can see from our pictures how green Kashmir has been eluding us, even though we have been searching for it. Supposedly, there are some 6", 7", and 8" plates to be had along with the two styles of cups and saucers, but we have never found any plates.

The stemware and tumbler line is #5099, which is the same line on which Trojan is found. This is the collector dubbed cascading "waterfall" stem.

Both styles of after dinner cups are shown in the picture on page 147. The square #2419 (Mayfair blank) saucer set is more difficult to find than the round; but we have only stumbled upon it in green.

30

		Yellow Green	Blue
	Ashtray	20.00	25.00
4	Bowl, cream soup	22.00	28.00
	Bowl, finger	15.00	30.00
13	Bowl, 5", fruit	12.00	20.00
	Bowl, 6", cereal	22.00	30.00
	Bowl, 7", soup	30.00	60.00
27	Bowl, 2 hdld., sweetmeat	22.00	
	Bowl, 8½", pickle	18.00	25.00
	Bowl, 9", baker	30.00	65.00
5	Bowl, 10", 2 hdld., Grecian Scroll	38.00	60.00
7	Bowl, 12", centerpiece	38.00	60.00
	Candlestick, 2"	15.00	25.00
	Candlestick, 3"	20.00	30.00
3	Candlestick, 5", Grecian "Scroll"	22.00	35.00
	Candlestick, 9½"	30.00	60.00
24	Candy, w/cover, #2430	75.00	150.00
	Cheese and cracker set	45.00	68.00
	Comport, 6"	30.00	40.00
14	Creamer, ftd.	14.00	18.00
1	Cup, #2375½	10.00	15.00
2	Cup, #2350½	10.00	15.00
23	Cup, after dinner, flat, #2350	25.00	
25	Cup, after dinner, ftd., #2375	25.00	35.00
	Grapefruit	40.00	
	Grapefruit liner	30.00	
30	Ice bucket, #2375	65.00	95.00
20	Mayo & liner w/spoon	65.00	95.00
	Oil, ftd.	245.00	395.00
18	Pitcher, ftd.	295.00	395.00
12	Plate, cream soup or mayo liner	6.00	8.00
	Plate, 6", bread & butter	4.00	6.00
29	Plate, 7", salad, rnd.	6.00	7.00
	Plate, 7", salad, sq.	6.00	7.00
9	Plate, 8", salad	8.00	10.00

		Yellow Green	Blue
10	Plate, 9", luncheon	9.00	15.00
11	Plate, 10", dinner	30.00	50.00
31	Plate, 10", grill	30.00	40.00
	Plate, cake, 10"	33.00	
	Salt & pepper, pr.	90.00	140.00
21	Sandwich, 11", center hdld., #2375	30.00	40.00
	Sauce boat, w/liner	90.00	135.00
1	Saucer, rnd., #2375	2.00	5.00
2	Saucer, sq., #2419	2.00	5.00
23	Saucer, after dinner, sq.	5.00	
25	Saucer, after dinner, rnd., #2375	5.00	8.00
	Stem, ¾ oz., cordial	65.00	90.00
	Stem, 2½ oz., ftd.	20.00	35.00
	Stem, 2 oz., ftd., whiskey	25.00	38.00
	Stem, 2½ oz., wine	25.00	38.00
	Stem, 3 oz., cocktail	16.00	20.00
15	Stem, 3½ oz., ftd., cocktail	16.00	20.00
	Stem, 4 oz., claret	28.00	40.00
	Stem, 4½ oz., oyster cocktail	12.00	14.00
19	Stem, 5 oz., low sherbet	10.00	16.00
16	Stem, 5½ oz., parfait	25.00	32.00
8	Stem, 6 oz., high sherbet, #5099	14.00	22.00
28	Stem, 9 oz., water, 8½", #5099	20.00	30.00
	Sugar, ftd.	14.00	18.00
	Sugar lid	35.00	60.00
22	Tumbler, 5 oz., 4½", ftd., juice	12.00	20.00
	Tumbler, 9 oz., 5⅜", ftd., water	15.00	24.00
	Tumbler, 10 oz., ftd., water	18.00	28.00
	Tumbler, 11 oz.	18.00	
6	Tumbler, 12 oz., ftd.	20.00	28.00
26	Tumbler, 13 oz., ftd., tea	20.00	
	Tumbler, 16 oz., ftd., tea	28.00	
	Vase, 8"	110.00	185.00

Note: See stemware identification on page 109.

LAFAYETTE, #2440, FOSTORIA GLASS COMPANY, C. 1931 – 1944; DISCONTINUED 1960

Colors: crystal, Topaz/Gold Tint (every piece of pattern); at least 12 pieces of Regal Blue, Empire Green, Burgundy; 6 pieces of Ruby & Silver Mist; some amber, green, Wisteria, and Rose

Lafayette #2440 is the mould line used for most of Fostoria's later crystal etchings, with Navarre and Meadow Rose being the most recognized. Colored pieces of Lafayette are well liked. The favored color is Wisteria, but yellow can also be gathered into a set. We finally found a burgundy piece (sugar). You might blend some of the colors with crystal in order to have more pieces, but finding crystal without an etching may be harder than you might think.

		Crystal Amber	Rose, Green Topaz	Wisteria	Regal Blue	Burgundy	Empire Green
	Almond, individual	8.00	12.00	25.00			
	Bonbon, 5", 2 hdld.	12.00	20.00	35.00	35.00	30.00	30.00
	Bowl, 4½", sweetmeat	15.00	20.00	35.00	35.00	35.00	30.00
	Bowl, cream soup	18.00	26.00	60.00			
	Bowl, 5", fruit		18.00	30.00			
	Bowl, 6", cereal	15.00	18.00	35.00			
	Bowl, 6½", olive	15.00	20.00	40.00			
	Bowl, 6½", 2-pt. relish	18.00	25.00	40.00	50.00	45.00	45.00
	Ruby 50.00; Silver Mist 25.00						
4	Bowl, 6½", oval sauce	22.00	28.00	75.00	50.00	50.00	45.00
	Ruby 65.00; Silver Mist 27.50						
	Bowl, 7", "D" cupped	26.00	30.00	75.00			
	Bowl, 7½", 3-pt. relish	22.00	28.00	70.00	50.00	45.00	45.00
	Ruby 55.00; Silver Mist 30.00						
	Bowl, 8", nappy	28.00	35.00	65.00			
	Bowl, 8½", pickle	16.00	28.00	50.00			
	Bowl, 10", oval baker	30.00		65.00	65.00		
	Bowl, 10", "B," flair	30.00	40.00				
	Bowl, 12", salad, flair	35.00	42.00	100.00			
	Cake, 10½", oval, 2 hdld.	33.00	42.00		60.00	65.00	65.00
	Celery, 11½"	26.00	28.00	75.00			
1	Creamer, 4½", ftd.	12.00	18.00	26.00	30.00	30.00	30.00
5	Cup	9.00	12.00	14.00	25.00	35.00	35.00
	Cup, demi	12.00	20.00	50.00			
	Tray, 5", 2-hdld., lemon	15.00	20.00	30.00	30.00	30.00	33.00
	Tray, 8½", oval, 2-hdld.	20.00	24.00	60.00	45.00	45.00	45.00
	Ruby 55.00; Silver Mist 25.00						
	Mayonnaise, 6½", 2 pt.	20.00	24.00	50.00	45.00	55.00	55.00
	Ruby 55.00; Silver Mist 30.00						
	Plate, 6"	6.00	8.00	10.00			
	Plate, 7¼"	6.00	10.00	14.00			
	Plate, 8½"	8.00	12.00	18.00			
3	Plate, 9½"	18.00	22.00	32.00			
	Plate, 10¼"	30.00	40.00	65.00			
	Plate, 13", torte	32.00	42.00	70.00	90.00	95.00	110.00
	Ruby 110.00; Silver Mist 40.00						
	Platter, 12"	30.00	48.00	95.00			
	Platter, 15"	40.00	60.00				
5	Saucer	2.00	3.00	4.00	5.00	8.00	30.00
	Saucer, demi	4.00	7.00	12.00			
2	Sugar, 3⅝", ftd.	12.00	18.00	26.00	30.00	30.00	40.00
	Vase, 7", rim ft., flair	40.00	60.00				

LE FLEUR, TIFFIN GLASS COMPANY, EARLY 1930S

Colors: Crystal, Mandarin (yellow), Rose (pink), and Mandarin or Rose with crystal stems

Le Fleur is found in Mandarin (yellow) more often than crystal or pink. We have seen pink advertised, but have yet to spot a piece for sale in our travels. Yellow is the apparent color choice if you find this a pleasing design. The pitcher, creamer, and sugar pictured here were bought by a stroke of fate. A few pieces of Cambridge yellow Gloria were priced to us from their listing by a couple wanting to sell their inherited set. As we were unpacking the boxes of glass, some pieces were not Gloria, but Tiffin's Le Fleur. It gave us a foundation for a new pattern, but not having a yellow Gloria pitcher as they thought was a disappointment at the time. You will find that people of yesteryear often bought matching colors rather than patterns. This is not the first time we've encountered such a mixture touted as being one pattern.

		All Colors				All Colors
	Bonbon, 2-handled	30.00			Stem, #15022, 3 oz., cocktail	22.00
	Bowl, 12", centerpiece, ftd.	60.00			Stem, #15022, 6 oz., champagne	24.00
	Bowl, finger, 8 oz., ftd.	30.00			Stem, #15022, 6 oz., sherbet	20.00
	Bowl, mayonnaise, ftd.	30.00			Stem, #15022, 9 oz., water goblet	35.00
2	Candle, #5831	28.00			Stem, #15024, 1½ oz., 5", cordial	58.00
	Celery, 10"	50.00			Stem, #15024, 3½ oz., 4¾", cocktail	22.00
	Creamer, #5831, ftd.	38.00			Stem, #15024, 4½ oz., 5⅝", cafe parfait	33.00
4	Creamer, #6, flat	40.00			Stem, #15024, 6 oz., 4½", sherbet	20.00
	Cup	40.00		1	Stem, #15024, 6 oz., 6¼", champagne	24.00
5	Jug	350.00			Stem, #15024, 9 oz.., 8¼", water goblet	35.00
	Jug w/cover	450.00			Sugar, #5831, ftd.	38.00
	Plate, 6", mayonnaise	12.00		3	Sugar, #6, flat	40.00
	Plate, 7½"	15.00			Tumbler, 9 oz., ftd.	30.00
	Saucer	10.00			Tumbler, 12 oz., ftd.	35.00

LILY OF THE VALLEY, DUNCAN & MILLER GLASS COMPANY, 1937

Color: crystal

Lily of the Valley is a design that is "noticed" whenever it is displayed. We were first impressed by its carved floral stem when collecting cordials years ago.

Duncan's Canterbury #115 and Pall Mall #30 blanks were employed for the cutting. The mayonnaise pictured is #30 and the bowl and plate are #115. If cup or saucers were cut in this pattern, we have never witnessed them.

Stemware has the Lily of the Valley in the stem itself, but the bowls on top of the stem are found with cutting or plain. The cutting on the bowl elicits exclamations from first time observers. Duncan's cataloging for this stem was D-4 and the cut variety was DC-4. Prices below are for deep cut (DC-4) bowl items; deduct about 50% for plain bowl stems. Once you see this pattern, you will understand why collectors want the cut version.

This is another pattern that usually is found in a grouping rather than a piece or two. Original owners seem to pass it down through the family, keeping it as an heirloom rather than discarding it — and we can see why!

#	Item	Price		#	Item	Price
8	Ashtray, 3"	25.00		5	Plate, 8"	35.00
	Ashtray, 6"	35.00			Plate, 9"	45.00
7	Bowl, 12"	60.00			Relish, 3-part	30.00
3	Candlestick, double, 5"	60.00		12	Stem, cocktail	25.00
15	Candy, w/lid	95.00		10	Stem, cordial	80.00
9	Celery, 10½"	40.00		13	Stem, high sherbet	25.00
	Cheese and cracker	75.00		2	Stem, water goblet	40.00
6	Creamer	30.00		11	Stem, wine	45.00
14	Mayonnaise	30.00		4	Sugar	30.00
14	Mayonnaise ladle	8.00		1	Tumbler, ftd. water	25.00
14	Mayonnaise liner	15.00				

"LIONS" (HERALDRY), LINE #34 "ADDIE," LINE #37 "MOONDROPS," NEW MARTINSVILLE GLASS COMPANY, C. 1934

Colors: amber, black, crystal, green, pink

We identified this New Martinsville "coat of arms style" etching as "Lions." We will revert to an original name if one can be ascertained.

Nearly all "Lions" etch is found on New Martinsville's Line #34 as pictured below except for crystal candle and sugar shown on Line #37 known as "Moondrops" to collectors. We have not found "Lions" on colored items of Line #37. We are picturing every different piece we have found, but are sure you will locate others.

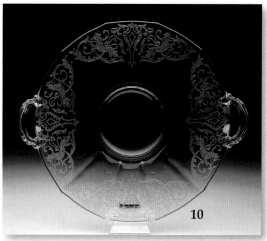

		Amber Crystal	Pink Green	Black
4	Bowl, creme soup, ftd., 2 hdld., #34	20.00		
3	Candleholder, #37	25.00		
	Candlestick, #34		30.00	
8	Candy w/lid		75.00	120.00
	Center handle server		35.00	
	Comport, cheese		20.00	30.00
7	Creamer, #34		20.00	30.00
	Creamer, #37	15.00		
6	Cup, #34		20.00	25.00
2	Plate, 8"		15.00	25.00
9	Plate, 12", cracker		30.00	40.00
6	Saucer, #34		5.00	7.00
1	Sugar, #34		20.00	30.00
5	Sugar, #37	15.00		
10	Tray, 2 hnd , 12"	30.00	35.00	40.00

LUCIANA, TIFFIN GLASS COMPANY, 1925 – 1931

Colors: crystal regular optic w/black and crystal wide optic w/green trim

Luciana is usually displayed at shows a piece or two at a time. Rarely is it found in a grouping which shows it to an impressive advantage. Luckily, we have bought two partial sets of Luciana. A black grouping with four different pieces was bought in an estate sale in Ohio; and a few months later, we ran into a larger set of seven different green pieces in Florida.

The green plates, especially the dinners, were well used, so the original owners obviously enjoyed them. The design on the black plate is frosted and not as pleasing to the eye as are the pieces in black with etched crystal. The pattern disappears into the black even when seeing it in person.

The pieces that appeared in internet auctions a few years ago brought some serious prices; but few are even being offered, now. Thus, prices have stopped skyrocketing, and have descended to more reasonable levels.

	Bonbon, 5" high	65.00		Stem, parfait, #016	35.00
	Candy w/cover, #9557	125.00		Stem, parfait, #043	35.00
	Creamer, #6	50.00		Stem, saucer champagne, #016	20.00
	Decanter w/stopper, #185	250.00	7	Stem, sundae, #016	16.00
	Finger bowl, ftd., #002	30.00	8	Stem, sundae, #043	16.00
	Finger bowl, ftd., #185	30.00	10	Stem, water, #043	40.00
	Pitcher w/cover, 2 qt., ftd., #194	350.00		Stem, water, 11 oz., #016	50.00
3	Plate, 6", #8833	9.00		Stem, wine, #043	30.00
	Plate, 7¼", #8814	12.00	9	Stem, wine, 2½ oz., #016	40.00
4	Plate, 8", #8833	15.00		Sugar, #6	50.00
1	Plate, 10", #8833	60.00	6	Tumbler, 5 oz., juice ftd., #194	30.00
	Stem, claret, #016	50.00	5	Tumbler, 9 oz., water ftd., #194	25.00
	Stem, cocktail, 3 oz., #016	28.00	2	Tumbler, 12 oz., ice tea, ftd., #194	35.00
	Stem, oyster cocktail, #043	18.00		Vase, 10½", bud, #004	135.00

MARDI GRAS, #42, DUNCAN GLASS COMPANY, LATE 1800S

Colors: crystal, crystal with ruby or gold, cobalt

Mardi Gras was produced for the most part in crystal, but you can find it with gold trim or ruby flashing; but beware, since these are frequently well worn. A few rare pieces surface in cobalt, but infrequently. The piece in cobalt that we have seen is a small tray, perhaps a pickle, which lies on a metal (chrome) base. There seems to be a profusion of Mardi Gras pieces obtainable and one could put together a small collection rather swiftly if so inclined. You may find a punch set reasonably priced when compared to other patterns of this era.

	Bottle, bitters	75.00			Plate, 5"	8.00
	Bottle, molasses, hdld.	85.00			Plate, 6"	9.00
	Bottle, oil, hdld.	40.00			Plate, 7"	9.00
8	Bottle, water	55.00			Plate, 8"	20.00
	Bowl, berry, 4"	15.00			Salt & pepper	55.00
	Bowl, shallow, 6"	20.00		11	Salt, open, individual	10.00
6	Bowl, round, 8"	50.00			Spooner, tall	65.00
	Bowl, fruit, 10"	65.00		15	Spooner, child's	60.00
	Bowl, punch, 13½", and stand	150.00			Stem, goblet	45.00
	Box, powder and cover	155.00			Stem, claret	50.00
	Butter and cover, domed	75.00			Stem, champagne/sherbet, 2 styles	22.00
14	Butter and cover, individual	165.00			Stem, cocktail	24.00
	Cake plate, ftd.	100.00		9	Stem, wine	28.00
	Celery, tall	55.00			Stem, sherry, straight sided and flared	35.00
	Cracker jar and cover, tall	145.00			Stem, cordial	60.00
	Creamer, regular	30.00		4	Sugar and cover, regular	40.00
12	Creamer, individual/child's	60.00		13	Sugar and cover, individual	120.00
2	Cup, punch	8.00			Toothpick	45.00
	Egg cup, ftd.	35.00			Tumbler, water	20.00
	Jug, honey, individual	65.00			Tumbler, juice	20.00
	Mustard and cover	75.00			Tumbler, bar (2 oz.)	20.00
3	Oil bottle	50.00		16	Vase, ball, individual, 1½"	150.00
1	Pitcher, straight sided	125.00			Vase, ball, 4"	40.00
	Pitcher, bulbous	175.00			Vase, tall, footed, 10"	55.00
10	Pitcher, syrup, individual	75.00		5	Vase, wall, 9½"	100.00
7	Plate, 3", butter	22.00				

MARJORIE, CAMBRIDGE GLASS COMPANY, LATE 1916 – 1940S; STEMLINE #7606, C. 1920; STEMLINE #3750 (HEXAGON STEM), C. 1940S

Colors: amethyst w/gold, crystal, Emerald green

Cambridge's early Marjorie pattern was changed to Fuchsia in the 1930s. The #7606 stems were promoted in the 1927 Sears catalog as shown here.

		Crystal
3	Bottle, oil & vinegar, 6 oz.	295.00
6	Candle, 3 lite, #1307	95.00
	Comport, #4011	70.00
	Comport, 5", #4004	60.00
	Comport, 5", jelly (sherbet), #2090	55.00
	Cream, flat, curved in side, #1917/10	90.00
10	Cream, flat, straight side, #1917/18	100.00
14	Cup	50.00
	Decanter, 28 oz., cut stop, #17	400.00
	Decanter, 28 oz. #7606	300.00
	Finger bowl, #7606	35.00
	Grapefruit w/liner inside, #7606	75.00
	Jug, 30 oz., #104	225.00
	Jug w/cover, 30 oz., #106	295.00
	Jug, 3 pint, #93	195.00
	Jug, 3½ pint, #108 short, flair bottom	195.00
	Jug, 3½ pint, rim bottom, bulbous, #111	195.00
	Jug, 54 oz., flat bottom, #51	295.00
	Jug w/cover, 66 oz., #106	295.00
1	Jug, 4 pint, tall, flat bottom, #110	295.00
	Jug, guest room 38 oz. w/tumbler fitting inside, #103	395.00
	Marmalade & cover, #145	75.00
	Nappie, 4", #4111	30.00
	Nappie, 4" ftd., #5000	35.00
	Nappie, 8", #4111	80.00
	Nappie, 8" ftd., #5000	85.00
	Night bottle, 20 oz. w/tumbler, #4002	395.00
2	Oil w/hex cone cut stop, #32	340.00
4	Plate, 7¾", salad, #7606	12.00
19	Plate, 7¼", finger bowl liner, #7606	12.00
	Saucer	20.00
15	Stem, 3⁵⁄₁₆", Brandy, #7606	100.00
16	Stem, 3¾", ⅞ oz., cordial, #7606	100.00
	Stem, 1 oz., cordial, #3750	100.00

		Crystal
	Stem, 2½ oz., wine, #7606	50.00
	Stem, 2 oz., creme de menthe, #7606	100.00
	Stem, 3 oz., cocktail, #7606	20.00
	Stem, 3 oz., wine, #3750	30.00
	Stem, 3½ oz., cocktail, #3750	20.00
17	Stem, 3⅞", pousse-cafe, #7606	100.00
	Stem, 4½ oz., claret, #3750	35.00
	Stem, 4½ oz., claret, #7606	35.00
20	Stem, 5½ oz., cafe parfait, #7606	50.00
	Stem, 6 oz., low sherbet, #3750	9.00
18	Stem, 6 oz., low fruit/sherbet, #7606	9.00
	Stem, 6 oz., high sherbet, #3750	12.00
	Stem, 6 oz., high sherbet, #7606	12.00
	Stem, 10 oz., water, #3750	18.00
21	Stem, 10 oz., water, #7606	18.00
5	Sugar, flat, curved in side, #1917/10	100.00
11	Sugar, flat, straight side, #1917/18	125.00
	Syrup & cover, 8 oz., #106	275.00
	Tumbler, #8851	18.00
9	Tumbler, 1½ oz. whiskey, #7606	25.00
	Tumbler, 4 oz., 2⁷⁄₁₆"	16.00
	Tumbler, 5 oz., #8858	15.00
	Tumbler, 5 oz., #7606	15.00
	Tumbler, 5 oz. ftd., #3750	18.00
	Tumbler, 6 oz., 3⁷⁄₁₆"	20.00
7	Tumbler, 8 oz., #7606	20.00
	Tumbler, 9 oz., #8858	20.00
	Tumbler, 10 oz., ftd. & hdld., #7606	35.00
	Tumbler, 10 oz., hdld. & ftd., #8023	35.00
8	Tumbler, 10 oz., table, #7606	22.00
	Tumbler, 10 oz., ftd., #3750	22.00
	Tumbler, 12 oz., #8858	22.00
13	Tumbler, 12 oz., ftd., #3750	22.00
	Tumbler, 12 oz., tea, #7606	20.00
12	Tumbler, 12 oz., hdld., #8858	28.00

MEADOW WREATH, ETCH # 26 ON #42 RADIANCE LINE, NEW MARTINSVILLE GLASS COMPANY, 1926 – 1944

Colors: crystal and some blue

Meadow Wreath, a New Martinsville etching, with little exclusion, was decorated on Radiance Line #42. Meadow Wreath's design sometimes frustrates Radiance collectors searching for light blue as larger pieces are found more often etched than not. We regularly see blue Meadow Wreath etched candles but rarely ones without an etching. If a collector were willing to mix the etched Meadow Wreath with non-etched wares, a wider range of blue pieces would be feasible.

There is a wealth of bowls and serving pieces available in Meadow Wreath, but fundamental luncheon items are the exception save for the ubiquitous sugars and creamers. We recommend using these serving items to balance other patterns where those items are scarce. Merging color is already a trend, so blending patterns won't seem such a stretch in this day of ever more expensive and hard to obtain vintage glassware.

1

		Crystal
	Bowl, 7", 2 hdld., bonbon	15.00
2	Bowl, 7", 2 pt. relish, #4223/26	15.00
	Bowl, 8", 3 pt. relish, #4228/26	25.00
	Bowl, 10", comport, #4218/26	30.00
	Bowl, 10", crimped, #4220/26	35.00
3	Bowl, 10", oval celery, #42/26	22.00
	Bowl, 10", flat, flared	28.00
	Bowl, 11", crimped, ftd. #4266/26	38.00
6	Bowl, 11", ftd., flared, #4265/26	38.00
	Bowl, 12", crimped, flat, #4212	38.00
	Bowl, 12", flat, flared, deep, #42/26	38.00
	Bowl, 12", flat, flared, #4213/26	38.00
	Bowl, 13", crimped, flat	42.00
	Bowl, 5 qt., punch, #4221/26	125.00

		Crystal
	Candle, 2 lite, rnd. ft.	28.00
	Candy box (3 pt.) & cover, #42/26	38.00
1	Cheese & cracker, 11", #42/26	35.00
4	Creamer, ftd., tab hdld., #42/26	10.00
	Cup, 4 oz., punch, tab hdld.	7.00
	Ladle, punch, #4226	40.00
	Mayonnaise set, liner & ladle, #42/26	32.00
	Plate, 11"	26.00
	Plate, 14", #42/26	33.00
	Salver, 12", ftd., #42/26	35.00
5	Sugar, ftd., tab hdld., #42/26	10.00
	Tray, oval for sugar & creamer, #42/26	12.00
	Vase, 10", crimped, #4232/26	50.00
	Vase, 10", flared, #42/26	48.00

MINUET, ETCHING #1530 ON QUEEN ANN BLANK, #1509; TOUJOURS BLANK, #1511; SYMPHONE BLANK, #5010, ET AL; A.H. HEISEY & CO., 1939 – 1950S

Color: crystal

Minuet has three different designs encircling each piece. Two of those are illustrated on the right and the third was supposed to be emphasized on the cocktail icer on the next page. Oh well, two out of three worked! Established prices have been adjusted for basic pieces of Minuet, i.e. dinner plates, creamers, and sugars. By the way, what we consider dinner plates are listed as service plates in Heisey catalogs. That was normally the case in other companies' catalogs, also, which explains their shortage today. Actual dinner plates were usually cataloged in the 9 – 9½" range, but collectors have always purchased the larger plates to use as dinners.

Minuet stemware is plentiful, but tumblers are rarely found. As with other Elegant patterns, Minuet stems were purchased to use with china settings. Glass serving pieces were often ignored since china was in vogue for serving guests. Only the three-part relish and three-footed bowls are found without difficulty.

	Item	Price
	Bell, dinner, #3408	75.00
9	Bowl, finger, #3309	50.00
	Bowl, 6", ftd., dolphin, mint	45.00
	Bowl, 6", ftd., 2 hdld., jelly	40.00
	Bowl, 6½", salad dressings	35.00
14	Bowl, 7", salad dressings, 2 part	40.00
	Bowl, 7", triplex, relish	60.00
	Bowl, 7½", sauce, ftd.	70.00
	Bowl, 9½", 3 pt., "5 o'clock," relish	50.00
	Bowl, 10", salad, #1511 Toujours	65.00
11	Bowl, 11", 3 pt., "5 o'clock," relish	60.00
	Bowl, 11", ftd., dolphin, floral	120.00
	Bowl, 12", oval, floral, #1511 Toujours	65.00
	Bowl, 12", oval, #1514	65.00
	Bowl, 13", floral, #1511 Toujours	60.00
	Bowl, 13", pickle & olive	45.00
	Bowl, 13½", shallow salad	75.00
	Candelabrum, 1-lite, w/prisms	110.00
	Candelabrum, 2-lite, bobeche & prisms	175.00
	Candlestick, 1-lite, #112	35.00
	Candlestick, 2-lite, #1511 Toujours	130.00
	Candlestick, 3-lite, #142 Cascade	80.00
	Candlestick, 5", 2-lite, #134 Trident	50.00
	Centerpiece vase & prisms, #1511 Toujours	200.00
1	Cocktail icer, w/liner, #3304 Universal	120.00
	Comport, 5½", #5010	40.00
	Comport, 7½", #1511 Toujours	60.00
	Creamer, #1511 Toujours	60.00
	Creamer, dolphin ft. #1509	35.00
	Creamer, indiv., #1509 Queen Ann	37.50
	Creamer, indiv., #1511 Toujours	70.00
	Cup	25.00
	Ice bucket, dolphin ft.	175.00
	Marmalade, w/cover, #1511 Toujours (apple shape)	150.00
12	Mayonnaise, 5½", dolphin ft. & ladle	50.00
3	Mayonnaise, ftd., #1511 Toujours	60.00
	Pitcher, 73 oz., #4164	300.00
2	Plate, 7", mayonnaise liner	10.00

	Item	Price
	Plate, 7", salad	14.00
	Plate, 7", salad, #1511 Toujours	10.00
	Plate, 8", luncheon	20.00
4	Plate, 8", luncheon, #1511 Toujours	15.00
	Plate, 10½", service	120.00
	Plate, 12", rnd., 2 hdld., sandwich	150.00
	Plate, 13", floral, salver, #1511 Toujours	60.00
	Plate, 14", torte, #1511 Toujours	60.00
	Plate, 15", sandwich, #1511 Toujours	50.00
	Plate, 16", snack rack, w/#1477 center	80.00
	Salt & pepper, pr. (#10)	200.00
	Saucer	8.00
15	Stem, #5010, Symphone, 1 oz., cordial	100.00
	Stem, #5010, 2½ oz., wine	40.00
6	Stem, #5010, 3½ oz., cocktail	20.00
	Stem, #5010, 4 oz., claret	30.00
10	Stem, #5010, 4½ oz., oyster cocktail	20.00
	Stem, #5010, 6 oz., saucer champagne	20.00
13	Stem, #5010, 6 oz., sherbet	18.00

MINUET

5	Stem, #5010, 9 oz., water	25.00
	Sugar, individual, #1511 Toujours	70.00
	Sugar, individual, #1509 Queen Ann	37.50
	Sugar, dolphin ftd., #1509 Queen Ann	35.00
	Sugar, #1511 Toujours	60.00
	Tray, 12", celery, #1511 Toujours	50.00
	Tray, 15", social hour	65.00
	Tray for individual sugar & creamer	30.00
8	Tumbler, #5010, 5 oz., fruit juice	22.00
	Tumbler, #5010, 9 oz., low ftd., water	25.00
7	Tumbler, #5010, 12 oz., tea, ftd.	50.00
	Tumbler, #2351, 12 oz., tea	50.00
	Vase, 5", #5013	50.00
	Vase, 5½", ftd., #1511 Toujours	95.00
	Vase, 6", urn, #5012	75.00
	Vase, 7½", urn, #5012	90.00
	Vase, 8", #4196	95.00
	Vase, 9", urn, #5012	110.00
	Vase, 10", #4192	110.00
	Vase, 10", #4192, Saturn optic	115.00

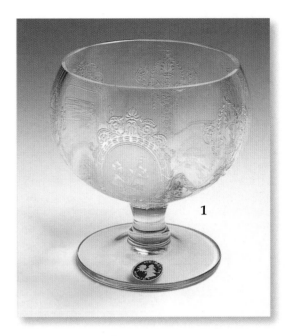

MORGAN, ETCH #412, CENTRAL GLASS WORKS, 1920S – 1930S

Colors: amber, amethyst, black, blue, crystal, green, pink, crystal stems w/colored bowls

Morgan Etch #412 is a Central Glass Works design by Joseph Balda. He was generally recognized for his Heisey designs. Rumor has it that a family named Morgan embraced this pattern for use in the West Virginia governor's mansion. Thus, their name bonded to this extraordinary seated fairy design.

We have been buying Morgan for about 25 years as Cathy found the pattern fascinating. We finally found an amethyst Morgan pitcher to show you, although it looks pink in the photo. After its introduction in our book, many collectors were equally charmed by this oh so scantily dispersed pattern.

Notice the three styles of center handled servers and straight and ruffled 10" vases pictured in green. The 10" slender bud vases are also found with straight or ruffled tops.

3

Amber pieces are turning up, but there are fewer collectors buying it. Black pieces being found include a candy, 6" bonbon, and a bud vase with a gold encrusted fairy. Does anyone have a gold decorated piece other than a bud vase?

The Morgan pattern is found only on the lid of any covered items. Colored cups and saucers are missing from most collections. Crystal ones can be found.

Morgan stemware has become more difficult to snare, with blue and amethyst stems commanding the highest prices. Internet auctions increased the demand for Morgan tremendously, but prices once commanded have presently slowed. There are five styles and shapes of stemware. The beaded stems seem to come in solid colors (crystal, pink, or green,) but are also found bi-colored with blue tops on crystal. The "wafer" stem is found all pink, in green stems with crystal bowls, and in crystal stems with blue bowls. All lilac stems are solid lilac, but the bowls are shaped differently from other colors. This lilac Morgan stemware line is the same mould line as shown in "Balda" on page 22.

1

		*All Colors
31	Bonbon, 6", two hdld.	50.00
36	Bonbon, 9", two hdld.	85.00
6	Bowl, 4¼", ftd., fruit	45.00
5	Bowl, 5", finger	50.00
7	Bowl, 10", console	75.00
35	Bowl, 13", console	110.00
	Candlestick, 3", pr	65.00
22	Candy, blown, pattern on top	495.00
25	Candy w/lid, diamond shaped, 4 ftd.	495.00
	Cheese & cracker	110.00
	Comport, 6½" tall, 5" wide	65.00
	Comport, 6½" tall, 6" wide	75.00
24	Creamer, ftd.	50.00
32	Cup	150.00
9	Decanter, w/stopper	350.00
30	Ice bucket, 4¾" x7½", 2 hdld.	450.00
	Mayonnaise	65.00
	Mayonnaise liner	15.00
	Oil bottle	250.00
20	Pitcher, 75 oz., flat w/optic, #411	895.00
28	Plate, 6½", fruit bowl liner	10.00
3	Plate, 6½", squared	25.00
	Plate, 7¼", salad	20.00
23	Plate, 7½", octagonal	15.00
29	Plate, 8½", luncheon	25.00
27	Plate, 9¼", dinner	75.00
	Salt & pepper, pr.	175.00
33	Saucer	10.00
14	Server, 9½", octagonal, center hdld.	75.00

		*All Colors
19	Server, 10⅜", round, center hdld.	75.00
17	Server, 11", octagonal, flat, center hdld.	75.00
	Stem, 3¼", sherbet	25.00
	Stem, 4⅜", sherbet, beaded stem	25.00
37	Stem, 5⅛", cocktail, beaded stem	30.00
16	Stem, 5⅝", high, sherbet, beaded stem	30.00
4	Stem, 5⅞", high sherbet	38.00
2	Stem, 5⅞", wine	40.00
	Stem, 6", wine, wafer & straight stem	40.00
1	Stem, 7¼", 10 oz., water, 2 styles	55.00
15	Stem, 8¼", water	55.00
34	Sugar, ftd.	50.00
21	Tray, 8" sq. (no pattern)	25.00
	Tumbler, oyster cocktail	30.00
10	Tumbler, 2⅛", whiskey	75.00
	Tumbler, 10 oz., flat water	30.00
26	Tumbler, 4⅜", ftd., juice	30.00
12	Tumbler, 5⅜", ftd., 10 oz., water	30.00
18	Tumbler, 5¾", ftd., water	30.00
11	Tumbler, 5⅞", ftd., 12 oz., tea	45.00
	Vase, fan shaped	350.00
	Vase, 8", drape optic	250.00
	Vase, 9⅞", straight w/flared top	350.00
38	Vase, 10", bud, straight or ruffled top**	175.00
8	Vase, 10", flared top	250.00
13	Vase, 10", ruffled top	450.00

*Crystal 25% to 30% lower. Blue, lilac 25% to 30% higher.
**Gold decorated $300.00.

20

7

8

5

4

6

16

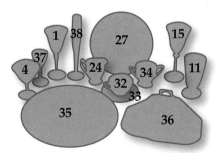

1 38
37
4
24
32
33
35
27
34
15
11
36

MT. VERNON, CAMBRIDGE GLASS COMPANY, LATE 1920S – 1940S

Colors: amber, crystal, Carmen, Royal blue, Heatherbloom, Emerald green (light and dark); rare in Violet

Mt. Vernon can be collected in amber or crystal, but few are trying to complete sets in it today. Some are buying colors when they find them, but it is usually for use rather than for display. You may be able to purchase small luncheon sets in red, cobalt blue, or Heatherbloom; but only a few extra pieces were made in those colors. However, we found that those sold well when we displayed them in Cambridge as long as they were priced reasonably. We doubled the prices listed (or a little less) for amber and crystal and that seemed to be the magic price to move it. Indiana's Diamond Point is often confused with Mt. Vernon; so be aware of that.

	Amber Crystal
Ashtray, 3½", #63	6.00
Ashtray, 4", #68	10.00
Ashtray, 6" x 4½", oval, #71	12.00
Bonbon, 7", ftd., #10	10.00
Bottle, bitters, 2½ oz., #62	50.00
Bottle, 7 oz., sq., toilet, #18	55.00
Bowl, finger, #23	8.00
Bowl, 4½", ivy ball or rose, ftd., #12	22.00
Bowl, 5¼", fruit, #6	8.00
Bowl, 6", cereal, #32	10.00
Bowl, 6", preserve, #76	10.00
Bowl, 6½", rose, #106	15.00
Bowl, 8", pickle, #65	15.00
Bowl, 8½", 4 pt., 2 hdld., sweetmeat, #105	26.00
Bowl, 10", 2 hdld., #39	18.00
Bowl, 10½", deep, #43	26.00
Bowl, 10½", salad, #120	22.00
Bowl, 11", oval, 4 ftd., #136	25.00
Bowl, 11", oval, #135	22.00
Bowl, 11½", belled, #128	26.00
Bowl, 11½", shallow, #126	26.00
Bowl, 11½", shallow cupped, #61	26.00
Bowl, 12", flanged, rolled edge, #129	30.00
Bowl, 12", oblong, crimped, #118	30.00
Bowl, 12", rolled edge, crimped, #117	30.00
Bowl, 12½", flanged, rolled edge, #45	32.00
Bowl, 12½", flared, #121	32.00

		Amber Crystal
	Bowl, 12½", flared, #44	32.00
	Bowl, 13", shallow, crimped, #116	32.00
	Box, 3", w/cover, round, #16	26.00
17	Box, 4", w/cover, sq., #17	30.00
	Box, 4½", w/cover, ftd., round, #15	32.00
5	Butter tub, w/cover, #73	48.00
	Cake stand, 10½", ftd., #150	30.00
	Candelabrum, 13½", #38	120.00
	Candlestick, 4", #130	8.00
	Candlestick, 5", 2-lite, #110	20.00
	Candlestick, 8", #35	24.00
	Candy, w/cover, 1 lb., ftd., #9	70.00
	Celery, 10½", #79	14.00
	Celery, 11", #98	15.00
	Celery, 12", #79	18.00
	Cigarette box, 6", w/cover, oval, #69	26.00
	Cigarette holder, #66	12.00
	Coaster, 3", plain, #60	5.00
	Coaster, 3", ribbed, #70	5.00
	Cocktail icer, 2 pc., #85	25.00
	Cologne, 2½ oz., w/stopper, #1340	35.00
	Comport, 4½", #33	10.00
	Comport, 5½", 2 hdld., #77	12.00
	Comport, 6", #34	13.00
	Comport, 6½", #97	15.00
	Comport, 6½", belled, #96	20.00
	Comport, 7½", #11	22.00

		Amber Crystal
	Comport, 8", #81	22.00
	Comport, 9", oval, 2 hdld., #100	33.00
	Comport, 9½", #99	25.00
9	Creamer, ftd., #8	8.00
	Creamer, individual, #4	8.00
	Creamer, #86	8.00
1	Cup, #7	5.00
	Decanter, 11 oz., #47	50.00
19	Decanter, 40 oz., w/stopper, #52	65.00
4	Honey jar, w/cover (marmalade), #74	30.00
	Ice bucket, w/tongs, #92	33.00
	Lamp, 9" hurricane, #1607	75.00
	Mayonnaise, divided, 2 spoons, #107	22.00
6	Mug, 14 oz., stein, #84	26.00
	Mustard, w/cover, 2½ oz., #28	22.00
	Pickle, 6", 1 hdld., #78	10.00
	Pitcher, 50 oz., #90	65.00
	Pitcher, 66 oz., #13	70.00
	Pitcher, 80 oz., ball, #95	90.00
	Pitcher, 86 oz., #91	110.00
	Plate, finger bowl liner, #23	3.00
	Plate, 6", bread & butter, #4	2.00
	Plate, 6⅜", bread & butter, #19	3.00
	Plate, 8½", salad, #5	5.00
2	Plate, 10½", dinner, #40	22.00
7	Plate, 11½", hdld., #37	18.00
	Relish, 6", 2 pt., 2 hdld., #106	10.00
	Relish, 8", 2 pt., hdld., #101	15.00
	Relish, 8", 3 pt., 3 hdld., #103	18.00
	Relish, 11", 3 part, #200	22.00
	Relish, 12", 2 part, #80	26.00
11	Relish, 12", 5 part, #104	26.00
	Salt, indiv., #24	5.00
	Salt, oval, 2 hdld., #102	8.00
	Salt & pepper, pr., #28	20.00

		Amber Crystal
	Salt & pepper, pr., short, #88	18.00
	Salt & pepper, tall, #89	22.00
	Salt dip, #24	7.00
	Sauce boat & ladle, tab hdld., #30-445	50.00
1	Saucer, #7	2.00
	Stem, 3 oz., wine, #27	12.00
	Stem, 3½ oz., cocktail, #26	8.00
	Stem, 4 oz., oyster cocktail, #41	7.00
16	Stem, 4½ oz., claret, #25	10.00
	Stem, 4½ oz., low sherbet, #42	5.00
13	Stem, 6½ oz., tall sherbet, #2	6.00
15	Stem, 10 oz., water, #1	12.00
	Sugar, ftd., #8	8.00
	Sugar, individual, #4	8.00
14	Sugar, #86	8.00
18	Tray, 8½", 4 pt., 2 hdld., sweetmeat	7.00
	Tray, for indiv., sugar & creamer, #4	9.00
	Tumbler, 1 oz., ftd., cordial, #87	12.00
8	Tumbler, 2 oz., whiskey, #55	8.00
3	Tumbler, 3 oz., ftd., juice, #22	6.00
	Tumbler, 5 oz., #56	7.00
	Tumbler, 5 oz., ftd., #21	7.00
	Tumbler, 7 oz., old-fashion, #57	10.00
10	Tumbler, 10 oz., ftd., water, #3	10.00
12	Tumbler, 10 oz., table, #51	10.00
	Tumbler, 10 oz., tall, #58	10.00
	Tumbler, 12 oz., barrel shape, #13	10.00
	Tumbler, 12 oz., ftd., tea, #20	12.00
	Tumbler, 14 oz., barrel shape, #14	14.00
	Tumbler, 14 oz., tall, #59	18.00
	Urn, w/cover (same as candy), #9	70.00
	Vase, 5", #42	12.00
	Vase, 6", crimped, #119	18.00
	Vase, 6", ftd., #50	22.00
	Vase, 6½", squat, #107	25.00
	Vase, 7", #58	28.00
	Vase, 7", ftd., #54	33.00
	Vase, 10", ftd., #46	50.00

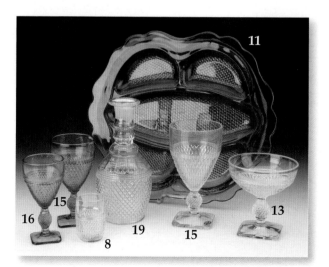

NAUTICAL, DUNCAN & MILLER GLASS COMPANY, LATE 1930S

Colors: crystal, blue, blue and pink opalescent

Nautical is readily recognized; but various pieces slip through the cracks. It is difficult to miss items with anchors and rope; however, some pieces do not have the anchor, which means they can elude you unless you are focused. We have cleaned out our folder of Nautical photographs to show you as many different pieces as we could. Enjoy!

Blue, particularly the opalescent, is the most coveted color; but admirers are prone to mix blue with crystal in order to have more pieces. We actually have seen little price decreases in this pattern probably due to so few pieces entering the marketplace. Prices for blue remain fairly steady, but opalescent prices have slipped a little due to the fact that those willing to pay the higher asking prices already have! Notice the difference in the decanter and covered jar that are pictured side by side in the bottom row on page 166. The jar is listed as a candy jar and the decanter is the taller opalescent covered piece in the photo. The decanter is taller and thinner and the lids are not interchangeable as we were once told.

That 7" comport with an anchor for the stem can be found with two different tops. The opalescent one pictured has a pointed edge around the top while the other style has a plain, rounded one.

The stand for the Nautical shakers pictured below created quite a stir among longtime connoisseurs of Nautical. A Duncan dealer actually told us that the only stand for the shakers was the one used in Caribbean, but this holder has an anchor in the center.

		*Blue	Crystal	Opalescent
6	Ashtray, 3"	45.00	8.00	80.00
	Ashtray, 6"	40.00	12.50	
22	Bowl, hdl	75.00	45.00	
19	Bowl, oval, 10"	225.00	60.00	
12	Candy jar, w/lid	550.00	295.00	750.00
	Cigarette holder	55.00	15.00	
21	Cigarette jar	100.00	45.00	175.00
17	Cocktail shaker (fish design)	195.00	65.00	
1	Comport, 7"	450.00	195.00	595.00
15	Creamer	95.00	15.00	
18	Decanter	695.00	225.00	750.00
2	Ice bucket	295.00	150.00	495.00
8	Marmalade	175.00	50.00	295.00
9	Plate, 6"	25.00	10.00	
10	Plate, 6½", 2 hdld., cake	35.00	12.00	
3	Plate, 8"	40.00	10.00	
16	Plate, 10"	125.00	25.00	
	Relish, 12", 7 part	75.00	35.00	
11	Relish, 3-part, 2 hdld., tray	45.00	22.50	
4	Shakers, pr., w/tray	500.00	65.00	
7	Relish, round, 2pt. hdl.	75.00	45.00	
	Sugar	95.00	15.00	
14	Tumbler, 2 oz., bar	55.00	12.50	
13	Tumbler, 8 oz., whiskey & soda	50.00	12.00	
	Tumbler, 9 oz., water, ftd.	50.00	15.00	
	Tumbler, cocktail	45.00	12.00	
20	Tumbler, ftd., orange juice	50.00	15.00	
	Tumbler, high ball	55.00	18.00	
5	Tray for shakers	300.00		

* Add 10% for satinized. ** 23 Anchor Bookend — not Duncan — goes well with Nautical

2

2

NAVARRE, PLATE ETCHING #327, FOSTORIA GLASS COMPANY, 1937 – 1980

Colors: crystal; all other colors found made very late

Navarre is the most collected crystal *etched* pattern made by Fostoria. (American is the most widely collected pressed Fostoria crystal pattern; but it had a run of nearly 70 years and at least three generations were exposed to it.) Navarre was only made for 44 years; and the thin delicate stems even enhance modern day china patterns. Navarre was promoted nationally, but prices on the West Coast were more expensive as a result of shipping costs. With the price of gasoline and postage regularly increasing, transportation costs are once again factoring into dealers' pricing glassware in today's market.

Only the older crystal pieces of Navarre are priced in this book. Pink and blue were made in the 1970s and 1980s as were additional crystal pieces not originally made in the late 1930s and 1940s. These later pieces include carafes, Roemer wines, continental champagnes, and brandies. You can find these later pieces in our *Collectible Glassware from the 40s, 50s, and 60s....* Many of these are acid signed on the base "Fostoria" although some carried only a sticker. We are informing you to make you mindful of the colors made in Navarre. You will even find a few pieces of Navarre that are signed Lenox. These were made after Fostoria closed and Lenox used some Fostoria moulds for a while. A few collectors ignore the colored Lenox pieces since the color seldom matched the original; but it does not seem to make much difference to most Navarre collectors. A few Depression era glass shows have forbidden these pieces or colors to be sold since they were of more recent manufacture. However, most shows are changing these arbitrary rules to allow patterns to be included as long as production began earlier.

18

		Crystal
	Bell, dinner	70.00
	Bowl, #2496, 4", sq., hdld.	15.00
17	Bowl, #2496, 4⅜", hdld.	14.00
	Bowl, #869, 4½", finger	50.00
	Bowl, #2496, 4⅝", tri-cornered	18.00
16	Bowl, #2496, 5", hdld., ftd.	18.00

		Crystal
	Bowl, #2496, 6", square, sweetmeat	20.00
	Bowl, #2496, 6¼", 3 ftd., nut	20.00
	Bowl, #2496, 7⅜", ftd., bonbon	22.00
	Bowl, #2496, 10", oval, floating garden	50.00
	Bowl, #2496, 10½", hdld., ftd.	65.00
4	Bowl, #2470½, 10½", ftd.	55.00
13	Bowl, #2496, 12", flared	60.00

NAVARRE

		Crystal
14	Bowl, #2545, 12½", oval, "Flame"	70.00
	Candlestick, #2496, 4"	16.00
	Candlestick, #2496, 4½", double	28.00
	Candlestick, #2472, 5", double	35.00
	Candlestick, #2496, 5½"	30.00
	Candlestick, #2496, 6", triple	40.00
	Candlestick, #2545, 6¾", double, "Flame"	65.00
1	Candlestick, #2482, 6¾", triple	48.00
	Candy, w/cover, #2496, 3 part	110.00
	Celery, #2440, 9"	30.00
	Celery, #2496, 11"	35.00
	Comport, #2496, 3¼", cheese	22.00
	Comport, #2400, 4½"	28.00
9	Comport, #2496, 4¾"	30.00
	Cracker, #2496, 11", plate	33.00
	Creamer, #2440, 4¼", ftd.	14.00
12	Creamer, #2496, individual	14.00
	Cup, #2440	14.00
	Ice bucket, #2496, 4⅜" high	90.00
	Ice bucket, #2375, 6" high	100.00
	Mayonnaise, #2375, 3 piece	48.00
	Mayonnaise, #2496½", 3 piece	48.00
	Pickle, #2496, 8"	23.00
	Pickle, #2440, 8½"	25.00
18	Pitcher, #5000, 48 oz., ftd.	295.00
	Plate, #2440, 6", bread/butter	6.00
	Plate, #2440, 7½", salad	8.00
	Plate, #2440, 8½", luncheon	14.00
	Plate, #2440, 9½", dinner	36.00
	Plate, #2496, 10", hdld., cake	40.00
	Plate, #2440, 10½", oval cake	48.00
	Plate, #2496, 14", torte	60.00

		Crystal
	Plate, #2464, 16", torte	95.00
10	Relish, #2496, 6", 2 part, sq.	24.00
15	Relish, #2496, 10" x 7½", 3 part	40.00
	Relish, #2496, 10", 4 part	40.00
5	Relish, #2419, 13¼", 5 part	60.00
	Salt & pepper, #2364, 3¼", flat, pr.	60.00
	Salt & pepper, #2375, 3½", ftd., pr.	80.00
	Salad dressing bottle, #2083, 6½"	395.00
	Sauce dish, #2496, div. mayonnaise, 6½"	30.00
	Sauce dish, #2496, 6½" x 5¼"	70.00
	Sauce dish liner, #2496, 8", oval	15.00
	Saucer, #2440	3.00
	Stem, #6016, 1 oz., cordial, 3⅞"	40.00
	Stem, #6106, 3¼ oz., wine, 5½"	26.00
	Stem, #6106, 3½ oz., cocktail, 6"	19.00
8	Stem, #6106, 4 oz., oyster cocktail, 3⅝"	19.00
	Stem, #6106, 4½ oz., claret, 6½"	28.00
2	Stem, #6106, 6 oz., low sherbet, 4⅜"	15.00
	Stem, #6106, 6 oz., saucer champagne, 5⅝"	17.00
	Stem, #6106, 10 oz., wate,r, 7⅝"	28.00
	Sugar, #2440, 3⅝", ftd.	13.00
11	Sugar, #2496, individual	13.00
	Syrup, #2586, metal cut-off top, 5½"	395.00
	Tidbit, #2496, 8¼", 3 ftd., turned up edge	22.00
	Tray, #2496½", for ind. sugar/creamer	15.00
3	Tumbler, #6106, 5 oz., ftd., juice, 4⅝"	17.00
7	Tumbler, #6106, 10 oz., ftd., water, 5⅜"	20.00
6	Tumbler, #6106, 13 oz., ftd., tea, 5⅞"	24.00
	Vase, #4128, 5"	125.00
	Vase, #4121, 5"	120.00
	Vase, #2470, 10", ftd.	185.00

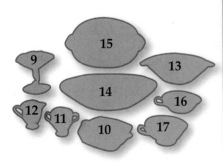

NEW GARLAND, PLATE ETCHING #284, FOSTORIA GLASS COMPANY, 1930 – 1934

Colors: Amber, Rose, and Topaz

New Garland is a Fostoria pattern that has not garnered much attention over the years. It may be the squared shapes or the inability to find it easily. Diligent searching at shows or on the internet should turn up a few pieces. If you like the older, squared mould shape of Fostoria's #2419 Mayfair line, this pattern is for you. New Garland was designed by George Sakier, the man behind many of Fostoria's more futuristic designs of that era.

Pink appears to be the color of choice; but we are getting a few requests for Topaz, recently. It has sold well for us when we have been able to acquire it for display.

		Amber Topaz	Rose
	Bonbon, 2 hdld.	12.00	18.00
	Bottle, salad dressing	175.00	225.00
	Bowl, 5", fruit	10.00	15.00
	Bowl, 6", cereal	12.00	20.00
8	Bowl, 7", soup	20.00	30.00
	Bowl, 7½"	25.00	40.00
10	Bowl, 10", baker	33.00	48.00
	Bowl, 11", ftd.	45.00	60.00
	Bowl, 12"	50.00	60.00
	Candlestick, 2"	15.00	20.00
	Candlestick, 3"	17.50	22.50
	Candlestick, 9½"	30.00	40.00
	Candy jar, cover, ½ lb.	50.00	80.00
	Celery, 11"	22.00	30.00
	Comport, 6"	20.00	28.00
	Comport, tall	30.00	40.00
12	Cream soup	15.00	20.00
	Creamer	11.00	15.00
	Creamer, ftd.	12.00	17.50
	Creamer, tea	15.00	20.00
7	Cup, after dinner, #2419	18.00	22.00
4	Cup, ftd., #2419	13.00	15.00
	Decanter	145.00	210.00
	Finger bowl, #4121	12.00	15.00
	Finger bowl, #6002, ftd.	15.00	18.00
	Ice bucket, #2375	75.00	120.00
	Ice dish	20.00	25.00
	Jelly, 7"	18.00	22.50
	Lemon dish, 2 hdld.	15.00	18.00
	Mayonnaise, 2 hdld.	18.00	22.50
	Mint, 5½"	12.50	16.00
	Nut, individual	10.00	13.00
	Oil, ftd.	125.00	200.00
	Pickle, 8½"	16.00	20.00
	Pitcher, ftd.	225.00	295.00
6	Plate, 6", #2419	4.00	6.00
11	Plate, 7"	7.00	10.00
3	Plate, 8"	12.00	15.00
1	Plate, 9", #2419	25.00	35.00

		Amber Topaz	Rose
	Plate, 10" cake, 2 hdld.	27.50	35.00
2	Platter, 12"	35.00	50.00
	Platter, 15"	50.00	80.00
	Relish, 4 part	20.00	27.50
	Relish, 8½"	14.00	18.00
	Sauce boat	50.00	75.00
	Sauce boat liner	20.00	25.00
4	Saucer, #2419	3.00	4.00
	Saucer, after dinner	7.00	8.00
	Shaker, pr.	40.00	60.00
	Shaker, pr., ftd.	75.00	100.00
	Stem, #4120, 2 oz., whiskey	20.00	30.00
	Stem, #4120, 3½ oz., cocktail	20.00	24.00
	Stem, #4120, 5 oz., low sherbet	14.00	16.00
	Stem, #4120, 7 oz., low sherbet	15.00	18.00
	Stem, #4120, high sherbet	18.00	20.00
	Stem, #4120, water goblet	22.00	28.00
	Stem, #6002, claret	25.00	35.00
	Stem, #6002, cordial	30.00	40.00
	Stem, #6002, goblet	22.00	28.00
	Stem, #6002, high sherbet	18.00	20.00
	Stem, #6002, low sherbet	14.00	16.00
	Stem, #6002, oyster cocktail	16.00	20.00
9	Stem, #6002, wine	22.00	28.00
	Sugar	11.00	15.00
	Sugar, ftd.	12.00	17.50
	Sugar, tea	15.00	20.00
	Tumbler, #4120, 5 oz.	12.00	18.00
	Tumbler, #4120, 10 oz.	14.00	20.00
	Tumbler, #4120, 13 oz.	15.00	22.00
	Tumbler, #4120, 16 oz.	20.00	28.00
	Tumbler, #6002, ftd., 2 oz.	18.00	25.00
5	Tumbler, #6002, ftd., 5 oz.	12.00	18.00
	Tumbler, #6002, ftd., 10 oz.	14.00	20.00
	Tumbler, #6002, ftd., 13 oz.	15.00	22.00
	Vase, 8"	75.00	95.00

NUMBER 520, "BYZANTINE," ROUND LINE, CAMBRIDGE GLASS COMPANY, C. 1931

Colors: amber, Emerald green, Peach Blo; #3095 colored Peach-blo w/ribbed bowl, crystal stem & foot, optic, amber

Cambridge's Number 520 and Numbers 703 and 704, which ensue, are usually referred to as "one of those Cambridge numbered patterns"; few dealers outside of those focusing on Cambridge take time to learn to differentiate them. There are collectors of these lines, and hopefully adding names "Byzantine," "Florentine," and "Windows Border" may help identify the patterns as did "Rosalie" for Number 731.

Since no factory name has been forthcoming for No. 520, we adopted an idea from a collector of Number 520. She told us it reminded her of the highly structured designs witnessed in her travels. "It's very Byzantine," she said.

We see similar quantities of Peach Blo (pink) and Emerald (green), but apparently, there are more fans of the Emerald. Amber pieces were shown previously.

		Peach Blo Green, Amber				Peach Blo Green, Amber
	Bouillon, 2 hdld. soup cup, #934	20.00		Plate, 11", club luncheon, grill		25.00
10	Bowl, 5¼", fruit, #928	20.00		Plate, finger bowl liner, #3060		9.00
9	Bowl, 6½", cereal or grapefruit, #466	26.00	12	Platter for gravy boat, #917		25.00
	Bowl, 12", oval, #914	40.00		Platter, 14½", oval/service, #903		65.00
11	Bowl, cream soup & liner	25.00	3	Saucer, #933		4.00
	Bowl, finger, #3060 & liner	25.00		Saucer, cupped, liner for bouillon		8.00
2	Butter w/cover	165.00		Stem, 2½ oz., cocktail, #3060		16.00
	Candy box, #300	110.00	4	Stem, 2½ oz., wine, #3060		25.00
	Comport, 7¼" h., #531	35.00		Stem, 6 oz., high sherbet, #3060		15.00
	Comport, jelly, #2900	30.00		Stem, 7 oz., sherbet, #3060		12.00
	Comport, #3095 (twist stem)	35.00		Stem, 9 oz., water, #3060		24.00
1	Creamer, rim ft., #138	16.00		Stem, cocktail, #3095		16.00
3	Cup, #933	15.00		Stem, high sherbet, #3095		16.00
	Gravy or sauce boat, double, #917	75.00		Stem, low sherbet, #3095		15.00
	Oil bottle, #193	175.00	7	Sugar, rim ft., #138		16.00
	Oil bottle w/cut flattened stop, 6 oz., #197	195.00		Tumbler, 3 oz., ftd., #3060		16.00
8	Plate, 6", sherbet	6.00		Tumbler, 5 oz., ftd., #3060		16.00
5	Plate, 8", luncheon	12.00		Tumbler, 10 oz., ftd., #3060		18.00
6	Plate, 9½" dinner, #810	35.00		Tumbler, 12 oz., low ft., #3095		20.00
	Plate, 10", grill	30.00				

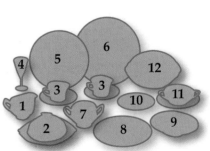

NUMBER 703, "FLORENTINE," CAMBRIDGE GLASS COMPANY, LATE 1920S

Colors: Emerald light green and w/gold, Peach-blo, amber

Cambridge's No. 703 is another of the numbered lines that collectors can never remember what the number is. Hopefully, the name "Florentine" may stick. Still, even experienced dealers often have to sneak a peek at a book to make certain of these numbered lines. We have previously only pictured "Florentine" in green. Enjoy the added amber and Peach-blo items this time. We bought a large set a few years ago of mixed numbered lines, but "Florentine" mostly sold at the first couple of shows where we had it displayed. It's exceedingly attractive!

6

		Green
2	Bouillon liner, 6", #934	5.00
3	Bouillon, 2-hdld., #934	14.00
	Bowl, 5¼", fruit, #928	10.00
	Bowl, 6½", cereal, #466	15.00
	Bowl, 8", #1004	40.00
4	Bowl, 8½" soup, #381	22.00
	Candlestick, #625	22.00
6	Creamer, #138	12.00
8	Cup, after dinner, #494	20.00
5	Cup, ftd., #494	10.00
	Finger bowl liner, #3060	5.00
	Finger bowl, #3060	11.00
	Fruit salad, 7 oz., #3060	16.00
	Platter, 12½", oval, #901	50.00
	Platter, 16", oval, #901	70.00
	Sandwich tray, 12" oval, center handle, #173	30.00
8	Saucer, after dinner	5.00
5	Saucer, #494	2.00
9	Stem, 1 oz., cordial, #3060	40.00
	Stem, 2½ oz., cocktail, #3060	16.00
	Stem, 2½ oz., wine, #3060	20.00

		Green
	Stem, 4½ oz., claret, #3060	22.00
	Stem, 5 oz., low sherbet, #3060	9.00
	Stem, 5½ oz., tall sherbet, #3060	10.00
	Stem, 6 oz., cafe parfait, #3060	15.00
	Stem, 9 oz., water, #3060	20.00
1	Sugar, #138	12.00
	Tumbler, 2 oz., bar, #3060	10.00
	Tumbler, 3 oz., ftd., #3060	12.00
7	Tumbler, 4 oz., oyster cocktail, #3060	10.00
	Tumbler, 5 oz., juice, #3060	12.00
	Tumbler, 5 oz., ftd. juice, #3060	14.00
	Tumbler, 8 oz., table, #3060	15.00
	Tumbler, 8 oz., ftd, #3060	16.00
	Tumbler, 10 oz., ftd., water, #3060	16.00
	Tumbler, 10 oz., water, #3060	16.00
	Tumbler, 12 oz., tea, #3060	18.00
	Tumbler, 12 oz., ftd., tea, #3060	20.00

NUMBER 704, "WINDOWS BORDER," CAMBRIDGE GLASS COMPANY, C. 1925

Colors: amber, Bluebell, crystal, Emerald, Peach-blo

Number 704 is a Cambridge numbered line whose name was suggested by a collector as "Windows Border"; and that might be recalled better than Number 704, which as a rule, is forgotten once it has been researched.

We have seen several sets of "Windows Border" exhibited in antique malls without any name, but identified as Cambridge since most pieces are marked with that enlightening C in a triangle signifying Cambridge. We hope its exposure in this book will enhance its appeal to collectors and bring it the recognition it merits.

1

		All Colors
	Bottle, decanter, #0315	175.00
	Bottle, decanter, #3075	195.00
	Bowl, 5¼", fruit	15.00
8	Bowl, 6", cereal	20.00
7	Bowl, 7", 3 ftd.	30.00
10	Bowl, 8", rolled edge, #460	32.00
	Bowl, 8½", soup	28.00
	Bowl, 8¾", oval	30.00
	Bowl, 10½", #912 casserole and cover	165.00
	Bowl, 12", oval, #914	45.00
	Bowl, 12", oval w/cover, #915	110.00
	Bowl, 2 hdld. cream soup, #922	18.00
	Bowl, finger, #3060	28.00
	Bowl, finger, #3075	28.00
	Butter and cover, #920	110.00
	Candlestick, 2", #227½	15.00
	Candlestick, 3½", #628	22.00
	Candlestick, 7½", #439	33.00
	Candlestick, 8½", #438	36.00
	Candlestick, 9½", #437	40.00
	Candy box and cover, 5", #98, 3-part, flat	85.00
	Candy box and cover, 5", #299, 3-ftd.	85.00

	All Colors
Candy box and cover, 6", #300, 3-ftd.	95.00
Celery, 11", #908	30.00
Celery tray, 11", #652	38.00
Cheese plate, #468	30.00
Cheese plate & cover, #3075	115.00
Cigarette box, #430	40.00
Cigarette box, #616	40.00
Cologne, 1 oz., #198 or #199	100.00
Comport, 5", #3075	25.00
Creamer, flat, #137	15.00
Creamer, flat, #942	15.00
Creamer, flat, #943	15.00
Creamer, flat, #944	15.00
Cup, #933	10.00
Cup, demi, #925	25.00
Gravy boat, double and stand, #917	110.00
Ice bucket w/bail, short, #970	90.00
Ice bucket w/bail, tall, #957	90.00

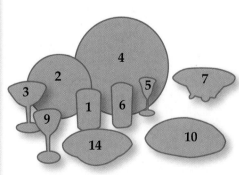

		All Colors
	Ice tub, straight up tab hdlds., #394	65.00
	Jug, night set, #103, 38 oz. w/tumbler	195.00
	Jug, #107	175.00
	Jug, #124, 68 oz., w/lid	250.00
	Jug, 62 oz., flat, #955	200.00
	Jug, #3077 w/lid	350.00
	Mayonnaise, 3 pc., #169	40.00
	Mayonnaise, 3 pc., #533	40.00
	Oil, 6 oz., #193	60.00
	Oyster cocktail, 4½ oz., ftd., #3060	10.00
	Pickle tray, 9", #907	25.00
	Plate, 6"	5.00
2	Plate, 7"	6.00
	Plate, 8"	12.00
	Plate, 8½"	12.00
11	Plate, 9½", dinner	40.00
4	Plate, 10½", service	50.00
12	Plate, 12", oval/cracker, #487	20.00
	Plate, 13½"	55.00
	Plate, cupped, liner for creme soup, #922	6.00
	Plate, liner for finger bowl, #3060	6.00
	Plate, liner for finger bowl, #3075	6.00
	Platter, 12½", oval service, #901	65.00
	Platter, 16", oval, #904	75.00
	Puff & cover, 3" or 4", #578, blown	85.00
	Puff & cover, 4", #582	60.00
	Saucer, #933	4.00
	Saucer, demi, #925	6.00
5	Stem, 1 oz., cordial, #3075	45.00
9	Stem, 2½ oz., cocktail (wide bowl), #3075	12.00
	Stem, 2½ oz., wine (slender bowl), #3075	20.00
	Stem, 4½ oz., claret, #3075	26.00

		All Colors
	Stem, 5 oz., parfait, #3060	28.00
	Stem, 5½ oz., cafe parfait, #3075	28.00
3	Stem, 6 oz., high sherbet, #3060	15.00
	Stem, 9 oz., #3060	24.00
	Stem, 9 oz., #3075	24.00
	Stem, low sherbet, #3075	10.00
	Stem, high sherbet, #3075	12.00
	Sugar, flat, #137	15.00
	Sugar, flat, #942	15.00
	Sugar, flat, #943	15.00
	Sugar, flat, #944	15.00
	Syrup, 9 oz., w/metal cover, #170	135.00
	Syrup, tall jug, #814	165.00
	Toast dish and cover, 9", #951	225.00
14	Tray, 10", center handle, #140	35.00
13	Tray, 12", oval, center handle, #173	35.00
	Tumbler, 2 oz., flat, #3060	22.00
	Tumbler, 2 oz., whiskey, #3075	22.00
	Tumbler, 3 oz., ftd., #3075	20.00
	Tumbler, 5 oz., ftd., #3075	15.00
	Tumbler, 5 oz., #3075	20.00
	Tumbler, 6 oz., ftd. fruit salad (sherbet)	12.00
	Tumbler, 8 oz., ftd., #3075	15.00
	Tumbler, 10 oz., #3075	16.00
1	Tumbler, 10 oz., flat, #3060	16.00
	Tumbler, 10 oz., ftd., #3075	20.00
	Tumbler, 12 oz., #3075	22.00
6	Tumbler, 12 oz., flat, #3060	22.00
	Tumbler, 12 oz., ftd., #3060	22.00
	Tumbler, 12 oz., ftd., #3075	22.00
	Vase, 6½", ftd., #1005	95.00
	Vase, 9½", ftd., #787	135.00

173

NYMPH, "FLYING NUN," TIFFIN GLASS COMPANY, EARLY 1930S

Colors: Nile Green and Nile Green with crystal

Our initiation to Nymph was back when it was identified as "Flying Nun" by Fred Bickenheuser. We questioned that term as it did not look like a nun to us, but that was the accepted terminology at the time.

We started buying a few pieces for photography as it became available. We regularly attended the National Tiffin show to keep up with that market until about 10 years ago. Amazingly, few Tiffin dinnerware lines were being displayed, and that was our interest for our books. What was being offered then were colors and an assortment of large vases and decorative pieces.

After deciding to add five Tiffin dinnerware lines to our Elegant book, we went back once more to observe dinnerware prices. We found dinnerware lines of Cambridge, Heisey, and Fostoria in evidence, but only four individual Tiffin dinnerware pieces were being offered for sale. Our trip was not very rewarding in that respect.

		Nile Green
	Candy jar, #9557, ½ lb., w/cover	165.00
1	Creamer	50.00
9	Jug w/cover	495.00
	Jug	395.00
3	Plate, 8", salad	16.00
8	Plate, 10", service	90.00
	Stem, #15011, 3 oz., cocktail	30.00
7	Stem, #15011, 6 oz., champagne	30.00
	Stem, #15011, 6 oz., sherbet	25.00
6	Stem, #15011, 9 oz., water goblet	40.00
2	Sugar	50.00
5	Tumbler, #14185, 2½ oz., ftd. whiskey	40.00
	Tumbler, #14185, 9 oz., ftd., water	30.00
4	Tumbler, #14185, 12 oz., ftd., iced tea	35.00
	Vase, 10", bud, #15004	85.00

OCTAGON, BLANK #1231 RIBBED, BLANK #500, AND BLACK #1229, A.H. HEISEY & CO.

Colors: crystal, Flamingo pink, Sahara yellow, Moongleam green, Hawthorne orchid, Marigold deep amber/yellow, and Dawn

Octagon was generally marked by Heisey's trademark **H** within a diamond. Since it is marked, you rarely see a piece reasonably priced even though it is one of Heisey's inexpensive patterns. Few collectors actively hunt for this unembellished pattern, which comes in an assortment of colors. In the price list below, the only pieces that attract much attention are the basket, ice tub, and the 12" four-part tray. Observe that ice tubs were sometimes cut or etched as shown here. That 12" tray can be found in the rare gray/black color called Dawn. Heisey's Octagon is sensibly priced for a beginning collector.

Marigold pieces are occasionally found in Octagon, and one such is shown in the photo on the next page. This rarely seen Heisey color is prone to peeling and crazing which cannot be undone. If that occurs, it becomes unappealing to collectors.

		Crystal	Flamingo	Sahara	Moongleam	Hawthorne	Marigold
5	Basket, 5", #500	500.00	300.00	300.00	350.00	450.00	800.00
	Bonbon, 6", sides up, #1229	10.00	40.00	25.00	25.00	40.00	
	Bowl, cream soup, 2 hdld.	10.00	20.00	25.00	30.00	40.00	
7	Bowl, 2 hdld, individual nut bowl	15.00	25.00	25.00	25.00	60.00	65.00
	Bowl, 5½", jelly, #1229	15.00	30.00	25.00	25.00	50.00	
	Bowl, 6", mint, #1229	10.00	20.00	25.00	25.00	45.00	30.00
	Bowl, 6", #500	14.00	20.00	22.00	25.00	35.00	
	Bowl, 6½", grapefruit	10.00	20.00	22.00	25.00	35.00	
2	Bowl, 8", #1209	20.00	45.00	45.00	45.00	65.00	
	Bowl, 8", ftd., #1229 comport	15.00	25.00	35.00	45.00	55.00	
	Bowl, 9", flat soup	10.00	15.00	20.00	27.50	30.00	
	Bowl, 9", vegetable	15.00	32.00	25.00	30.00	50.00	
3	Bowl, 12", #1203	25.00	55.00	50.00	55.00	65.00	
	Candlestick, 3", 1-lite	15.00	30.00	30.00	40.00	50.00	
	Cheese dish, 6", 2 hdld., #1229	7.00	15.00	10.00	15.00	15.00	
	Creamer, #500	10.00	30.00	35.00	35.00	50.00	
	Creamer, hotel	10.00	30.00	30.00	35.00	50.00	
	Cup, after dinner	10.00	20.00	20.00	25.00	42.00	
	Cup, #1231	5.00	15.00	20.00	20.00	35.00	
	Dish, frozen dessert, #500	15.00	30.00	20.00	30.00	35.00	50.00
4	Frozen dessert	10.00	22.00		22.00		30.00
1	Ice tub, #500	30.00	65.00	80.00	85.00	129.00	150.00
	Mayonnaise, 5½", ftd., #1229	10.00	25.00	30.00	35.00	55.00	
6	Nut, two hdld.	10.00	25.00	20.00	25.00	65.00	70.00
	Plate, cream soup liner	3.00	5.00	7.00	9.00	12.00	
	Plate, 6"	4.00	8.00	8.00	10.00	15.00	
	Plate, 7", bread	5.00	10.00	10.00	15.00	20.00	
9	Plate, 8", luncheon	7.00	10.00	10.00	15.00	25.00	

1   1   1

175

		Crystal	Flamingo	Sahara	Moongleam	Hawthorne	Marigold
	Plate, 10", sand., #1229	15.00	20.00	25.00	30.00	80.00	
	Plate, 10", muffin, #1229, sides up	15.00	25.00	30.00	35.00	40.00	
	Plate, 10½"	17.00	25.00	30.00	35.00	45.00	
	Plate, 10½", ctr. hdld., sandwich	25.00	40.00	40.00	45.00	70.00	
	Plate, 12", muffin, #1229, sides up	20.00	27.00	30.00	35.00	45.00	
	Plate, 13", hors d'oeuvre, #1229	20.00	35.00	35.00	45.00	60.00	
	Plate, 14"	22.00	25.00	30.00	35.00	50.00	
	Platter, 12¾", oval	20.00	25.00	30.00	40.00	50.00	
	Saucer, after dinner	5.00	8.00	10.00	10.00	12.00	
	Saucer, #1231	5.00	8.00	10.00	10.00	12.00	
	Sugar, #500	10.00	25.00	35.00	35.00	50.00	
	Sugar, hotel	10.00	30.00	30.00	35.00	50.00	
	Tray, 6", oblong, #500	8.00	15.00	15.00	15.00	30.00	
	Tray, 9", celery	10.00	20.00	20.00	25.00	45.00	
	Tray, 12", celery	10.00	25.00	25.00	30.00	50.00	
8	Tray, 12", 4 pt., #500 variety*	40.00	90.00	110.00	120.00	250.00	*350.00

*Dawn

OLD COLONY, EMPRESS BLANK #1401, CARACASSONE BLANK #3390, AND OLD DOMINION BLANK #3380, A.H. HEISEY & CO., 1930 – 1939

Colors: crystal, Flamingo pink, Sahara yellow, Moongleam green, Marigold deep amber/yellow

Due to the wealth of Sahara (yellow), Old Colony pricing will be based on Sahara. Price crystal at 60% less and Flamingo at 10% less; for Moongleam, add 10% and Marigold, add 20%. Space does not permit pricing each color separately. If you like Heisey's Sahara, this might be the perfect pattern to collect due to its availability.

		Sahara
	Bouillon cup, 2 hdld., ftd.	25.00
	Bowl, finger, #4075	15.00
	Bowl, ftd., finger, #3390	25.00
	Bowl, 4½", nappy	14.00
	Bowl, 5", ftd., 2 hdld.	20.00
	Bowl, 6", ftd., 2 hdld., jelly	25.00
	Bowl, 6", dolphin ftd., mint	30.00
	Bowl, 7", triplex, dish	40.00
	Bowl, 7½", dolphin ftd., nappy	45.00
	Bowl, 8", nappy	35.00
	Bowl, 8½", ftd., floral, 2 hdld.	50.00
	Bowl, 9", 3 hdld.	80.00
	Bowl, 10", rnd., 2 hdld., salad	50.00
	Bowl, 10", sq., salad, 2 hdld.	50.00
	Bowl, 10", oval, dessert, 2 hdld.	45.00
	Bowl, 10", oval, veg.	60.00
	Bowl, 11", floral, dolphin ft.	70.00
	Bowl, 13", ftd., flared	35.00
	Bowl, 13", 2 pt., pickle & olive	40.00
	Cigarette holder, #3390	44.00
	Comport, 7", oval, ftd.	80.00
	Comport, 7", ftd., #3368	70.00
	Cream soup, 2 hdld.	22.00
1	Creamer, dolphin ft.	40.00
	Creamer, indiv.	40.00
	Cup, after dinner	40.00
9	Cup	24.00
	Decanter, 1 pt.	325.00
	Flagon, 12 oz., #3390	90.00
	Grapefruit, 6"	30.00
	Grapefruit, ftd., #3380	20.00
	Ice tub, dolphin ft.	100.00
	Mayonnaise, 5½", dolphin ft.	40.00
6	Nut dish, individual, dolphin ft.	25.00
	Oil, 4 oz., ftd.	105.00
	Pitcher, 3 pt., #3390	200.00
	Pitcher, 3 pt., dolphin ft.	200.00
	Plate, bouillon	15.00

		Sahara
	Plate, cream soup	12.00
	Plate, 4½", rnd.	5.00
	Plate, 6", rnd.	12.00
	Plate, 6", sq.	12.00
	Plate, 7", rnd.	15.00
8	Plate, 7", sq.	15.00
	Plate, 8", rnd.	18.00
2	Plate, 8", sq.	18.00
	Plate, 9", rnd.	26.00
	Plate, 10½", rnd.	120.00
	Plate, 10½", sq.	110.00
	Plate, 12", rnd.	75.00
	Plate, 12", 2 hdld., rnd., muffin	75.00
	Plate, 12", 2 hdld., rnd., sand.	50.00
	Plate, 13", 2 hdld., sq., sand.	50.00
	Plate, 13", 2 hdld., sq., muffin	50.00
	Platter, 14", oval	55.00
	Salt & pepper, pr.	100.00
	Saucer, sq.	10.00
10	Saucer, rnd.	7.00
5	Stem, #3380, 1 oz., cordial	75.00
	Stem, #3380, 2½ oz., wine	20.00
	Stem, #3380, 3 oz., cocktail	12.00
	Stem, #3380, 4 oz., oyster/cocktail	15.00
	Stem, #3380, 4 oz., claret	30.00
	Stem, #3380, 5 oz., parfait	16.00
	Stem, #3380, 6 oz., champagne	14.00
	Stem, #3380, 6 oz., sherbet	14.00
	Stem, #3380, 10 oz., short soda	14.00
	Stem, #3380, 10 oz., tall soda	18.00
	Stem, #3390, 1 oz., cordial	75.00
	Stem, #3390, 2½ oz., wine	20.00
	Stem, #3390, 3 oz., cocktail	12.00
	Stem, #3390, 3 oz., oyster/cocktail	15.00
	Stem, #3390, 4 oz., claret	24.00
4	Stem, #3390, 6 oz., champagne	18.00
	Stem, #3390, 6 oz., sherbet	15.00
	Stem, #3390, 11 oz., low water	20.00

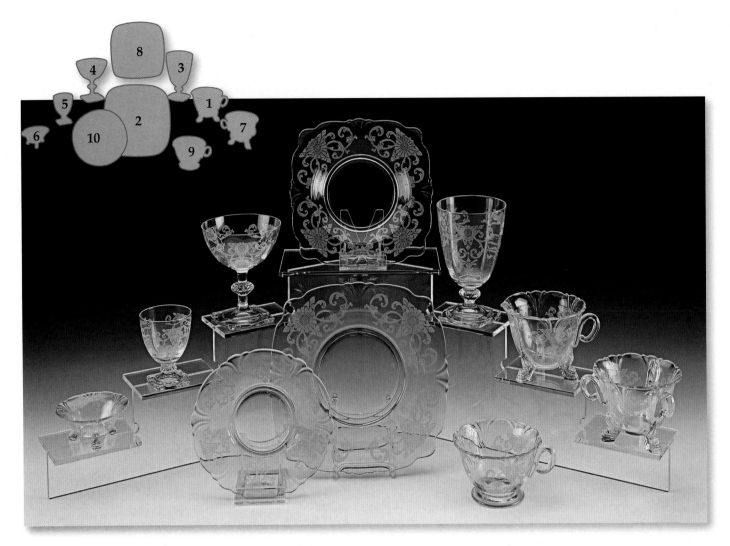

		Sahara
	Stem, #3390, 11 oz., tall water	22.00
7	Sugar, dolphin ft.	45.00
	Sugar, individual	40.00
	Tray, 10", celery	30.00
	Tray, 12", ctr. hdld., sandwich	50.00
	Tray, 12", ctr. hdld., sq.	50.00
	Tray, 13", celery	40.00
	Tray, 13", 2 hdld., hors d'oeuvre	75.00
	Tumbler, dolphin ft.	165.00
	Tumbler, #3380, 1 oz., ftd., bar	40.00

		Sahara
	Tumbler, #3380, 2 oz., ftd., bar	20.00
	Tumbler, #3380, 5 oz., ftd., bar	14.00
	Tumbler, #3380, 8 oz., ftd., soda	16.00
	Tumbler, #3380, 10 oz., ftd., soda	16.00
3	Tumbler, #3380, 12 oz., ftd., tea	18.00
	Tumbler, #3390, 2 oz., ftd.	20.00
	Tumbler, #3390, 5 oz., ftd., juice	18.00
	Tumbler, #3390, 8 oz., ftd., soda	22.00
	Tumbler, #3390, 12 oz., ftd., tea	25.00
	Vase, 9", dolphin ftd.	150.00

OLD SANDWICH, BLANK #1404, A.H. HEISEY & CO.

Colors: crystal, Flamingo pink, Sahara yellow, Moongleam green, cobalt, amber

Old Sandwich Moongleam is the preferred color as is true of its sister pattern Ipswich which is sometimes mistaken for old Sandwich. We are showing you Moongleam (green) and Flamingo (pink) this time. Collecting sets almost seems to be a thing of the past, but crystal settings would be considerably less expensive than any of the colors listed. There are four sizes of creamers, but only an oval sugar. Old Sandwich cobalt blue pieces are scarce and expensive as you can see by our price listing.

		Crystal	Flamingo	Sahara	Moongleam	Cobalt
15	Ashtray, individual	9.00	45.00	25.00	45.00	45.00
9	Beer mug, 12 oz.	50.00	400.00	180.00	250.00	240.00
6	Beer mug, 14 oz.*	55.00	375.00	180.00	250.00	250.00
	Beer mug, 18 oz.	65.00	400.00	170.00	400.00	380.00
	Bottle, catsup, w/#3 stopper (like large cruet)	70.00	200.00	175.00	225.00	
	Bowl, finger	12.00	50.00	60.00	60.00	
	Bowl, ftd., popcorn, cupped	80.00	110.00	110.00	135.00	
19	Bowl, 11", rnd., ftd., floral	50.00	85.00	65.00	100.00	
20	Bowl, 12", oval, ftd., floral	30.00	50.00	50.00	80.00	
1	Candlestick, 6"	40.00	100.00	100.00	130.00	250.00
2	Cigarette holder	60.00	70.00	80.00	100.00	
7	Comport, 6"	65.00	95.00	90.00	100.00	
17	Creamer, oval	25.00	90.00	85.00	50.00	
	Creamer, 12 oz.	32.00	185.00	170.00	175.00	575.00
	Creamer, 14 oz.	35.00	175.00	180.00	185.00	
	Creamer, 18 oz.	40.00	185.00	190.00	195.00	
16	Cup	40.00	65.00	65.00	125.00	
23	Catsup bottle	60.00	185.00	200.00	225.00	
	Floral block, #22	15.00	25.00	30.00	35.00	
14	Oil bottle, 2½ oz., #85 stopper	50.00	140.00	140.00	250.00	
	Parfait, 4½ oz.	15.00	50.00	50.00	60.00	

		Crystal	Flamingo	Sahara	Moongleam	Cobalt
	Pilsner, 8 oz.	14.00	28.00	32.00	38.00	
	Pilsner, 10 oz.	16.00	32.00	37.00	42.00	
	Pitcher, ½ gallon, ice lip	80.00	140.00	140.00	340.00	
4	Pitcher, ½ gallon, reg.	100.00	175.00	165.00	185.00	
	Plate, 6", sq., ground bottom	10.00	20.00	17.00	22.00	
	Plate, 7", sq.	10.00	27.00	25.00	30.00	
3	Plate, 8", sq.	15.00	30.00	27.00	32.00	
5	Salt & pepper, pr.	40.00	110.00	140.00	275.00	
16	Saucer	10.00	15.00	15.00	25.00	
18	Stem, 2½ oz., wine	18.00	45.00	45.00	55.00	
	Stem, 3 oz., cocktail	20.00	30.00	32.00	40.00	
	Stem, 4 oz., claret	17.00	35.00	35.00	50.00	150.00
13	Stem, 4 oz., oyster cocktail	12.00	22.00	22.00	28.00	
12	Stem, 4 oz., sherbet	7.00	14.00	14.00	17.00	
	Stem, 5 oz., saucer champagne	12.00	28.00	28.00	40.00	
21	Stem, 10 oz., low ft.	15.00	50.00	50.00	140.00	
22	Sugar, oval	25.00	90.00	55.00	60.00	
	Sundae, 6 oz.	18.00	30.00	30.00	35.00	
	Tumbler, 1½ oz., bar, ground bottom	45.00	340.00	200.00	200.00	240.00
	Tumbler, 5 oz., juice	7.00	35.00	20.00	35.00	
	Tumbler, 6½ oz., toddy	20.00	35.00	40.00	40.00	
	Tumbler, 8 oz., ground bottom, cupped & straight rim	20.00	35.00	35.00	40.00	
11	Tumbler, 10 oz.	20.00	40.00	40.00	45.00	
	Tumbler, 10 oz., low ft.	15.00	40.00	42.00	45.00	
8	Tumbler, 12 oz., ftd., iced tea	15.00	75.00	35.00	55.00	45.00
10	Tumbler, 12 oz., iced tea	20.00	45.00	45.00	55.00	

ORIENTAL, ETCHING #250, FOSTORIA GLASS CO., 1918 – 1929

Color: crystal

A pheasant is the notable attribute of Fostoria's Oriental. That Oriental name might normally have you on the lookout for a pagoda or a junk in the design. We've bought and sold quite a few unusual Oriental pieces over the years before deciding to add this to the Elegant book. Sorry, our photo inventory did not come across the cigarette box which we photographed and subsequently sold. Lost photos have happened a few times over the 37 years of writing, but thankfully, just a few.

This is an extensive pattern including six different pitchers (jugs in Fostoria's catalog listing). We rarely see single items for sale, rather small groupings, particularly tumblers and a random pitcher. Optimistically, publicity here will flush more Oriental into the market. As it is, few dealers, other than those who appreciate Fostoria, know what this pattern actually is. You might consider adding some to your table before it all flies the coop.

	Almond #766	16.00
	Bonbon, 4½", #880	24.00
	Bottle, oil, 5 oz., cut neck, #1465	65.00
	Bottle, oil, 7 oz., cut neck, #1465	75.00
	Bottle, salad dressing, #2083	85.00
	Bottle, salad dressing, #2169	85.00
	Bowl, finger, #766	16.00
	Bowl, punch bowl and foot, #1227	395.00
	Box, cigarette w/cover, #2618	50.00
2	Carafe, #1697, 23 oz.	95.00
1	Carafe tumbler, 6 oz., #4023	30.00
	Carafe whiskey, 2½ oz., #981	32.00
	Comport, 5", #803	22.00
	Comport, 6", #803	25.00
	Creamer, #1851	20.00
	Creamer, #2133	20.00
	Custard, 4 oz., #766	7.50
	Decanter, qt., cut neck, #300	150.00
	Grapefruit, #945	35.00
	Grapefruit liner, #945½	25.00
	Horseradish, #979	55.00
	Jug, 300/7	195.00
	Jug, 303/7	195.00
	Jug, 724/7	210.00
5	Jug w/cover, #317½	210.00
	Jug, claret, #1761	210.00
	Marmalade w/cover, #1968	45.00
	Mayonnaise, #2138	35.00
	Mayonnaise plate, 6", #2138	7.00
	Mustard w/cover, #1831	38.00
	Nappy, 4½", #1227	20.00
	Nappy, 5", ftd., #803	20.00
	Nappy, 6", ftd., #803	22.50
	Nappy, 7", ftd., #803	25.00
	Nappy, 8", #1227	30.00
	Plate, 5", tumbler underliner, #701	7.00
	Plate, 5", sherbet	7.00
	Plate, 6", finger bowl, #766	7.00
	Plate, 7", salad, #1897	11.00
	Plate, 9", sandwich, #1848	17.50
	Plate, 10½", sandwich, #1719	25.00
	Shakers, pr., #2022	75.00
	Stem, #766½, parfait	26.00
	Stem, #766, ¾ oz., brandy	26.00
	Stem, #766, ¾ oz., cordial	32.00

ORIENTAL

	Stem, #766, 2 oz., sherry	20.00
	Stem, #766, 2¾ oz., wine	22.00
	Stem, #766, 3 oz., cocktail	12.00
	Stem, #766, 4½ oz., claret	24.00
7	Stem, #766, 5 oz., champagne	16.00
4	Stem, #766, 9 oz., water goblet	20.00
3	Stem, #766, fruit	9.00
	Stem, #766, parfait	26.00
	Stem, #766, sherbet	9.00
	Sugar, #1851	20.00
	Sugar, #2133	20.00
	Sweetmeat, #858	26.00
	Tumbler, #837, oyster cocktail	12.00
	Tumbler, 3 oz., #4011	30.00
	Tumbler, 3 oz., #887	30.00
	Tumbler, 5 oz., #4011	15.00
	Tumbler, 5 oz., #889	15.00
	Tumbler, 8 oz., #4011	17.50
	Tumbler, 8 oz., #701	17.50
	Tumbler, 12 oz., #4011	20.00
6	Tumbler, 14 oz., #701	22.50
	Tumbler, 14 oz., handled, #701	35.00
	Tumbler, 15 oz., #4011	22.50
	Tumbler, ftd. ice tea, handled, #4061	30.00
	Tumbler, ftd. ice tea, handled, #766	30.00
	Tumbler, table, #4011½	16.00
	Tumbler, table, #820	16.00

PERSIAN PHEASANT, TIFFIN GLASS COMPANY, EARLY 1930S

Colors: crystal, Nile Green, Rose and Nile Green w/crystal

Collectors are attracted to bird patterns and Tiffin produced a sufficient amount of birds to give them options. When we were acquiring additional patterns for this book, we didn't realize that three of the nine were bird designs until we commenced laying out the book. This Tiffin pheasant design is reminiscent of Fostoria's Oriental pattern which also integrates pheasants. Add to that Tiffin's Empire and a third of our newest additions made use of our feathered friends.

Pricing below is for crystal, as that is what we are finding in the market. Rose and Nile Green are rarely encountered. A few colored stems turn up, but that seems to be all that is ever offered for sale. Rose stems are completely Rose but Nile Green stems have crystal stems with green bowls.

		*Crystal
	Bowl, #5902, 6½", fruit or nut	14.00
	Bowl, #526, 9"	38.00
	Bowl, #526, 10", cupped	42.00
	Bowl, #5902, 10", salad, deep	45.00
	Bowl, #5902, 12½", cone	60.00
	Bowl, #5902, 13", crimped	65.00
	Bowl, #5902, 13", shallow	58.00
	Bowl, #8153, 12", center console	55.00
	Bowl, 13", center console	58.00
4	Bowl, finger	22.00
6	Bowl, finger, ftd.	25.00
	Candle, #9758	35.00
	Candleholder, #5902, 5⅝", w/fan center, 2-lite	50.00
	Celery, #5902, 10½"	40.00
	Comport, #004, 6", high	40.00
	Comport, #185, 6", wide, low	35.00
	Creamer, #185	35.00
	Creamer, #5902	35.00
	Cup	45.00
	Grapefruit, #251, w/plain liner	55.00
	Jug, ftd.	250.00
	Jug, ftd., w/cover	295.00
	Jug, 60 oz.	225.00
	Mayonnaise, #5902, flat	35.00
	Nappy, #5902, 7"	35.00
	Plate, #5902, 6¼", mayonnaise liner	7.00
	Plate, #5902, 8¼", salad	12.00
	Plate, #5902, 10½", 2-hdld.	40.00
	Plate, #5902, 13", lily	50.00
	Plate, #5902, 14", sandwich	50.00

		*Crystal
	Relish, #5902, 6⅜", 3-pt.	40.00
	Relish, #5902, 10½", 3-pt.	45.00
	Saucer	8.00
	Server, #5905, center handle	35.00
	Shaker, #2, pr.	75.00
	Stem, #15037, 1½ oz., cordial	40.00
	Stem, #15037, 3 oz., wine	28.00
	Stem, #15037, 3½ oz., cocktail	18.00
	Stem, #15037, 4½ oz., claret	26.00
	Stem, #15037, 5 oz., parfait	22.00
	Stem, #15037, 5½ oz., champagne	20.00
	Stem, #15037, 6 oz., sherbet	16.00
	Stem, #15037, 9 oz., water goblet	26.00
3	Stem, #17358, 1½ oz., cordial	40.00
	Stem, #17358, 3 oz., wine	28.00
2	Stem, #17358, 3½ oz., 5¼" cocktail	18.00
5	Stem, #17358, 4½ oz., 6¼", claret	25.00
	Stem, #17358, 5½ oz., 6¾", champagne	20.00
	Stem, #17358, 6 oz., sherbet	16.00
	Stem, #17358, 9 oz., 8¼", water goblet	26.00
	Sugar, #185	35.00
7	Sugar, #5902	35.00
	Tumbler, #15037, 9 oz., water	20.00
1	Tumbler, #17358, 9 oz., water	20.00
	Tumbler, #17358, 12 oz., 6¾", ice tea	25.00
	Vase, #14185, 6½", bud	45.00
	Vase, #14185, 8¼", bud	60.00
	Vase, #14185, 10½", bud	75.00
	Vase, #15082, 11", bud	85.00

*Add 50% for Rose or Nile Green

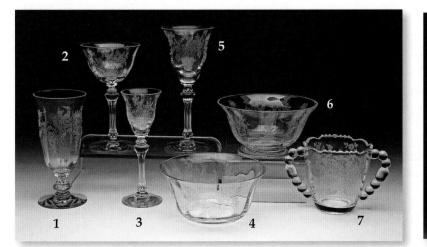

183

PIONEER, #2350, FOSTORIA GLASS COMPANY, C. 1926

Colors: amber, Blue, crystal, green, Rose, Ebony, Topaz, Azure, Orchid

Fostoria's Pioneer #2350 is the mould blank employed for both Seville and Vesper etchings. Few Pioneer collectors search for the less expensive non-etched blank. Blue, as the color pictured here was called, is the color gathered. It is often used to fill for missing pieces of etched patterns since prices are a fraction of those for etched designs. The Blue butter dish pictured could be bought for $100.00 or less, but add an etching and the price skyrockets. Repeatedly, collectors have discussed with us that they feel it better to have an undecorated piece in their set than nothing at all.

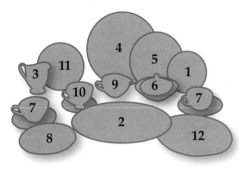

		Crystal Amber Green	Ebony	Rose Topaz	Azure Orchid	Blue
	Ashtray, 3¾"	12.00	15.00	16.00	18.00	
	Ashtray, lg., deep	14.00	15.00	16.00	20.00	
	Bouillon, flat	12.00				14.00
	Bouillon, ftd., #2350½	10.00				
8	Bowl, 5", fruit, shallow	8.00				15.00
	Bowl, 6", cereal	12.00				18.00
12	Bowl, 7", rnd. soup	15.00				25.00
	Bowl, 8", nappy	20.00				25.00
	Bowl, 8", oval pickle	17.50				22.50
	Bowl, 9", nappy	17.50				25.00
	Bowl, 9", oval baker	28.00				42.00
	Bowl, 10", oval baker	30.00				50.00
	Bowl, 10", salad	25.00				40.00
	Bowl, creme soup, flat	15.00				27.50
	Bowl, creme soup, ftd., #2350½	18.00				
6	Butter & cover	60.00				90.00
	Celery, 11", oval narrow	20.00				24.00
	Comport, 8"	27.50		30.00	40.00	
9	Creamer, flat	9.00				15.00
3	Creamer, ftd., #2350½*	9.00	10.00	12.00		15.00
	Cup, after dinner	10.00	14.00			16.00
7	Cup, flat	10.00				15.00
10	Cup, ftd., #2350½	10.00	12.50			15.00
	Egg cup	18.00		25.00		

		Crystal Amber Green	Ebony	Rose Topaz	Azure Orchid	Blue
	Grapefruit liner**	5.00				
	Grapefruit, strt. side	25.00				33.00
1	Plate, 5", bouillon liner	4.00				8.00
11	Plate, 6"	4.00	8.00			
5	Plate, 7", salad	5.00	9.00			9.00
	Plate, 8"	7.00	10.00			15.00
	Plate, 9"	10.00	14.00			20.00
	Plate, 10"	15.00	20.00			30.00
4	Plate, 12", chop	18.00				35.00
	Plate, 15", service	25.00				40.00
	Plate, creme soup	5.00				7.00
	Plate, oval sauce boat	9.00				12.50
2	Platter, 10½"	22.50				30.00
	Platter, 12"	25.00				35.00
	Platter, 15"	30.00				40.00
	Relish, rnd., 3 pt.	12.50		15.00	20.00	
	Sauce boat, flat	22.50				35.00
7	Saucer	3.00	4.00			5.00
10	Saucer, after dinner	3.00	4.00			4.00
	Sugar cover	14.00				30.00
	Sugar, flat	9.00				15.00
	Sugar, ftd., #2350½*	9.00	10.00	12.00		15.00
	Tumbler, ftd., water					25.00

*Ruby $17.50
** Looks like straight crystal glass

PLAZA, #21, DUNCAN & MILLER GLASS COMPANY, LATE 1920S – EARLY 1930S

Colors: amber, crystal, green, pink, cobalt blue, red

Plaza was Duncan & Miller's pattern #21, which was made in an array of colors. Amber jumps out at us in our travels as evidenced by our photograph. As a matter of fact, amber seems to be the only color inhabiting Florida. You buy what you happen upon when you are motivated to add to a new book.

Pink and green, of course, are sought more than other colors. Were blue and red more available, those would be favored; but that lone cocktail is the only blue piece we have. We catch sight of very few items in those colors except in the Pittsburgh area; and in that part of the country, everyone knows Duncan and it is highly cherished!

		Amber Crystal	*Pink Green				Amber Crystal	*Pink Green
12	Bowl, 4⅜", finger	4.00	13.00		9	Salt and pepper, pr.	32.00	
13	Bowl, 6¼", cereal	6.00	15.00		11	Saucer	1.00	3.00
	Bowl, 9", oval vegetable	22.00	45.00		6	Stem, cocktail	8.00	14.00
	Bowl, 10", deep vegetable	24.00	40.00			Stem, cordial	16.00	30.00
	Bowl, 14", flared, console	38.00	60.00		1	Stem, parfait	9.00	20.00
	Candle, 4¾"h. x 7"w. double	15.00	30.00		14	Stem, saucer champagne	7.00	14.00
2	Candy and lid, 4½", round	15.00	30.00			Stem, 3¾, sherbet	5.00	10.00
11	Cup	4.00	10.00			Stem, water	12.00	18.00
4	Mustard, w/slotted lid	15.00	28.00			Stem, wine	12.00	18.00
	Oil bottle	22.00	50.00			Tumbler, flat juice	5.00	12.00
	Parfait	10.00	24.00			Tumbler, flat tea	9.00	16.00
	Pitcher, flat	35.00	75.00			Tumbler, flat water	7.00	15.00
5	Plate, 5¼", finger bowl liner	3.00	8.00			Tumbler, flat whiskey	7.00	12.00
	Plate, 6½", bread and butter	2.00	8.00		3	Tumbler, 3½", ftd., juice	6.00	12.00
	Plate, 7½", salad	3.00	10.00		8	Tumbler, ftd., tea	10.00	20.00
10	Plate, 8½", luncheon	4.00	12.00		7	Tumbler, ftd., water	8.00	16.00
	Plate, 10½", hdld.	15.00	24.00			Vase, 8"	28.00	75.00

*Add 50% for any cobalt blue or red.

PLEAT & PANEL, BLANK #1170, A.H. HEISEY & CO., 1926

Colors: crystal, Flamingo pink, Moongleam green, and amber

Many consider Pleat and Panel to be Depression glass; and some influential Heisey dealers would prefer to put Pleat and Panel in that category as its quality and color renditions are deemed not up to usual Heisey standards. Although passionate Heisey connoisseurs do not like to admit it, not all Heisey was first quality.

There are considerable color variations in the Flamingo pink. It can be very light to an orange shade. Pink was a volatile color to manage in the days before there were precise temperature controls on glass vats. Only economically driven Depression glass companies were supposed to have color deviations. Yes, even Heisey had difficulty sustaining color!

Pleat and Panel does echo an early Deco inspiration in its design and probably doesn't deserve the snubbing it endures from collectors. Most pieces carry the well-known **H** in a diamond mark; so rarely do you spot pieces priced inexpensively. Truthfully, though, thus far our problem with the pattern has been pricing it cheaply enough so someone will buy it.

Stems are normally marked on the stem itself and not the foot; look there if you are searching for a mark. Remember, it does not have to be marked to actually be Heisey.

		Crystal	Flamingo	Moon-gleam
	Bowl, 4", chow chow	6.00	11.00	14.00
	Bowl, 4½", nappy	6.00	11.00	14.00
9	Bowl, 5", 2 hdld., bouillon	7.00	14.00	17.50
	Bowl, 5", 2 hdld., jelly	9.00	14.00	17.50
10	Bowl, 5", lemon, w/cover	20.00	50.00	60.00
13	Bowl, 6½", grapefruit/cereal	5.00	14.00	17.50
	Bowl, 8", nappy	10.00	32.50	40.00
	Bowl, 9", oval, vegetable	12.50	35.00	40.00
	Cheese & cracker set, 10½", tray, w/compote	25.00	75.00	80.00
1	Compotier, w/cover, 5", high ftd.	35.00	75.00	80.00
	Creamer, hotel	10.00	20.00	25.00
	Cup	7.00	15.00	17.50
8	Marmalade, 4¾"	10.00	30.00	35.00
11	Oil bottle, 3 oz., w/pressed stopper*	30.00	75.00	110.00
	Pitcher, 3 pint, ice lip	45.00	140.00	165.00
3	Pitcher, 3 pint	45.00	140.00	165.00

		Crystal	Flamingo	Moon-gleam
	Plate, 6"	4.00	8.00	8.00
	Plate, 6¾", bouillon underliner	4.00	8.00	8.00
	Plate, 7", bread	4.00	8.00	10.00
4	Plate, 8", luncheon	5.00	12.50	15.00
	Plate, 10¾", dinner	15.00	48.00	52.00
12	Plate, 14", sandwich	15.00	32.50	40.00
	Platter, 12", oval	15.00	42.50	47.50
	Saucer	3.00	5.00	5.00
6	Sherbet, 5 oz., footed	4.00	8.00	10.00
	Stem, 5 oz., saucer champagne	5.00	12.00	14.00
5	Stem, 7½ oz., low foot	8.00	20.00	30.00
7	Stem, 8 oz.	12.00	28.00	35.00
	Sugar w/lid, hotel	10.00	20.00	30.00
	Tray, 10", compartmented spice	10.00	25.00	30.00
	Tumbler, 8 oz., ground bottom	5.00	17.50	22.50
	Tumbler, 12 oz., tea, ground bottom	7.00	25.00	30.00
2	Vase, 8"	30.00	110.00	120.00

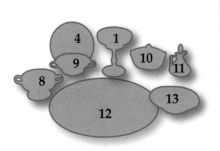

PORTIA, CAMBRIDGE GLASS COMPANY, 1932 – EARLY 1950S

Colors: crystal, yellow, Heatherbloom, green, amber, Carmen, and Crown Tuscan w/gold

Portia crystal items missing in our listing here may be found under Rose Point, which has a more detailed listing of Cambridge pieces. Prices for the Portia items will generally run 25% to 35% less than the same item in Rose Point.

		Crystal
	Basket, 2 hdld. (upturned sides)	28.00
	Basket, 7", 1 hdld.	295.00
	Bowl, 3", individual nut, 4 ftd.	45.00
	Bowl, 3½", cranberry	38.00
	Bowl, 3½", sq., cranberry	38.00
21	Bowl, 5¼", 2 hdld., bonbon, #3400/180	26.00
	Bowl, 6", 2 pt., relish	22.00
	Bowl, 6", ftd., 2 hdld., bonbon	22.00

	Crystal
Bowl, 6", grapefruit or oyster	28.00
Bowl, 6½", 3 pt., relish	28.00
Bowl, 7", 2 pt., relish	30.00
Bowl, 7", ftd., bonbon, tab hdld.	28.00
Bowl, 7", pickle or relish	30.00
Bowl, 9", 3 pt., celery & relish, tab hdld.	38.00
Bowl, 9½", ftd., pickle (like corn bowl)	28.00
Bowl, 10", flared, 4 ftd.	45.00
Bowl, 11", 2 pt., 2 hdld., "figure 8" relish	30.00
Bowl, 11", 2 hdld.	48.00
Bowl, 12", 3 pt., celery & relish, tab hdld.	42.00
Bowl, 12", 5 pt., celery & relish	48.00
Bowl, 12", flared, 4 ftd.	48.00
Bowl, 12", oval, 4 ftd., "ears" handles	60.00

20

PORTIA

		Crystal
	Bowl, finger, w/liner, #3124	30.00
28	Bowl, 10", hndl., #3500/28	48.00
	Bowl, seafood (fruit cocktail w/liner)	38.00
9	Candlestick, 5", keyhole, #3400/646	28.00
24	Candlestick, 5½", double, #502	50.00
	Candlestick, 6", 2-lite, keyhole, #3400/647	38.00
	Candlestick, 6", 3-lite, keyhole, #3400/648	42.00
	Candy box, w/cover, rnd.	110.00
2	Candy box, w/cover, 6", Ram's head, #3500/78	175.00
	Cigarette holder, urn shape	40.00
	Cocktail icer, 2 pt.	48.00
	Cocktail shaker, w/glass stopper	175.00
	Cocktail shaker, 80 oz., hdld. ball w/chrome top	225.00
15	Cologne, 2 oz., hdld. ball w/stopper, #3400/97	175.00
	Comport, 5½"	35.00
	Comport, 5⅜", blown	38.00
11	Creamer, ftd., #3400/68	18.00
	Creamer, hdld. ball	38.00
	Creamer, indiv.	16.00

2

1

		Crystal
	Cup, ftd., sq.	20.00
17	Cup, rd., #3400/54	14.00
20	Cup, after dinner, #3400/69	75.00
	Decanter, 29 oz., ftd., sherry, w/stopper	250.00
1	Decanter, 35 oz., flat, hdld., #3400/113	193.00
	Hurricane lamp, candlestick base	175.00
	Hurricane lamp, keyhole base, w/prisms	225.00
	Ice bucket, w/chrome handle	90.00
	Ivy ball, 5¼"	75.00
	Mayonnaise, div. bowl, w/liner & 2 ladles	45.00
23	Mayonnaise, w/liner & ladle, #3400/11	45.00
	Oil, 6 oz., loop hdld., w/stopper	90.00
	Oil, 6 oz., hdld. ball, w/stopper	80.00
	Pitcher, ball, 80 oz., #3400/38	175.00
	Pitcher, Doulton, 76 oz., #3400/152	310.00
6	Pitcher, 76 oz., #3400/100	175.00
	Plate, 6", 2 hdld.	12.00
4	Plate, 6½", bread/butter	6.00
26	Plate, 7", tab hndl., mayonnaise/liner, #3400/15	12.00
	Plate, 8", salad	12.00
	Plate, 8", ftd., 2 hdld.	15.00
	Plate, 8", ftd., bonbon, tab hdld.	18.00
	Plate, 8½", sq.	15.00
25	Plate, 10½", dinner	50.00
	Plate, 13", 4 ftd., torte	50.00
	Plate, 13½", 2 hdld., cake	50.00
	Plate, 14", torte	60.00
	Puff box, 3½", ball shape, w/lid	210.00
16	Salt & pepper, pr., ftd., #3400/77	35.00
17	Saucer, rnd., #3400/54	4.00
20	Saucer, after dinner, #3400/69	20.00
	Set: 3 pc. frappe (bowl, 2 plain inserts)	55.00
13	Stem, #3121, 1 oz., cordial	45.00
	Stem, #3121, 1 oz., low ftd., brandy	40.00
	Stem, #3121, 2½ oz., wine	28.00
	Stem, #3121, 3 oz., cocktail	20.00
	Stem, #3121, 4½ oz., claret	28.00
	Stem, #3121, 4½ oz., oyster cocktail	15.00
	Stem, #3121, 5 oz., parfait	28.00
	Stem, #3121, 6 oz., low sherbet	14.00
	Stem, #3121, 6 oz., tall sherbet	16.00
	Stem, #3121, 10 oz., goblet	24.00
7	Stem, #3122, 1 oz., cordial	45.00
18	Stem, #3122, 5 oz., ftd., juice	22.00
	Stem, #3124, 3 oz., cocktail	16.00
	Stem, #3124, 3 oz., wine	24.00
	Stem, #3124, 4½ oz., claret	28.00
	Stem, #3124, 7 oz., low sherbet	14.00
	Stem, #3124, 7 oz., tall sherbet	16.00
	Stem, #3124, 10 oz., goblet	24.00
14	Stem, #3126, 1 oz., cordial	45.00
	Stem, #3126, 1 oz., low ft., brandy	45.00
22	Stem, #3126, 2½ oz., wine	28.00
	Stem, #3126, 3 oz., cocktail	16.00
	Stem, #3126, 4½ oz., claret	28.00

		Crystal
	Stem, #3126, 4½ oz., low ft., oyster cocktail	14.00
	Stem, #3126, 7 oz., low sherbet	14.00
3	Stem, #3126, 7 oz., tall sherbet	16.00
	Stem, #3126, 9 oz., goblet	24.00
12	Stem, #3130, 1 oz., cordial	45.00
	Stem, #3130, 2½ oz., wine	28.00
	Stem, #3130, 3 oz., cocktail	16.00
	Stem, #3130, 4½ oz., claret	28.00
27	Stem, #3130, 4½ oz., fruit/oyster cocktail	14.00
	Stem, #3130, 7 oz., low sherbet	14.00
	Stem, #3130, 7 oz., tall sherbet	16.00
	Stem, #3130, 9 oz., goblet	24.00
	Sugar, ftd., hdld. ball	38.00
10	Sugar, ftd., #3400/68	18.00
	Sugar, individual	16.00
	Tray, 11", celery	33.00
8	Tray, 11", hdld., sandwich	33.00
19	Tumbler, 1 oz., cordial, #1344	38.00
	Tumbler, #3121, 2½ oz., bar	33.00
	Tumbler, #3121, 5 oz., ftd., juice	16.00
	Tumbler, #3121, 10 oz., ftd., water	20.00
	Tumbler, #3121, 12 oz., ftd., tea	25.00

		Crystal
	Tumbler, #3124, 3 oz.	15.00
	Tumbler, #3124, 5 oz., juice	18.00
	Tumbler, #3124, 10 oz., water	20.00
	Tumbler, #3124, 12 oz., tea	25.00
	Tumbler, #3126, 2½ oz.	28.00
	Tumbler, #3126, 5 oz., juice	16.00
	Tumbler, #3126, 10 oz., water	20.00
	Tumbler, #3126, 12 oz., tea	25.00
	Tumbler, #3130, 5 oz., juice	18.00
	Tumbler, #3130, 10 oz., water	20.00
	Tumbler, #3130, 12 oz., tea	25.00
29	Tumbler, #3400/38, 12 oz.	25.00
	Vase, 5", globe	48.00
	Vase, 6", ftd.	65.00
	Vase, 8", ftd.	90.00
	Vase, 9", keyhole ft.	75.00
5	Vase, 10", #1242	60.00
	Vase, 11", flower	90.00
	Vase, 11", pedestal ft.	95.00
	Vase, 12", keyhole ft.	110.00
	Vase, 13", flower	175.00

PRINCESS FEATHER, #201, WESTMORELAND GLASS COMPANY, LATE 1924 – EARLY 1950S; REISSUED AS GOLDEN SUNSET (AMBER) IN 1960S

Colors: amber, blue, crystal, crystal w/black base, crystal w/lavender or red flash, green, pink

Princess Feather is continually confused with other companies' Sandwich patterns. Notice the back-to-back quarter moons tied together in the pattern. If you keep that image in mind, you won't confuse it with any other Sandwich again.

Golden Sunset (amber) was not made until the 60s, so it is found more easily than other colors. Crystal was introduced in the mid-20s and can be collected without great difficulty should you wish. However, gathering a set in color other than amber will be a chore — though gratifying!

Pink or green catches the eye of more collectors, but there is not enough now available to satisfy collectors' needs. That is why gathering a complete set is no longer the typical practice as in the past. Lavender and red flashed pieces turn up occasionally and are usually blended as complementary accessories.

		Amber Crystal	*Pink Green
	Basket, 8", hdld.	40.00	
	Bonbon, 6", hdld.	18.00	
	Bonbon, 7½", crimped	22.00	
	Bowl, finger	6.00	14.00
6	Bowl, 5", nappy	6.00	14.00
	Bowl, 6½", nappy	10.00	18.00
	Bowl, 6½", grapefruit	10.00	18.00
	Bowl, 9½", bell, ftd.	30.00	
	Bowl, 10", banana, ftd.	50.00	
	Bowl, 10", crimped, ftd.	45.00	
15	Bowl, 11" x 8", oval, hdld.	40.00	
	Bowl, 12", nappy	30.00	50.00
	Cake salver, 10"	40.00	
	Candle, one lite	12.00	22.00
	Candle, double	22.00	38.00
13	Creamer	8.00	18.00
14	Cup	6.00	8.00
	Decanter w/stopper	50.00	
	Jelly w/lid, 5"	25.00	
	Pitcher, 54 oz.	85.00	
	Plate, 6", #3400/60	4.00	8.00
	Plate, 6½", liner finger bowl	4.00	8.00

		Amber Crystal	*Pink Green
	Plate, 7"	5.00	10.00
	Plate, 8"	7.00	15.00
	Plate, 10½", dinner	28.00	55.00
	Plate, 13", service	32.00	60.00
	Plate, 18"	60.00	
	Relish, 5 part, 2 hdld.	30.00	
1	Salt and pepper	22.00	60.00
14	Saucer	2.00	3.00
	Stem, 2 oz., cordial	16.00	
4	Stem, 2½ oz., wine	10.00	20.00
	Stem, 3 oz., cocktail	8.00	18.00
	Stem, 5 oz., high sherbet	8.00	18.00
9	Stem, 5 oz., saucer champagne	8.00	18.00
8	Stem, 6 oz., sherbet	6.00	14.00
5	Stem, 8 oz., water	10.00	24.00
12	Sugar	8.00	18.00
	Tray, creamer/sugar	10.00	
	Tumbler, 6 oz., juice	6.00	14.00
11	Tumbler, 9 oz., ftd.	8.00	20.00
	Tumbler, 10 oz., water, flat	10.00	22.00
	Tumbler, 12 oz., ice tea, flat	12.00	26.00
	Vase, 14", flat	65.00	

* Add 25% for blue or ruby/lavender flash.

PRISCILLA, #2321 FOSTORIA GLASS COMPANY, 1925 – 1931

Colors: amber, black, Blue, crystal, green, pink

Priscilla is a mid 20s Fostoria pattern that has very few pieces, but is bailed out by its colors and design. The blue color pictured was simply called Blue by Fostoria. Unfortunately, we found a Blue 48 ounce pitcher and five handled tumblers a few weeks too late to include a picture for this book. We did make a couple of collectors happy when we offered them for sale.

There are contradictory viewpoints as to whether the handled custard (as pictured) or sherbet goes on the canapé plate, but the handled custard base fits that ring quite well. Of course, our photographer decided to place the bouillon on the plate instead of one of those. You will probably find more amber than any other color Priscilla although we bought more Blue to photograph.

6

		Amber Green	Blue
	Ashtray, 3", sq.		11.00
2	Bouillon	8.00	15.00
	Cream soup	12.00	18.00
1	Creamer	8.00	12.50
	Cup	7.00	12.00
3	Custard, ftd., hdld.	8.00	15.00
	Pitcher, 48 oz., ftd.	75.00	125.00
	Plate, 8"	6.00	12.00
4	Plate, 8" w/indent (Mah Jongg)	6.00	10.00
	Saucer	2.00	4.00
	Stem, 7 oz.	8.00	18.00
	Stem, 9 oz., water	10.00	20.00
	Stem, saucer champagne	8.00	18.00
5	Sugar	8.00	12.50
6	Tumbler, ftd.	8.00	18.00
	Tumbler, ftd., hdld.	10.00	22.00

3

Colors: crystal, Limelight green

Provincial was originally launched as Whirlpool in the 1930s; but Heisey changed its name to Provincial for a 1952 reissue. This reissue introduced Limelight which was Heisey's attempt at reviving the earlier, popular Zircon color.

		Crystal	Limelight Green
	Ashtray, 3", sq.	12.50	
	Bonbon dish, 7", 2 hdld., upturned sides	12.00	45.00
	Bowl, 5 quart, punch	100.00	
	Bowl, individual, nut/jelly	12.00	40.00
16	Bowl, 4½", nappy	12.00	70.00
10	Bowl, 5", 2 hdld., nut/jelly	12.00	
	Bowl, 5½", nappy	20.00	40.00
	Bowl, 5½", round, hdld., nappy	20.00	
17	Bowl, 5½", tri-corner, hdld., nappy, mayo	22.00	80.00
5	Bowl, 10", 4 part, relish	25.00	150.00
	Bowl, 12", floral	30.00	
	Bowl, 13", gardenia	30.00	
15	Box, 5½", footed, candy, w/cover	65.00	425.00
	Butter dish, w/cover	80.00	
	Candle, 1-lite, block	20.00	
6	Candle, 2-lite	60.00	
	Candle, 3-lite, #4233, 5", vase	80.00	
	Cigarette box w/cover	40.00	
	Cigarette lighter	30.00	
	Coaster, 4"	15.00	
8	Creamer, ftd.	12.00	85.00
	Creamer & sugar, w/tray, individual	70.00	

		Crystal	Limelight Green
	Cup, punch	8.00	
	Marmalade	45.00	
	Mayonnaise, 7" (plate, ladle, bowl)	40.00	150.00
	Mustard	140.00	
	Oil bottle, 4 oz., #1 stopper	25.00	
7	Oil & vinegar bottle (French dressing)	35.00	
9	Plate, 5", footed, cheese	20.00	
	Plate, 7", 2 hdld., snack	25.00	
12	Plate, 7", bread	8.00	
3	Plate, 8", luncheon	11.00	50.00
	Plate, 14", torte	30.00	
	Plate, 18", buffet	35.00	250.00
	Salt & pepper, pr.	35.00	
	Stem, 3½ oz., oyster cocktail	10.00	
1	Stem, 3½ oz., wine	10.00	
13	Stem, 5 oz., sherbet/champagne	8.00	
	Stem, 10 oz.	12.00	
4	Sugar, footed	12.00	85.00
	Tray, 13", oval, celery	20.00	
14	Tumbler, 5 oz., ftd., juice	8.00	60.00
11	Tumbler, 8 oz.	10.00	
2	Tumbler, 9 oz., ftd.	10.00	75.00
18	Tumbler, 12 oz., ftd., iced tea	12.00	140.00
	Tumbler, 13", flat, ice tea	15.00	
19	Vase, 3½", violet	20.00	95.00
	Vase, 4", pansy	30.00	
	Vase, 6", sweet pea	35.00	

PSYCHE, U.S. GLASS COMPANY FACTORY "R." 1926 – 1931

Color: crystal and crystal w/green

Psyche is a Tiffin pattern that has mesmerized collectors for years. It is not a prolific pattern, but enough can be obtained to motivate your quest.

As with most Elegant patterns from this era, you can come by tumblers and stems more easily than basic serving pieces. We finally found a creamer, but no sugar has been forthcoming. The green stemware and handled pieces appear more than all crystal pieces, but finding plates or bowls is a whole different ballgame. Remember, people pretty much shunned using glass dishes back then.

The cordial shown is from our cordial collection and was purchased almost 25 years ago out of a set of Tiffin cordials displayed at the national Heisey show. A dealer displayed a large set of Tiffin with a floral cutting on the same stemware line as Psyche. Mixed within that set were some Psyche cordials. We bought one, as did a couple of other collectors. Since those floral stems were priced the same as the Psyche ones, they were still in the inventory when we last saw him several years ago. What something ought to be worth because of its age and beauty and what it actually will bring in the marketplace are often two very different things. Demand stimulates price — not necessarily age or beauty.

	Bonbon	55.00		4	Stem, cocktail	30.00
	Bowl, 13", centerpiece	110.00		7	Stem, cordial	110.00
	Bowl, finger, ftd.	35.00			Stem, grapefruit w/liner	85.00
	Candleholder, #9758	65.00		2	Stem, saucer champagne	25.00
6	Creamer	50.00			Stem, sherbet	22.00
	Cup	75.00			Stem, water goblet	45.00
	Pitcher	395.00			Stem, wine	50.00
	Pitcher w/cover	495.00			Sugar	50.00
3	Plate, 6"	15.00		1	Tumbler, iced tea	42.00
	Plate, 8"	22.00		5	Tumbler, juice	32.00
	Plate, 10"	95.00			Tumbler, oyster cocktail	25.00
	Saucer	15.00			Tumbler, water	30.00
	Stem, café parfait	50.00			Vase, bud	110.00
	Stem, claret	50.00				

PURITAN, DUNCAN & MILLER GLASS COMPANY, LATE 1920S – EARLY 1930S

Colors: crystal, green, pink

Puritan has not been an easy pattern for us to locate except in travels to western Pennsylvania. We did score a green pitcher and a fairly representative assortment of pink last year; so you can see several pieces we have never pictured before.

We still get a laugh when we see the assorted pieces of green Puritan we bought in an antique mall about 100 miles south of us. A dealer approached us at a show later and asked us what the green pattern was we had bought down south. She bought all that we left (even though she did not know what it was) because the mall owner had convinced her it must be good, since we bought it. Since we need everything for a book, from the sublime to the ridiculous, we're not sure that's a good yardstick — but it worked for the mall owner.

Many crystal pieces we find have cuttings or etches on them, possibly from a separate decorating firm.

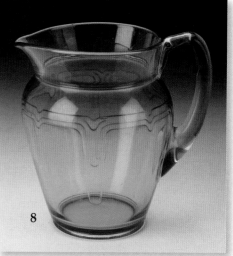

8

		*All Colors
	Bowl, cream soup, 2-hdld.	16.00
5	Bowl, 5"	10.00
7	Bowl, 6½", soup	14.00
	Bowl, 9", oval vegetable	40.00
4	Bowl, 9¼"	45.00
	Bowl, 12", rolled console	45.00
	Candlestick	20.00
	Comport	30.00
6	Creamer	15.00
1	Cup	10.00
	Cup, demi	12.00
	Ice bucket	70.00
8	Pitcher	125.00
9	Plate, 7½", salad	7.00

		*All Colors
	Plate, 10", dinner	18.00
	Plate, cream soup liner	5.00
3	Saucer	2.00
	Saucer, demi	4.00
	Server, center hdld.	32.00
	Stem, sherbet	8.00
	Stem, water goblet	17.00
2	Sugar	15.00
	Tumbler, flat tea	18.00
	Tumbler, ftd. juice	8.00
	Vase, 8"	60.00

* Crystal 25% less

QUEEN LOUISE, #7614 HAMPTON DRAWN (PULLED) STEM LINE; MORGANTOWN GLASS WORKS, C. 1928

Color: crystal bowl w/Anna Rose (pink) stem and foot

Queen Louise captivates anyone who sees it. Not everyone can afford this silkscreen decorated glassware, but almost all who have seen it, would like to own it. Fortunately, for those who were wishing prices were lower, they have softened some, but not as much as many had hoped.

Looking for Queen Louise has been an adventure, but we have discovered it in groups of five pieces or more every time we've come across it. Like other expensive glassware sets of that time, Queen Louise has evidently been handed down intact rather than divided among heirs. Apparently, it was distributed in the Chicago and St. Louis areas, since that is where it used to be found. Even the internet auctions have been void of listings for this pattern recently.

All stems are selling about the same price with waters being found the most often, but also being most sought. Champagnes and parfaits may be the most difficult stems to find. Plates are rare and the footed finger bowl is seldom seen.

8	Bowl, finger, ftd.	195.00
	Plate, 6", finger bowl liner	85.00
4	Plate, salad	110.00
6	Stem, 2½ oz., wine	300.00
5	Stem, 3 oz., cocktail	300.00
2	Stem, 5½ oz., saucer champagne	250.00
	Stem, 5½ oz., sherbet	260.00
7	Stem, 7 oz., parfait	395.00
3	Stem, 9 oz., water	395.00
1	Tumbler, 9 oz., ftd.	350.00

Colors: crystal, Sahara, Zircon, rare

		Crystal
	Ashtray, rnd.	14.00
10	Ashtray, sq.	10.00
	Ashtray, 4", rnd.	22.00
	Ashtray, 6", sq.	35.00
15	Ashtray, 6", sq. w/oval cig. holder	95.00
	Ashtrays, bridge set (heart, diamond, spade, club)	85.00
	Basket, bonbon, metal handle	25.00
	Bottle, rock & rye, w/#104 stopper	240.00
14	Bottle, 4 oz., cologne	90.00
	Bottle, 5 oz., bitters, w/tube	85.00
	Bowl, indiv., nut	10.00
13	Bowl, oval, indiv., jelly	15.00
19	Bowl, indiv., nut, 2 part	20.00
	Bowl, 4½", nappy, bell or cupped	20.00
	Bowl, 4½", nappy, scalloped	20.00
	Bowl, 5", lemon, w/cover	65.00
	Bowl, 5", nappy, straight	18.00
	Bowl, 5", nappy, sq.	25.00
	Bowl, 6", 2 hdld., div., jelly	40.00
	Bowl, 6", 2 hdld., jelly	30.00
	Bowl, 7", 2 part, oval, relish	30.00
	Bowl, 8", centerpiece	55.00
	Bowl, 8", nappy, sq.	55.00
	Bowl, 9", nappy, sq.	65.00
	Bowl, 9", salad	50.00
	Bowl, 10", flared, fruit	45.00
	Bowl, 10", floral	45.00
	Bowl, 11", centerpiece	50.00
	Bowl, 11", cone beverage	195.00
	Bowl, 11", punch	175.00
	Bowl, 11½", floral	50.00
8	Bowl, 12", oval, floral	40.00
	Bowl, 12", flared, fruit	50.00
	Bowl, 13", cone, floral	65.00
	Bowl, 14", oblong, floral	70.00
	Bowl, 14", oblong, swan hdld., floral	280.00

		Crystal
	Box, 8", floral	70.00
16	Candle block, 3", #1469½	30.00
	Candle vase, 6"	35.00
	Candlestick, 2", 1-lite	35.00
	Candlestick, 2-lite, bobeche & "A" prisms	80.00
6	Candlestick, 7", w/bobeche & "A" prisms	120.00
20	Candlestick, 7" w/bobeche & "A" prisms (1469½)	120.00
	Cheese, 6", 2 hdld.	22.00
12	Cigarette box, w/cover, oval	90.00
	Cigarette box, w/cover, 6"	35.00
	Cigarette holder, oval, w/2 comp. ashtrays	70.00
18	Cigarette holder, rnd.	18.00
	Cigarette holder, sq.	18.00
	Cigarette holder, w/cover	30.00
	Coaster or cocktail rest	10.00
	Cocktail shaker, 1 qt., w/#1 strainer & #86 stopper	350.00
	Comport, 6", low ft., flared	25.00
	Comport, 6", low ft., w/cover	65.00
	Creamer	15.00
25	Creamer, indiv.	20.00
	Cup	16.00
	Cup, beverage	18.00
	Cup, punch	8.00
	Decanter, 1 pint, w/#95 stopper	210.00
	Ice tub, 2 hdld., & underplate	80.00
	Marmalade, w/cover (scarce)	85.00
	Mayonnaise and under plate	45.00
	Mustard, w/cover	60.00
	Oil bottle, 3 oz., w/#103 stopper	35.00
	Pitcher, ½ gallon, ball shape	380.00
	Pitcher, ½ gallon, ice lip, ball shape	380.00
11	Plate, oval, hors d'oeuvres	850.00
	Plate, 2 hdld., ice tub liner	50.00
	Plate, 6", rnd.	10.00
	Plate, 6", sq.	18.00
	Plate, 7", sq.	20.00
	Plate, 8", rnd.	18.00
	Plate, 8", sq.	27.00
	Plate, 13½", sandwich	35.00
	Plate, 13½", ftd., torte	35.00
	Plate, 14", salver	35.00
	Plate, 20", punch bowl underplate	140.00

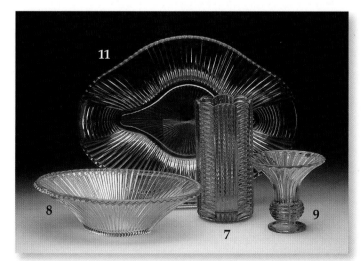

RIDGELEIGH

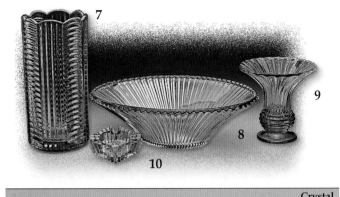

		Crystal
	Puff box, 5", and cover	65.00
	Salt & pepper, pr.	45.00
23	Salt dip, indiv.	10.00
	Saucer	5.00
	Soda, 12 oz., ftd., no knob in stem (rare)	50.00
1	Stem, cocktail, pressed	12.00
	Stem, claret, pressed	45.00
22	Stem, oyster cocktail, pressed	30.00
	Stem, sherbet, pressed	12.00
2	Stem, saucer champagne, pressed	20.00
	Stem, wine, pressed	45.00
	Stem, 1 oz., cordial, blown	160.00
	Stem, 2 oz., sherry, blown	90.00
	Stem, 2½ oz., wine, blown	80.00
	Stem, 3½ oz., cocktail, blown	35.00
	Stem, 4 oz., claret, blown	55.00
	Stem, 4 oz., oyster cocktail, blown	30.00

		Crystal
	Stem, 5 oz., saucer champagne, blown	25.00
	Stem, 5 oz., sherbet, blown	20.00
	Stem, 8 oz., luncheon, low stem	30.00
3	Stem, 9 oz., goblet, pressed	35.00
	Sugar	15.00
24	Sugar, indiv.	20.00
26	Tray, for indiv. sugar & creamer	20.00
	Tray, 10½", oblong	40.00
	Tray, 11", 3 part, relish	50.00
	Tray, 12", celery & olive, divided	50.00
	Tray, 12", celery	40.00
17	Tumbler, 2½ oz., bar, pressed	40.00
	Tumbler, 5 oz., juice, blown	30.00
21	Tumbler, 5 oz., soda, ftd., pressed	30.00
	Tumbler, 8 oz., #1469¾, pressed	35.00
4	Tumbler, 8 oz., 4½" (rare)	75.00
	Tumbler, 8 oz., old-fashion, pressed	25.00
	Tumbler, 8 oz., soda, blown	40.00
	Tumbler, 10 oz., #1469½, pressed	45.00
27	Tumbler, 12 oz., ftd., soda, pressed	55.00
5	Tumbler, 12 oz., soda, #1469½, pressed	50.00
	Tumbler, 13 oz., iced tea, blown	40.00
	Vase, #1 indiv., cuspidor shape	40.00
	Vase, #2 indiv., cupped top	45.00
	Vase, #3 indiv., flared rim	30.00
	Vase, #4 indiv., fan out top	55.00
	Vase, #5 indiv., scalloped top	55.00
	Vase, 3½"	25.00
9	Vase, 6" (also flared)	35.00
7	Vase, 8"	75.00
	Vase, 8", triangular, #1469¾	110.00

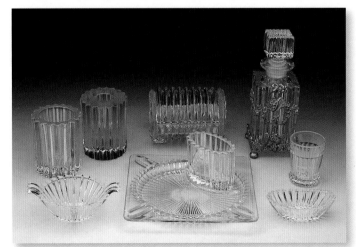

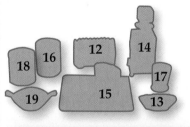

ROGENE, ETCH #269, FOSTORIA GLASS COMPANY, C. 1924 – 1929

Color: crystal

Rogene, etch #269, is an early 20s Fostoria pattern that has a multitude of pieces that are realistically priced for their age and beauty. There are five pitchers available for your choosing as well as 10 different tumblers and 8 stems not including the grapefruit and liner.

	Almond, ftd., #4095	9.00
	Comport, 5" tall, #5078	25.00
	Comport, 6", #5078	25.00
9	Creamer, flat, #1851	25.00
	Decanter, qt., cut neck, #300	75.00
	Finger bowl, #766	18.00
	Jelly, #825	20.00
	Jelly & cover, #825	32.00
	Jug 4, ftd., #4095	100.00
	Jug 7, #318	125.00
	Jug 7, #2270	150.00
	Jug 7, #4095	175.00
	Jug 7, covered, #2270	225.00
	Marmalade & cover, #1968	40.00
	Mayonnaise bowl, #766	22.00
	Mayonnaise ladle	15.00
5	Mayonnaise set, 3 pc., #2138 (ftd. compote, ladle, liner)	50.00
	Nappy, 5" ftd. (comport/sherbet), #5078	15.00
	Nappy, 6" ftd., #5078	22.00
	Nappy, 7" ftd., #5078	28.00
	Night set, 2 pc., #1697 (carafe & tumbler)	145.00
	Oil bottle w/cut stop, 5 oz., #1495	70.00
	Oyster cocktail, ftd., #837	10.00
	Plate, 5"	4.00
	Plate, 6"	5.00
	Plate, 6", #2283	5.00
	Plate, 7", salad, #2283	8.00
4	Plate, 8"	12.00

	Plate, 11"	25.00
	Plate, 11", w/cut star	27.50
	Plate, finger bowl liner	5.00
	Plate, mayonnaise liner, #766	10.00
	Shaker, pr., glass (pearl) top, #2283	50.00
	Stem, ¾ oz., cordial, #5082	32.00
	Stem, 2½ oz., wine, #5082	17.00
	Stem, 3 oz., cocktail, #5082	12.00
	Stem, 4½ oz., claret, #5082	20.00
10	Stem, 5 oz., fruit, #5082	10.00
	Stem, 5 oz., saucer champagne, #5082	12.00
	Stem, 6 oz., parfait, #5082	18.00
1	Stem, 9 oz., #5082	20.00
	Stem, grapefruit, #945½	28.00
	Stem, grapefruit liner, #945½	17.00
6	Sugar, flat, #1851	25.00
	Tumbler, 2½ oz., whiskey, #887	16.00
	Tumbler, 2½ oz., ftd., #4095	16.00
8	Tumbler, 5 oz., flat, #889	10.00
	Tumbler, 5 oz., ftd., #4095	10.00
	Tumbler, 8 oz., flat,, #889	11.00
3	Tumbler, 10 oz., ftd., #4095	12.00
	Tumbler, 12 oz., flat, hdld., #837	25.00
7	Tumbler, 13 oz., flat, #889	15.00
2	Tumbler, 13 oz., ftd., #4095	18.00
	Tumbler, flat, table, #4076	12.00
	Vase, 8½" rolled edge	110.00

ROSALIE, OR #731, CAMBRIDGE GLASS COMPANY, LATE 1920S – 1930S

Colors: Amber, Bluebell, Carmen, crystal, Ebony, Emerald green, Heatherbloom, Peach-Blo, Topaz, Willow blue

Rosalie, Cambridge's #731 line, is a pattern that can be observed in an array of colors; but few are attempting to purchase a set in any one color. Usable items and a combination of hues seem to be the newest trend. The delightful news is that Rosalie is one of Cambridge's least expensive, etched colored wares, predominantly available in pink and green. Realistically, a small arrangement of Willow Blue is feasible; but Carmen, Bluebell, or Heatherbloom are colors that are too seldom seen to be organized into sets. Note how well the pattern shows on the blue console bowl that was adorned with enamel. These were factory made; and for photography purposes, we wish all patterns were embellished that way.

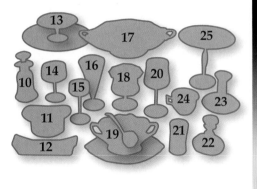

		Blue Pink Green	Amber Crystal
	Bottle, French dressing	175.00	110.00
	Bowl, bouillon, 2 hdld.	25.00	12.00
	Bowl, cream soup	25.00	12.00
1	Bowl, finger, w/liner	55.00	40.00
	Bowl, finger, ftd., w/liner	50.00	38.00
	Bowl, 3½", cranberry	38.00	26.00
	Bowl, 5½", fruit	20.00	14.00
	Bowl, 5½", 2 hdld., bonbon	22.00	14.00
	Bowl, 6¼", 2 hdld., bonbon	22.00	15.00
	Bowl, 7", basket, 2 hdld.	28.00	18.00
	Bowl, 8½", soup	40.00	25.00
	Bowl, 8½", 2 hdld.	65.00	30.00
	Bowl, 8½", w/cover, 3 pt.	150.00	75.00
	Bowl, 10", rolled edge	65.00	30.00
17	Bowl, 10", 2 hdld.	65.00	30.00
	Bowl, 11"	65.00	30.00
	Bowl, 11", basket, 2 hdld.	70.00	40.00
	Bowl, 11½"	70.00	40.00
	Bowl, 12", decagon	100.00	70.00
3	Bowl, 13", console	110.00	

		Blue Pink Green	Amber Crystal
	Bowl, 14", decagon, deep	195.00	150.00
	Bowl, 15", oval console	110.00	70.00
	Bowl, 15", oval, flanged	115.00	70.00
	Bowl, 15½", oval	115.00	70.00
22	Candle, 3½", #627	30.00	22.00
2	Candlestick, 4", #627	28.00	20.00
23	Candlestick, 4¼"x5"	30.00	22.00
	Candlestick, 5", keyhole	35.00	25.00
	Candlestick, 6", 3-lite keyhole	38.00	30.00
	Candy and cover, 6", #864	150.00	75.00
	Candy and cover, 6", #104		110.00
	Celery, 11"	33.00	22.00
13	Cheese & cracker, 11", plate	60.00	35.00
	Cigarette jar & cover	75.00	40.00
	Comport, 5½", 2 hdld.	28.00	15.00
	Comport, 5¾"	28.00	15.00
	Comport, 6", ftd., almond	38.00	28.00
	Comport, 6½", low ft.	38.00	28.00
25	Comport, 6½", high ft.	38.00	28.00
	Comport, 6¾"	38.00	26.00

		Blue Pink Green	Amber Crystal
7	Creamer, ftd., #867	18.00	12.00
	Creamer, #979	18.00	12.00
	Creamer, ftd., tall, ewer	65.00	33.00
24	Cup	20.00	15.00
19	Gravy, double, w/platter, #1147	165.00	90.00
	Ice bucket or pail	90.00	60.00
18	Icer, w/liner	60.00	38.00
	Ice tub	90.00	60.00
12	Loaf sugar, #1018	110.00	65.00
11	Mayonnaise, w/liner & spoon	50.00	30.00
19	Mayonnaise, w/plate & spoon, #983	100.00	75.00
	Nut, 2½", ftd.	55.00	40.00
10	Oil bottle, #2973	90.00	70.00
	Pitcher, 62 oz., #955	295.00	195.00
	Plate, 6¾", bread/butter	6.00	4.00
	Plate, 7", 2 hdld.	14.00	9.00
	Plate, 7½", salad, #1176	12.00	6.00
	Plate, 8⅜"	15.00	8.00
	Plate, 9½", dinner	40.00	28.00
	Plate, 11", 2 hdld.	38.00	22.00
	Platter, 12"	75.00	40.00
	Platter, 15"	115.00	60.00
	Relish, 9", 2 pt.	35.00	16.00
	Relish, 11", 2 pt.	42.00	26.00
	Salt dip, 1½", ftd.	40.00	26.00
	Saucer	4.00	2.00
4	Stem, 1 oz., cordial		30.00
	Stem, 1 oz., cordial, #3077	75.00	40.00
6	Stem, 3 oz., cocktail	12.00	

		Blue Pink Green	Amber Crystal
15	Stem, 3 oz., cocktail, #7606	20.00	12.00
	Stem, 3½ oz., cocktail, #3077	18.00	12.00
	Stem, 3½ oz., cocktail, #3115	20.00	
	Stem, 4½ oz., claret, #7606	28.00	18.00
14	Stem, 6 oz., saucer/champagne, #7606	24.00	16.00
	Stem, 6 oz., low sherbet, #3077	14.00	10.00
5	Stem, 6 oz., high sherbet, #3077	16.00	12.00
	Stem, 9 oz., water goblet, #3077	24.00	16.00
	Stem, 9 oz., water goblet, #3115	30.00	
	Stem, 10 oz., goblet, #801	28.00	18.00
20	Stem, 10 oz., water goblet, #7606	33.00	24.00
8	Sugar, ftd., #867	18.00	12.00
	Sugar shaker	250.00	195.00
	Tray for sugar shaker/creamer	30.00	20.00
	Tray, ctr. hdld., for sugar/creamer	20.00	14.00
	Tray, 11", ctr. hdld.	35.00	28.00
	Tumbler, 2½ oz., ftd., #3115	30.00	16.00
	Tumbler, 5 oz., ftd., #3077	22.00	15.00
	Tumbler, 8 oz., ftd., #3077	16.00	14.00
21	Tumbler, 8 oz., #9024	28.00	15.00
	Tumbler, 10 oz., ftd., #3077	24.00	14.00
16	Tumbler, 10 oz., ftd., #3115	24.00	14.00
	Tumbler, 12 oz., ftd., #3077	30.00	18.00
9	Tumbler, 12 oz., tea	16.00	
	Vase, 5½", ftd.	85.00	48.00
	Vase, 6"	90.00	52.00
	Vase, 6½", ftd.	125.00	55.00
	Vase, 12", w/rim (black), #402	195.00	

ROSE POINT, CAMBRIDGE GLASS COMPANY, 1936 – 1953

Colors: crystal; some crystal with gold; Ebony, Carmen, Crown Tuscan, and amber, all with gold

Rose Point is the most collected and possibly the most recognized pattern in this book. Only Fostoria's American might come close to the recognition levels of Rose Point; but American is known more as Fostoria to the public than for its actual name. Pages 202 and 203 show a Rose Point brochure with a listing where pieces are identified by number that should aid in distinguishing pieces. There are space limitations to how much catalog information we can do and still show you the actual glass. A challenge to new collectors is distinguishing the different mould blanks on which Rose Point is discovered. Be sure to examine the brochure to see the different line numbers of #3400, #3500, and #3900. These are the major Cambridge mould lines upon which Rose Point was etched. This will also aid in identifying pieces from other Cambridge patterns that refer you to Rose Point for help in pricing.

Collectors are not limited to choosing only one line in which to acquire pieces. Consequently, not all are always searching for the same items. Be sure to see the two gold encrusted nude stem goblets pictured on page 205. These were the first Rose Point Statuesque table stems to be found gold decorated and our understanding is that the original owner of these bought a car from the proceeds of selling a dozen of each. Gold "encrusted" items always draw attention no matter what pattern.

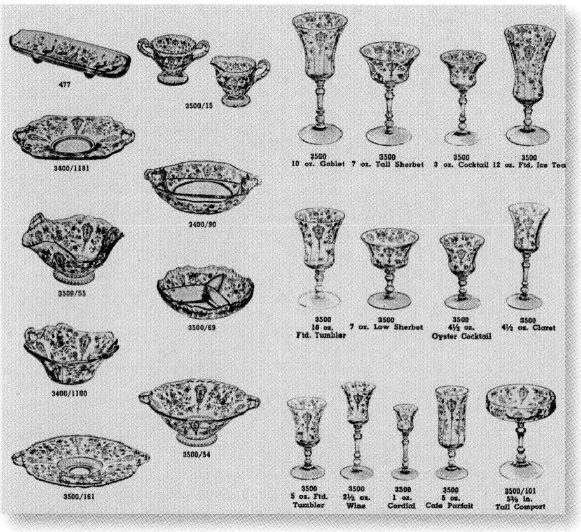

LIST OF ROSE POINT ITEMS

3500	10 oz. Goblet
3500	7 oz. Tall Sherbet
3500	7 oz. Low Sherbet
3500	3 oz. Cocktail
3500	2½ oz. Wine
3500	4½ oz. Claret
3500	4½ oz. Oyster Cocktail
3500	1 oz. Cordial
3500	5 oz Cafe Parfait
3500	12 oz. Ftd. Ice Tea
3500	10 oz. Ftd. Tumbler
3500	5 oz. Ftd. Tumbler
477	9½ in. Pickle
3400/1180	5¼ in. 2 Hdl. Bonbon
3400/1181	6 in. 2 Hdl. Plate
3400/90	6 in. 2 part Relish
3500/15	Ind. Sugar & Cream
3500/54	6 in. 2 Hdl. Ftd. Bonbon
3500/55	6 in. 2 Hdl. Ftd. Basket
3500/69	6½ in. 3 part Relish
3500/161	8 in. 2 Hdl. Ftd. Plate
3400/91	8 in. 3 part Relish
3500/57	8 in. 3 part Candy Box & Cover
3500/101	5⅜ in. Tall Comport
3900/17	Cup & Saucer
3900/19	2 pc. Mayonnaise Set
3900/20	6½ in. Bread & Butter Plate
3900/22	8 in. Salad Plate
3900/24	10½ in. Dinner Plate
3900/26	12 in. 4 Ftd. Plate
3900/28	11½ in. Ftd. Bowl
3900/33	13 in. 4 Ftd. Torte Plate, R. E.
3900/34	11 in. 2 Handled Bowl
3900/35	13½ in. 2 Handled Cake Plate
3900/40	Ind. Sugar & Cream
3900/41	Sugar & Cream
3900/54	10 in. 4 Ftd. Bowl, flared
3900/62	12 in. 4 Ftd. Bowl, flared
3900/65	12 in. 4 Ftd. Oval Bowl
3900/67	5 in. Candlestick
3900/72	6 in. 2 lite Candlestick
3900/74	6 in. 3 lite Candlestick
3900/100	6 oz. Oil, g. s.
3900/111	4 pc. Mayonnaise Set
3900/115	13 oz. Tumbler
3900/120	12 in. 5 part Celery & Relish
3900/123	7 in. Relish or Pickle
3900/124	7 in. 2 part Relish
3900/125	9 in. 3 part Celery & Relish
3900/126	12 in. 3 part Celery & Relish
3900/129	3 pc. Mayonnaise Set
3900/130	7 in. 2 handled Ftd. Bonbon
3900/131	8 in. 2 handled Ftd. Bonbon Plate
3900/136	5½ in. Comport
3900/165	Candy Box & Cover
3900/166	14 in. Plate, r. e.
3900/671	Ice Bucket
3900/671	Ice Bucket with chrome Handle
	Chrome Ice Tongs (long)
3900/1177	Salt & Pepper Shaker (doz. pr.)
274	10 in. Bud Flower Holder
278	11 in. Ftd. Flower Holder
279	13 in. Ftd. Flower Holder
968	2 pc. Cocktail Icer
1237	9 in. Ftd. Flower Holder
1238	12 in. Ftd. Flower Holder
1299	11 in. Ftd. Flower Holder
1309	5 in. Glode Flower Holder
1603	Hurricane Lamp (Etch. Chimney only)
1617	Hurricane Lamp (Etch. Chimney only)
6004	6 in. Ftd. Flower Holder
6004	8 in. Ftd. Flower Holder
P. 101	Cocktail Shaker (Patent—D133,198)

	Crystal
Ashtray, stack set on metal pole, #1715	210.00
Ashtray, 2½", sq., #721	22.00
Ashtray, 3¼", #3500/124	28.00
Ashtray, 3¼", sq., #3500/129	38.00
Ashtray, 3½", #3500/125	30.00
Ashtray, 4", #3500/126	33.00
Ashtray, 4", oval, #3500/130	60.00
Ashtray, 4¼", #3500/127	32.00
Ashtray, 4½", #3500/128	38.00
Ashtray, 4½", oval, #3500/131	48.00
Basket, 3", favor, #3500/79	435.00
Basket, 5", 1 hdld., #3500/51	360.00
Basket, 6", 1 hdld., #3500/52	375.00
Basket, 6", 2 hdld., #3400/1182	29.00
Basket, 6", sq., ftd., 2 hdld, #3500/55	35.00
Basket, 7", 1 hdld., #119	595.00
Basket, 7", wide, #3500/56	45.00
Basket, sugar, w/handle and tongs, #3500/13	295.00
Bell, dinner, #3121	110.00
Bowl, 3", 4 ftd., nut, #3400/71	50.00
Bowl, 3½", bonbon, cupped, deep, #3400/204	65.00
Bowl, 3½", cranberry, #3400/70	60.00
Bowl, 5", hdld., #3500/49	38.00
Bowl, 5", fruit, #3500/10	60.00
Bowl, 5", fruit, blown, #1534	65.00

	Crystal
Bowl, 5¼", fruit, #3400/56	60.00
Bowl, 5½", nappy, #3400/56	55.00
Bowl, 5½", 2 hdld., bonbon, #3400/1179	33.00
Bowl, 5½", 2 hdld., bonbon, #3400/1180	33.00
Bowl, 6", bonbon, crimped, #3400/203	60.00
Bowl, 6", bonbon, cupped, shallow, #3400/205	60.00
Bowl, 6", cereal, #3400/53	75.00
Bowl, 6", cereal, #3400/10	75.00
Bowl, 6", cereal, #3500/11	75.00
Bowl, 6", hdld., #3500/50	35.00
Bowl, 6", 2 hdld., #1402/89	35.00
Bowl, 6", 2 hdld., ftd., bonbon, #3500/54	32.00
Bowl, 6", 4 ftd., fancy rim, #3400/136	100.00
Bowl, 6½", bonbon, crimped, #3400/202	60.00
Bowl, 7", bonbon, crimped, shallow, #3400/201	75.00
Bowl, 7", tab hdld., ftd., bonbon, #3900/130	28.00
Bowl, 8", ram's head, squared, #3500/27	395.00
Bowl, 8½", rimmed soup, #361	200.00
Bowl, 8½", 3 part, #221	195.00
Bowl, 9", 4 ftd., #3400/135	200.00
Bowl, 9", ram's head, #3500/25	395.00
Bowl, 9½", pickle like corn, #477	35.00
Bowl, 9½", ftd., w/hdl., #115	110.00
Bowl, 9½", 2 hdld., #3400/34	60.00
Bowl, 9½", 2 part, blown, #225	495.00

3900/131

3900/165

1309

3900/129

3900/166

1603

1617

1237

6004-6

6004-8

3900/136

3900/125

3900/671

P. 101

274

1299

1238

278

279

968

3900/1177

3900/54

3900/126

3900/123

3900/65

3900/130

3900/124

3900/111

3500/57

3900/74

3900/120

3900/100

3400/91

3900/62

3900/35

3900/33

3900/72

		Crystal
	Bowl, 2 hdld., #3400/1185	75.00
	Bowl, 10", 2 hdld., #3500/28	75.00
	Bowl, 10", 4 tab ftd., flared, #3900/54	65.00
	Bowl, 10", salad, Pristine, #427	160.00
	Bowl, 10½", crimp edge, #1351	85.00
	Bowl, 10½", flared, #3400/168	70.00
	Bowl, 10½", 3 part, #222	295.00
	Bowl, 10½", 3 part, #1401/122	295.00
	Bowl, 11", ftd., #3500/16	90.00
	Bowl, 11", ftd., fancy edge, #3500/19	145.00
	Bowl, 11", 4 ftd., oval, #3500/109	310.00
	Bowl, 11", 4 ftd., shallow, fancy edge, #3400/48	85.00
	Bowl, 11", fruit, #3400/1188	85.00
	Bowl, 11", low foot, #3400/3	135.00
	Bowl, 11", tab hdld., #3900/34	70.00
	Bowl, 11½", ftd., w/tab hdl., #3900/28	75.00
	Bowl, 12", crimped, pan, Pristine, #136	350.00
	Bowl, 12", 4 ftd., oval, #3400/1240	110.00
	Bowl, 12", 4 ftd., oval, w/"ears" hdl., #3900/65	85.00
	Bowl, 12", 4 ftd., fancy rim oblong, #3400/160	80.00
	Bowl, 12", 4 ftd., flared, #3400/4	80.00
	Bowl, 12", 4 tab ftd., flared, #3900/62	80.00
	Bowl, 12", ftd., #3500/17	110.00
	Bowl, 12", ftd., oblong, #3500/118	145.00
	Bowl, 12", ftd., oval w/hdld., #3500/21	195.00
	Bowl, 12½", flared, rolled edge, #3400/2	150.00
	Bowl, 12½", 4 ftd., #993	75.00
	Bowl, 13", #1398	125.00
	Bowl, 13", 4 ftd., narrow, crimped, #3400/47	125.00
	Bowl, 13", flared, #3400/1	75.00
	Bowl, 14", 4 ftd., crimp edge, oblong, #1247	125.00
	Bowl, 18", crimped, pan Pristine, #136	650.00
	Bowl, cream soup, w/liner, #3400	150.00
	Bowl, cream soup, w/liner, #3500/2	150.00
	Bowl, finger, w/liner, #3106	90.00
	Bowl, finger, w/liner, #3121	90.00
3	Butter, w/cover, round, #506	140.00
	Butter, w/cover, 5", #3400/52	140.00
	Butter dish, ¼ lb., #3900/52	350.00
	Candelabrum, 2-lite w/bobeches & prisms, #1268	195.00
	Candelabrum, 2-lite, #3500/94	125.00
	Candelabrum, 3-lite, #1338	55.00
	Candelabrum, 5½", 3-lite w/#19 bobeche & #1 prisms, #1545	150.00
	Candelabrum, 6½", 2-lite, w/bobeches & prisms Martha, #496	150.00
	Candle, torchere, cup ft., #3500/90	225.00
	Candle, torchere, flat ft., #3500/88	210.00
	Candlestick, Pristine, #500	100.00
	Candlestick, sq. base & lites, #1700/501	195.00
	Candlestick, 2½", #3500/108	25.00
	Candlestick, 3½", #628	32.00
	Candlestick, 4", #627	50.00
	Candlestick, 4", ram's head, #3500/74	110.00
	Candlestick, 5", 1-lite keyhole, #3400/646	35.00

		Crystal
	Candlestick, 5", inverts to comport, #3900/68	40.00
	Candlestick, 5½", 2-lite Martha, #495	85.00
	Candlestick, 6", #3500/31	95.00
	Candlestick, 6", 2-lite keyhole, #3400/647	38.00
	Candlestick, 6", 2-lite, #3900/72	45.00
	Candlestick, 6", 3-lite, #3900/74	50.00
	Candlestick, 6", 3-lite keyhole, #3400/638	50.00
	Candlestick, 6", 3-tiered lite, #1338	55.00
	Candlestick, 6½", Calla Lily, #499	100.00
	Candlestick, 7", #3121	75.00
	Candlestick, 7½", w/prism, Martha, #497	110.00
	Candy box, w/cover, 5", apple shape, #316	1,250.00
	Candy box, w/cover, 5⅜", #1066 stem	200.00
	Candy box, w/cover, 5⅜", tall stem, #3121/3	165.00
	Candy box, w/cover, 5⅜", short stem, #3121/4	150.00
	Candy box, w/cover, blown, 5⅜", #3500/103	195.00
	Candy box, w/cover, 6", ram's head, #3500/78	295.00
	Candy box, w/rose finial, 6", 3 ftd., #300	295.00
6	Candy box, w/cover, 7", 3 ftd., #300	150.00
	Candy box, w/cover, 7", #3400/9	150.00
	Candy box, w/cover, 7", rnd., 3 pt., #103	140.00
	Candy box, w/cover, 8", 3 pt., #3500/57	90.00
	Candy box, w/cover, rnd., #3900/165	125.00
	Celery, 12", #3400/652	45.00
	Celery, 12", #3500/652	45.00
	Celery, 12", 5 pt., #3400/67	60.00
	Celery, 14", 4 pt., 2 hdld., #3500/97	125.00
	Celery & relish, 9", 3 pt., #3900/125	45.00
	Celery & relish, 12", 3 pt., #3900/126	55.00
	Celery & relish, 12", 5 pt., #3900/120	70.00
	Cheese, 5", comport & cracker, 13", plate, #3900/135	125.00
	Cheese, 5½", comport & cracker, 11½", plate, #3400/6	125.00
	Cheese, 6", comport & cracker, 12", plate, #3500/162	140.00
	Cheese dish, w/cover, 5", #980	525.00
	Cigarette box, w/cover, #615	150.00
	Cigarette box, w/cover, #747	155.00
	Cigarette holder, oval, w/ashtray ft., #1066	150.00
	Cigarette holder, rnd., w/ashtray ft., #1337	135.00
	Coaster, 3½", #1628	38.00
	Cocktail icer, 2 pc., #3600	60.00
	Cocktail shaker, metal top, #3400/157	190.00
	Cocktail shaker, metal top, #3400/175	190.00
	Cocktail shaker, 12 oz., metal top, #97	350.00
	Cocktail shaker, 32 oz., w/glass stopper, #101	265.00
	Cocktail shaker, 46 oz., metal top, #98	195.00
	Cocktail shaker, 48 oz., glass stopper, #102	195.00
	Comport, 5", #3900/135	35.00
	Comport, 5", 4 ftd., #3400/74	45.00
	Comport, 5½", scalloped edge, #3900/136	52.00
	Comport, 5⅜", blown, #3500/101	60.00
	Comport, 5⅜", blown, #3121 stem	65.00
	Comport, 5⅜", blown, #1066 stem	65.00
	Comport, 6", #3500/36	120.00
	Comport, 6", #3500/111	150.00
	Comport, 6", 4 ftd., #3400/13	45.00

		Crystal
5	Comport, 7", #3400/14	125.00
	Comport, 7", 2 hdld., #3500/37	120.00
	Comport, 7", keyhole, #3400/29	125.00
	Comport, 7", keyhole, low, #3400/28	80.00
	Creamer, #3400/68	18.00
	Creamer, #3500/14	22.00
	Creamer, flat, #137	110.00
	Creamer, flat, #944	125.00
	Creamer, ftd., #3400/16	70.00
	Creamer, ftd., #3900/41	18.00
	Creamer, indiv., #3500/15, pie crust edge	20.00
	Creamer, indiv., #3900/40, scalloped edge	20.00
	Cup, 3 styles, #3400/54, #3500/1, #3900/17	22.00
	Cup, 5 oz., punch, #488	35.00
	Cup, after dinner, #3400/69	250.00
	Decanter, 12 oz., ball, w/stopper, #3400/119	350.00
	Decanter, 14 oz., ftd., #1320	425.00
	Decanter, 26 oz., sq., #1380	695.00
	Decanter, 28 oz., tall, #1372	695.00
	Decanter, 28 oz., w/stopper, #1321	395.00
	Decanter, 32 oz., ball, w/stopper, #3400/92	450.00
	Dressing bottle, flat, #1263	395.00
	Dressing bottle, ftd., #1261	350.00
	Epergne candle w/vases, #3900/75	375.00
	Grapefruit, w/liner, #187	95.00
	Hat, 5", #1704	450.00
	Hat, 6", #1703	495.00
	Hat, 8", #1702	595.00
	Hat, 9", #1701	650.00
	Honey dish, w/cover, #3500/139	350.00
	Hot plate or trivet	95.00
	Hurricane lamp, w/prisms, #1613	350.00
	Hurricane lamp, candlestick base, #1617	290.00
	Hurricane lamp, keyhole base, w/prisms, #1603	290.00
	Hurricane lamp, 8", etched chimney, #1601	290.00
	Hurricane lamp, 10", etched chimney & base, #1604	395.00
	Ice bucket, #1402/52	150.00
	Ice bucket, w/chrome hdld., #3900/671	145.00
	Ice bucket, P.672	150.00
	Ice bucket, #3400 & #3900	150.00
	Ice pail, P.1705	225.00
	Ice pail, #3400/851	160.00
	Ice tub, Pristine, P.671	275.00
	Icer, cocktail, #968 or, #18	60.00
	Marmalade, 8 oz., #147	175.00
	Marmalade, w/cover, 7 oz., ftd., #157	195.00
	Mayonnaise sherbet type w/ladle, #19	60.00
	Mayonnaise, div., w/liner & 2 ladles, #3900/111	65.00
	Mayonnaise, 3 pc., #3400/11	65.00
	Mayonnaise, 3 pc., #3900/129	65.00
	Mayonnaise, w/liner & ladle, #3500/59	65.00
	Mustard, 3 oz., #151	150.00
	Mustard, 4½ oz., ftd., #1329	350.00
	Oil, 2 oz., ball, w/stopper, #3400/96	125.00
	Oil, 6 oz., ball, w/stopper, #3400/99	150.00

	Crystal
Oil, 6 oz., hdld., #3400/193	110.00
Oil, 6 oz., loop hdld., w/stopper, #3900/100	150.00
Oil, 6 oz., w/stopper, ftd., hdld., #3400/161	250.00
Pickle, 9", #3400/59	55.00
Pickle or relish, 7", #3900/123	33.00
Pitcher, 20 oz., #3900/117	350.00
Pitcher, 20 oz., w/ice lip, #70	350.00
Pitcher, 32 oz., #3900/118	350.00
Pitcher, 32 oz., martini slender, w/metal insert, #3900/114	550.00
Pitcher, 60 oz., martini, #1408	1,750.00
Pitcher, 76 oz., #3900/115	295.00
Pitcher, 76 oz., ice lip, #3400/100	195.00
Pitcher, 76 oz., ice lip, #3400/152	350.00
Pitcher, 80 oz., ball, #3400/38	210.00
Pitcher, 80 oz., ball, #3900/116	210.00
Pitcher, 80 oz., Doulton, #3400/141	310.00
Pitcher, nite set, 2 pc., w/tumbler insert top, #103	895.00
Plate, 6", bread/butter, #3400/60	10.00
Plate, 6", bread/butter, #3500/3	10.00
Plate, 6", 2 hdld., #3400/1181	18.00
Plate, 6⅛", canape, #693	150.00
Plate, 6½", bread/butter, #3900/20	10.00
Plate, 7½", #3500/4	12.00
Plate, 7½", salad, #3400/176	12.00
Plate, 8", salad, #3900/22	15.00
Plate, 8", 2 hdld., ftd., #3500/161	33.00
Plate, 8", tab hdld., ftd., bonbon, #3900/131	35.00
Plate, 8½", breakfast, #3400/62	16.00
Plate, 8½", salad, #3500/5	16.00
Plate, 9½", crescent salad, #485	195.00
Plate, 9½", luncheon, #3400/63	24.00
Plate, 10½", dinner, #3400/64	125.00
Plate, 10½", dinner, #3900/24	125.00
Plate, 11", 2 hdld., #3400/35	55.00
Plate, 12", 4 ftd., service, #3900/26	55.00
Plate, 12", ftd., #3500/39	68.00
Plate, 12½", 2 hdld., #3400/1186	60.00
Plate, 13", rolled edge, ftd., #3900/33	65.00
Plate, 13", 4 ftd., torte, #3500/110	110.00
Plate, 13", ftd., cake, Martha, #170	195.00

1   2   4

ROSE POINT

	Crystal
Plate, 13", torte, #3500/38	150.00
Plate, 13½", #242	125.00
Plate, 13½", rolled edge, #1397	60.00
Plate, 13½", tab hdld., cake, #3900/35	65.00
Plate, 14", rolled edge, #3900/166	70.00
Plate, 14", service, #3900/167	70.00
Plate, 14", torte, #3400/65	120.00
Plate, 18", punch bowl liner, Martha, #129	600.00
Punch bowl, 15", Martha, #478	4,500.00
Punch set, 15-pc., Martha	6,000.00
Relish, 5½", 2 pt., #3500/68	25.00
Relish, 5½", 2 pt., hdld., #3500/60	32.00
Relish, 6", 2 pt., #3400/90	32.00
Relish, 6", 2 pt., 1 hdl., #3400/1093	70.00
Relish, 6½", 3 pt., #3500/69	50.00
Relish, 6½", 3 pt., hdld., #3500/61	60.00
Relish, 7", 2 pt., #3900/124	32.00
Relish, 7½", 3 pt., center hdld., #3500/71	110.00
Relish, 7½", 4 pt., #3500/70	50.00
Relish, 7½", 4 pt., 2 hdld., #3500/62	65.00
Relish, 8", 3 pt., 3 hdld., #3400/91	35.00
Relish, 10", 2 hdld., #3500/85	75.00
Relish, 10", 3 pt., 2 hdld., #3500/86	70.00
Relish, 10", 3 pt., 4 ftd., 2 hdld., #3500/64	55.00
Relish, 10", 4 pt., 4 ftd., #3500/65	65.00
Relish, 10", 4 pt., 2 hdld., #3500/87	65.00
Relish, 11", 2 pt., 2 hdld., #3400/89	75.00
Relish, 11", 3 pt., #3400/200	60.00
Relish, 12", 5 pt., #3400/67	70.00
Relish, 12", 5 pt., Pristine, #419	260.00
Relish, 12", 6 pc., #3500/67	210.00
Relish, 14", w/cover, 4 pt., 2 hdld., #3500/142	1,200.00
Relish, 15", 4 pt., hdld., #3500/113	195.00
Salt & pepper, egg shape, pr., #1468	100.00
Salt & pepper, individual, rnd., glass base, pr., #1470	90.00
Salt & pepper, individual, w/chrome tops, pr., #360	60.00
Salt & pepper, lg., rnd., glass base, pr., #1471	100.00
Salt & pepper, w/chrome tops, pr., ftd. 3400/77	45.00
Salt & pepper w/chrome tops, pr., flat, #3900/1177	40.00
Sandwich tray, 11", center handled, #3400/10	110.00
Saucer, after dinner, #3400/69	40.00
Saucer, 3 styles, #3400, #3500, #3900	5.00
1 Statusque, cocktail	2,500.00
2 Statusque, banquet goblet	3,500.00
Stem, #3104, 3½ oz., cocktail	295.00
Stem, #3106, ¾ oz., brandy	100.00
Stem, #3106, 1 oz., cordial	100.00
Stem, #3106, 1 oz., pousse cafe	100.00
Stem, #3106, 2 oz., sherry	50.00
Stem, #3106, 2½ oz., wine	45.00
Stem, #3106, 3 oz., cocktail	25.00
Stem, #3106, 4½ oz., claret	40.00
Stem, #3106, 5 oz., oyster cocktail	24.00
Stem, #3106, 7 oz., high sherbet	24.00
Stem, #3106, 7 oz., low sherbet	18.00

6

	Crystal
Stem, #3106, 10 oz., water goblet	30.00
Stem, #3121, 1 oz., brandy	100.00
Stem, #3121, 1 oz., cordial	55.00
Stem, #3121, 3 oz., cocktail	20.00
Stem, #3121, 3½ oz., wine	42.00
Stem, #3121, 4½ oz., claret	50.00
Stem, #3121, 4½ oz., low oyster cocktail	22.00
Stem, #3121, 5 oz., low ft. parfait	65.00
Stem, #3121, 6 oz., low sherbet	14.00
Stem, #3121, 6 oz., tall sherbet	16.00
Stem, #3121, 10 oz., water	28.00
Stem, #3500, 1 oz., cordial	55.00
Stem, #3500, 2½ oz., wine	45.00
Stem, #3500, 3 oz., cocktail	25.00
Stem, #3500, 4½ oz., claret	55.00
Stem, #3500, 4½ oz., low oyster cocktail	24.00
Stem, #3500, 5 oz., low ft. parfait	70.00
Stem, #3500, 7 oz., low ft. sherbet	14.00
Stem, #3500, 7 oz., tall sherbet	18.00
Stem, #3500, 10 oz., water	30.00
Stem, #7801, 4 oz., cocktail, plain stem	30.00
Stem, #7966, 1 oz., cordial, plain ft.	110.00
Stem, #7966, 2 oz., sherry, plain ft.	100.00
Sugar, #3400/68	18.00
Sugar, #3500/14	20.00
Sugar, flat, #137	110.00
Sugar, flat, #944	125.00
Sugar, ftd., #3400/16	70.00
Sugar, ftd., #3900/41	18.00
Sugar, indiv., #3500/15, pie crust edge	20.00
Sugar, indiv., #3900/40, scalloped edge	18.00
Syrup, w/drip stop top, #1670	350.00
Tray, 6", 2 hdld., sq., #3500/91	150.00
Tray, 12", 2 hdld., oval, service, #3500/99	225.00
Tray, 12", rnd., #3500/67	175.00
Tray, 13", 2 hdld., rnd., #3500/72	165.00
Tray, sugar/creamer, #3900/37	22.00
Tumbler, #498, 2 oz., straight side	100.00
Tumbler, #498, 5 oz., straight side	40.00
Tumbler, #498, 8 oz., straight side	40.00
Tumbler, #498, 10 oz., straight side	40.00
Tumbler, #498, 12 oz., straight side	65.00
Tumbler, #3000, 3½ oz., cone, ftd.	90.00
Tumbler, #3000, 5 oz., cone, ftd.	90.00
Tumbler, #3106, 3 oz., ftd.	30.00

	Crystal
Tumbler, #3106, 5 oz., ftd.	30.00
Tumbler, #3106, 9 oz., ftd.	30.00
Tumbler, #3106, 12 oz., ftd.	34.00
Tumbler, #3121, 2½ oz., ftd.	55.00
Tumbler, #3121, 5 oz., low ft., juice	28.00
Tumbler, #3121, 10 oz., low ft., water	26.00
Tumbler, #3121, 12 oz., low ft., ice tea	30.00
Tumbler, #3400/1341, 1 oz., cordial	90.00
Tumbler, #3400/92, 2½ oz.	90.00
Tumbler, #3400/38, 5 oz.	90.00
Tumbler, #3400/38, 12 oz.	50.00
Tumbler, #3900/115, 13 oz.	55.00
Tumbler, #3500, 2½ oz., ftd.	55.00
Tumbler, #3500, 5 oz., low ft., juice	30.00
Tumbler, #3500, 10 oz., low ft., water	26.00
Tumbler, #3500, 13 oz., low ftd.	30.00
Tumbler, #3500, 12 oz., tall ft., ice tea	30.00
Tumbler, #7801, 5 oz., ftd.	33.00
Tumbler, #7801, 12 oz., ftd., ice tea	55.00
Tumbler, #3900/117, 5 oz.	55.00
Tumbler, #3400/115, 13 oz.	45.00
Urn, 10", w/cover, #3500/41	595.00
Urn, 12", w/cover, #3500/42	695.00
Vase, 5", #1309	90.00
Vase, 5", globe, #3400/102	80.00
Vase, 5", ftd., #6004	60.00
Vase, 6", high ftd., flower, #6004	60.00
Vase, 6", #572	175.00
Vase, 6½", globe, #3400/103	90.00
Vase, 7", ivy, ftd., ball, #1066	295.00
Vase, 8", #1430	275.00
Vase, 8", flat, flared, #797	195.00
Vase, 8", ftd., #3500/44	175.00
Vase, 8", high ftd., flower, #6004	65.00
Vase, 9", ftd., keyhole, #1237	95.00
Vase, 9", ftd., #1620	175.00
Vase, 9½" ftd., keyhole, #1233	110.00

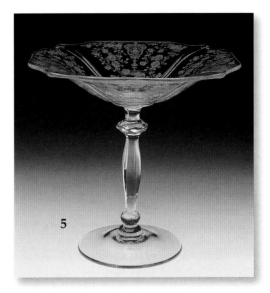

5

	Crystal
Vase, 10", ball bottom, #400	250.00
Vase, 10", bud, #1528	120.00
Vase, 10", cornucopia, #3900/575	275.00
Vase, 10", flat, #1242	175.00
Vase, 10", ftd., #1301	110.00
Vase, 10", ftd., #6004	110.00
Vase, 10", ftd., #3500/45	195.00
Vase, 10", slender, #274	55.00
Vase, 11", ftd., flower, #278	155.00
Vase, 11", ped. ftd., flower, #1299	195.00
Vase, 12", ftd., #6004	120.00
Vase, 12", ftd., keyhole, #1234	165.00
Vase, 12", ftd., keyhole, #1238	175.00
Vase, 13", ftd., flower, #279	275.00
Vase 18", #1336	2,750.00
Vase, sweet pea, #629	375.00

3

ROYAL, PLATE ETCHING #273, FOSTORIA GLASS COMPANY, 1925 – 1932

Colors: amber, Ebony, blue, green

Fostoria's Royal is sporadically identified as Vesper, since both etchings are comparable, are found on the #2350 blank, and were created in the same colors. Royal does not entice as many admirers as Vesper, possibly do to an inadequate distribution. Inexperienced collectors should find Royal's pricing more to their taste because of less demand. Remember that demand boosts prices more than scarcity.

Enough amber or green Royal can be gathered to acquire a set, though that does not seem to be a major concern. Only a very small number of pieces can be found in blue or black. Fostoria's blue color found with the Royal etching was called Blue as opposed to the Azure blue which is a lighter hue found etched with June or other patterns. We have spent years accumulating the Blue pictured.

Rare and hard to find pieces of Royal include both styles of pitchers, covered cheese and butter dishes, cologne bottles, and sugar lids. The cologne bottle is a combination powder jar and cologne. The stopper is the hardest part of the three-piece set to find. It has a pointed end which is often absent.

26

Published material indicates production of Royal continued until 1934, although the January 1, 1933, Fostoria catalog no longer listed Royal as being for sale. We have changed our cutoff date of production to 1932. If you can locate a May 1928 copy of *House and Garden*, there is an enjoyable Fostoria Royal advertisement displayed.

		*Amber Green
	Almond, #4095	24.00
	Ashtray, #2350, 3½"	18.00
	Bowl, #2350, bouillon, flat	12.00
	Bowl, #2350½, bouillon, ftd.	15.00
	Bowl, #2350, cream soup, flat	15.00
	Bowl, #2350½, cream soup, ftd.	18.00
	Bowl, #869, 4½", finger	18.00
	Bowl, #2350, 5½", fruit	12.00
	Bowl, #2350, 6½", cereal	20.00
	Bowl, #2267, 7", ftd.	22.00
	Bowl, #2350, 7¾", soup	22.00
	Bowl, #2350, 8", nappy	24.00
	Bowl, #2350, 9", nappy	26.00

		*Amber Green
	Bowl, #2350, 9", oval, baker	33.00
24	Bowl, #2324, 10", ftd.	38.00
	Bowl, #2350, 10", salad	30.00
	Bowl, #2350, 10½", oval, baker	38.00
	Bowl, #2315, 10½", ftd.	38.00
	Bowl, #2329, 11", console	20.00
	Bowl, #2297, 12", deep	20.00
	Bowl, #2329, 13", console	28.00
	Bowl, #2324, 13", ftd.	40.00
	Bowl, #2371, 13", oval, w/flower frog	130.00
2	Butter, w/cover, #2350	225.00
1	Candlestick, #2324, 4"	15.00
	Candlestick, #2324, 9"	50.00

*Add up to 50% more for blue or black.

ROYAL

		*Amber Green
	Candy, w/cover, #2331, 3 part	75.00
3	Candy, w/cover, ftd., ½ lb.	125.00
	Celery, #2350, 11"	22.00
	Cheese, w/cover/plate, #2276 (plate 11")	150.00
	Cologne, #2322, tall	110.00
	Cologne, #2323, short	90.00
	Cologne/powder jar combination	250.00
	Comport, #1861½, 6", jelly	20.00
	Comport, #2327, 7"	22.00
	Comport, #2358, 8" wide	25.00
	Creamer, flat	12.00
	Creamer, #2315½, ftd., fat	12.00
17	Creamer, #2350½, ftd.	10.00
	Cup, #2350, flat	8.00
20	Cup, #2350½, ftd.	9.00
4	Cup, #2350, demi	18.00
	Egg cup, #2350	25.00
	Grapefruit, w/insert	60.00
	Grapefruit, #2315	22.00
	Grapefruit, #2350	30.00
	Ice bucket, #2378	55.00
	Mayonnaise, #2315	20.00
	Pickle, 8", #2350	18.00
	Pitcher, #1236	295.00
	Pitcher, #5000, 48 oz.	250.00
	Plate, 8½", deep soup/underplate	30.00
	Plate, #2350, 6", bread/butter	2.00
	Plate, #2350, 7½", salad	3.00
18	Plate, #2350, 8½", luncheon	7.00
21	Plate, #2321, 8¾, Maj Jongg (canape)	22.00
	Plate, #2350, 9½", small dinner	10.00
	Plate, #2350, 10½", dinner	22.00

		*Amber Green
	Plate, #2350, 13", chop	26.00
	Plate, #2350, 15", chop	33.00
	Platter, #2350, 10½"	22.00
	Platter, #2350, 12"	32.00
	Platter, #2350, 15½"	60.00
	Salt and pepper, #5100, pr.	55.00
	Sauce boat, w/liner	95.00
20	Saucer, #2350/#2350½	2.00
6	Saucer, #2350, demi	5.00
	Server, #2287, 11", center hdld.	25.00
	Stem, #869, ¾ oz., cordial	45.00
	Stem, #869, 2¾ oz., wine	20.00
	Stem, #869, 3 oz., cocktail	12.00
25	Stem, #869, 5½ oz., oyster cocktail	12.00
	Stem, #869, 5½ oz., parfait	18.00
	Stem, #869, 6 oz., low sherbet	8.00
	Stem, #869, 6 oz., high sherbet	10.00
22	Stem, #869, 9 oz., water	18.00
26	Sugar, flat, w/lid	145.00
	Sugar, #2315, ftd., fat	12.00
19	Sugar, #2350½, ftd.	10.00
	Sugar lid, #2350½	100.00
	Tumbler, #869, 5 oz., flat	15.00
	Tumbler, #859, 9 oz., flat	18.00
5	Tumbler, #859, 12 oz., flat	22.00
	Tumbler, #5000, 2½ oz., ftd.	22.00
	Tumbler, #5000, 5 oz., ftd.	8.00
23	Tumbler, #5000, 9 oz., ftd.	10.00
	Tumbler, #5000, 12 oz., ftd.	17.00
	Vase, #2324, urn, ftd.	100.00
	Vase, #2292, flared	110.00

209

RUBA ROMBIC, CONSOLIDATED LAMP AND GLASS COMPANY, 1928 – 1933

Colors: Smokey topaz, Jungle green, French Crystal, Silver Gray, Lilac, Sunshine, Jade; some milk glass, Apple green, black, French Opalescent

Ruba Rombic has seen a few price alterations, possibly because there is not enough product being offered. Mostly prices have remained uniform, but Ruba Rombic items were already way beyond the spending limits set by most collectors of glass. There are some who feel this is the most wonderful pattern in the book, while others ridicule anyone who thinks it is. Should you see a piece, inexpensively priced, buy it in spite of your feelings. Someone will find it irresistible.

The frosted powder jar (10) shown is often thought to be Ruba Rhombic, but is only a look-alike.

The color most prominent in the photo is Smokey Topaz, priced below with Jungle Green. Both of these colors are transparent as opposed to the other colors that are cased (layered). Smokey Topaz will be the color you are most likely to find if you are lucky enough to see a piece. Not long ago, we spotted a Smokey Topaz decanter. Both top and bottom were badly damaged and the inside was cloudy to the point of looking frosted. While turning it around to see the price, we were told that we could buy it for only $1,500.00 since it was worth $1,800.00. Sorry! Damaged glassware does have some value if rare, but not within hand grenade range of mint price under those conditions.

The cased color column below includes three colors. They are Lilac (lavender), Sunshine (yellow), and Jade (green). French crystal is a white, applied color except that the raised edges are crystal with no white coloring at all. Silver is sometimes called Gray Silver.

Ruba Rombic has always sold to a specialized market that eluded most dealers who did not have such an outlet. The internet is changing that to some extent. Once a piece of glass reaches a price of four digits, there are a limited number of die-hards willing, or able, to pay that price. Once five digit prices are attained, there are few who can afford it; and then finding that one who wants it that badly is another problem. You can buy a good used car, a new import, or make a down payment on an abode in that range!

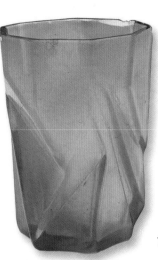

1

		Smokey Topaz, Jungle Green	Cased Color	French Opal, French Crystal, Silver
	Ashtray, 3½"	500.00	650.00	750.00
	Bonbon, flat, 3 part	200.00	300.00	350.00
2	Bottle, decanter, 9"	1,500.00	1,800.00	2,200.00
	Bottle, perfume, 4¾"	1,500.00	1,500.00	1,800.00
	Bottle, toilet, 7½"	1,050.00	1,250.00	1,500.00
	Bowl, 3", almond	225.00	250.00	350.00
9	Bowl, 8", cupped	900.00	1,100.00	1,200.00
8	Bowl, 9", flared	850.00	1,100.00	1,200.00
5	Bowl, 12", oval	1,250.00	1,500.00	1,500.00
	Bowl, bouillon	150.00	200.00	225.00
4	Bowl, finger	90.00	115.00	125.00
	Box, cigarette, 3½" x 4¼"	750.00	1,100.00	1,250.00
	Box, powder, 5", round	750.00	1,100.00	1,250.00
	Candlestick, 2½" high, pr.	400.00	550.00	650.00
	Celery, 10", 3 part	750.00	850.00	900.00
	Comport, 7", wide	750.00	850.00	900.00
3	Creamer	175.00	200.00	250.00
	Light, ceiling fixture, 10"		1,250.00	1,250.00
	Light, ceiling fixture, 16"		2,000.00	2,000.00
	Light, table light		1,000.00	1,000.00

		Smokey Topaz, Jungle Green	Cased Color	French Opal, French Crystal, Silver
	Light, wall sconce		1,250.00	1,250.00
	Pitcher, 8¼"	2,000.00	2,500.00	3,500.00
	Plate, 7"	60.00	85.00	125.00
	Plate, 8"	60.00	85.00	125.00
	Plate, 10"	200.00	225.00	250.00
	Plate, 15"	1,100.00	1,250.00	1,250.00
	Relish, 2 part	300.00	400.00	450.00
	Sugar	175.00	200.00	250.00
	Sundae	85.00	110.00	125.00
	Tray for decanter set	1,500.00	1,800.00	2,000.00
1	Tumbler, 2 oz., flat, 2¾"	100.00	120.00	140.00
	Tumbler, 3 oz., ftd.	110.00	130.00	155.00
	Tumbler, 9 oz., flat	110.00	150.00	175.00
	Tumbler, 10 oz., ftd.	150.00	250.00	300.00
	Tumbler, 12 oz., flat	175.00	250.00	300.00
	Tumbler, 15 oz., ftd., 7"	275.00	400.00	450.00
7	Vase, 6"	750.00	900.00	1,200.00
6	Vase, 9½"	1,250.00	2,000.00	2,500.00
	Vase, 16"	10,000.00	12,000.00	12,000.00

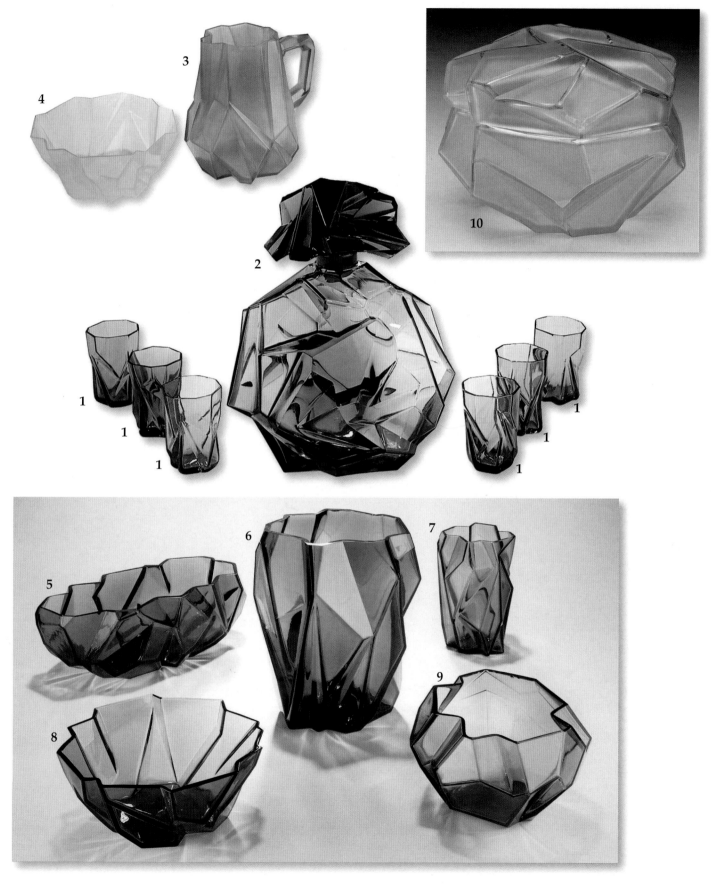

Colors: crystal, amber, pink, green, red, cobalt blue

Lancaster Colony continued to produce some Sandwich pieces in their lines at the Indiana Glass factory until it closed. The bright blue, green, or amberina color combinations were made by Indiana from Duncan moulds and were sold by Montgomery Ward in the early 1970s. We noticed a small set of Sunset (amberina) at a recent antique extravaganza priced as rare Early American Sandwich. Early American 1970s is more like it, but we have learned to shake our heads and move on. Usually, the seller would rather argue about his wares, than learn the truth which he probably knows anyway. There are a few collectors beginning to ask for these colors, but most Depression glass shows do not allow 1970s glass to be displayed; so the internet, antique malls, and flea markets are where these colors are being sold. Remember, they are only about 30 years old and not Depression era; pay accordingly.

Cobalt blue and true red Sandwich items stimulate a few Duncan collectors. Tiffin also made a few Sandwich pieces in milk glass and Chartreuse out of Duncan moulds before they were turned over to Lancaster Colony. As of now, few seem to desire those colors. If you like them, latch onto them inexpensively.

An abundance of crystal Sandwich stemware makes it as cost-effective to buy as nearly all currently made imported stemware sold in department stores. If you enjoy this design, now would be a good time to start picking it up while you can still afford the gasoline needed to search for it.

	Crystal
Ashtray, 2½" x 3¾", rect.	7.00
Ashtray, 2¾", sq.	5.00
Basket, 6½", w/loop hdl.	110.00
Basket, 10", crimped, w/loop hdl.	150.00
Basket, 10", oval, w/loop hdl.	195.00
Basket, 11½", w/loop hdl.	185.00
Bonbon, 5", heart shape, w/ring hdl.	12.00
Bonbon, 5½", heart shape, hdld.	12.00
Bonbon, 6", heart shape, w/ring hdl.	16.00
Bonbon, 7½", ftd., w/cover	40.00
Bowl, 2½", salted almond	10.00
Bowl, 3½", nut	9.00
Bowl, 4", finger	10.00
Bowl, 5½", hdld.	10.00
Bowl, 5½", ftd., grapefruit, w/rim liner	12.00
Bowl, 5½", ftd., grapefruit, w/fruit cup liner	12.00

	Crystal
Bowl, 5", 2 pt., nappy	9.00
Bowl, 5", ftd., crimped ivy	28.00
Bowl, 5", fruit	8.00
Bowl, 5", nappy, w/ring hdl.	10.00
Bowl, 6", 2 pt., nappy	12.00
Bowl, 6", fruit salad	10.00
Bowl, 6", grapefruit, rimmed edge	12.00
Bowl, 6", nappy, w/ring hdl.	12.00
Bowl, 10", salad, deep	48.00
Bowl, 10", 3 pt., fruit	50.00
Bowl, 10", lily, vertical edge	38.00
Bowl, 11", cupped nut	40.00
Bowl, 11½", crimped flower	40.00
Bowl, 11½", gardenia	34.00
Bowl, 11½", ftd., crimped fruit	38.00
Bowl, 12", fruit, flared edge	34.00

		Crystal
	Bowl, 12", shallow salad	30.00
	Bowl, 12", oblong console	33.00
	Bowl, 12", epergne, w/ctr. hole	90.00
	Butter, w/cover, ¼ lb.	40.00
	Cake stand, 11½", ftd., rolled edge	65.00
	Cake stand, 12", ftd., rolled edge, plain pedestal	60.00
	Cake stand, 13", ftd., plain pedestal	60.00
	Candelabra, 10", 1-lite, w/bobeche & prisms	60.00
	Candelabra, 10", 3-lite, w/bobeche & prisms	150.00
	Candelabra, 16", 3-lite, w/bobeche & prisms	195.00
	Candlestick, 4", 1-lite	10.00
	Candlestick, 4", 1-lite, w/bobeche & stub. prisms	28.00
	Candlestick, 5", 3-lite	32.00
	Candlestick, 5", 3-lite, w/bobeche & stub. prisms	85.00
	Candlestick, 5", 2-lite, w/bobeche & stub. prisms	85.00
	Candlestick, 5", 2-lite	28.00
	Candy, 6", sq.	295.00
	Candy box, w/cover, 5", flat	40.00
	Candy jar, w/cover, 8½", ftd.	65.00
	Cheese, w/cover (cover 4¾", plate 8")	90.00
	Cheese/cracker (3" compote, 13" plate)	40.00
	Cigarette box, w/cover, 3½"	20.00
	Cigarette holder, 3", ftd.	20.00
5	Coaster, 5"	8.00
	Comport, 2¼"	10.00
	Comport, 3¼", low ft., crimped candy	18.00
	Comport, 3¼", low ft., flared candy	12.00
	Comport, 4¼", ftd.	18.00
	Comport, 5", low ft.	22.00
	Comport, 5½", ftd., low crimped	25.00
	Comport, 6", low ft., flared	22.00
	Condiment set (2 cruets, 3¾" salt & pepper, 4 pt. tray)	90.00
	Creamer, 4", 7 oz., ftd.	7.00
	Cup, 6 oz., tea	7.00
	Epergne, 9", garden	135.00
	Epergne, 12", 3 pt., fruit or flower	250.00
	Jelly, 3", indiv.	8.00
4	Mayonnaise set, 3 pc.: ladle, 5" bowl, 7" plate	26.00
	Oil bottle, 5¾"	26.00
	Pan, 6¾" x 10½", oblong, camelia	50.00
	Pitcher, 13 oz., syrup top	48.00
	Pitcher, w/ice lip, 8", 64 oz.	125.00
	Plate, 3", indiv. jelly	5.00
	Plate, 6", bread/butter	4.00
	Plate, 6½", finger bowl liner	5.00
	Plate, 7", dessert	6.00
	Plate, 8", mayonnaise liner, w/ring	8.00
	Plate, 8", salad	8.00
	Plate, 9½", dinner	22.00
	Plate, 11½", hdld., service	30.00
	Plate, 12", torte	32.00
	Plate, 12", ice cream, rolled edge	40.00
	Plate, 12", deviled egg	60.00
	Plate, 13", salad dressing, w/ring	35.00
	Plate, 13", service	35.00

		Crystal
	Plate, 13", service, rolled edge	35.00
	Plate, 13", cracker, w/ring	26.00
	Plate, 16", lazy susan, w/turntable	85.00
	Plate, 16", hostess	75.00
	Relish, 5½", 2 pt., rnd., ring hdl.	15.00
	Relish, 6", 2 pt., rnd., ring hdl.	18.00
	Relish, 7", 2 pt., oval	18.00
	Relish, 10", 4 pt., hdld.	24.00
	Relish, 10", 3 pt., oblong	26.00
	Relish, 10½", 3 pt., oblong	26.00
	Relish, 12", 3 pt.	36.00
	Salad dressing set: (2 ladles, 5" ftd. mayonnaise, 13" plate w/ring)	60.00
	Salad dressing set: (2 ladles, 6" ftd. div. bowl, 8" plate w/ring)	65.00
	Salt & pepper, 2½", w/glass tops, pr.	18.00
	Salt & pepper, 2½", w/metal tops, pr.	18.00
	Salt & pepper, 3¾", w/metal top (on 6" tray), 3 pc.	26.00
	Saucer, 6", w/ring	2.00
	Stem, 2½", 6 oz., ftd., fruit cup/jello	8.00
	Stem, 2¾", 5 oz., ftd., oyster cocktail	10.00
8	Stem, 3½", 5 oz., sundae (flared rim)	8.00
2	Stem, 4¼", 3 oz., cocktail	9.00
	Stem, 4¼", 5 oz., ice cream	7.00
7	Stem, 4¼", 3 oz., wine	12.00
	Stem, 5¼", 4 oz., ftd., parfait	18.00
9	Stem, 5¼", 5 oz., champagne	12.00
10	Stem, 6", 9 oz., goblet	15.00
	Sugar, 3¼", ftd., 9 oz.	8.00
	Sugar, 5 oz.	8.00
	Sugar (cheese) shaker, 13 oz., metal top	50.00
	Tray, oval (for sugar/creamer)	9.00
	Tray, 6" mint, rolled edge, w/ring hdl.	15.00
	Tray, 7", oval, pickle	12.00
	Tray, 7", mint, rolled edge, w/ring hdl.	18.00
	Tray, 8", oval	16.00
	Tray, 8", for oil/vinegar	18.00
	Tray, 10", oval, celery	15.00
	Tray, 12", fruit epergne	38.00
	Tray, 12", ice cream, rolled edge	38.00
1	Tumbler, 3¾", 5 oz., ftd., juice	8.00
3	Tumbler, 4½", 9 oz., flat, water	7.00
	Tumbler, 4¾", 9 oz., ftd., water	10.00
6	Tumbler, 5¼", 13 oz., flat, iced tea	15.00
11	Tumbler, 5¼", 12 oz., ftd., iced tea	15.00
	Urn, w/cover, 12", ftd.	135.00
	Vase, 3", ftd., crimped	20.00
	Vase, 3", ftd., flared rim	18.00
	Vase, 4", hat shape	22.00
	Vase, 4½", flat base, crimped	26.00
	Vase, 5", ftd., flared rim	22.00
	Vase, 5", ftd., crimped	38.00
	Vase, 5", ftd., fan	50.00
	Vase, 7½", epergne, threaded base	65.00
	Vase, 10", ftd.	75.00

Colors: crystal, Zircon or Limelight green, Dawn

Limelight and Zircon are to all intents and purposes the same color. Zircon was originally introduced in 1937. In the 1950s, it was reintroduced by Heisey, but identified as Limelight. Zircon prices are holding steadier than most colors of Heisey with few exceptions. Saturn plates of all sizes, pitchers, and shakers are hard to find. Some items have a tendency to look more green than others. The greener hue often goes unsold since it does not match well and is closer to the Aqua found in Duncan's Festive pattern from the 50s. Once in a while, a Duncan Festive vase is found labeled Heisey, but not as frequently as in the past.

Crystal Saturn prices are declining due to lack of buyer interest.

		Crystal	Zircon Limelight
	Ashtray	10.00	150.00
	Bitters bottle, w/short tube, blown	90.00	
9	Bowl, baked apple	25.00	100.00
	Bowl, finger	10.00	100.00
	Bowl, 4½", nappy	10.00	
	Bowl, 5", nappy	10.00	90.00
	Bowl, 5", whipped cream	25.00	80.00
	Bowl, 7", pickle	35.00	
	Bowl, 9", 3 part, relish	20.00	
	Bowl, 10", celery	15.00	
	Bowl, 10", gardenia	35.00	110.00
19	Bowl, 11", salad	40.00	140.00
	Bowl, 12", fruit, flared rim	35.00	100.00
	Bowl, 13", floral, rolled edge	37.00	
	Bowl, 13", floral	37.00	
21	Candelabrum, w/"e" ball drops, 2-lite	175.00	500.00
20	Candle block, 2-lite	95.00	425.00
	Candlestick, 3", ftd., 1-lite	30.00	500.00
16	Comport, 7"	50.00	400.00
7	Creamer	15.00	160.00
1	Cup	10.00	135.00
	Hostess Set, 8 pc. (low bowl w/ftd. ctr. bowl, 3 toothpick holders & clips)	65.00	240.00
	Marmalade, w/cover	45.00	500.00
8	Mayonnaise, liner & ladle	8.00	80.00
6	Mustard, w/cover and paddle, attached	95.00	*550.00
4	Oil bottle, 3 oz.	55.00	500.00
5	Pitcher, 70 oz., w/ice lip, blown	65.00	550.00
11	Pitcher, juice	40.00	500.00

* Zircon $800.00 at 1998 auction.

		Crystal	Zircon Limelight
	Plate, 6"	5.00	50.00
	Plate, 7", bread	5.00	55.00
10	Plate, 8", luncheon	10.00	50.00
	Plate, 13", torte	25.00	
	Plate, 15", torte	20.00	
12	Salt & pepper, pr.	30.00	600.00
2	Saucer	5.00	25.00
	Stem, 3 oz., cocktail	15.00	70.00
	Stem, 4 oz., fruit cocktail or oyster cocktail, no ball in stem, ftd.	10.00	75.00
	Stem, 4½ oz., sherbet	8.00	50.00
	Stem, 5 oz., parfait	15.00	110.00
	Stem, 6 oz., saucer champagne	10.00	95.00
	Stem, 10 oz.	20.00	90.00
3	Sugar	15.00	160.00
	Sugar shaker (pourer)	70.00	
	Sugar, w/cover, no handles	25.00	
	Tray, tidbit, 2 sides turned as fan	25.00	110.00
14	Tumbler, 5 oz., juice	8.00	75.00
15	Tumbler, 7 oz., old-fashion	10.00	
	Tumbler, 8 oz., old-fashion	10.00	
	Tumbler, 9 oz., luncheon	15.00	
13	Tumbler, 10 oz.	20.00	80.00
	Tumbler, 12 oz., soda	20.00	85.00
	Vase, violet	35.00	160.00
22	Vase, 6", ball	40.00	240.00
17	Vase, 8½", flared	55.00	225.00
	Vase, 8½", straight	55.00	235.00
	Vase, 9", ball		600.00
18	Vase, 10½"	50.00	260.00

SEVILLE, FOSTORIA GLASS COMPANY, 1920 – 1931

Colors: amber, green

Seville is the "Rodney Dangerfield" of Fostoria glassware patterns. As the comedian moaned, "I don't get no respect." We have never understood why it has never caught on with enthusiasts for either green or amber. It is eye-catching, 77 to 88 years old, and made by Fostoria, one of the major glass companies of the time which is no longer in business.

Seville would be a worthwhile Elegant pattern to search for even though there probably won't be massive displays at shows. You might have to ask for it. It might surprise you what dealers have in inventory that often is not exhibited at shows. They only have so much table space, and our theory is that you ought to display only what you think will sell.

Green would be easier to obtain than amber as you may note by the lack of amber in our photo. The butter dish, pitcher, grapefruit and liner, and sugar lid are all tricky to find, but oh, so heartwarming when you do run across them.

1

		Amber	Green
	Ashtray, #2350, 4"	12.00	15.00
10	Bowl, #2350, fruit, 5½"	8.00	12.00
	Bowl, #2350, cereal, 6½"	15.00	20.00
	Bowl, #2350, soup, 7¾"	18.00	25.00
	Bowl, #2315, low foot, 7"	15.00	20.00
	Bowl, #2350, vegetable	20.00	27.50
	Bowl, #2350, nappy, 9"	25.00	35.00
	Bowl, #2350, oval, baker, 9"	22.00	30.00
	Bowl, #2315, flared, 10½", ftd.	22.00	30.00
	Bowl, #2350, oval, baker, 10½"	30.00	38.00
	Bowl, 10", ftd.	32.00	38.00
	Bowl, #2350, salad, 10"	28.00	32.00
20	Bowl, #2329, rolled edge, console, 11"	27.50	35.00
	Bowl, #2297, deep, flared, 12"	30.00	35.00
	Bowl, #2371, oval, console, 13"	32.00	38.00
	Bowl, #2329, rolled edge, console, 13"	32.00	40.00
	Bowl, #2350, bouillon, flat	12.00	15.00
19	Bowl, #2350½, bouillon, ftd.	12.00	15.00
	Bowl, #2350, cream soup, flat, w/liner	14.00	18.00
12	Bowl, #2350½, cream soup, ftd.	12.00	15.00
	Bowl, #869/2283, finger, w/6" liner	18.00	25.00
11	Butter, w/cover, #2350, round	175.00	250.00
	Candlestick, #2324, 2"	14.00	18.00
13	Candlestick, #2324, 4"	14.00	18.00
	Candlestick, #2324, 9"	38.00	45.00
	Candy jar, w/cover, #2250, ½ lb., ftd.	90.00	145.00
	Candy jar, w/cover, #2331, 3 pt., flat	60.00	85.00
	Celery, #2350, 11"	14.00	17.50
	Cheese and cracker, #2368 (11" plate)	32.00	38.00
3	Comport, #2327, 7½" (twisted stem)	20.00	24.00
	Comport, #2350, 8"	25.00	35.00
	Creamer, #2315½, flat, ftd.	12.00	15.00
16	Creamer, #2350½, ftd.	12.00	14.00
	Cup, #2350, after dinner	15.00	22.00
	Cup, #2350, flat	8.00	11.00
17	Cup, #2350½, ftd.	8.00	11.00
	Egg cup, #2350	22.00	25.00
	Grapefruit, #945½, blown	30.00	40.00
1	Grapefruit, #945½, liner, blown	25.00	25.00

		Amber	Green
	Grapefruit, #2315, molded	22.00	25.00
	Ice bucket, #2378	50.00	60.00
	Pickle, #2350, 8"	12.00	15.00
4	Pitcher, #5084, ftd.	195.00	250.00
14	Plate, #2350, bread and butter, 6"	3.00	3.00
21	Plate, #2350, salad, 7½"	4.50	5.00
	Plate, #2350, luncheon, 8½"	5.00	6.00
	Plate, #2321, Maj Jongg (canape), 8¾"	18.00	25.00
15	Plate, #2350, sm. dinner, 9½"	10.00	12.00
	Plate, #2350, dinner, 10½"	25.00	30.00
	Plate, #2350, chop, 13¾"	28.00	30.00
	Plate, #2350, round, 15"	38.00	38.00
	Plate, #2350, cream soup liner	4.00	5.00
	Platter, #2350, 10½"	30.00	35.00
23	Platter, #2350, 12"	32.00	40.00
	Platter, #2350, 15"	50.00	65.00
5	Salt and pepper shaker, #5100, pr.	40.00	60.00
	Sauce boat liner, #2350	15.00	20.00
	Sauce boat, #2350	40.00	45.00
18	Saucer, #2350	2.00	3.00
	Saucer, after dinner, #2350	3.00	4.00
	Stem, #870, cocktail	10.00	12.00
7	Stem, #870, cordial	35.00	45.00
8	Stem, #870, high sherbet	10.00	10.00
6	Stem, #870, low sherbet	8.00	8.00
	Stem, #870, oyster cocktail	10.00	10.00
	Stem, #870, parfait	18.00	22.00
2	Stem, #870, water	18.00	22.00
9	Stem, #870, wine	18.00	22.00
	Sugar cover, #2350½	50.00	70.00
	Sugar, fat, ftd., #2315	12.00	12.00
	Sugar, ftd., #2350½	12.00	12.00
22	Tray, 11", center hdld., #2287	25.00	28.00
	Tumbler, #5084, ftd., 2 oz.	22.00	28.00
	Tumbler, #5084, ftd., 5 oz.	10.00	11.00
	Tumbler, #5084, ftd., 9 oz.	12.00	15.00
	Tumbler, #5084, ftd., 12 oz.	16.00	18.00
	Urn, small, #2324	75.00	100.00
	Vase, #2292, 8"	80.00	95.00

"SPIRAL FLUTES," DUNCAN & MILLER GLASS COMPANY, INTRODUCED 1924

Colors: amber, green, pink, crystal

"Spiral Flutes" is a striking Duncan & Miller pattern that is collected less than many of the other "swirling or spiraling" Depression patterns. Most Duncan & Miller patterns have suffered a lack of collector esteem due to limited information available on that company's wares. For some preposterous reason, Duncan collectors seem to want to keep their knowledge to themselves. Thankfully, that attitude is slowly changing; but it has come at a great price to Duncan glass collectibility. Our experience has been that the more people aware of a company's patterns, the more of said glass will be exposed. Once known, there are those who diligently root it out of basements, garages, and attics. Hopefully, it is not too late!

		Amber Green Pink			Amber Green Pink
16	Bowl, 2", almond	8.00		Bowl, 9", nappy	25.00
15	Bowl, 3¾", bouillon	12.50	14	Bowl, 10", oval, veg., two styles	40.00
19	Bowl, 4⅜", finger	6.00		Bowl, 10½", lily pond	35.00
	Bowl, 4¾", ftd., cream soup	12.00		Bowl, 11¾" w. x 3¾" t., console, flared	25.00
	Bowl, 4" w., mayonnaise	16.00		Bowl, 11", nappy	25.00
	Bowl, 5", nappy	5.00		Bowl, 12", cupped console	25.00
	Bowl, 6½", cereal, sm. flange	22.00		Candle, 3½"	18.00
	Bowl, 6¾", grapefruit	7.00		Candle, 7½"	50.00
	Bowl, 6", hdld. nappy	18.00		Candle, 9½"	70.00
	Bowl, 6", hdld. nappy, w/cover	60.00		Candle, 11½"	75.00
	Bowl, 7", nappy	12.00	8	Candy w/cover	38.00
	Bowl, 7½", flanged (baked apple)	20.00		Celery, 10¾" x 4¾"	15.00
	Bowl, 8", nappy	16.00		Chocolate jar, w/cover*	175.00
	Bowl, 8½", flanged (oyster plate)	20.00	9	Cigarette holder, 4"	30.00

		Amber Green Pink
4	Comport, 4⅜"x7" high	12.00
17	Comport, 6⅝"	15.00
	Comport, 9", low ft., flared	45.00
	Console stand, 1½" h. x 4⅝" w.	10.00
	Creamer, oval	7.00
18	Cup	8.00
12	Cup, demi	20.00
	Fernery, 10" x 5½", 4 ftd., flower box*	250.00
	Grapefruit, ftd.	18.00
	Ice tub, handled	75.00
	Lamp, 10½", countess	250.00
	Mug, 6½", 9 oz., handled	22.00
	Mug, 7", 9 oz., handled	24.00
	Oil, w/stopper, 6 oz.	135.00
	Pickle, 8⅝"	12.00
	Pitcher, ½ gal.	150.00
	Plate, 6", pie	3.00
	Plate, 7½", salad	4.00
	Plate, 8⅜", luncheon	4.00
	Plate, 10⅜", dinner	20.00
	Plate, 13⅝", torte	25.00
	Plate, w/star, 6" (fingerbowl item)	6.00
	Platter, 11"	33.00

		Amber Green Pink
10	Platter, 13"	50.00
	Relish, 10" x 7⅜", oval, 3 pc. (2 inserts)	90.00
	Saucer	2.00
12	Saucer, demi	4.00
13	Seafood sauce cup, 3" w. x 2½" h.	18.00
	Stem, 3¾", 3½ oz., wine	12.00
	Stem, 3¾", 5 oz., low sherbet	6.00
3	Stem, 4¾", 6 oz., tall sherbet	8.00
	Stem, 5⅝", 4½ oz., parfait	12.00
6	Stem, 6¼", 7 oz., water	14.00
	Sugar, oval	7.00
	Sweetmeat, w/cover, 7½"	80.00
11	Tumbler, 3⅜", ftd., 2½ oz., cocktail (no stem)	6.00
	Tumbler, 4¼", 8 oz., flat	16.00
1	Tumbler, 4⅜", ftd., 5½ oz., juice (no stem)	12.00
	Tumbler, 4¾", 7 oz., flat, soda	20.00
	Tumbler, 5⅛", ftd., 7 oz., water (1 knob)	6.00
7	Tumbler, 5⅛", ftd., 9 oz., water (no stem)	18.00
2	Tumbler, 5½", 11 oz., ginger ale	40.00
	Vase, 6½"	20.00
	Vase, 8½"	30.00
5	Vase, 10½"	38.00

* Crystal, $135.00

SHIRLEY, #331, FOSTORIA GLASS COMPANY, 1939 – 1957

Color: crystal

Shirley was etched upon a number of major Fostoria mould blanks. All items listed as #2496 refer to the Baroque line and #2545 refer to what is known as "flame." Stems are found on line #6017 which is also called Sceptre. This is an extensive pattern that does not presently have enough buyers to push the prices. It sells well for us when we find pieces. Stems are around, but not as prevalent as stemware in other Elegant patterns.

This floral design is regularly referred to as a poppy which was a popular floral design. Tiffin used Poppies for Flanders and another pattern called Poppy. Cambridge's Gloria is based upon a poppy, but Fostoria did poppies proud with three different etchings, Rogene, Legion, and Shirley. Unfortunately, our individual candle pictured does not exhibit the pattern as well as we would have liked.

	Bonbon, #2496	30.00
	Bowl, #2496, 5", fruit	20.00
	Bowl, #2496, 9½", oval	50.00
	Bowl, #2496, 10½", 2-hdld.	55.00
	Bowl, #2496, 12", flared	55.00
	Bowl, #2496, cream soup	30.00
1	Bowl, #2496, 3-ftd. nut	28.00
	Bowl, #2545, 12½", oval	60.00
	Bowl, #766, finger	22.00
	Candelabrum, #2545, 2-lite w/prisms	90.00
	Candlestick, #2496, 4"	20.00
	Candlestick, #2496, duo	30.00
	Candlestick, #2545, 4½"	25.00
10	Candlestick, #2545, 6"	35.00
	Candlestick, #2545, duo	60.00
	Candy w/lid, #2496	85.00
	Celery, #2496, 11"	28.00
	Cheese comport, #2496, 4¾"	25.00
9	Comport, #2496, 5½"	25.00
8	Creamer, #2496, ftd.	16.00
	Creamer, #2496, individual	20.00
4	Cup, #2496	15.00
2	Ice bucket, #2496, w/metal handle	65.00
	Mayonnaise, #2496, 6½", 2-part	20.00
	Mayonnaise or sauce dish, #2496, 6½"	30.00
	Nappy, #2496, flared	18.00
	Nappy, #2496, round	18.00
	Nappy, #2496, square	18.00
	Nappy, #2496, tri-cornered	18.00
	Pickle, #2496, 8¼"	22.00
	Pitcher, #6011, ftd.	195.00
	Plate, #2337, 6"	7.00
	Plate, #2337, 7"	8.00
6	Plate, #2337, 8¼", luncheon	11.00
	Plate, #2496, 6¼, cream soup liner	7.00
	Plate, #2496, 9½", dinner	26.00
	Plate, #2496, 10", cake plate, 2-hdld.	32.00
5	Plate, #2496, 10", cracker	30.00
	Plate, #2496,14", torte	55.00
	Platter, #2496, 12"	50.00
	Relish, #2496, 6", 2-part, square	20.00

2

3	Relish, #2496, 10", 3-part	33.00
4	Saucer, #2496	4.00
	Shaker, #2496, pr.	60.00
	Stem, #6017, 3⅜", ¾ oz., cordial	40.00
	Stem, #6017, 4½", 6 oz., sherbet	15.00
	Stem, #6017, 4⅞", 3½ oz., cocktail	16.00
	Stem, #6017, 5½", 3 oz., wine	20.00
	Stem, #6017, 5½", 6 oz., champagne	16.00
	Stem, #6017, 5⅞", 4 oz., claret	20.00
7	Stem, #6017, 7⅜", 9 oz., water goblet	24.00
	Sugar, #2496, ftd.	16.00
	Sugar, #2496, individual	20.00
	Sweetmeat, #2496, 6", square	20.00
	Tray, #2496, individual sugar/cream	20.00
	Tumbler, #6017, 3⅝", 4 oz., oyster cocktail	18.00
	Tumbler, #6017, 4¾", 5 oz., ftd. juice	18.00
	Tumbler, #6017, 5½", 9 oz., ftd. water	16.00
	Tumbler, #6017, 6", 12 oz., ftd. ice tea	20.00
	Vase, #2545, 10"	135.00

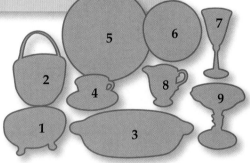

SPARTA, DECORATION #769, MORGANTOWN, EARLY 1930S

Colors: Ebony, Ritz Blue

Sparta is Morgantown Decoration #769 that was applied in gold or platinum (possibly white gold) on a number of their mould blanks. Golf Ball, #7643, is the most recognized decorated line. In that line we can attribute a water goblet; sherbet, wine, and a footed water tumbler with Sparta etch on Ritz blue. A water tumbler is pictured. If there are any regularly found Sparta items, it would be the Lynward decanter pictured. It will not be found priced economically; but we have seen at least four over the years. Collectors of barware are snatching these as fast as Morgantown enthusiasts. That cross-over interest keeps the supply well in check so that demand is usually ahead of the small supply.

The Majesty candleholder pictured in the bottom row is often mistaken as a sherbet. These were marketed with a 13" console bowl, but the curious thing was that the bowl was sold with four candles contrasting to the routinely offered single pair with a console set.

		All Colors
	Bowl, #4355 Janice, 13", console	175.00
4	Candle, #7662 Majesty, 4"	125.00
2	Decanter, 10½", Lynward	295.00
3	Plate, 8"	30.00
	Stem, #7643, 4⅛", 3½ oz., sherbet	65.00
	Stem, #7643, 4¾", 3 oz., wine	100.00

		All Colors
	Stem, #7643, 5", 5½ oz., champagne	75.00
	Stem, #7643, 6¾", 9 oz., water	110.00
5	Tumbler, #7643, 6⅛", 9 oz., water	90.00
1	Tumbler, #9051, 1½ oz., bar	65.00
	Tumbler, #8701 Garrett, 9 oz.	90.00
	Vase, #67 Grecian, 6"	150.00

STANHOPE, #1483, A.H. HEISEY CO., 1936 – 1941

Colors: crystal, some blown stemware in Zircon

Heisey's Stanhope is a Deco pattern that collectors of that genre are pursuing as well as Heisey devotees. Deco fans have a high regard for the red or black "T" knobs, which were incorporated into all the open round handles of Stanhope. The "T" knob, in the price listings, are insert handles (black or red, round, wooden knobs) which are like wooden dowel rods that act as horizontal handles. The insert handles are quirky to some; but others think them magnificent and will not purchase a piece missing them. Although items are listed with or without the knobs, you can expect items to be worth a minimum of 20% to 25% less if "T" knobs are absent. We had a tough time marketing that rarely seen flat candy in the photo below since it was missing the "T" knob on the lid. If you ever see these inserts presented for sale, buy them even if you do not own any Stanhope, because someone will want them.

Some people mistake the 11" salad bowl shown at the bottom of page 222 for a punch bowl; it would not hold much punch. Notice that prices for the omnipresent stemware have softened.

		Crystal
	Ashtray, indiv.	65.00
19	Bottle, oil, 3 oz., w or w/o rd. knob	300.00
	Bowl, 6", mint, 2 hdld., w or w/o rd. knobs	35.00
	Bowl, 6", mint, 2 pt., 2 hdld., w or w/o rd. knobs	35.00
2	Bowl, 11", salad	90.00
15	Bowl, 11", floral, 2 hdld.	75.00
	Bowl, finger, #4080 (blown, plain)	10.00
	Bowl, floral, 11", 2 hdld., w or w/o "T" knobs	80.00
1	Candelabra, 2-lite, w bobeche & prisms	175.00
12	Candy box & lid, rnd., w or w/o rd. knob	140.00
	Cigarette box & lid, w or w/o rd. knob	200.00
13	Creamer, 2 hdld., w or w/o rd. knobs	35.00
6	Cup, w or w/o rd. knob.	18.00
17	Ice tub, 2 hdld., w or w/o "T" knobs	70.00
	Jelly, 6", 1 hdld., w or w/o rd. knobs	30.00
7	Jelly, 6", 3 pt., 1 hdld., w or w/o rd. knobs	30.00
20	Mayonnaise, 2 hdld.	35.00
	Nappy, 4½", 1 hdld., w or w/o rd. knob	30.00

		Crystal
	Nut, indiv., 1 hdld., w or w/o rd. knob	80.00
11	Plate, 7"	20.00
16	Plate, 12", torte, 2 hdld., w or w/o "T" knobs	45.00
3	Plate, 15", torte, rnd. or salad liner	65.00
21	Relish, 11", triplex buffet, 2 hdld., w or w/o "T" knobs	45.00
	Relish, 12", 4 pt., 2 hdld., w or w/o "T" knobs	55.00
	Relish, 12", 5 pt., 2 hdld., w or w/o "T" knobs	55.00
	Salt & pepper, #60 top	140.00
6	Saucer	5.00
	Stem, 1 oz., cordial, #4083 (blown)	70.00
	Stem, 2½ oz., pressed wine	35.00
9	Stem, 2½ oz., wine, #4083	20.00
10	Stem, 3½ oz., cocktail, #4083	15.00
	Stem, 3½ oz., pressed cocktail	25.00
	Stem, 4 oz., claret, #4083	20.00
	Stem, 4 oz., oyster cocktail, #4083	10.00
	Stem, 5½ oz., pressed saucer champagne	20.00
	Stem, 5½ oz., saucer champagne, #4083	10.00
	Stem, 9 oz., pressed goblet	45.00
5	Stem, 10 oz., goblet, #4083	*22.50
	Stem, 12 oz., pressed soda	45.00
14	Sugar, 2 hdld., w or w/o rd. knobs	35.00
	Tray, 12" celery, 2 hdld., w or w/o "T" knobs	55.00
8	Tumbler, 5 oz., soda, #4083	20.00
	Tumbler, 8 oz., soda, #4083	22.50
18	Tumbler, 12 oz., soda, #4083	**25.00
	Vase, 7", ball	100.00
4	Vase, 9", 2 hdld., w or w/o "T" knobs	125.00

*Limelight – 110.00   **Limelight – 95.00

Color: crystal, crystal w/gold

This early Heisey pattern was produced in crystal only. You might find an occasional piece or two with gold accoutrements, but frequently that is timeworn to the point of being off-putting. Sunburst items may have a modification in the pattern consisting of punties (thumbprints) around the item just above the sunburst. This is not deemed another distinct pattern although some collectors dispute that point.

	Bottle, molasses, 13 oz.	175.00
	Bottle, oil, 2 oz.	65.00
	Bottle, oil, 4 oz.	65.00
	Bottle, oil, 6 oz.	75.00
2	Bottle, water	75.00
	Bridge set: approx. 5" each	
	Club	65.00
	Diamond	75.00
	Heart	75.00
	Spade	65.00
	Bowl, 4", round, scalloped top	22.00
18	Bowl, 4½", round, scalloped top	22.00
6	Bowl, 5", round, scalloped top, flared	25.00
15	Bowl, 5", finger	25.00
	Bowl, 5", hdld.	25.00
	Bowl, 5", three corner, hdld.	30.00
	Bowl, 6", round	30.00
	Bowl, 7", round	35.00

9	Bowl, 7", oblong	35.00
	Bowl, 8", round	40.00
	Bowl, 8", round, ftd.	40.00
	Bowl, 9", round	40.00
	Bowl, 9", round, ftd.	65.00
	Bowl, 9", oblong	45.00
	Bowl, 10", round	50.00
	Bowl, 10", round, ftd.	85.00
	Bowl, 10", oblong	45.00
13	Bowl, 10", round punch, pegged bottom & stand	400.00
	Bowl, 12", round, punch & stand	225.00
	Bowl, 12", oblong	55.00
	Bowl, 14", round, punch & stand	250.00

	Bowl, 15", round, punch & stand		275.00		Pitcher, 3 pt., upright	150.00
8	Butter and domed cover		125.00		Pitcher, 3 pt., bulbous	150.00
	Cake plate, 9", ftd.		150.00		Pitcher, ½ gal., upright	175.00
	Cake plate, 10, ftd.		150.00		Pitcher, ½ gal., straight sided	175.00
	Celery tray, 12"		65.00	12	Pitcher, ½ gal., bulbous	185.00
	Comport, 5", ftd.		45.00		Pitcher, 3 qt., upright	225.00
1	Comport, 6", ftd.		45.00		Plate, torte, 13"	35.00
	Creamer, lg.		45.00		Pitcher, 3 qt., bulbous	235.00
	Creamer, hotel		40.00	10	Plate, 9", oval underliner	30.00
	Creamer, individual		45.00	3	Rose bowl, 3", footed	250.00
14	Cup, punch, two styles		20.00		Salt & pepper, 3 styles	100.00
11	Egg cup, ftd.		55.00		Spooner	100.00
4	Goblet, water		150.00		Sugar, lg.	45.00
	Mayonnaise and underplate		55.00		Sugar, hotel	40.00
16	Pickle jar and stopper		145.00		Sugar, individual	45.00
	Pickle tray, 6"		35.00	7	Toothpick holder	135.00
	Pitcher, 1 qt., upright		145.00	17	Tumbler, 2 styles	40.00
	Pitcher, 1 qt., bulbous		145.00	5	Vase, orchid, 6"	125.00

SUNRAY, LINE #2510, FOSTORIA GLASS COMPANY, 1935 – 1944

Colors: crystal, red, blue, green, yellow

Sunray's pricing is still thorny due to the inconsistencies we are seeing. Be sure to see Glacier (page 121) which consists of frosted panels added to Sunray. Some Sunray enthusiasts are willing to mix the two, but most gather one or the other. Both patterns sell in the same price range, although Glacier's supply is more limited.

We price only crystal; but be aware of pieces that are found in red, blue, green, and yellow. A sample of each of those colors are shown on page 227. A few colored pieces in the midst of your crystal would likely enhance its appeal.

If you are just learning about Sunray, you should know that Duncan & Miller made a similar, but heavier and thicker pattern; so if you see a punch set that you assume is Sunray, it is not. There is no Sunray punch set. The cream soup is tab handled, but by adding a lid on it, it becomes an onion soup according to Fostoria's catalogs. The condiment tray with cruets and mustards is shaped like a cloverleaf, comparable to the one in Fostoria's American pattern. It is unmistakably in smaller supply than the American one; but not as many collectors are inclined to own one.

		Crystal
24	Almond, ftd., ind.	10.00
	Ashtray, ind., 2510½	6.00
	Ashtray, sq.	10.00
22	Bonbon, 6½", hdld.	14.00
	Bonbon, 7", 3 toed	15.00
	Bowl, 5", fruit	9.00
	Bowl, 9½", flared	25.00
	Bowl, 12", salad	30.00
	Bowl, 13", rolled edge	35.00
23	Bowl, custard, 2¼", high	9.00
12	Bowl, 10", hdld.	32.00
	Butter, w/lid, ¼ lb.	30.00
	Candelabra, 2-lite, bobeche & prisms	75.00
	Candlestick, 3"	15.00
4	Candlestick, 5½"	22.00
8	Candlestick, duo	30.00
16	Candy jar, w/cover	50.00

		Crystal
	Celery, hdld.	20.00
15	Cigarette and cover	18.00
	Cigarette box, oblong	20.00
	Coaster, 4"	6.00
9	Comport	18.00
	Cream soup	20.00
	Cream soup liner	5.00
	Cream, ftd.	9.00
	Cream, individual	9.00
14	Cup	10.00
	Decanter, w/stopper, 18 oz.	60.00
	Decanter, w/stopper, oblong, 26 oz.	65.00
	Ice bucket, no handle	50.00
3	Ice bucket, w/handle	55.00
	Jelly	14.00
7	Jelly, w/cover	30.00
11	Mayonnaise, w/liner, ladle	30.00

		Crystal
19	Mustard, w/cover, spoon	38.00
	Nappy, hdld., flared	10.00
6	Nappy, hdld., reg.	10.00
	Nappy, hdld., sq.	11.00
	Nappy, hdld., tri-corner	12.00
10	Oil bottle, w/stopper, 3 oz.	30.00
21	Onion soup, w/cover	40.00
	Pickle, hdld.	18.00
	Pitcher, 16 oz., cereal	40.00
	Pitcher, 64 oz.	75.00
5	Pitcher, 64 oz., ice lip	95.00
	Plate, 6"	4.00
	Plate, 7½"	6.00
17	Plate, 8½"	10.00
	Plate, 9½"	18.00
	Plate, 11", torte	24.00
	Plate, 12", sandwich	24.00
	Plate, 15", torte	38.00
	Plate, 16"	48.00
13	Relish, 6½", 3 part	18.00
	Relish, 8", 4 part	18.00
	Relish, 10", 2 part	16.00
	Salt dip	10.00

		Crystal
14	Saucer	2.00
22	Shaker, 4", pr.	38.00
	Shaker, individual, 2¼", #2510½, pr.	38.00
	Stem, 3½", 5½ oz., sherbet, low	8.00
	Stem, 3¼", 3½ oz., fruit cocktail	8.00
	Stem, 3", 4 oz., cocktail, ftd.	8.00
	Stem, 4⅞", 4½ oz., claret	18.00
1	Stem, 5¾", 9 oz., goblet	16.00
	Sugar, ftd.	8.00
	Sugar, individual	8.00
	Sweetmeat, hdld., divided, 6"	20.00
	Tray, 6½", ind. sugar/cream	8.00
	Tray, 10½", oblong	32.00
	Tray, 10", sq.	34.00
18	Tray, condiment, 8½", cloverleaf	38.00
	Tray, oval hdld.	22.00
25	Tumbler, 2¼", 2 oz., whiskey, #2510½	10.00
	Tumbler, 3½", 5 oz., juice, #2510½	10.00
20	Tumbler, 3½", 6 oz., old-fashion, #2510½	12.00
	Tumbler, 4⅛", 9 oz., table, #2510½	12.00
2	Tumbler, 4¾", 9 oz., ftd., table	12.00
	Tumbler, 4⅝", 5 oz., ftd., juice	12.00
	Tumbler, 5¼", 13 oz., ftd., tea	15.00
26	Tumbler, 5⅛", 13 oz., tea, #2510½	16.00
27	Vase, 3½", rose bowl	25.00
	Vase, 5", rose bowl	32.50
	Vase, 6", crimped	40.00
	Vase, 7"	50.00
	Vase, 9", sq. ftd.	60.00
	Vase, sweet pea	75.00

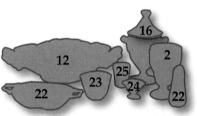

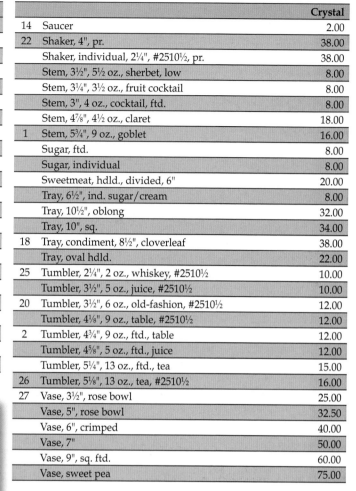

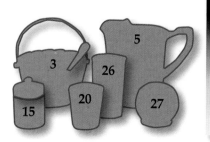

SUNRISE MEDALLION, "DANCING GIRL," #758, MORGANTOWN GLASS WORKS, LATE 1920S – EARLY 1930S

Colors: pink, green, blue, crystal

Collectors routinely had identified Sunrise Medallion (Morgantown's etching #758) as "Dancing Girl" which it was referred to by an earlier author on glassware. Contemporary collectors are more comfortable using the correct Sunrise Medallion name.

Catalog measurements were constantly recorded in ounces, not heights. Measurements for height in this book came from essentially measuring the items ourselves.

Twisted stem wares (#7664 Queen Anne) are slightly taller than their plain stem counterparts (#7630 Ballerina, "Lady Leg" stems). Measurements listed here are primarily from the #7630 line of which we have owned more than twisted ones. Twisted blue and crystal champagnes, sherbets, and waters are the only #7664 stems we have possessed. Should you have others, we would appreciate your input on measurements (height and capacity to top edge).

Blue is the preferred color of collectors, something true in nearly all patterns. Crystal turns up frequently and is not as highly priced because of a lack of demand. Pink stemware and tumblers are available, though not as popular as blue; however, other pink items are not often seen. Green appears to be rare with only a very few pieces surfacing. We have only owned a green sugar and 10" vase, but have seen a picture of a creamer. It was not for sale. Speaking of creamers and sugars, they are the most difficult pieces to find.

For such a highly prized pitcher, the blue one turns up frequently in the Northwest. There are two different styled oyster cocktails, which look something like a bar tumbler. We owned six at one time and their capacities ranged from a little under to a little over four ounces.

Cordials can be found in crystal, but only a few blue ones have materialized. We have never seen a twisted stem cordial in any color.

		Crystal	Blue	Pink Green
9	Bowl, finger, ftd.		65.00	
	Creamer		250.00	250.00
	Cup	30.00	80.00	60.00
	Parfait, 5 oz.	30.00	90.00	75.00
	Pitcher		495.00	
10	Plate, 5⅞", sherbet	4.00	10.00	6.00
	Plate, 7½", salad	8.00	15.00	15.00
12	Plate, 8⅜"	10.00	18.00	18.00
	Saucer	10.00	18.00	15.00
17	Sherbet, cone	16.00		
	Stem, 1½ oz., cordial	75.00	200.00	150.00
8	Stem, 2½ oz., wine	20.00	60.00	40.00
1	Stem, 6 oz., low sherbet	15.00	25.00	20.00
16	Stem, 6¼", 7 oz., champagne	18.00	30.00	25.00
14	Stem, 6¾", 7 oz., champagne, twist stem	18.00	30.00	25.00
	Stem, 6⅛", cocktail	18.00	35.00	25.00
3	Stem, 7¾", 9 oz., water	25.00	50.00	40.00
13	Stem, 8¼", 9 oz., water, twist stem	25.00	50.00	40.00
18	Sugar		250.00	250.00
	Tumbler, 2½", 4 oz., ftd.	20.00	75.00	
4	Tumbler, 3½", 4 oz., ftd.			30.00
	Tumbler, 4¼", 5 oz., ftd.	25.00	50.00	40.00
19	Tumbler, 4¼", flat	15.00		
15	Tumbler, 4¾", 9 oz., ftd.	15.00	40.00	30.00
	Tumbler, 5½", 11 oz., ftd.	22.00	60.00	45.00
6	Tumbler, 5½", flat	22.00		65.00
	Vase, 6" tall, 5" wide			350.00
2	Vase, 10", slender, bud	65.00	450.00	350.00
	Vase, 10", bulbous bottom			395.00

1

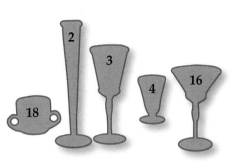

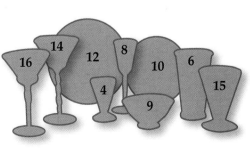

SYLVAN, TIFFIN GLASS COMPANY, LATE 1920S

Colors: Nile Green, Rose

   Tiffin's Sylvan was produced for 11 years (1925 – 1935); so, there should be more available today than there appears to be. Maybe it was so well used that it was tossed away and little was saved. Most Sylvan pieces are found on the same blanks as the popular Deerwood, but flowers are not as coveted as animals by collectors. You may find additional pieces not in the listing.

		Green/Pink				Green/Pink
	Bowl, 10", salad, straight edge #8105	60.00	3	Plate, 10", dinner, #8859		32.00
	Candleholder, 5", #101	28.00		Salver, 10", low ftd., #330		55.00
	Candy jar w/cover, ftd., cone, #330	75.00		Saucer, #9395		4.00
	Candy w/cover, 6", flat, #329	65.00		Server, 10", center handled, #330		35.00
4	Celery, 10", #151	35.00		Stem, #2809, 3 oz. wine		20.00
	Comport, 10", low ftd., #330	50.00	1	Stem, #2809, 3½ oz., cocktail		18.00
	Comport, cheese, #330	20.00		Stem, # 2809, 6 oz., champagne		15.00
	Creamer, #179	20.00		Stem, # 2809, 9 oz., water goblet		20.00
	Cup, #9395	15.00		Sugar, #179		20.00
	Plate, 5½", bread/butter, #8859	6.00		Tumbler, #2809, water		14.00
2	Plate, 7½", salad, #8859	8.00		Tumbler, #2809, ice tea		20.00
	Plate, 10", cracker w/indent, #330	22.00		Vase, 7", sweet pea, rolled edge, #151		65.00
				Whipped cream, ftd., #330		32.00

TALLY HO, #1402, CAMBRIDGE GLASS COMPANY, LATE 1920S – 1930S

Colors: amber, Carmen, crystal, Forest Green, Royal Blue

Tally Ho is an enormous Cambridge pattern in both manufacture and the magnitude of many of its pieces. It has formerly been represented in this book in various etched patterns from Elaine to Valencia. For identification, the heavy pressed one-color stems are listed as goblets in the listing below and the blown, thin, tall crystal stems with colored bowls are listed as stems. We have tried to illustrate as many of these as we could find.

We helped a friend liquidate his collection of Tally Ho at Cambridge last year. Funny, but it was the stemware that sold out. The bowls and other serving items were remaining after the sale. Tally Ho crystal punch bowl sets can be found with cups and ladles with colored handles as well as entirely crystal. The ones with colored handles are more desirable as are those of Duncan's Caribbean.

	Amber Crystal	Carmen Royal	Forest Green
Ashtray, 4"	10.00	20.00	15.00
Ashtray, 4", w/ctr. hdld.	15.00	25.00	22.00
Ash well, 2 pc., ctr. hdld.	18.00	30.00	25.00
Bowl, 4½", ftd., fruit/sherbet	10.00	16.00	14.00
Bowl, 5", frappe cocktail, 10 side rim	14.00	22.00	20.00
Bowl, 6", iced fruit, 10 side rim	20.00	30.00	25.00
Bowl, 6", 2 hdld.	14.00	22.00	20.00
Bowl, 6", 2 hdld. nappy	15.00	22.00	20.00
Bowl, 6½", grapefruit, flat rim	15.00	26.00	22.00
Bowl, 6½", 2 hdld.	15.00	26.00	22.00
Bowl, 7", fruit, 10 side rim	15.00	26.00	22.00
Bowl, 8"	25.00	38.00	33.00
Bowl, 8½", 3 comp.	38.00	65.00	55.00
Bowl, 9"	26.00	50.00	45.00
Bowl, 9", pan	26.00	50.00	45.00
Bowl, 10", pan	26.00	50.00	45.00
Bowl, 10½", belled	30.00	52.00	48.00

		Amber Crystal	Carmen Royal	Forest Green
	Bowl, 10½", 2 comp. salad	30.00	55.00	45.00
	Bowl, 10½", 2 hdld.	30.00	55.00	45.00
	Bowl, 10½", 3 comp.	40.00	65.00	55.00
	Bowl, 10½", low ft.	35.00	70.00	60.00
	Bowl, 11", flat, flared	35.00	65.00	50.00
	Bowl, 12", oval celery	25.00	32.00	28.00
	Bowl, 12", pan	32.00	70.00	60.00
	Bowl, 12½", flat rim	32.00	70.00	60.00
	Bowl, 12½", belled	32.00	70.00	60.00
17	Bowl, 13", ftd., punch	175.00	350.00	250.00
	Bowl, 13½", salad, flared	30.00	75.00	60.00
	Bowl, 17", pan	35.00	85.00	75.00
	Bowl, 2 comp., 2 ladle, salad dressing, flared	30.00	75.00	65.00
	Bowl, 2 comp., 2 ladle, salad dressing, rnd.	30.00	75.00	65.00

#		Amber Crystal	Carmen Royal	Forest Green
	Bowl, 2 ladle, spouted, salad dressing	25.00	60.00	45.00
	Bowl, finger	15.00	22.00	20.00
	Bowl, sauce boat	20.00	40.00	30.00
	Candelabrum, 6½", w/bobeche & prism	40.00	65.00	48.00
	Candlestick, 5"	20.00	35.00	30.00
	Candlestick, 6"	25.00	40.00	35.00
	Candlestick, 6½"	35.00	50.00	40.00
	Cheese & cracker, 11½", 2 hdld.	50.00	70.00	55.00
	Cheese & cracker, 13½"	50.00	70.00	65.00
	Cheese & cracker, 17½"	60.00	80.00	75.00
	Cheese & cracker, 18"	75.00	105.00	80.00
	Coaster, 4"	8.00	12.00	12.00
	Cocktail shaker, 50 oz., ftd., chrome top	60.00	125.00	95.00
	Cocktail shaker, hdld., ftd., chrome top	60.00	135.00	100.00
	Comport, tall frappe cocktail, 10 side rim	30.00	50.00	40.00
	Comport, 4½" tall	15.00	22.00	20.00
	Comport, 6", tall ft., flat, mint	20.00	40.00	35.00
	Comport, 6½", tall ft., raised edge	20.00	40.00	35.00
	Comport, 7", low ft.	20.00	45.00	35.00
	Comport, 8", low ft.	25.00	50.00	40.00
	Comport, 9", low ft., raised edge	35.00	60.00	55.00
	Comport, low ft., mint	15.00	22.00	20.00
	Cookie jar w/lid, chrome hdld. (ice pail w/lid)	85.00	175.00	140.00
28	Creamer, ftd.	12.00	24.00	20.00
20	Cup, 2½ oz., hdld., whiskey	12.00	22.00	18.00
21	Cup, ftd.	10.00	20.00	17.50
18	Cup, punch, flat	10.00	20.00	17.50
25	Decanter, 16 oz., hdld.	30.00	75.00	55.00
24	Decanter, 34 oz.	40.00	90.00	65.00
	Decanter, 34 oz., hdld.	40.00	95.00	75.00
	Goblet, brandy inhaler, #1402	35.00	55.00	40.00
	Goblet, claret, #1402	15.00	35.00	20.00
	Goblet, cocktail, #1402	14.00	26.00	16.00
13	Goblet, cordial, #1402	25.00	40.00	30.00
8	Goblet, water, #1402	18.00	30.00	22.00
	Goblet, low ft., brandy inhaler, #1402	20.00	50.00	38.00
	Goblet, low sherbet, #1402	10.00	20.00	15.00
	Goblet, oyster cocktail, #1402	12.00	20.00	15.00
10	Goblet, tall sherbet, #1402	14.00	22.00	18.00
	Goblet, wine, #1402	16.00	28.00	22.00
16	Ice pail, chrome hdld.	55.00	110.00	100.00
	Jug, 74 oz., tankard, flat bottom	110.00	250.00	175.00
	Jug, 88 oz., rnd. bottom	115.00	395.00	195.00
27	Mug, 6 oz., punch	10.00	20.00	15.00
26	Mug, 12 oz., hdld. stein	18.00	25.00	22.00

#		Amber Crystal	Carmen Royal	Forest Green
	Mug, 14 oz., hdld. stein, rnd. bottom	25.00	40.00	28.00
	Plate, 6", bread & butter	6.00	10.00	8.00
	Plate, 7", 2 hdld.	10.00	20.00	18.00
	Plate, 7½", salad	10.00	16.00	14.00
	Plate, 8", salad	12.00	16.00	14.00
	Plate, 9½", lunch	20.00	45.00	32.00
	Plate, 10½", dinner	28.00	85.00	
	Plate, 11½", 2 hdld., sandwich	28.00	55.00	45.00
	Plate, 13½", raised edge	30.00	60.00	50.00
	Plate, 14", chop	30.00	60.00	50.00
	Plate, 14", w/4" seat in center	30.00	60.00	50.00
	Plate, 17½", Sunday night supper	40.00	85.00	55.00
	Plate, 17½"	40.00	85.00	55.00
	Plate, 18", w/4" seat in center	45.00	95.00	65.00
	Plate, 18", buffet lunch	45.00	95.00	65.00
	Plate, 18", ftd., weekend supper	45.00	95.00	70.00
	Plate, finger bowl	7.00	12.00	10.00
	Plate, salad dressing liner	10.00	15.00	12.00
	Plate, sauce boat liner	10.00	15.00	12.00
	Relish, 6", 2 comp., 2 hdld.	15.00	25.00	20.00
	Relish, 8", 2 hdld., 3 comp.	20.00	30.00	25.00
	Relish, 10", 4 comp.	20.00	30.00	25.00
21	Saucer	2.00	4.00	3.00
23	Shaker, w/glass top	20.00	55.00	35.00
12	Stem, 1 oz., cordial	20.00	50.00	40.00
4	Stem, 2½ oz., high stem wine	15.00	30.00	25.00
	Stem, 3 oz., ftd., tumbler	12.00	25.00	20.00
5	Stem, 3 oz., high stem cocktail	12.00	25.00	20.00
	Stem, 4 oz., low stem cocktail	12.00	25.00	20.00
	Stem, 4½ oz., low sherbet	10.00	16.00	14.00
3	Stem, 4½ oz., high stem claret	12.00	30.00	22.00
	Stem, 5 oz., ftd., tumbler	10.00	22.00	16.00
7	Stem, 5 oz., low stem juice	10.00	22.00	16.00
	Stem, 6 oz., high stem juice	11.00	22.00	16.00
6	Stem, 6½ oz., low stem sherbet	11.00	18.00	16.00
2	Stem, 7½ oz., high sherbet	12.00	22.00	20.00
1	Stem, 10 oz., high stem	12.00	25.00	22.00
14	Stem, 10 oz., low stem lunch	12.00	25.00	22.00
15	Stem, 12 oz., ftd. tumbler	12.00	28.00	22.00
	Stem, 14 oz., high stem	12.00	32.00	26.00
	Stem, 16 oz., ftd., tumbler	12.00	35.00	26.00
	Stem, 18 oz., tall stem	15.00	45.00	30.00
22	Sugar, ftd.	12.00	24.00	20.00
19	Top hat, 10", vase	110.00	295.00	195.00
11	Tumbler, 2½ oz.	20.00	35.00	30.00
9	Tumbler, 5 oz.	20.00	35.00	28.00
	Tumbler, 7 oz., old-fashion	22.00	35.00	30.00
	Tumbler, 10 oz., short	20.00	35.00	30.00
	Tumbler, 10 oz., tall	20.00	35.00	30.00
	Tumbler, 14 oz., rnd. bottom	15.00	30.00	24.00
	Tumbler, 15 oz.	20.00	35.00	28.00
	Vase, 12", ftd.	75.00	225.00	175.00

TEAR DROP, #301, DUNCAN & MILLER GLASS COMPANY, 1936 – 1955

Colors: crystal, some yellow and cobalt blue

As with Duncan's Sandwich, Tear Drop stemware can be found at such a bargain price that you could use it today cheaper than you could buy almost any newly made stems. Tear Drop was heavily used exhibited by what is uncovered today; so, mint condition dinner plates and matching serving pieces are not easily encountered. This is an unparalleled starting point for anyone looking for an easily found and reasonably priced Elegant crystal pattern.

Colored pieces being found may have been produced at Tiffin from Duncan moulds. Reprints of original Duncan catalogs showing Tear Drop stemware and tumblers can be found in earlier editions of this book. In order to have room for the newly listed patterns and additional pictures, we removed catalog pages.

		Crystal
13	Ashtray, 3", indiv.	5.00
14	Ashtray, 5"	6.00
	Bonbon, 6", 4 hdld.	10.00
	Bottle, w/stopper, 12", bar	135.00
	Bowl, 4¼", finger	6.00
	Bowl, 5", fruit nappy	7.00
	Bowl, 5", 2 hdld., nappy	8.00
	Bowl, 6", dessert, nappy	7.00
	Bowl, 6", fruit, nappy	7.00
	Bowl, 7", fruit, nappy	8.00
	Bowl, 7", 2 hdld., nappy	9.00
	Bowl, 8" x 12", oval, flower	42.00
	Bowl, 9", salad	28.00
	Bowl, 9", 2 hdld., nappy	22.00
	Bowl, 10", crimped console, 2 hdld.	30.00
	Bowl, 10", flared, fruit	28.00
	Bowl, 11½", crimped, flower	32.00
	Bowl, 11½", flared, flower	30.00
	Bowl, 12", salad	35.00
	Bowl, 12", crimped, low foot	35.00
	Bowl, 12", ftd., flower	40.00
	Bowl, 12", sq., 4 hdld.	40.00
	Bowl, 13", gardenia	35.00
	Bowl, 15½", 2½ gal., punch	90.00
12	Butter, w/cover, ¼ lb., 2 hdld.	25.00
	Cake salver, 13", ftd.	50.00
	Canape set (6" plate w/ring, 4 oz., ftd., cocktail)	26.00
	Candlestick, 4"	10.00
	Candlestick, 7", 2-lite, ball loop ctr.	28.00
	Candlestick, 7", lg. ball ctr. w/bobeches, prisms	75.00
	Candy basket, 5½" x 7½", 2 hdld., oval	75.00
	Candy box, w/cover, 7", 2 pt., 2 hdld.	60.00
	Candy box, w/cover, 8", 3 pt., 3 hdld.	65.00
	Candy dish, 7½", heart shape	20.00
	Celery, 11", 2 hdld.	20.00
	Celery, 11", 2 pt., 2 hdld.	20.00
	Celery, 12", 3 pt.	22.00
	Cheese & cracker (3½" comport, 11" 2 hdld. plate)	40.00
10	Coaster/ashtray, 3", rolled edge	6.00
	Comport, 4¾", ftd.	11.00
	Comport, 6", low foot., hdld.	14.00

		Crystal
4,5,6	Condiment set, 5 pc. (salt/pepper, two 3 oz. cruets, 9", 2 hdld. tray)	75.00
8	Creamer, 3 oz.	7.00
	Creamer, 6 oz.	5.00
	Creamer, 8 oz.	7.00
	Cup, 2½ oz., demi	10.00
	Cup, 6 oz., tea	5.00
	Flower basket, 12", loop hdl.	90.00
	Ice bucket, 5½"	65.00
	Marmalade, w/cover, 4"	35.00
	Mayonnaise, 4½" (2 hdld. bowl, ladle, 6" plate)	35.00
	Mayonnaise set, 3 pc. (4½" bowl, ladle, 8" hdld. plate)	35.00
	Mustard jar, w/cover, 4¼"	30.00
	Nut dish, 6", 2 pt.	9.00
4	Oil bottle, 3 oz.	15.00
	Olive dish, 4¼", 2 hdld., oval	14.00
	Olive dish, 6", 2 pt.	14.00
	Pickle dish, 6"	14.00
	Pitcher, 5", 16 oz., milk	40.00
	Pitcher, 8½", 64 oz., w/ice lip	90.00
	Plate, 6", bread/butter	3.00
	Plate, 6", canape	8.00
	Plate, 7", 2 hdld., lemon	10.00
	Plate, 7½", salad	5.00
	Plate, 8½", luncheon	7.00
	Plate, 10½", dinner	28.00
15	Plate, 11", 2 hdld.	25.00

Unidentified stem line

13

		Crystal
	Plate, 13", 4 hdld.	30.00
	Plate, 13", salad liner, rolled edge	30.00
	Plate, 13", torte, rolled edge	30.00
	Plate, 14", torte	35.00
	Plate, 14", torte, rolled edge	35.00
	Plate, 16", torte, rolled edge	38.00
	Plate, 18", lazy susan	60.00
	Plate, 18", punch liner, rolled edge	50.00
12	Relish, 7", 2 pt., 2 hdld.	12.00
11	Relish, 7½", 2 pt., heart shape	18.00
	Relish, 9", 3 pt., 3 hdld.	27.00
	Relish, 11", 3 pt., 2 hdld.	30.00
	Relish, 12", 3 pt.	30.00
	Relish, 12", 5 pt., rnd.	35.00
	Relish, 12", 6 pt., rnd.	38.00
	Relish, 12", sq., 4 pt., 4 hdld.	38.00
	Salad set, 6" (compote, 11", hdld. plate)	35.00
	Salad set, 9" (2 pt. bowl, 13" rolled edge plate)	65.00
5	Salt & pepper, 5"	22.00
	Saucer, 4½", demi	3.00
	Saucer, 6"	1.50
	Stem, 2½", 5 oz., ftd., sherbet	4.00
	Stem, 2¾", 3½ oz., ftd., oyster cocktail	5.00
	Stem, 3½", 5 oz., sherbet	5.00
3	Stem, 4", 1 oz., cordial	22.00
	Stem, 4½", 1¾ oz., sherry	20.00
7	Stem, 4½", 3½ oz., cocktail	10.00
	Stem, 4¾", 3 oz., wine	13.00
	Stem, 5", 5 oz., champagne	8.00
	Stem, 5½", 4 oz., claret	13.00
9	Stem, 5¾", 9 oz.	10.00
	Stem, 6¼", 8 oz., ale	12.00

		Crystal
	Stem, 7", 9 oz.	14.00
	Sugar, 3 oz.	6.00
	Sugar, 6 oz.	5.00
	Sugar, 8 oz.	6.00
	Sweetmeat, 5½", star shape, 2 hdld.	30.00
	Sweetmeat, 6½", ctr. hdld.	25.00
	Sweetmeat, 7", star shape, 2 hdld.	35.00
	Tray, 5½", ctr. hdld. (for mustard jar)	12.00
	Tray, 6", 2 hdld. (for salt/pepper)	12.00
	Tray, 7¾", ctr. hdld. (for cruets)	12.50
	Tray, 8", 2 hdld. (for oil/vinegar)	12.50
	Tray, 8", 2 hdld. (for sugar/creamer)	10.00
6	Tray, 9" (for salt, pepper, 2 cruets)	20.00
	Tray, 10", 2 hdld. (for sugar/creamer)	10.00
	Tumbler, 2¼", 2 oz., flat, whiskey	14.00
	Tumbler, 2¼", 2 oz., ftd., whiskey	12.00
	Tumbler, 3", 3 oz., ftd., whiskey	12.00
	Tumbler, 3¼", 3½ oz., flat, juice	7.00
13	Tumbler, 3¼", 7 oz., flat, old-fashion	10.00
	Tumbler, 3½", 5 oz., flat, juice	8.00
	Tumbler, 4", 4½ oz., ftd., juice	8.00
	Tumbler, 4¼", 9 oz., flat	9.00
	Tumbler, 4½", 8 oz., flat, split	9.00
1	Tumbler, 4½", 9 oz., ftd.	9.00
	Tumbler, 4¾", 10 oz., flat, hi-ball	10.00
	Tumbler, 5", 8 oz., ftd., party	10.00
	Tumbler, 5¼", 12 oz., flat, iced tea	14.00
	Tumbler, 5¾", 14 oz., flat, hi-ball	16.00
2	Tumbler, 6", 14 oz., ftd., iced tea	16.00
	Urn, w/cover, 9", ftd.	125.00
	Vase, 9", ftd., fan	33.00
	Vase, 9", ftd., round	38.00

TERRACE, NO. 111, DUNCAN & MILLER GLASS COMPANY, 1937

Colors: crystal, amber, cobalt, red

Terrace with its Deco influenced design is a Duncan pattern that has been somewhat unnoticed over the years by collectors outside the western Pennsylvania area due to limited distribution and insufficient information about it. The internet auctions have dispensed more information over the last few years than the few books on Duncan glassware ever attempted.

Red and cobalt are the colors being hunted with little collector attention being given to amber or crystal. Small amounts of amber are available and most of that found has a gold decoration on it. Those desiring crystal openly look for First Love or some other etching rather than for Terrace itself.

Be cognizant of the crystal bowls and plates having cobalt or red bases. Learn to recognize that base pattern so you do not pass one of these.

1

		Crystal Amber	Cobalt Red
10	Ashtray, 3½", sq.	15.00	25.00
	Ashtray, 4¾", sq.	18.00	55.00
23	Bowl, 4", crystal top	26.00	
	Bowl, 4¼", finger, #5111½	25.00	55.00
22	Bowl, 4¾", turned up edge	10.00	22.00
26	Bowl, 6", crystal top	20.00	
	Bowl, 6¾" x 4¼", ftd., flared rim	25.00	
	Bowl, 8" sq. x 2½", hdld.	45.00	
	Bowl, 9" x 4½", ftd.	40.00	
	Bowl, 9½" x 2½", hdld.	40.00	
	Bowl, 10" x 3¾", ftd., flared rim	50.00	
	Bowl, 10¼" x 4¾", ftd.*	60.00	135.00
	Bowl, 11" x 3¼", flared rim	30.00	
	Butter or cheese, 7" sq. x 1¼"	100.00	
14	Candle, 3", 1-lite	20.00	50.00
	Candle, 4", low	22.00	
	Candlestick, 1-lite, bobeche & prisms	60.00	
	Candlestick 2-lite, 7" x 9¼", bobeche & prisms	85.00	
8	Candy dish, hdld.	30.00	100.00
	Candy urn, w/lid	100.00	395.00
	Cheese stand, 3" x 5¼"	20.00	33.00
	Cocktail shaker, metal lid	75.00	195.00
	Comport, w/lid, 8¾" x 5½"	135.00	395.00
1	Comport, 3½" x 4¾" w	26.00	65.00
2	Creamer, 3", 10 oz.	15.00	33.00
18	Cup	12.00	38.00
5	Cup, demi	15.00	
11	Ice bucket	50.00	
	Mayonnaise, 5½" x 2½", ftd., hdld., #111	30.00	
	Mayonnaise, 5½" x 3½", crimped	28.00	
	Mayonnaise, 5¾" x 3", w/dish hdld. tray	30.00	65.00
	Mayonnaise, w/7" tray, hdld.	30.00	
	Nappy, 5½" x 2", div., hdld.	15.00	
21	Nappy, 6" x 1¾", hdld.	20.00	35.00
	Pitcher	250.00	895.00
	Plate, 6"	8.00	15.00
25	Plate, 6", hdld., lemon	10.00	25.00
13	Plate, 6", sq.	10.00	25.00
	Plate, 7"	12.00	24.00
	Plate, 7½"	12.00	24.00
16	Plate, 7½", sq.	12.00	24.00

		Crystal Amber	Cobalt Red
	Plate, 8½"	15.00	25.00
15	Plate, 9", sq.	18.00	75.00
6	Plate, 11", sq.	26.00	95.00
	Plate, 11", hdld.	28.00	
	Plate, 11", hdld., cracker w/ring	28.00	90.00
	Plate, 11", hdld., sandwich	28.00	
	Plate, 12", torte, rolled edge	32.50	
24	Plate, 13", cake, ftd., crystal top*		165.00
	Plate, 13", torte, flat edge	35.00	
	Plate, 13", torte, rolled edge	37.50	
	Plate, 13¼", torte	35.00	150.00
28	Relish, 6" x 4¾", hdld., 2 pt.	20.00	48.00
	Relish, 9", 4 pt.	30.00	90.00
	Relish, 10½" x 1½", hdld., 5 pt.	55.00	
20	Relish, 12", 4 pt., hdld.	38.00	90.00
	Relish, 12", 5 pt., hdld.	38.00	
12	Relish, 12", 5 pt., w/lid	100.00	275.00
19	Salad dressing bowl, 2 pt., 5½" x 4¼"	38.00	75.00
18	Saucer, sq.	5.00	10.00
5	Saucer, demi	5.00	
	Stem, 3¾", 1 oz., cordial, #5111½	35.00	
	Stem, 3¾", 4½ oz., oyster cocktail, #5111½	18.00	
	Stem, 4", 5 oz., ice cream, #5111½	12.00	
	Stem, 4½", 3½ oz., cocktail, #5111½	20.00	
7	Stem, 5", 5 oz., saucer champagne, #5111½	12.00	40.00
	Stem, 5¼", 3 oz., wine, #5111½	28.00	
	Stem, 5¼", 5 oz., ftd. juice, #5111½	18.00	
	Stem, 5¾", 10 oz., low luncheon goblet, #5111½	20.00	
	Stem, 6", 4½ oz., claret, #5111½	36.00	
	Stem, 6½", 12 oz., ftd. ice tea, #5111½	28.00	
9	Stem, 6¾", 10 oz., tall water goblet, #5111½	22.00	
	Stem, 6¾", 14 oz., ftd. ice tea, #5111½	28.00	
4	Sugar, 3", 10 oz.	15.00	33.00
4	Sugar lid	10.00	85.00
17	Tumbler, 2 oz., shot	14.00	38.00
27	Tumbler, 4", 9 oz., water	16.00	60.00
	Tray, 8" x 2", hdld., celery	17.50	
	Urn, 4½" x 4½"	27.50	
	Urn, 10½" x 4½"	120.00	310.00
	Vase, 10, ftd.	100.00	

*Colored foot

THISTLE, ETCHED 10 OPTIC, CENTRAL GLASS COMPANY, 1900 – EARLY 1920S; TIFFIN GLASS COMPANY, 1924 – EARLY 1930S

Color: crystal

Both Tiffin and Central made this specific Thistle etching. The designs are precisely alike; thus mould shapes are the determining factors in deciding which company prepared an individual piece. There ought to be more of this pattern accessible to collectors with two different makers marketing Thistle over the years; truth is, few are presently concerned with this thorny problem.

6

1	Bowl, 14 oz. finger	11.00
	Bowl, 8½", soup	18.00
	Comport, 5" high	20.00
	Comport, 6" high	22.00
	Comport, low, 4½" diameter	15.00
	Comport, low, 6" diameter	18.00
	Comport, low, 7" diameter	20.00
	Cup, 4½ oz. handled custard	10.00
	Decanter, 32 oz., w/stopper	75.00
	Marmalade, 8 oz., w/lid	30.00
	Marmalade liner/coaster, 4½"	4.00
	Night bottle	85.00
	Night set tumbler	15.00
5	Pitcher w/cover., 80 oz.	85.00
6	Plate, 5", sherbet	4.00
	Plate, 6", finger bowl liner	5.00
	Stem, 3 oz., cocktail	10.00
3	Stem, 3 oz., wine	12.00
	Stem, 4 oz. or 5 oz., claret	14.00
	Stem, 4 oz., small sherbet	6.00
	Stem, 6 oz., large sherbet	8.00
	Stem, 6 oz., saucer champagne	10.00
	Stem, 10 oz., water	15.00
	Teapot with lid	100.00
	Tumbler, 2½ oz., flared shot	8.00

4	Tumbler, 3¼ oz., flared	6.00
	Tumbler, 5 oz., flared	7.00
	Tumbler, 5½ oz., flared	9.00
	Tumbler, 6½ oz., ale (like vase)	20.00
	Tumbler, 7 oz., flared	9.00
	Tumbler, 8 oz., flared	10.00
	Tumbler, 8 oz., narrow, high ball	10.00
2	Tumbler, 9 oz., flared	10.00
	Tumbler, 9 oz., straight	10.00
	Tumbler, 10 oz., flared	10.00
	Tumbler, 11 oz., handled tea	18.00
	Tumbler, 11 oz., flared	12.00
	Tumbler, 12 oz., flared	12.00
	Tumbler, 14 oz., flared	14.00

THISTLE CUT, LINE 3101 & LINE 3104, H.C. FRY GLASS COMPANY, 1930S

Colors: blue, green, and pink

Thistle Cut exists on two Fry dinnerware lines, which are both in the photo below. Line #3101 is shown by the round pieces; and Line #3104 by the octagon shaped ones. The stems with the disc connectors (beehive shape) are usually observed in groups with the round line. You can find this cutting on pink (Rose), green (Emerald), or blue (Azure). There are other cuttings on these Fry lines; so be sure to study this pattern to pinpoint this Thistle design. Most collectors have nicknamed the blue color "Cornflower."

We purchased this set over 30 years ago at Washington Court House, Ohio, simply because of the blue color. At that time, no one seemed to know what the glass was, so it remained incognito until researching our first *Glassware Pattern Identification Guide*. As with Duncan patterns, we rarely find Fry patterns outside a semi-circle of 100 miles south of Pittsburgh.

		All Colors
8	Bowl, 9", round, ftd.	50.00
4	Candlestick	30.00
6	Cup	20.00
5	Plate, 6", round, bread & butter	6.00
	Plate, 8", octagonal, luncheon	12.00
7	Plate, 8", round, luncheon	12.00
2	Plate, 10½", octagonal, dinner	38.00
	Plate, 10", round, dinner	38.00
6	Saucer	4.00
1	Stem, high sherbet	18.00
	Stem, juice, ftd.	20.00
	Stem, low sherbet	14.00
3	Stem, water goblet	24.00

THOUSAND EYE, WESTMORELAND GLASS COMPANY, C. 1934

Colors: crystal and crystal w/pale burgundy, champagne (yellow), and green-blue lustre stain; more intense ruby color replaced pale burgundy later; black turtles in 1952

Thousand Eye is almost certainly Westmoreland's most famous non-milk glass pattern and had one of their longest production runs outside of English Hobnail. It was introduced in 1934 and produced continuously, except for turtles and fairy lamps, until 1956. The turtle cigarette box was reissued. Obviously these were customers' favorite pieces as there are so many existing today. Fairy lamps, both footed and flat, were created into the late 1970s.

We often run into a 13" bowl on an 18" plate which are misguidedly labeled as Westmoreland's Thousand Eye line, but are actually Canton's Glass Line 100. They are usually found in crystal, but are seen in blue, red, or amber. These colored wares were originally Paden City, but Canton did advertise in 1954 that they would make standard colors as well as special colors if the customer so requested. Canton acquired many of Paden City's moulds after that company closed.

Various Westmoreland Thousand Eye pieces are reminiscent of earlier pattern glass items. It seems to be another one of those patterns that collectors hold in the highest regard or cannot tolerate. Stemware abounds; and like some of Duncan's patterns, you can buy these older pieces and use them less expensively than scores of today's glassware lines sold in department stores. Thousand Eye is durable, but it was used extensively, and it shows. You need to check plates and other flat pieces for wear. Mint condition flatware is more challenging to find than any of the stems and tumblers.

		Crystal
11	Ashtray (sm. turtle)	8.00
	Basket, 8", hdld., oval	40.00
8	Bowl, 4½", nappy	8.00
	Bowl, 5½", nappy	10.00
	Bowl, 7½", hdld.	16.00
	Bowl, 10", 2 hdld.	30.00
	Bowl, 11", belled	30.00
	Bowl, 11", crimped, oblong	35.00
	Bowl, 11", triangular	35.00
	Bowl, 11, round	35.00
	Bowl, 12", 2 hdld., flared	40.00
	Candelabra, 2 light	30.00
7	Cigarette box & cover (lg. turtle)	30.00
	Comport, 5", high ft.	20.00
	Creamer, high ft.	10.00
1	Creamer, low rim	10.00
6	Cup, ftd., bead hdld.	5.00
	Fairy lamp, flat	40.00
	Fairy lamp, ftd.	40.00
	Jug, ½ gal.	75.00
	Mayonnaise, ftd., w/ladle	25.00
	Plate, 6"	5.00
	Plate, 7"	6.00
4	Plate, 8½"	9.00
3	Plate, 10", service	18.00
	Plate, 16"	26.00

		Crystal
	Plate, 18"	40.00
9	Relish, 10", rnd., 6 part	25.00
6	Saucer	2.00
	Shaker, ftd., pr.	28.00
	Stem, 1 oz., cordial	12.00
	Stem, 2 oz., wine	9.00
	Stem, 3 oz., sherry	9.00
	Stem, 3½ oz., cocktail	7.00
	Stem, 5 oz., claret	9.00
	Stem, 8 oz.	10.00
	Stem, high ft., sherbet	8.00
	Stem, low ft., sherbet	6.00
	Stem, parfait, ftd.	10.00
	Sugar, high ft.	10.00
2	Sugar, low rim	10.00
	Tumbler, 1½ oz., whiskey	10.00
	Tumbler, 5 oz., flat ginger ale	8.00
	Tumbler, 5 oz., ftd.	8.00
	Tumbler, 6 oz., old-fashion	9.00
10	Tumbler, 7 oz., ftd.	9.00
	Tumbler, 8 oz., flat	9.00
	Tumbler, 9 oz., ftd.	10.00
5	Tumbler, 12 oz., ftd., tea	11.00
	Vase, crimped bowl	30.00
	Vase, flair rim	30.00

"TINKERBELL," ETCH #756, MORGANTOWN GLASS WORKS, C. 1927

Colors: azure, green, Pink

We routinely dubbed this etch "Tinkerbell," when we first bought 16 stems 30 years ago. About 10 years later we discovered that they were Morgantown's #7631 Jewel stem and that Morgantown collectors were also calling them "Tinkerbell."

A year later we displayed half our goblets and champagnes at the Heisey show, and found they sold very fast. We kept one of each and finally added a wine to our set. Later we were able to add the bottle from the medicine bottle/night set, but the rest of that four-piece set has dodged us for now. The only complete set we've seen was in a not-for-sale display at the Morgantown convention.

That green bud vase is 10" tall and was found in an antique mall in Ohio. It remains the only piece of green "Tinkerbell" we have seen.

		Azure Green
	Bowl, finger, ftd.	90.00
5	Night or medicine set bottle, 4 pc. (med. bottle w/stop, night glass, w/water bottle)	750.00
	Plate, finger bowl liner	25.00
	Stem, 1½ oz., cordial	195.00
3	Stem, 2½ oz., wine	125.00
	Stem, 3½ oz., cocktail	100.00
4	Stem, 5½ oz., saucer champagne	100.00
	Stem, 5½ oz., sherbet	80.00
2	Stem, 9 oz., goblet	150.00
6	Tumbler, 9 oz., ftd.	75.00
	Vase, 10", plain top, ftd., #36 Uranus	395.00
1	Vase, 10", ruffled top, ftd., #36 Uranus	495.00

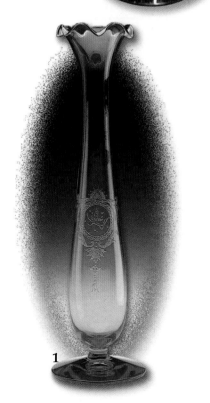

TROJAN, FOSTORIA GLASS COMPANY, 1929 – 1944

Colors: Rose pink, Topaz, yellow

Ancient stockpiles of Topaz and Rose Trojan are becoming increasingly meager. All of the pieces pictured are from a long-time collection in Florida.

Topaz used to sell quite well, as it was more copious in the market than pink. That oversupply of Topaz has been thinned, as well as those seeking it. Dealers are having trouble finding collectors for the harder to find items. The smaller supply of pink had discouraged collectors; but even that lesser supply is adequate for today's demand.

Trojan stemware can be found save for cordials and clarets in either color. Clarets are nearly impossible to find in most Fostoria patterns. The claret has the same shape as the wine, but holds four ounces as opposed to the three ounces of the wine. The scarcity of clarets and wines is not making much difference in today's market. Wine glasses in those days held 2 to 3½ ounces of liquid. This confuses today's admirers who are used to wine goblets holding eight ounces or more. In those days, that larger capacity was reserved for water. Due to the penchant of the public to buy water goblets to use as wines, prices for clarets and the previous sized wines are slipping drastically.

Soup and cereal bowl shortages were notable by rising prices over the years. Today, collectors are not obsessed with owning 4, 6, 8 or even 12 of each piece as used to be the case. Rare items that were on everyone's "want list," are being omitted from collections in favor of obtainable, usable items.

The following Fostoria facts need to be learned: liner plates for cream soup and mayonnaise dishes are the same piece; two-handled cake plates come with and without an indent in the center (the indented version also serves as a plate for cheese comports); bonbon, lemon dish, sweetmeat, and whipped cream bowls all come with loop or bow handles; and sugars come with a straight or ruffled edge. Surprisingly, it is the ruffled top sugar that takes a lid.

35

		Rose	Topaz
	Ashtray, #2350, lg.	25.00	20.00
19	Ashtray, #2350, sm.	20.00	16.00
	Bottle, salad dressing, #2983	495.00	350.00
39	Bowl, baker, #2375, 9"		60.00
	Bowl, bonbon, #2375		20.00
	Bowl, bouillon, #2375, ftd.		20.00
26	Bowl, cream soup, #2375, ftd.	28.00	25.00
18	Bowl, finger, #869/2283, w/6¼" liner	38.00	35.00
	Bowl, lemon, #2375	20.00	18.00
23	Bowl, #2394, 3 ftd., 4½", mint	20.00	18.00
36	Bowl, #2375, fruit, 5"	20.00	16.00
	Bowl, #2354, 3 ftd., 6"	38.00	33.00
27	Bowl, cereal, #2375, 6½"	38.00	33.00
	Bowl, soup, #2375, 7"	85.00	75.00
	Bowl, lg. dessert, #2375, 2 hdld.	80.00	65.00
	Bowl, #2395, 10"	95.00	65.00
7	Bowl, #2395, scroll, 10"	95.00	75.00
	Bowl, combination #2415, w/ candleholder handles	210.00	150.00
	Bowl, #2375, centerpiece, flared optic, 12"	65.00	50.00
	Bowl, #2394, centerpiece, ftd., 12"	70.00	65.00
	Bowl, #2375, centerpiece, mushroom, 12"	75.00	60.00
	Candlestick, #2394, 2"	20.00	18.00
11	Candlestick, 3", #2375	22.00	20.00
	Candlestick, #2375, flared, 3"	24.00	20.00
	Candlestick, #2395½, scroll, 5"	45.00	40.00
12	Candy, w/cover, #2394, ¼ lb.	250.00	200.00
13	Candy, w/cover, #2394, ½ lb.	150.00	135.00
	Celery, #2375, 11½"	38.00	32.00
5	Cheese & cracker, set, #2375, #2368	65.00	60.00
25	Comport, #5299 or #2400, 6"	45.00	38.00

		Rose	Topaz
	Comport, #2375, 7"	45.00	38.00
37	Creamer, #2375, ftd.	20.00	16.00
9	Creamer, tea, #2375½	40.00	35.00
29	Cup, after dinner, #2375	33.00	26.00
10	Cup, #2375½, ftd.	15.00	14.00
	Decanter, #2439, 9"	1,295.00	895.00
	Goblet, claret, #5099, 4 oz., 6"	70.00	50.00
40	Goblet, cocktail, #5099, 3 oz., 5¼"	22.00	18.00
	Goblet, cordial, #5099, ¾ oz., 4"	75.00	50.00
44	Goblet, water, #5299, 10 oz., 8¼"	33.00	27.00
	Goblet, wine, #5099, 3 oz., 5½"	40.00	32.00
16	Grapefruit, #5282½	40.00	33.00
17	Grapefruit liner, #945½	40.00	33.00
35	Ice bucket, #2375	90.00	80.00
14	Ice dish, #2451, #2455	35.00	30.00
15	Ice dish liner (tomato, crab, fruit), #2451	15.00	5.00
31	Mayonnaise ladle	25.00	15.00
31	Mayonnaise, w/liner, #2375	50.00	40.00
	Oil, ftd., #2375	325.00	275.00
30	Oyster, cocktail, #5099, ftd.	24.00	19.00
43	Parfait, #5099	45.00	35.00
	Pitcher, #5000	395.00	295.00
24	Plate, #2375, canape, 6¼"	22.00	18.00
	Plate, #2375, bread/butter, 6"	5.00	4.00
	Plate, #2375, salad, 7½"	8.00	7.00
	Plate, 2375, cream soup or mayo liner, 7½"	10.00	7.00
33	Plate, #2375, luncheon, 8¾"	15.00	12.00
	Plate, #2375, sm., dinner, 9½"	24.00	20.00
6	Plate, #2375, cake, handled, 10"	42.00	38.00
	Plate, #2375, grill, rare, 10¼"	70.00	65.00
34	Plate, #2375, dinner, 10¼"	50.00	40.00

		Rose	Topaz
	Plate, #2375, chop, 13"	50.00	40.00
32	Plate, #2375, round, 14"	50.00	45.00
	Platter, #2375, 12"	60.00	50.00
	Platter, #2375, 15"	100.00	85.00
	Relish, #2375, 8½"		35.00
	Relish, #2350, 3 pt., rnd., 8¾"	40.00	35.00
	Sauce boat, #2375	95.00	70.00
	Sauce plate, #2375	30.00	25.00
29	Saucer, #2375, after dinner	7.00	7.00
10	Saucer, #2375	4.00	3.00
	Shaker, #2375, pr., ftd.	90.00	75.00
3	Sherbet, #5099, high, 6"	23.00	19.00
2	Sherbet, #5099, low, 4¼"	16.00	14.00
28	Sugar, #2375½, ftd.	20.00	16.00
21	Sugar cover, #2375½	90.00	75.00

		Rose	Topaz
	Sugar pail, #2378	165.00	140.00
8	Sugar, tea, #2375½	40.00	30.00
4	Sweetmeat, #2375	18.00	16.00
1	Tray, 11", ctr. hdld., #2375	35.00	30.00
22	Tray, #2429, service & lemon insert		195.00
	Tumbler, #5099, ftd., 2½ oz.	40.00	30.00
42	Tumbler, #5099, ftd., 5 oz., 4½"	24.00	20.00
38	Tumbler, #5099, ftd., 9 oz., 5¼"	19.00	16.00
41	Tumbler, #5099, ftd., 12 oz., 6"	33.00	25.00
	Vase, #2417, 8"	195.00	125.00
	Vase, #4105, 8"	240.00	175.00
	Vase, #2369, 9"		225.00
	Whipped cream bowl, #2375	28.00	20.00
20	Whipped cream pail, #2378	110.00	85.00

"TURKEY TRACKS," POSSIBLY MCKEE GLASS COMPANY OR STEVENS & WILLIAMS, LATE 1920S

Colors: amber, amber w/green, amber w/red, rose w/green, green

"Turkey Tracks" is what this pattern has been called for years. It tends to turn up in quantities when it is found. We certainly opened a Pandora's Box with inclusion of this several years ago. Debates upon manufacturer and pricing concerns have made the most headlines. Our prices were originally garnered from dealers who were selling it and quoting us their realized prices. These have been significantly revamped due to our own familiarity in selling our finds.

The color combinations are attention-grabbing with the colors fluorescing. Amber is ordinarily a color we ignore, but this amber is quite different from most amber colors in that it even shows luminosity under a black light, not the normal circumstance. Wonder if all the people calling green glass "vaseline" will add this to their mix also? "Vaseline" is canary yellow, not green, which fluoresces because of uranium in its composition.

You will find some highly priced bi-colored stems and footed tumblers in "Turkey Tracks"; but then, bi-colored items have many admirers by themselves — without the added unusual design. Flat tumblers and plates seem to be available in all amber or green; other colors may be possible. Not seen, but reported is a compote style bowl.

		All Colors
5	Plate, 6", sherbet	7.00
6	Plate, 7⅞", salad	12.00
	Plate, 9⅛" dinner	30.00
4	Stem, 1½ oz., 5⅛", cordial	125.00
	Stem, 3 oz., cocktail	40.00
3	Stem, 3 oz., wine	45.00
	Stem, 6 oz., 4", high sherbet	40.00
2	Stem, 6 oz., low sherbet	30.00
	Tumbler, 3 oz., bar	30.00
	Tumbler, 6 oz., old-fashion	40.00
8	Tumbler, 6 oz., 4", ftd., juice	25.00
	Tumbler, 9 oz., ftd.	30.00
1	Tumbler, 10 oz., 4¼" ftd. water	35.00
	Tumbler, 12 oz., 5½", ftd. tea	40.00
7	Tumbler, 13 oz., 5⅞", ftd. ice tea	45.00

TWIST, BLANK #1252, A.H. HEISEY & CO., LATE 1920S – LATE 1930S

Colors: crystal, Flamingo pink, Moongleam green, Marigold amber/yellow, Sahara yellow, some Alexandrite (rare)

There is a faction paying attention to Deco influenced glass patterns and Twist certainly fits their criteria.

That amber/yellow color pictured on 248 is Marigold; and the pink/purple colored bucket on the right below is Alexandrite. Both are rare Heisey colors. Be aware that Marigold is arduous to find in mint condition because that applied color has an inclination to flake, scrape, or peel. Items that are beginning to deteriorate will continue to do so. If you have an option of owning a piece of this rarely seen color that has some problems, ignore it unless it is cheaply priced. Nothing can be done to renew it, but we understand there have been many who have tried.

Price adjustments have been seen in colored Twist lately, and those have not been on the positive side. Most Twist items are marked with the **H** in diamond, but this is one pattern that does not need a mark to be identified. Oil bottles, large bowls, and the three-footed utility plates are being found in quantities unknown before — thanks to internet shopping. The individual sugar and creamer have both all but disappeared into collections; buy those if you have an opportunity.

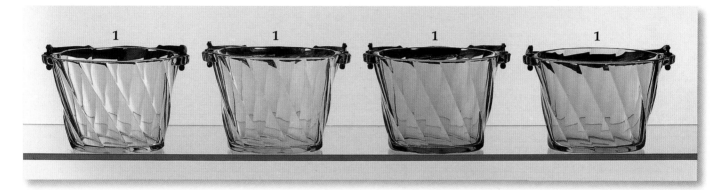

		Crystal	Flamingo	Moongleam	Marigold	Alexandrite	Sahara
	Baker, 9", oval	25.00	35.00	45.00	60.00		
	Bonbon, individual	15.00	35.00	40.00	40.00		
22	Bonbon, 6", 2 hdld.	10.00	20.00	25.00	30.00		
35	Bottle, French dressing	50.00	100.00	110.00	135.00		100.00
	Bowl, cream soup/bouillon	15.00	40.00	60.00	50.00		
31	Bowl, ftd., almond/indiv. sugar (unusual)	30.00	50.00	60.00	65.00		
	Bowl, indiv. nut	10.00	25.00	40.00	45.00		
8	Bowl, 4", nappy	10.00	30.00	35.00	40.00		
25	Bowl, 6", 2 hdld.	7.00	20.00	20.00	25.00		
3	Bowl, 6", 2 hdld., jelly	10.00	20.00	28.00	30.00		
	Bowl, 6", 2 hdld., mint	7.00	20.00	35.00	30.00		20.00
	Bowl, 8", low ftd.		80.00	80.00	85.00		
18	Bowl, 8", nappy, ground bottom	20.00	50.00	55.00	60.00		
	Bowl, 8", nasturtium, rnd.	45.00	70.00	120.00	80.00	450.00	80.00
	Bowl, 8", nasturtium, oval	45.00	70.00	90.00	80.00		
	Bowl, 9", floral	25.00	40.00	50.00	65.00		
	Bowl, 9", floral, rolled edge	30.00	40.00	45.00	65.00		
6	Bowl, 12", floral, oval, 4 ft.	45.00	100.00	110.00	90.00	550.00	85.00
21	Bowl, 12", floral, rnd., 4 ft.	30.00	40.00	50.00	65.00		
5	Candlestick, 2", 1-lite		40.00	50.00	75.00		
	Cheese dish, 6", 2 hdld.	10.00	20.00	25.00	30.00		
	Claret, 4 oz.	15.00	30.00	40.00	50.00		
2	Cocktail shaker, metal top			900.00			
4	Comport, 7", tall	40.00	60.00	120.00	120.00		
19	Creamer, hotel, oval	25.00	40.00	45.00	40.00		
30	Creamer, individual (unusual)	30.00	50.00	60.00	65.00		
32	Creamer, zigzag handles, ftd.	20.00	40.00	50.00	70.00		
7	Cup, zigzag handles	10.00	25.00	32.00	35.00		

TWIST

		Crystal	Flamingo	Moongleam	Marigold	Alexandrite	Sahara
	Grapefruit, ftd.	15.00	25.00	35.00	60.00		
1	Ice bucket w/metal handle	50.00	150.00	140.00	135.00	480.00	125.00
15	Mayonnaise	35.00	65.00	80.00	80.00		
14	Mayonnaise, #1252½	20.00	35.00	60.00	50.00		
26	Mustard, w/cover, spoon	40.00	90.00	140.00	100.00		70.00
	Oil bottle, 2½ oz., w/#78 stopper	50.00	140.00	170.00	200.00		
33	Oil bottle, 4 oz., w/#78 stopper	50.00	110.00	120.00	120.00		90.00
16	Pitcher, 3 pint	95.00	175.00	230.00			
	Plate, cream soup liner	5.00	7.00	10.00	15.00		
	Plate, 8", Kraft cheese	20.00	40.00	60.00	50.00		
28	Plate, 8", ground bottom	7.00	14.00	20.00	30.00		20.00
27	Plate, 9", ground bottom	7.00	14.00	20.00	30.00		20.00
37	Plate, 10", service, 4-feet			160.00			
9	Plate, 10½", dinner	40.00	80.00	140.00	120.00		90.00
	Plate, 12", 2 hdld., sandwich	30.00	60.00	90.00	80.00		
	Plate, 12", muffin, 2 hdld., turned sides	40.00	80.00	90.00	80.00		
	Plate, 13", 3 part, relish	10.00	17.00	22.00	35.00		
12	Platter, 12"	15.00	50.00	60.00	75.00		
29	Salt & pepper, ftd.	100.00	140.00	160.00	200.00		140.00
10	Salt & pepper, flat	50.00	120.00	160.00	190.00		140.00
7	Saucer	3.00	5.00	7.00	10.00	140.00	
	Stem, 2½ oz., wine, 2 block stem	40.00	90.00	110.00	125.00		
	Stem, 3 oz., oyster cocktail, ftd.	10.00	35.00	40.00	50.00		
	Stem, 3 oz., cocktail, 2 block stem	10.00	30.00	45.00	50.00		
	Stem, 5 oz., saucer champagne, 2 block stem	35.00	25.00	30.00			
	Stem, 5 oz., sherbet, 2 block stem	10.00	18.00	40.00	28.00		
	Stem, 9 oz., luncheon (1 block in stem)	40.00	60.00	70.00	75.00		
11	Stem, 9 oz., goblet (2 block in stem)	30.00	50.00	60.00	50.00		
	Sugar, ftd.	20.00	30.00	37.50	60.00		
20	Sugar, hotel, oval	25.00	45.00	50.00	40.00		

	Crystal	Flamingo	Moongleam	Marigold	Alexandrite	Sahara
31 Sugar, individual (unusual)	30.00	50.00	60.00	65.00		
34 Sugar, w/cover, zigzag handles	25.00	40.00	60.00	80.00		
Tray, 7", pickle, ground bottom	7.00	35.00	35.00	45.00		
24 Tray, 10", celery	30.00	50.00	50.00	50.00		40.00
Tray, 13", celery	25.00	50.00	60.00	50.00		
17 Tumbler, 5 oz., soda, flat bottom	10.00	35.00	38.00	38.00		
Tumbler, 6 oz., ftd., soda	10.00	25.00	32.00	36.00		
23 Tumbler, 8 oz., flat, ground bottom	15.00	45.00	70.00	40.00		
Tumbler, 8 oz., soda, straight & flared	12.00	35.00	40.00	40.00		
13 Tumbler, 9 oz., ftd., soda	20.00	45.00	50.00	60.00		
Tumbler, 12 oz., iced tea, flat bottom	20.00	50.00	60.00	70.00		
36 Tumbler, 12 oz., ftd., iced tea	20.00	45.00	50.00	60.00		

VALENCIA, CAMBRIDGE GLASS COMPANY, LATE 1930S

Colors: crystal, pink

Cambridge's Valencia is regularly confused with its Minerva pattern. Although these Cambridge patterns are similar, there are telltale ways to tell them apart. Notice in the photo of Valencia that the lines in the pattern are perpendicular to each other (think Tic Tac Toe). On Minerva, the lines in the pattern are on a diagonal forming diamonds instead of squares. Valencia had an insufficient production compared to other patterns, so dealers are not as familiar with it as with other Cambridge patterns.

Valencia has several pieces that would be sold for significant sums in other patterns where demand often exceeds the supply. However, with Valencia, there are so few collectors that rare pieces often are very under valued and even harder to sell. Many pieces pictured would be enthusiastically snatched up were they etched Rose Point, but are only just being recognized in Valencia. Valencia items are, unquestionably, rarer than the enormously popular Rose Point. However, rarity is not always as important in collecting as demand, the motivating force.

Some of the more exceptional pieces pictured include the square, covered honey dish, the Doulton pitcher, and that small metal-handled piece that Cambridge called a sugar basket. This is similar to Fostoria's sugar pail, but closer in size to Fostoria's whipped cream pail. Jargon used by glass companies in those days sometimes confuses today's collectors since they often differ.

		Crystal				Crystal
16	Ashtray, #3500/16, 3¼", square	9.00		Plate, #1402, 11½", sandwich, hdld.	25.00
17	Ashtray, #3500/124, 3¼", round	9.00	4	Plate, #3500/39, 12", ftd.	33.00
	Ashtray, #3500/126, 4", round	10.00		Plate, #3500/67, 12"	33.00
18	Ashtray, #3500/128, 4½", round	12.00	1	Plate, #3500/38, 13", torte	42.00
3	Ashtray/soapdish, #3500/130, 4", oval	50.00		Relish, #3500/68, 5½", 2 comp.	25.00
	Basket, #3500/55, 6", 2 hdld., ftd.	25.00		Relish, #3500/69, 6½", 3 comp.	30.00
	Bowl, #3500/49, 5", hdld.	12.00	10	Relish, #3500/71, 7½", 3 part, hdld.	70.00
	Bowl, #3500/37, 6", cereal	20.00		Relish, #1402/91, 8", 3 comp.	40.00
	Bowl, #1402/89, 6", 2 hdld.	15.00		Relish, #3500/64, 10", 3 comp.	45.00
	Bowl, #1402/88, 6", 2 hdld., div.	15.00		Relish, #3500/65, 10", 4 comp.	50.00
22	Bowl, #3500/115, 9½", 2 hdld., ftd.	28.00		Relish, #3500/67, 12", 6 pc.	160.00
	Bowl, #1402/82, 10"	40.00	15	Relish, #3500/112, 15", 3 pt., 2 hdld.	65.00
	Bowl, #1402/88, 11"	45.00		Relish, #3500/13, 15", 4 pt., 2 hdld.	65.00
	Bowl, #1402/95, salad dressing, div.	30.00	11	Salt and pepper, #3400/18	50.00
	Bowl, #1402/100, finger, w/liner	32.00	21	Saucer, #3500/1	3.00
	Bowl, #3500, ftd., finger	26.00		Stem, #1402, cordial	45.00
	Candy dish, w/cover, #3500/103	135.00		Stem, #1402, wine	28.00
	Celery, #1402/94, 12"	26.00		Stem, #1402, cocktail	18.00
	Cigarette holder, #1066, ftd.	50.00		Stem, #1402, claret	28.00
6	Comport, #3500/36, 6"	25.00		Stem, #1402, oyster cocktail	14.00
	Comport, #3500/37, 7"	35.00		Stem, #1402, low sherbet	10.00
	Creamer, #3500/14	14.00		Stem, #1402, tall sherbet	12.00
	Creamer, #3500/15, individual	15.00		Stem, #1402, goblet	24.00
21	Cup, #3500/1	13.00		Stem, #3500, cordial	45.00
	Decanter, #3400/92, 32 oz., ball	175.00		Stem, #3500, wine, 2½ oz.	28.00
	Decanter, #3400/119, 12 oz., ball	165.00		Stem, #3500, cocktail, 3 oz.	15.00
20	Honey dish, w/cover, #3500/139	165.00		Stem, #3500, claret, 4½ oz.	28.00
12	Ice pail, #1402/52	90.00		Stem, #3500, oyster cocktail, 4½ oz.	14.00
	Mayonnaise, #3500/59, 3 pc.	35.00		Stem, #3500, low sherbet, 7 oz.	10.00
	Nut, #3400/71, 3", 4 ftd.	45.00		Stem, #3500, tall sherbet, 7 oz.	12.00
	Perfume, #3400/97, 2 oz., perfume	150.00		Stem, #3500, goblet, long bowl	24.00
2	Pitcher, 80 oz., Doulton, #3400/141	295.00	19	Stem, #3500, goblet, short bowl	24.00
8	Plate, #3500/167, 7½", salad	7.00	14	Sugar, #3500/14	14.00
	Plate, #3500/5, 8½", breakfast	9.00		Sugar, #3500/15, individual	15.00

VALENCIA

		Crystal
13	Sugar basket, #3500/13	135.00
9	Tumbler, #3400/92, 2½ oz.	20.00
7	Tumbler, #3400/100, 13 oz.	20.00
	Tumbler, #3400/115, 14 oz.	22.00
	Tumbler, #3500, 2½ oz., ftd.	20.00
	Tumbler, #3500, 3 oz., ftd.	18.00

		Crystal
	Tumbler, #3500, 5 oz., ftd.	16.00
	Tumbler, #3500, 10 oz., ftd.	18.00
5	Tumbler, #3500, 12 oz., ftd.	20.00
	Tumbler, #3500, 13 oz., ftd.	22.00
	Tumbler, #3500, 16 oz., ftd.	25.00

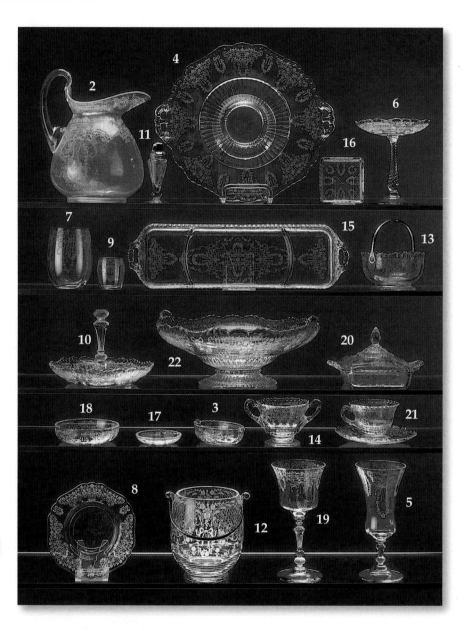

VERSAILLES, FOSTORIA GLASS COMPANY, 1928 – 1944

Colors: blue, yellow, pink, green

Fostoria line numbers (also relative to June and Fairfax listings) are recorded here for each piece of Versailles. The demand for Versailles has dwindled somewhat so that the supply has caught up to requirements for now, although the prices may not indicate that at shows. Be sure to check out internet listings by dealers and auctions where that is more noticeable. Superlative blue Versailles has almost been surpassed by green in collectors now seeking it. We used to steer clear of buying green Versailles, as it was more difficult to sell; but that is no longer true.

Be sure to see page 109 for various types of Fostoria stemware. Confusion reigns because stem heights are similar. Here, shapes and capacities are more important. Yellow Versailles is always found on stem line #5099, which has a cascading stem; all other Versailles is found on stem line #5098, shown on page 254.

		Green	Blue	Pink Yellow
	Ashtray, #2350	22.00	28.00	20.00
	Bottle, #2083, salad dressing, crystal glass top	595.00	895.00	450.00
	Bottle, #2375, salad dressing, w/ sterling top or colored top	550.00	850.00	450.00
	Bowl, #2375, baker, 9"	75.00	125.00	65.00
	Bowl, #2375, bonbon	25.00	28.00	20.00
25	Bowl, #2375, bouillon, ftd.	25.00	35.00	22.00
24	Bowl, #2375, cream soup, ftd.	30.00	40.00	25.00
5	Bowl, #869/2283, finger, w/6" liner	45.00	60.00	35.00
	Bowl, lemon	20.00	26.00	22.00
	Bowl, 4½", mint, 3 ftd.	26.00	38.00	26.00
	Bowl, #2375, fruit, 5"	24.00	36.00	24.00
	Bowl, #2394, 3 ftd., 6"			33.00
	Bowl, #2375, cereal, 6½"	38.00	48.00	33.00
16	Bowl, #2375, soup, 7"	90.00	125.00	65.00
	Bowl, #2375, lg., dessert, 2 hdld.	75.00	110.00	70.00
	Bowl, #2375, baker, 10", oval	75.00	110.00	70.00
	Bowl, #2395, centerpiece, scroll, 10"	75.00	115.00	70.00
22	Bowl, #2375, centerpiece, flared top, 12"	70.00	90.00	60.00
	Bowl, #2394, ftd., 12"	70.00	90.00	60.00
33	Bowl, #2375½, oval, centerpiece, 13"	70.00	90.00	
	Candlestick, #2394, 2"	20.00	28.00	22.00
35	Candlestick, #2375½, 2½"	25.00	35.00	22.00
32	Candlestick, #2395, 3"	25.00	35.00	22.00
15	Candlestick, #2395½, scroll, 3"	40.00	45.00	30.00
11	Candy, w/cover, #2331, 3 pt.	165.00	225.00	
	Candy, w/cover, #2394, ¼ lb.			175.00
	Candy, w/cover, #2394, ½ lb.			140.00
29	Celery, #2375, 11½"	65.00	90.00	55.00
	Cheese & cracker, #2375 or #2368, set	70.00	90.00	70.00
	Comport, #5098, 3"	30.00	42.00	28.00
21	Comport, #5099/2400, 6"	60.00	85.00	60.00
9	Comport, #2375, 7½"	40.00	85.00	
	Comport, #2400, 8"	65.00	110.00	
6	Creamer, #2375½, ftd.	22.00	25.00	18.00
13	Creamer, #2375½, tea	35.00	40.00	30.00
31	Cup, #2375, after dinner	40.00	65.00	30.00
	Cup, #2375½, ftd.	16.00	30.00	16.00
	Decanter, #2439, 9"	1,000.00	1,500.00	795.00
17	Goblet, cordial, #5098 or #5099, ¾ oz., 4"	110.00	110.00	60.00
18	Goblet, #5098 or #5099, claret, 4 oz., 6"	60.00	90.00	55.00
1	Goblet, cocktail, #5098 or #5099, 3 oz., 5¼"	28.00	33.00	26.00

		Green	Blue	Pink Yellow
23	Goblet, water, #5098 or #5099, 10 oz., 8¼"	90.00	70.00	50.00
30	Goblet, wine, #5098 or #5099, 3 oz., 5½"	55.00	65.00	50.00
4	Grapefruit, #5082½	40.00	50.00	40.00
4	Grapefruit liner, #945½, etched	40.00	50.00	40.00
10	Ice bucket, #2375	85.00	110.00	80.00
	Ice dish, #2451	40.00	50.00	38.00
	Ice dish liner (tomato, crab, fruit), #2451	20.00	20.00	10.00
34	Mayonnaise, w/liner, #2375	50.00	60.00	45.00
34	Mayonnaise ladle	20.00	30.00	15.00
	Oil, #2375, ftd.	450.00	550.00	350.00
	Oyster cocktail, #5098 or #5099	24.00	30.00	22.00
	Parfait, #5098 or #5099	55.00	65.00	45.00
14	Pitcher, #5000	495.00	595.00	395.00
	Plate, #2375, bread/butter, 6"	7.00	9.00	6.00
	Plate, #2375, canape, 6"	20.00	24.00	20.00
	Plate, #2375, salad, 7½"	10.00	12.00	10.00
	Plate, #2375, cream soup or mayo liner, 7½"	10.00	12.00	10.00
	Plate, #2375, luncheon, 8¾"	15.00	18.00	14.00
	Plate, #2375, sm., dinner, 9½"	30.00	35.00	25.00
	Plate, #2375, cake, 2 hdld., 10"	45.00	55.00	40.00
26	Plate, #2375, dinner, 10¼"	70.00	85.00	70.00
	Plate, #2375, chop, 13"	70.00	75.00	55.00
	Platter, #2375, 12"	65.00	75.00	60.00
	Platter, #2375, 15"	110.00	160.00	100.00
28	Relish, #2375, 8½", 2-part			33.00
	Sauce boat, #2375	125.00	175.00	90.00
	Sauce boat plate, #2375	25.00	35.00	20.00
31	Saucer, #2375, after dinner	10.00	15.00	9.00
	Saucer, #2375	3.00	4.00	3.00
27	Shaker, #2375, pr., ftd.	120.00	135.00	100.00
20	Sherbet, #5098/5099, high, 6"	24.00	28.00	23.00
2	Sherbet, #5098/5099, low, 4¼"	20.00	22.00	18.00
7	Sugar, #2375½, ftd.	22.00	25.00	18.00
	Sugar cover, #2375½	130.00	150.00	110.00
	Sugar pail, #2378	200.00	275.00	165.00
12	Sugar, #2375½, tea	35.00	40.00	30.00
36	Sweetmeat, #2375	24.00	24.00	20.00
	Tray, #2375, ctr. hdld., 11"	40.00	45.00	35.00
8	Tray, service & lemon	300.00	350.00	200.00
	Tumbler, flat, old-fashion (pink only)			110.00
	Tumbler, flat, tea (pink only)			110.00
	Tumbler, #5098 or #5099 2½ oz., ftd.	50.00	60.00	40.00
3	Tumbler, #5098 or #5099, 5 oz., ftd., 4½"	28.00	32.00	22.00

VERSAILLES

		Green	Blue	Pink Yellow			Green	Blue	Pink Yellow
	Tumbler, #5098 or #5099, 9 oz., ftd., 5¼"	32.00	35.00	22.00	Vase, #2385, fan, ftd., 8½"	250.00	350.00	
19	Tumbler, #5098 or #5099 12 oz., ftd., 6"	43.00	45.00	32.00	Whipped cream bowl, #2375	24.00	30.00	20.00
	Vase, #2417, 8"			215.00	Whipped cream pail, #2378	150.00	225.00	150.00
	Vase, #4100, 8"	250.00	325.00					

Note: See page 109 for stem identification.

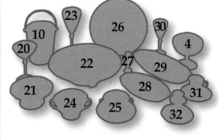

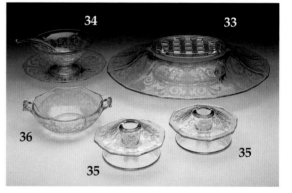

Colors: amber, green; some blue

We purchased a large set of Fostoria's Vesper pattern to keep one of each piece for photography. We're showing you as much Vesper as room allows. Amber Vesper is the color often observed, but wanes in popularity when compared to other colors. Obviously, from the abundance of amber glassware made in the late 1920s and 1930s, that was a trendy color then. Don't be mislead. We have sold hundreds of pieces of amber Vesper. The trick is pricing it within the range buyers are willing to pay.

Today, there is little blue Vesper to be found for sale. However, minor accumulations do appear when older Fostoria collections are being dispersed. Blue is the official Fostoria name for the intense blue color.

Hard to find, attractive, colored glassware is often priced out of the reach of the younger collector; but more realistic prices are now surfacing. With $4.00 a gallon gasoline prices likely in our future, there will be serious adjustments to what is collected in any field, not just glass.

Difficult Vesper items to acquire are the vanity set (combination perfume and powder jar), moulded and blown grapefruits, egg cup, butter dish, both styles of candy dishes, and the Maj Jongg (8¾" canapé) plate. It is the high sherbet that actually fits the ring on that plate (page 257).

Vesper comes on stem line #5093 and tumbler line #5100. The shapes are slightly different from etches found on the Fostoria Fairfax blank (page 109). Cordials, clarets, and parfaits are the most difficult stems to acquire while the footed, 12-ounce iced tea and two-ounce footed bar are the least available tumblers. As with other Elegant patterns, prices for clarets and wines have slipped while ones for water goblets have increased a bit.

There will never be a better time to start collecting Vesper; so if this is your fancy, better start now.

			Green	Amber	Blue
47		Ashtray, #2350, small	15.00	15.00	
		Ashtray, #2350, large	20.00	20.00	
		Bowl, #2350, bouillon, ftd.	18.00	22.00	30.00
		Bowl, #2350, cream soup, flat	22.00	22.00	
		Bowl, #2350, cream soup, ftd.	20.00	22.00	30.00
16		Bowl, #2350, fruit, 5½"	10.00	14.00	25.00
43		Bowl, #2350, cereal, sq. or rnd., 6½"	22.00	22.00	40.00
		Bowl, #2267, low, ftd., 7"	22.00	25.00	
22		Bowl, #2350, soup, shallow, 7¾"	24.00	28.00	55.00
		Bowl, soup, deep, 8¼"		32.00	
		Bowl, 8⅞"	30.00	32.00	
		Bowl, #2350, baker, oval, 9"	48.00	50.00	90.00
		Bowl, #2350, rd.	40.00	42.00	
		Bowl, #2350, baker, oval, 10½"	60.00	60.00	125.00
		Bowl, #2375, flared bowl, 10½"	45.00	45.00	
46		Bowl, #2350, ped., ftd., 10½"	45.00	55.00	
20		Bowl, #2329, console, rolled edge, 11"	35.00	38.00	
37		Bowl, #2375, 3 ftd., 12½"	45.00	45.00	110.00
		Bowl, #2371, oval, 13"	48.00	48.00	
25		Bowl, #2329, rolled edge, 13"	45.00	45.00	
		Bowl, #2329, rolled edge, 14"	48.00	45.00	125.00
		Butter dish, #2350	350.00	695.00	
39		Candlestick, #2324, 2"	18.00	18.00	
19		Candlestick, #2394, 3"	20.00	20.00	
		Candlestick, #2324, 4"	22.00	20.00	40.00
		Candlestick, #2394, 9"	60.00	65.00	90.00
36		Candy jar, w/cover, #2331, 3 pt.	100.00	90.00	225.00
31		Candy jar, w/cover, #2250, ftd., ½ lb.	225.00	175.00	
34		Celery, #2350	25.00	25.00	40.00
		Cheese, #2368, ftd.	20.00	20.00	
		Comport, 6"	25.00	25.00	40.00
27		Comport, #2327 (twisted stem), 7½"	33.00	35.00	65.00
		Comport, 8"	50.00	50.00	70.00
42		Creamer, #2350½, ftd.	15.00	15.00	
33		Creamer, #2315½, fat, ftd.	20.00	20.00	30.00
		Creamer, #2350½, flat		20.00	
23		Cup, #2350	12.00	12.00	25.00

255

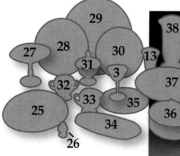

		Green	Amber	Blue
24	Cup, #2350, after dinner	35.00	25.00	70.00
17	Cup, #2350½, ftd.	12.00	12.00	25.00
	Egg cup, #2350		35.00	
	Finger bowl and liner, #869/2283, 6"	30.00	30.00	60.00
15	Grapefruit, #5082½, blown	45.00	35.00	75.00
14	Grapefruit liner, #945½, blown	45.00	35.00	50.00
	Grapefruit, #2315, molded	45.00	35.00	
44	Ice bucket, #2378	75.00	65.00	210.00
10	Oyster cocktail, #5100	20.00	20.00	33.00
	Pickle, #2350	28.00	25.00	48.00
38	Pitcher, #5100, ftd.	275.00	295.00	495.00
	Plate, #2350, bread/butter, 6"	6.00	4.00	12.00
	Plate, #2350, salad, 7½"	8.00	7.00	16.00
	Plate, #2350, luncheon, 8½"	12.00	12.00	22.00
35	Plate, #2321, Maj Jongg (canape), 8¾"		25.00	
30	Plate, #2350, sm., dinner, 9½"	20.00	20.00	35.00
28	Plate, dinner, 10½"	40.00	45.00	
	Plate, #2287, ctr. hand., 11"	30.00	33.00	60.00
21	Plate, chop, 13¾"	35.00	35.00	80.00
29	Plate, #2350, server, 14"	45.00	45.00	95.00
	Plate, w/indent for cheese, 11"	25.00	25.00	
	Platter, #2350, 10½"	40.00	40.00	
3	Platter, #2350, 12"	50.00	50.00	125.00
45	Platter, #2350, 15",	75.00	75.00	195.00
26	Salt & pepper, #5100, pr.	60.00	60.00	
	Sauce boat, w/liner, #2350	135.00	125.00	
24	Saucer, #2350, after dinner	8.00	7.00	22.00

		Green	Amber	Blue
17, 23	Saucer, #2350, #2350½	4.00	3.00	8.00
3	Stem, #5093, high sherbet	16.00	14.00	30.00
4	Stem, #5093, water goblet	25.00	22.00	50.00
1	Stem, #5093, low sherbet	14.00	12.00	26.00
5	Stem, #5093, parfait	32.00	32.00	65.00
8	Stem, #5093, cordial, ¾ oz.	40.00	40.00	110.00
7	Stem, #5093, wine, 2¾ oz.	30.00	24.00	60.00
2	Stem, #5093, cocktail, 3 oz.	20.00	18.00	40.00
6	Stem, #5093, claret, 4 oz.	40.00	40.00	
	Sugar, #2350½, flat		20.00	
32	Sugar, #2315, fat, ftd.	20.00	20.00	35.00
41	Sugar, #2350½, ftd.	14.00	14.00	
40	Sugar, lid	125.00	125.00	
9	Tumbler, #5100, ftd., 2 oz.	30.00	30.00	60.00
11	Tumbler, #5100, ftd., 5 oz.	16.00	14.00	40.00
13	Tumbler, #5100, ftd., 9 oz.	16.00	16.00	40.00
12	Tumbler, #5100, ftd., 12 oz.	28.00	25.00	60.00
	Urn, #2324, small	90.00	90.00	
	Urn, large	100.00	110.00	
18	Vase, #2292, 8"	100.00	100.00	200.00
	Vanity set, combination cologne/powder & stopper	195.00	225.00	350.00

Note: See stemware identification on page 109.

VICTORIAN, #1425, A.H. HEISEY CO., 1933 – 1953

Colors: crystal, Sahara, Cobalt, rare in pale Zircon

Notice the two tumblers used as a pattern shot on the right. The taller one is Victorian while the shorter one is Duncan's Block. Block is an older ware often confused with Victorian and you can understand why. Thankfully, Victorian pieces are usually marked with the Heisey **H** inside a diamond.

We have found Victorian in a number of venues recently, although most were pieces made by Imperial rather than Heisey. Heisey Victorian was only made in the colors listed. If you see pink (Azalea), green (Verde), or amber Victorian in your travels, then you have Imperial's reissue of the pattern made in 1964 and 1965. These colors are usually also marked with the **H** in diamond trademark but were made from Heisey moulds after Heisey was no longer in business; Imperial did not remove Heisey's mark at first which creates confusion for those who depend upon that mark as their only point of reference. In some cases marked Heisey is not Heisey at all — but Imperial.

We caught sight of a set of amber Victorian offered at an outdoor extravaganza a few months ago, with a sign announcing *rare Heisey amber* at $3.00 each. How rare and $3.00 each can be synonymous is beyond us. Kind of reminds you off all the internet auctions touting rare items priced for $0.99. Right now collectors of older Heisey tend to look down on Imperial made wares. We suppose that will change someday, particularly since Imperial is out of business — but not to date.

Rarely found items are still selling if suitably priced, but not all covet them. Items being priced above market are sitting. Another thing we note is the dust ring or faded price sticker when picking up a piece. That usually suggests a less than agreeable price.

Imperial made a few pieces in crystal Victorian, but we know no magical wand to separate crystal made by Heisey from Imperial's. These items are not as ignored by Heisey collectors, as are the colored Imperial Victorian pieces, since they are tricky to tell apart.

		Crystal
	Bottle, 3 oz., oil	50.00
10	Bottle, 27 oz., rye	120.00
	Bottle, French dressing	80.00
	Bowl, 10½", floral	50.00
	Bowl, finger	25.00
	Bowl, punch	250.00
	Bowl, rose	90.00
	Bowl, triplex, w/flared or cupped rim	125.00
	Butter dish, ¼ lb.	50.00
18	Candlestick, 2-lite	80.00
17	Cigarette box, 4"	70.00
19	Cigarette box, 6"	90.00
20	Cigarette holder & ashtray, ind.	20.00
	Comport, 5"	50.00
14	Comport, 6", 3 ball stem	120.00
	Compote, cheese (for center sandwich)	35.00
	Creamer	20.00
	Cup, punch, 5 oz.	8.00
	Decanter and stopper, 32 oz.	70.00
5	Jug, 54 oz.	400.00
15	Mayonnaise, footed	125.00
	Nappy, 8"	40.00
	Plate, 6", liner for finger bowl	10.00
	Plate, 7"	15.00
	Plate, 8"	20.00
	Plate, 12", cracker	75.00

		Crystal
	Plate, 13", sandwich	60.00
	Plate, 21", buffet or punch bowl liner	200.00
	Relish, 11", 3 pt.	50.00
	Salt & pepper	65.00
11	Stem, 2½ oz., wine	25.00
7	Stem, 3 oz., claret	25.00
8	Stem, 5 oz., oyster cocktail	22.00
12	Stem, 5 oz., saucer champagne	15.00
	Stem, 5 oz., sherbet	15.00
3	Stem, 9 oz., goblet (one ball)	*20.00
	Stem, 9 oz., high goblet (two ball)	20.00
	Sugar	20.00
	Tray, 12", celery	40.00
	Tray, condiment (s/p & mustard)	140.00
9	Tumbler, 2 oz., bar	25.00
2	Tumbler, 5 oz., soda (straight or curved edge)	25.00
	Tumbler, 8 oz., old-fashion	35.00
4	Tumbler, 10 oz., w/rim foot	35.00
6	Tumbler, 12 oz., ftd. soda	40.00
1	Tumbler, 12 oz., soda (straight or curved edge)	28.00
	Vase, 4"	45.00
	Vase, 5½"	60.00
13	Vase, 6", ftd.	100.00
16	Vase, 7½" (pitcher mold), rare	600.00
	Vase, 9", ftd., w/flared rim	150.00

*Sahara 100.00

WAVERLY, BLANK #1519, A.H. HEISEY & CO., 1940 – 1957

Colors: crystal; rare in amber

Heisey's Waverly #1519 mould blank is renowned for the Orchid and Rose etchings appearing on it rather than for its own shape identity. Having seen large displays of Waverly, it's a magnificent, fashionable pattern on its own.

		Crystal
	Bowl, 6", oval, lemon, w/cover	45.00
6	Bowl, 6", relish, 2 part, 3 ftd.	10.00
	Bowl, 6½", 2 hdld., ice	70.00
	Bowl, 7", 3 part, relish, oblong	30.00
	Bowl, 7", salad	20.00
	Bowl, 9", 4 part, relish, round	25.00
	Bowl, 9", fruit	25.00
	Bowl, 9", vegetable	25.00
	Bowl, 10", crimped edge	25.00
	Bowl, 10", gardenia	20.00
	Bowl, 11", seahorse foot, floral	45.00
	Bowl, 12", crimped edge	25.00
5	Bowl, 13", gardenia, w/candleholder center	60.00
	Box, 5", chocolate, w/cover	50.00
	Box, 5" tall, ftd., w/cover, seahorse hdl.	60.00
1	Box, 6", candy, w/bow tie knob	45.00
	Box, trinket, lion cover (rare)	700.00

		Crystal
	Butter dish, w/cover, 6", square	50.00
	Candleholder, 1-lite, block (rare)	80.00
	Candleholder, 2-lite	30.00
	Candleholder, 2-lite, "flame" center	65.00
2	Candleholder, 3-lite	70.00
3	Candle epergnette, 5"	20.00
	Candle epergnette, 6", deep	25.00
	Candle epergnette, 6½"	15.00
	Cheese dish, 5½", ftd.	20.00
	Cigarette holder, seahorse hdl.	100.00
	Comport, 6", low ftd.	15.00
	Comport, 6½", jelly	25.00
	Comport, 7", low ftd., oval	35.00
15	Creamer, ftd.	12.00
20-21	Creamer & sugar, individual, w/tray	50.00
4	Cruet, 3 oz., w/#122 stopper	50.00
16	Cup	10.00

		Crystal
	Honey dish, 6½", ftd.	40.00
	Mayonnaise, w/liner & ladle, 5½"	40.00
11	Plate, 7", salad	7.00
	Plate, 8", luncheon	8.00
8	Plate, 10½", dinner	95.00
	Plate, 11", sandwich	20.00
	Plate, 13½", ftd., cake salver	50.00
	Plate, 14", center handle, sandwich	40.00
	Plate, 14", sandwich	35.00
18	Salt & pepper, pr, #12-1519	35.00
19	Salt & pepper, pr, #13-1519	50.00
17	Saucer	2.00

		Crystal
	Stem, #5019, 1 oz., cordial	50.00
	Stem, #5019, 3 oz., wine, blown	20.00
10	Stem, #5019, 3½ oz., cocktail	15.00
9	Stem, #5019, 5½ oz., sherbet/champagne	9.00
7	Stem, #5019, 10 oz., blown	20.00
14	Sugar, ftd.	12.00
	Tray, 12", celery	20.00
12	Tumbler, #5019, 5 oz., ftd., juice, blown	20.00
13	Tumbler, #5019, 13 oz., ftd., tea, blown	22.00
	Vase, 3½", violet	35.00
	Vase, 7", ftd.	30.00
	Vase, 7", ftd., fan shape	35.00

WILDFLOWER, CAMBRIDGE GLASS COMPANY, 1940S – 1950S

Colors: amber, crystal, Ebony w/gold, Emerald green

Wildflower etchings surface on various Cambridge dinnerware blanks, but it is by and large found on #3121 stems. We have endeavored to price a selection of this wide-ranging pattern. Like Rose Point, almost any Cambridge blank may have been used to etch Wildflower. Price gold encrusted crystal items up to 25% higher and colored items about 50% higher, except for gold-encrusted Ebony, which brings double or triple the prices listed. A majority of collectors are now buying crystal because that is still obtainable.

		Crystal
	Basket, #3400/1182, 2 hdld., ftd., 6"	28.00
	Bowl, #3500/54, 2 hdld., ftd.	26.00
10	Bowl, #3500/69, 3 pt. relish	26.00
	Bowl, finger, blown, 4½"	28.00
	Bowl, #3400/1180, bonbon, 2 hdld., 5¼"	28.00
	Bowl, bonbon, 2 hdld., ftd., 6"	28.00
18	Bowl, #3400/90, 2 pt., relish, 6"	27.00
	Bowl, #3500/61, 3 pt., relish, hdld., 6½"	40.00
	Bowl, #3900/123, relish, 7"	30.00
	Bowl, #3900/130, bonbon, 2 hdld., 7"	30.00
8	Bowl, #3400/88, 2 pt., relish, 8"	30.00
2	Bowl, #3400/91, 3 pt., relish, 3 hdld., 8"	32.00
	Bowl, #3900/125, 3 pt., celery & relish, 9"	35.00
	Bowl, #477, pickle (corn), ftd., 9½"	28.00
	Bowl, #3900/1185, 10"	50.00
9	Bowl, #3900/34, 2 hdld., 11"	55.00
	Bowl, #3900/28, w/tab hand., ftd., 11½"	65.00
17	Bowl, #3900/126, 3 pt., celery & relish, 12"	48.00
	Bowl, #3400/4, 4 ft., flared, 12"	60.00
	Bowl, #3400/1240, 4 ft., oval, "ears" hdld., 12"	65.00
	Bowl, #3900/120, 5 pt., celery & relish, 12"	40.00
	Butter dish, #3900/52, ¼ lb.	210.00
22	Butter dish, #3400/52, 5"	130.00
	Cake plate, 13", #170	60.00
	Candlestick, #3400/638, 3-lite, ea.	42.00
	Candlestick, #3400/646, 5"	35.00
	Candlestick, #3400/647, 2-lite, "keyhole", 6"	35.00
19	Candlestick, #3121, 7"	70.00
	Candlestick, P.500	40.00
	Candy box, w/cover, #3400/9, 4 ftd.	120.00
	Candy box, w/cover, #3900/165, rnd.	105.00
	Candy box, w/cover, #1066, 5½"	110.00
	Cocktail icer, #968, 2 pc.	45.00
	Cocktail shaker, P.101, w/top	125.00
3	Cocktail shaker w/glass top	125.00
	Cocktail shaker, #3400/175	125.00
	Comport, #3900/136, 5½"	40.00
	Comport, #3121, blown, 5⅜"	40.00
	Comport, #3500/148, 6"	32.00
	Creamer, #3900/41	16.00
	Creamer, #3900/40, individual	20.00
14	Creamer, #3500/15, individual	20.00
	Cup, #3900/17 or #3400/54	16.00
	Hat, #1704, 5"	250.00
	Hat, #1703, 6"	350.00
	Hurricane lamp, #1617, candlestick base	175.00
	Hurricane lamp, #1603, keyhole base & prisms	195.00
	Ice bucket, w/chrome hand., #3900/671	95.00

		Crystal
11	Mayonnaise set, 3 pc., #3400/11	45.00
	Mayonnaise, #3900/19, sherbet style	30.00
1	Oil, w/stopper, #3900/100, 6 oz.	110.00
	Pitcher, ball, #3400/38, 80 oz.	195.00
	Pitcher, #3900/115, 76 oz.	195.00
	Pitcher, Doulton, #3400/141	310.00
	Plate, crescent salad	90.00
	Plate, #3900/20, bread/butter, 6½"	6.00
	Plate, #3400/176, 7½"	8.00
	Plate, #3900/161, 2 hdld., ftd., 8"	16.00
	Plate, #3900/22, salad, 8"	15.00
	Plate, #3400/62, 8½"	15.00
	Plate, #3900/24, dinner, 10½"	55.00
	Plate, #3900/26, service, 4 ftd., 12"	45.00
7	Plate, #3900/35, cake, 2 hdld., 13½"	65.00
	Plate, #3900/167, torte, 14"	50.00
	Plate, #3900/65, torte, 14"	50.00
	Salt & pepper, #3400/77, pr.	40.00
	Salt & pepper, #3900/1177	40.00
	Saucer, #3900/17 or #3400/54	3.00
	Set: 2 pc. Mayonnaise, #3900/19 (ftd. sherbet w/ladle)	45.00
	Set: 3 pc. Mayonnaise, #3900/129 (bowl, liner, ladle)	50.00
	Set: 4 pc. Mayonnaise, #3900/111 (div. bowl, liner, 2 ladles)	55.00
	Stem, #3121, cordial, 1 oz.	45.00
	Stem, #3121, cocktail, 3 oz.	20.00
	Stem, #3121, wine, 3½ oz.	30.00
	Stem, #3121, claret, 4½ oz.	33.00
	Stem, #3121, 4½ oz., low oyster cocktail	14.00
	Stem, #3121, 5 oz., low parfait	28.00
5	Stem, #3121, 6 oz., low sherbet	14.00
6	Stem, #3121, 6 oz., tall sherbet	18.00
13	Stem, #3121, 10 oz., water	28.00
20	Stem, #3725, 10 oz., water	28.00
15	Sugar, 3400/16	16.00
	Sugar, 3400/68	16.00
16	Sugar, indiv., 3500/15	20.00
4	Sugar, indiv., 3900/40	20.00
	Tray, creamer & sugar, 3900/37	12.00
	Tumbler, #3121, 5 oz., juice	20.00
12	Tumbler, #3121, 10 oz., water	22.00
	Tumbler, #3121, 12 oz., tea	24.00
	Tumbler, #3900/115, 13 oz.	30.00
	Vase, #3400/102, globe, 5"	50.00

WILDFLOWER

		Crystal			Crystal
	Vase, #6004, flower, ftd., 6"	75.00		Vase, #278, flower, ftd., 11"	100.00
	Vase, #6004, flower, ftd., 8"	75.00		Vase, #1299, ped. ft., 11"	125.00
	Vase, #1237, keyhole ft., 9"	95.00		Vase, #1238, keyhole ft., 12"	110.00
21	Vase, #1528, bud, 10"	95.00		Vase, #279, ftd., flower, 13"	195.00

WOODLAND, ETCHING #264, FOSTORIA GLASS COMPANY, 1922 – 1929

Color: crystal; crystal with gold named Goldwood

Woodland is an early Fostoria pattern that is being noticed by a few collectors. A varied assortment of items are found; per usual, stemware steps to the forefront. The pattern was specified as Goldwood when found with gold trim. We are sure gold trim increased the production cost; thus, it was a way to supply a new pattern with an increased price tag and not have to make extra moulds. Today, the gold rim does not add to the price; in fact, to most, it is an agitation.

	Item	Price			Item	Price
	Bottle, salad dressing w/ stopper, #2083	75.00		3	Pitcher, 65 oz., #300	155.00
	Bowl, 4½", finger, #766	12.00			Plate, 5", sherbet, #840	5.00
	Candy jar w/lid, ½ lb., #2250	55.00			Plate, 6", fingerbowl liner, #1736	6.00
	Candy jar w/lid, ¼ lb., #2250	45.00			Plate, 7", salad, #1897	6.00
	Comport, 5"	22.00			Plate, 8¼", luncheon, #2238	8.00
	Comport, 6"	22.00			Plate, 11", torte, #2238	14.00
	Creamer, flat, #1851	15.00			Shaker, pr., #2022	35.00
	Decanter, 32 oz., #300	70.00			Stem, ¾ oz., cordial	20.00
	Jelly w/cover, #825	25.00			Stem, 2¾ oz., wine	12.00
	Marmalade w/cover, #4089	35.00			Stem, 3 oz., cocktail	11.00
	Mayonnaise liner, 6"	7.00			Stem, 5 oz., low sherbet	9.00
	Mayonnaise, ftd., #2138	30.00		2	Stem, 5 oz., saucer champagne	9.00
	Mustard w/cover, #1831	30.00			Stem, 6 oz., parfait	12.00
	Nappy, 5", ftd.	18.00		1	Stem, 9 oz., water	12.00
	Nappy, 6", ftd.	20.00		4	Sugar, flat, #1851	15.00
	Nappy, 7", ftd.	22.50			Sweetmeat, #766	22.00
	Night bottle, 23 oz., #1697	65.00			Syrup, 8 oz. w/cut-off top, #2194	85.00
	Night tumbler, 6 oz., #4023	15.00			Tumbler, 3½", 5 oz., juice, #889	8.00
	Oil bottle, 5 oz., w/stopper, #1465	42.00			Tumbler, 4½", 10½", water, #4076	10.00
	Oil bottle, 7 oz., w/stopper, #1465	52.00			Tumbler, 5½", 14 oz., tea, #889	14.00

YEOMAN, BLANK #1184, A.H. HEISEY & CO., C. 1915

Colors: crystal, Flamingo pink, Sahara yellow, Moongleam green, Hawthorne orchid/pink, Marigold deep, amber/yellow; some cobalt, and Alexandrite

Yeoman is pictured here in Hawthorne (a consistent pale amethyst) regardless of lighting. It is not the rare Alexandrite which changes its color in different light sources.

Etched designs are often found on Yeoman blank #1184 and sell for 10% to 25% more than the prices listed below for Yeoman. Empress is the most found etching on Yeoman, as well as the most beloved. Yeoman can be seen with sterling silver decoration; these were not originally added at the Heisey factory. Sterling decoration, today, does not add to the price and often will keep an item from selling. Heisey admirers are meticulous about their productions.

Yeoman has some sought pieces for item collectors such as cologne and oil bottles as well as sugar shakers.

		Crystal	Flamingo	Sahara	Moongleam	Hawthorne	Marigold
	Ashtray, 4", hdld. (bow tie)	10.00	20.00	22.00	25.00	30.00	35.00
	Bowl, 2 hdld., cream soup	12.00	20.00	25.00	30.00	35.00	40.00
	Bowl, finger	5.00	11.00	17.00	20.00	27.50	30.00
	Bowl, ftd., banana split	7.00	23.00	30.00	35.00	40.00	45.00
6	Bowl, ftd., 2 hdld., bouillon, w/liner	10.00	20.00	25.00	30.00	35.00	40.00
	Bowl, 4½", nappy	4.00	7.50	10.00	12.50	15.00	17.00
	Bowl, 5", low, ftd., jelly	12.00	20.00	25.00	27.00	30.00	40.00
	Bowl, 5", oval, lemon and cover	30.00	60.00	65.00	75.00	90.00	90.00
	Bowl, 5", rnd., lemon and cover	30.00	60.00	65.00	75.00	90.00	90.00
	Bowl, 5", rnd., lemon, w/cover	15.00	20.00	25.00	30.00	40.00	50.00
	Bowl, 6", oval, preserve	7.00	12.00	17.00	22.00	27.00	30.00
	Bowl, 6", vegetable	5.00	10.00	14.00	16.00	20.00	24.00
	Bowl, 6½", hdld., bonbon	5.00	10.00	14.00	16.00	20.00	24.00
	Bowl, 8", rect., pickle/olive	12.00	15.00	20.00	25.00	30.00	35.00
	Bowl, 8½", berry, 2 hdld.	14.00	22.00	25.00	30.00	35.00	50.00
	Bowl, 9", 2 hdld., veg., w/cover	35.00	60.00	60.00	70.00	95.00	175.00
	Bowl, 9", oval, fruit	20.00	25.00	35.00	45.00	55.00	55.00
	Bowl, 9", baker	20.00	25.00	35.00	45.00	55.00	55.00

		Crystal	Flamingo	Sahara	Moongleam	Hawthorne	Marigold
7	Bowl, 10", floral plateau #10	30.00	40.00		45.00	65.00	
	Bowl, 12", low, floral	15.00	25.00	35.00	45.00	60.00	55.00
	Box, puff w/insert	95.00	150.00		175.00	120.00	
	Candle vase, single, w/short prisms & inserts	90.00			150.00		
	Candy, hdld., 8½"	25.00	45.00		50.00		90.00
	Cigarette holder (ashtray), bottom	25.00	60.00	65.00	70.00	80.00	100.00
	Cologne bottle, w/stopper	60.00	160.00	160.00	160.00	170.00	180.00
15	Comport, 5", high ftd., shallow	15.00	25.00	37.00	45.00	55.00	70.00
	Comport, 6", low ftd., deep	20.00	30.00	34.00	40.00	42.00	48.00
	Comport and cover, #3350	55.00	85.00		85.00	110.00	175.00
	Creamer, #1189	20.00	35.00	35.00	40.00		
14	Creamer	10.00	25.00	20.00	22.00	50.00	28.00
	Creamer, #1001	40.00	60.00				
	Cruet, 2 oz., oil	20.00	70.00	80.00	85.00	90.00	85.00
	Cruet, 4 oz., oil	30.00	70.00	80.00	85.00		
11	Cup	5.00	20.00	20.00	25.00	22.00	
	Cup, after dinner	20.00	40.00	40.00	45.00	50.00	60.00
	Cup, coffee, Russian, 5 oz., #3312		45.00				
	Egg cup	20.00	25.00	35.00	35.00	60.00	35.00
	Goblet, #3325		40.00		65.00		
	Gravy (or dressing) boat, w/underliner	13.00	25.00	30.00	45.00	50.00	45.00
	Marmalade jar, w/cover	25.00	35.00	40.00	45.00	55.00	65.00
	Mustard and cover	60.00	80.00	125.00	125.00		
	Parfait, 5 oz.	10.00	15.00	20.00	25.00	30.00	35.00
	Pitcher, quart	50.00	100.00	100.00	100.00	140.00	160.00
	Plate, 2 hdld., cheese	5.00	10.00	13.00	15.00	17.00	25.00
	Plate, cream soup underliner	5.00	7.00	9.00	12.00	14.00	16.00

YEOMAN

		Crystal	Flamingo	Sahara	Moongleam	Hawthorne	Marigold
	Plate, finger bowl underliner	3.00	5.00	7.00	9.00	11.00	13.00
	Plate, 4½", coaster	3.00	5.00	10.00	12.00		
	Plate, 6"	3.00	6.00	8.00	10.00	13.00	15.00
	Plate, 6", bouillon underliner	3.00	6.00	8.00	10.00	13.00	15.00
	Plate, 6½", grapefruit bowl	7.00	12.00	15.00	19.00	27.00	32.00
2	Plate, 7"	5.00	8.00	10.00	14.00	17.00	22.00
	Plate, 8", oyster cocktail	9.00					
	Plate, 8", soup	9.00					
	Plate, 9", oyster cocktail	10.00					
1	Plate, 10½"	20.00	35.00		35.00	60.00	
	Plate, 10½", ctr. hdld., oval, div.	15.00	26.00		32.00		
	Plate, 11", 4 pt., relish	20.00	27.00		32.00		
8	Plate, 14"	20.00					
5	Platter, 12", oval	10.00	17.00	19.00	26.00	50.00	
9	Salt and pepper, #49	30.00	40.00				
	Salt, ind. tub (cobalt: $30.00)	10.00	20.00		30.00		
	Salver, 10", low ftd.	15.00	50.00		70.00		
	Salver, 12", low ftd.	10.00	50.00		70.00		
12	Saucer	3.00	5.00	7.00	7.00	6.00	10.00
	Saucer, after dinner	3.00	5.00	7.00	8.00	10.00	10.00
	Stem, 2¾ oz., ftd., oyster cocktail	4.00	8.00	10.00	12.00	14.00	
	Stem, 3 oz., cocktail	10.00	12.00	17.00	20.00		
	Stem, 3½ oz., sherbet	5.00	8.00	11.00	12.00		
	Stem, 4 oz., fruit cocktail	3.00	10.00	10.00	12.00		
	Stem, 4½ oz., sherbet	3.00	10.00	10.00	12.00		
	Stem, 5 oz., soda	9.00	8.00	30.00	20.00		
	Stem, 5 oz., sherbet	5.00	7.00	9.00	9.00		
	Stem, 6 oz., champagne	6.00	16.00	18.00	22.00		
	Stem, 8 oz.	5.00	12.00	18.00	20.00		
4	Stem, 10 oz., goblet	8.00	15.00	60.00	25.00	45.00*	
13	Sugar, w/cover	15.00	45.00	45.00	50.00	70.00	40.00
	Sugar and cover, #1189	25.00	45.00	45.00	55.00		
	Sugar shaker, ftd.	50.00	95.00		110.00		
	Syrup, 7 oz., saucer ftd.	30.00	75.00				
	Tray, 7" x 10", rect.	26.00	30.00	40.00	35.00		
	Tray, 9", celery	10.00	14.00	16.00	15.00		
	Tray, 11", ctr. hdld., 3 pt.	15.00	35.00	40.00			
	Tray, 12", oblong	16.00	60.00	65.00			
	Tray, 13", 3 pt., relish	20.00	27.00	32.00			
	Tray, 13", celery	20.00	27.00	32.00			
	Tray, 13", hors d'oeuvre, w/cov. ctr.	32.00	42.00	52.00	75.00		
	Tray insert, 3½" x 4½"	4.00	6.00	7.00	8.00		
	Tumbler, 2½ oz., whiskey	3.00	40.00	25.00	40.00		
	Tumbler, 4½ oz., soda	4.00	6.00	10.00	15.00		
	Tumbler, 8 oz.	4.00	15.00	20.00	20.00		
	Tumbler, 10 oz., cupped rim	4.00	15.00	20.00	22.50		
	Tumbler, 10 oz., straight side	5.00	15.00	20.00	22.50		
	Tumbler, 12 oz., tea	5.00	20.00	25.00	30.00		
	Tumbler cover (unusual)	35.00					
	Vase, 5½", #4157	40.00	65.00	75.00	70.00	85.00	
3	Vase, 6", #516-2		50.00		60.00	75.00	
10	Vase, 7", floral bowl, #3480		55.00		65.00	85.00	

* #3325

OTHER BOOKS BY CATHY AND GENE FLORENCE

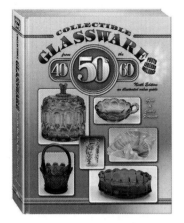

Collectible Glassware from the 40s, 50s & 60s, 9th Edition

Covering collectible glassware made after the Depression era, this is the only book available that deals exclusively with the glassware from this period. It is completely updated, featuring some original company catalog pages and six new patterns — making a total of 136 patterns from Anniversary to Yorktown, with many of the most popular Fire-King patterns in between. Each pattern is alphabetically listed, all known pieces in each pattern are described and priced, and 400 color photographs showcase both common and very rare pieces. All the pieces in the photographs are identified and cross-referenced with their listings. The Florences' descriptive text offers insight into each pattern's history, popularity, and value. 2008 values.
Item # 7524 ISBN: 978-1-57432-557-7 8½ x 11 256 Pgs HB $19.95

Collectible' Encyclopedia of Depression Glass, 18th Edition

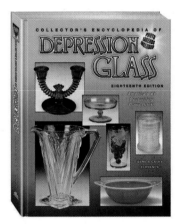

The Florences present this completely revised edition of America's #1 bestselling glass book with 156 patterns and more than 400 beautiful color photographs. With the assistance of several nationally known dealers, this book illustrates, as well as realistically prices, items in demand. Dealing primarily with the glass made from the 1920s through the 1030s, this beautiful reference book contains stunning color photographs, updated values, and a special section on reissues and fakes. All the pieces in the photographs are identified and cross-referenced with their listings. This dependable information comes from years of research and experience by full-time glass dealers Gene and Cathy Florence, America's leading glassware authorities. 2008 values.
Item # 7526 ISBN: 978-1-57432-559-1 8½ x 11 256 Pgs HB $19.95

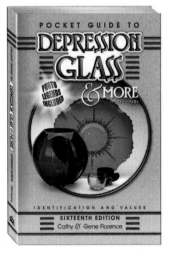

Pocket Guide to Depression Glass & More 16th Edition

Over 4,000 values have been updated in this edition of *Pocket Guide to Depression Glass & More*, to represent the ever-changing market. Many of the photographs have been replaced to add new finds and showcase other available items. The more than 200 color photographs and the listings of the patterns make identification simple. All pieces in photographs are identified and cross-referenced with their listings. There is even a section on re-issues and fakes. This book is the perfect companion to the Florences' *Collector's Encyclopedia of Depression Glass*. 2007 values.
Item # 7027 ISBN: 978-1-57432-512-6 8½ x 11 224 Pgs HB $12.95

Glass Candlesticks of the Depression Era

The Florences have compiled these books to help identify the candlestick patterns made during the Depression era. More than 500 different candlesticks are shown in each book. The books are arranged according to color, and many famous glass makers are represented. Volume 1 has 2000 values; Volume 2 has 2006 values.
Volume 1 Item # 5354 ISBN: 978-1-57432-136-4 8½ x 11 176 Pgs HB $24.95
Volume 2 Item # 6934 ISBN: 978-1-57432-495-2 8½ x 11 224 Pgs HB $24.95

OTHER BOOKS BY CATHY AND GENE FLORENCE

Anchor Hocking's Fire-King & More, 3rd Edition

From the 1940s through 2000, Anchor Hocking Glass Corporation of Lancaster, Ohio, produced an extensive line of heat resistant oven glassware called Fire-King. The Fire-King line included not only dinnerware but also a plethora of glass kitchen items — measuring cups, mixing bowls, mugs, and more. Loaded with over 2,500 pieces photographed in full color, vintage catalog pages, company morgue items, facts, new information, and values, this new edition will be a hit once again with collectors. It has everything readers expect from glassware authorities Gene and Cathy Florence. 2006 values.
Item # 6930 ISBN: 978-1-57432-491-4 8½ x 11 224 Pgs HB $24.95

Florences' Ovenware from the 1920s to the Present

This book is dedicated to the various collectible ovenware items from the 1920s to the present, often overlooked and once regarded as everyday, non-collectible dishes. Featuring bakeware products like casseroles, mixing bowls, and other dishes, this book showcases hundreds of large shelf and group shots. Companies include Pyrex, McKee, Federal, Glassbake, Safe bake, Fry, and Jeannette. There are also vintage catalog pages that add interest for collectors. 2005 values.
Item # 6641 ISBN: 978-1-57432-449-5 8½ x 11 208 Pgs HB $24.95

Florences' Glass Kitchen Shakers, 1930 – 1950s

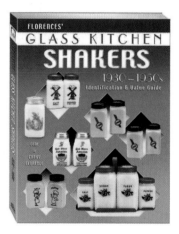

Gene and Cathy Florence, foremost authorities on glassware, have produced a fantastic guide for collectors. Over 1,000 glass kitchen shakers, including sugar shakers, are pictured in this volume of full-color photographs. Catalog identifications of previously unknown shaker names are provided, as well as name, company, and value given for each item shown. Companies featured include hazel-Atlas, Anchor Hocking, Jeannette, McKee, Owens-Illinois, and Tipp City Decorations. 2004 values.
Item # 6462 ISBN: 978-1-57432-389-4 8½ x 11 160 Pgs HB $19.95

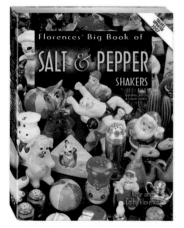

Florences' Big Book of Salt & Pepper Shakers

Over 5,000 shakers photographed in full color are featured in this book. Categories include advertising products, animals, chefs, Christmas, ethnic groups, famous characters, gambling, garden items, glass, heads, metal, miniature, musical, nodders, Occupied Japan, plastic/celluloid, pottery, religious, risqué, singles, souvenir, sports, steins, Western themes, and World's Fairs. Many famous potteries are represented — Lefton, Holt Howard, Vandor, Shawnee, and more. 2007 values.
Item # 5918 ISBN: 978-1-57432-257-6 8½x 11 272 Pgs HB $24.95

To order books:

Cathy Florence
P.O. Box 22186 • Lexington, KY 40522
or
Cathy Florence
P.O. Box 64 • Astatula, FL 34705

COLLECTOR BOOKS
P.O. Box 3009 • Paducah, KY 42002–3009
www.collectorbooks.com

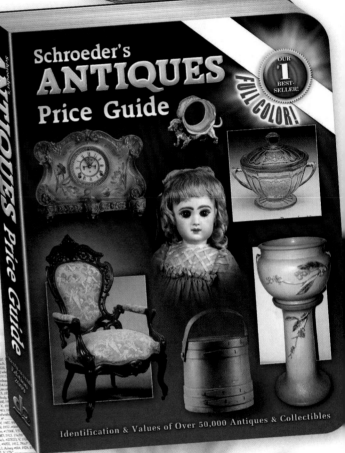